Shakespeare and Joyce

SHAKESPEARE and JOYCE
A Study of *Finnegans Wake*

Vincent John Cheng

The Pennsylvania State University Press
University Park and London

Library of Congress Cataloging in Publication Data

Cheng, Vincent John, 1951–
Shakespeare and Joyce.

Includes bibliography and index.
1. Joyce, James, 1882–1941. Finnegans Wake—Sources.
2. Shakespeare, William, 1564–1616—Influence—Joyce.
I. Joyce, James, 1882–1941. Finnegans Wake. II. Title.
PR6019.09F574   1983   823'.912   82-42781
ISBN 0-271-00342-1

Published in the United States of America by
The Pennsylvania State University Press

Published in Great Britain by
Colin Smythe Limited, Gerrards Cross, Buckinghamshire

Copyright © 1984 The Pennsylvania State University
All rights reserved
Designed by Dolly Carr
Printed in the United States of America

Contents

	Preface	vii
	Acknowledgments	ix
	Abbreviations	xi
1	Introduction	1

Part I

2	History and Possibility	17
3	All the World's a Stage	32
4	The Purchypatch of Hamlock: *Hamlet* and the *Wake*	54
5	Fathers and Sons: Shakespeare and Joyce	73
6	The Strife Between Brothers	90

Part II

| Shakespearean Allusions in *Finnegans Wake* | 113 |

Part III

Shakespearean Allusions: Appendixes	195
Notes	245
Bibliography	265
Index	269

Preface

Some years ago I became aware that there was a considerable amount of Shakespeare and Shakespeareana in *Finnegans Wake*. This situation was already obvious to more seasoned readers of James Joyce, but I was surprised to find that no extensive work had been done on the topic. And so I launched myself into what has proven to be a continuously enjoyable and exciting endeavor: after all, I had now both opportunity and excuse to spend my time rereading and studying two of the greatest writers of the English language. The study thus became both a lark and a labor of love: I would wander for days through Shakespeare's plays, and would then step into the thickets of *Finnegans Wake* to rediscover groves of Shakespeare. Within months the small monograph I had originally envisioned had become a referential jungle of its own. This book, consequently, has been quite some time in the making.

I little expected to find so many Shakespearean allusions, and certainly there are more that I have not uncovered. I am sure that careful readers have found some allusions of their own that have eluded me, and no doubt they will disagree with some of my identifications. Joyceans are likely to want to add to or subtract from my lists, which serve as both a referential collection and a point of departure.

This study aims to be a reference work, collecting and explicating the multitudinous Shakespearean allusions in the *Wake*, as well as an interpretive discussion of the major significances of Shakespeare in Joyce's book. In the introduction I explain how the three parts of this study can most profitably and efficiently be used by readers who wish to identify and understand particular Shakespearean allusions in the *Wake*. All studies of *Finnegans Wake* finally must have as their aim to be exegetically useful to readers lost in the thickets of Joyce's "pure and simple jumble of words": "You is feeling like you was lost in the bush, boy? You says: It is a puling sample jungle of woods. You most shouts out: Bethicket me for a stump of a beech if I have the poultriest notions what the farest he all means" (112.03–6).

Acknowledgments

A recurrent theme in *Finnegans Wake* is that nothing is original work, that all works depend on the previous efforts of others. Similarly, this study could not have been written without the aid and efforts of a large number of people, to whom I am much indebted.

A study like this is only possible, to begin with, because of the previous studies by fine commentators of Joyce. Several of them have been especially helpful, furthermore, in reading and emending the manuscript at its various stages of development. Matthew Hodgart pored over my rough and early drafts, and his suggestions and additions helped to shape my later ideas. Jackson Cope's insights and advice have been invaluable, and his watchful eye kept this from growing into some rough beast. Mike Begnal and Robert Boyle, S.J., both were very open with their encouragement, suggestions, and emendations. Finally, publishing a work about Shakespeare in the *Wake* would have been foolish without the imprimatur of Adaline Glasheen, who has been generous and supportive in reading the manuscript and in sharing her knowledge.

At Stanford University, where this study began as a doctoral dissertation, I was indebted to the acute readings of William Chace, David Riggs, and John Bishop. This early work was made possible by a Whiting Fellowship in the Humanities.

My colleagues at the University of Southern California have been equally helpful and generous with their encouragement and advice—especially Marjorie Perloff, Virginia Tufte, Allan Casson, and Sylvia Manning. I am grateful to Irwin C. Lieb and to the late David S. Wiesen, as, respectively, the university's vice-president and dean of Humanities, for encouragement and help in funding this project.

I would like to thank my editors, Jack Pickering and Patricia Coryell, at The Pennsylvania State University Press: Joyce no doubt was aware that in *Finnegans Wake* he had created the ultimate challenge, not only to readers, but also to editors.

Finally, Rob Polhemus has been most instrumental in the gestation and growth of this study—providing advice, encouragement, and enthusiasm.

For all this relief, much thanks.

Abbreviations

References to the works of Joyce and Shakespeare appear in parentheses within the text. *Finnegans Wake* (New York: Viking Press, 1959) references are by page and line. References to other works by Joyce are indicated by the following symbols:

> *P: A Portrait of the Artist as a Young Man* (New York: Viking Press, 1964).
> *U: Ulysses* (New York: Random House, 1961).
> *D: Dubliners* (New York: Viking Press, 1961).
> *Letters: The Letters of James Joyce,* Vols. 1–3, edited by Stuart Gilbert and Richard Ellmann (New York: Viking Press, 1957, 1966).

Books and articles frequently cited are referred to by the following short titles:

> Atherton: James S. Atherton, *The Books at the Wake.*
> *AWN: A Wake Newslitter.*
> Gifford and Seidman: Don Gifford and Robert J. Seidman, *Notes for Joyce.*
> Glasheen: Adaline Glasheen, *Third Census of* Finnegans Wake.
> Hodgart: M.J.C. Hodgart, "Shakespeare and *Finnegans Wake.*"
> McHugh: Roland McHugh, *Annotations to* Finnegans Wake.
> Peery: William Peery, "Shakhisbeard at *Finnegans Wake.*"
> *RES: The Reader's Encyclopedia of Shakespeare,* edited by Oscar J. Campbell and Edward G. Quinn.
> Schoenbaum: S. Schoenbaum, *Shakespeare's Lives.*
> Tindall: William York Tindall, *A Reader's Guide to* Finnegans Wake.

The edition of Shakespeare's plays that I have used throughout is *The Complete Pelican Shakespeare,* General Ed. Alfred Harbage.

Complete bibliographical entries are provided following the Notes.

1
Introduction

"Ah, there's only one man he's got to get the better of now, and that's that Shakespeare!"
                                                                Nora Joyce[1]

In *Ulysses*, John Eglinton (quoting Alexandre Dumas senior) asserts that "After God, Shakespeare has created most"; while Stephen Dedalus makes an equation between Shakespeare and the Creator, "the playwright who wrote the folio of this world" (*U*, 212, 213—"and wrote it badly," Stephen adds). In *Finnegans Wake*, James Joyce confirms and restates this notion, referring to Shakespeare as "Great Shapesphere" (295.04). To Joyce, artist and god were equivalent—the quintessential artist was the greatest bard of all, the lord of language at the Globe.

As the reputed comment by his wife, Nora, indicates, Joyce was in the habit of comparing himself with England's national poet. It was a lifelong habit. In 1903 the young and arrogant Irishman, upon finishing a poem, declared: "I have written the most perfect lyric since Shakespeare."[2] In *Ulysses*, amid a catalogue of famous men transformed into fictitious Irishmen, we find the name "Patrick W. Shakespeare" (*U*, 297). Though Joyce may have been jesting with the speculation that either Hamlet or Shakespeare was an Irishman,[3] he chose for his Irish Shakespeare a cryptogram of a real Irishman, Patrick W. Joyce (1827–1914), a scholar and historian (of no relation to James Joyce) whose books Joyce used in writing *Ulysses* and the *Wake*;[4] we see again Joyce's preoccupation with equating his name with Shakespeare's. In the course of this study, we shall discover Joyce making this comparison repeatedly and at every level. In James Atherton's words, "Joyce saw himself as Shakespeare's rival—possibly his greatest rival."[5]

Furthermore, besides equating himself with Shakespeare as fellow artist-creators and playwrights who write the folios of their worlds, Joyce conceived of the world of the *Wake* as drama, as a Shakespearean play. Like Shakespeare, Joyce viewed the world as a stage, the "worldstage" (33.03) of the *Wake;* this notion will be referred to in this study as the dramatic metaphor.

The aim of this study is to establish beyond doubt the centrality and omnipresence of Shakespeare, of the Shakespearean corpus, and of the dramatic metaphor in *Finnegans Wake*, and to provide a useful reference work for *Wake* readers: a guide to Shakespearean usage and allusion in *Finnegans Wake*.

Joyce has been very well served by his critics; we have come a long way toward an understanding of *Ulysses*, and, through the efforts of a dedicated handful of scholars, we are approaching a grasp of the *Wake*. Much of *Finnegans Wake*, however, remains a literary outland that is still barely mapped out. One area which cries out for exploration is the role of Shakespeare in the *Wake*. Early critics acknowledged the importance of Shakespeare in *Ulysses;* and that topic has been thoroughly treated by a number of them, culminating in William Schutte's excellent book.[6] These scholars have shown us, as has the text of *Ulysses* itself, the importance of Shakespeare to Joyce as an artist: Harry Levin writes that "Joyce seeks a guide in Homer, and a father in Shakespeare";[7] and Samuel Goldberg maintains that "when we look for real artistic affinities rather than influences or symbolic techniques, I think the closest analogue is not Dante, or Mallarmé, or Blake, or Flaubert, or even Ibsen, but Shakespeare. . . . above all there is Shakespeare."[8]

Similarly, all the major *Wake* critics have acknowledged the importance of Shakespeare in *Finnegans Wake*. Adaline Glasheen, for example, asserts that "Shakespeare (man, works) is the matrix of *Finnegans Wake*" and that *"Finnegans Wake* is about Shakespeare";[9] James Atherton writes: "I think there is at least one quotation from every single play by Shakespeare."[10] However, the only published works on this topic (to my knowledge) have been William Peery's 1951 article, "Shakhisbeard at *Finnegans Wake,*" and M.J.C. Hodgart's 1953 essay, "Shakespeare and *Finnegans Wake.*" These comprise fifteen and seventeen pages, respectively, of loose notes on some Shakespearean allusions.[11] In his volume *The Books at the Wake: A Study of Literary Allusions in James Joyce's* Finnegans Wake, Atherton acknowledges that "Joyce saw himself as Shakespeare's . . . greatest rival"; nevertheless, he devotes full chapters to Swift and to Lewis Carroll, and accords only two and a half pages to Shakespeare. There is a need, then, for more critical study on the role and importance of Shakespeare in *Finnegans Wake*—and in Joyce's vision (in the *Wake*) of himself as an artist.

A disparity exists between the acknowledged importance of this topic and its actual treatment by the critics; as a result, the magnitude of its importance has been repeatedly underestimated. M.J.C. Hodgart, to whose essay this study is most indebted, wrote in 1953 that: "Already Mr. L.A.G. Strong and Mr. William Peery have identified a number of allusions to Shakespeare. It is difficult to say just how many allusions there are in *Finnegans Wake*. . . . But, roughly, Mr. Strong has noted about 75 allusions and Mr. Peery discusses 55, of which about 30 are in Strong. I believe I have seen about 180 more: my total of nearly 300 may be well below the true figure."[12] Hodgart's conservative estimate is also very wide of the mark, as this study has compiled well over 1,000 allusions, and no doubt many more have yet to be discovered. Similarly, Atherton points out that "all the plays of Shakespeare are quoted at some point or other" and that "Mr. Hodgart's article and its appendix lists about 300 'unit' allusions to Shakespeare and his plays. Like all the other lists of Joycean allusions—including those in this volume [*The Books at the Wake*]—it is probably far from complete, although it supplies about one for every two pages of the *Wake*."[13]

Atherton continues: "But many of the more frequently recurring allusions are to such well-known tags as 'To be or not to be,' and it is reasonable to expect anyone capable of reading *Finnegans Wake* to find these for himself."[14] Perhaps he is right, although his expectation may be too generous. Who (and where) *is* that "anyone capable of reading *Finnegans Wake*" who can find such things for himself? As if, with a dreambook like the *Wake*, such an ideal encyclopedist-scholar-decoder-reader is common or even exists![15] Who is capable of reading *Finnegans Wake* without the help of readers' guides and lexicons? Also, it would be reasonable to say that anyone can discover the references to *Hamlet* if they were, in fact, all well-known tags, like "To me or not to me. Satis thy quest on" (269.19–20), but what about the hundreds of lesser-known references, like "a kiber galler" (321.11) and "till navel, spokes, and felloes hum like hymn" (447.04)?[16] Finally, even the familiar tags can be obscure: how many readers can be trusted, without some clue, to recognize in "*Hanno, o Nonanno, acce'l brubblemm'as*" (182.20–21) that well-known question, "To be or not to be, that is the question"? Will some sense be made, then, of what that allusion does in that particular context and on that page in the *Wake*? Such information is what this guidebook hopes to provide for the reader of the *Wake*.

Method and Organization

My aim is both interpretive and scholarly; accordingly, this study falls into two major sections. Part I attempts to make critical and interpretive sense of some important and recurring Shakespearean allusions and motifs. The individual chapters are organized thematically, according to the general patterns of allusion and motif. "History and Possibility" describes some of the theoretical foundations of *Ulysses* and *Finnegans Wake*, and suggests how references to Shakespeare and to his plays elucidate and reinforce these notions. "All the World's a Stage" shows, first, how Joyce conceived the *Wake* essentially as a drama, specifically a Shakespearean drama, performed on the "worldstage" by a Shakespearean stock company, and, second, how this theme underlies all the "action" of *Finnegans Wake*. "The Purchypatch of Hamlock" is an exposition of how *Hamlet* functions as a central matrix, a symbolic framework, for the action on this worldstage. "Fathers and Sons" and "The Strife Between Brothers" are analyses of how Joyce repeatedly employs certain insistent Shakespearean allusions and motifs to illuminate his vision of history, of change and replacement, of repetition and originality, of reproduction and re-production. There are, however, numerous allusions whose thematic significances, beyond the immediate and particular explanations in Part II, remain elusive. I hope that the interpretations in Part I will serve as a threshold for further study and critical comprehension of the Shakespearean allusions.

Part II is the foundation of this study and perhaps the more useful section as a reference work: annotations and explanatory notes to every Shakespearean allusion found in this study are organized by page and line. These allusions include both those noted by previous critics, compiled here, and those uncovered by this study. The discovery of Shakespearean allusions has been an arduous task: my method was to steep myself in Shakespeareana and to carefully read the plays, then to read and re-read *Finnegans Wake* just as carefully, with ears cocked and eyes open for any Shakespearean echoes (blank verse rhythms were often a tip-off), references, and allusions. Needless to say, the process involved a great deal of crosschecking and comparison between the plays and the *Wake*, with indispensable aid provided by the available concordances to both works. I hope that the corresponding notes will serve as a Shakespearean companion to reading *Finnegans Wake* as the available German, Scandinavian, Classical, and Gaelic lexicons function for the *Wake*.

Finally, the first two parts are followed by a third, the appendixes, a set of indices in which allusions to specific lines in Shakespeare are listed by play, act, scene, and line; in addition, other allusions are grouped into various relevant categories. These appendixes should prove useful for looking up allusions, for comparing similar allusions, and for general referential purposes.

Thus, for example, a reader who is studying the paragraph beginning midway down page 58 of the *Wake* would first turn to Part II and find the entries listed for page 58; there he would read:

58.25   *cappapee:* Horatio's description of the ghost of Hamlet's father was "A figure like your father, / Armèd at point exactly, cap-a-pe [head to foot]" (I. ii. 199–200). "Cap-a-pe" seems to be a leitmotif for HCE. See chapter 4 and Hodgart, p. 739. Compare "cap-a-pipe" in 220.26, "from grosskopp to megapod" in 78.05, "capapee" in 583.29, "Reclined from cape to pede" in 619.27, etc.

In context, the three soldiers in 58.24 are referred to as "cappapee"—armed from head to foot.

The reader who is curious about the scope of this verbal motif can turn to the *Hamlet* section of appendix 2 and find listed under "I. ii. 200 *Horatio: Armèd at point exactly, cap-a-pe* / (see also entries under I. ii. 228 *From top to toe*)" a total of nine allusions in the *Wake* to this line from *Hamlet;* then, under the cognate line, "I. ii. 228 *Hamlet: [Armed] from top to toe? / All: My lord, from head to foot,*" he would find four similar allusions. The reader might wish to locate in Part II some of these other twelve allusions for comparison—for example, 583.29 *waxened capapee.* Or, more likely, seeing that the motif is an extensive one, the reader might (as suggested in the entry for 58.25) turn to the appropriate pages in chapter 4, a section on *Hamlet,* to discover how this line from that play is used as a leitmotif in the *Wake* and how it operates in the contextual usage of *Hamlet* in the *Wake.* He would then be prepared to identify and, possibly, to interpret or understand any of the other twelve allusions to this motif when he finds them in his reading of the *Wake.*

This study is composed for readers who are already somewhat familiar with the *Wake* and for first-time readers who are using other sources for a more general understanding of the *Wake.*[17] Consequently, I will assume that the reader already knows the basic elements of the *Wake*—Viconian *ricorso,* Bruno's union of opposites, the "Ballad of Finnegan's Wake," and so forth—as well as the basic structure of the book. This Shakespearean guidebook cannot be understood (nor could it have been written) without the more general works of previous scholars.

I will, however, provide here the briefest of all introductory descriptions of this marvelous book. I quote the *Encyclopaedia Britannica:*

> Basically, the book is, in one sense, the story of a publican in Chapelizod, near Dublin, his wife, and their three children; but Mr. Humphrey Chimpden Earwicker, Mrs. Anna Livia, Shem, Shaun, and Isobel, are every family of mankind, the archetypal family about whom all mankind is dreaming. The 18th-Century Italian Giambattista Vico provides the basic theory that history is cyclic; to demonstrate this the book begins with the end of a sentence left unfinished on the last page. Ideally it should be bound in

a circle. It is thousands of dreams in one. Languages merge. . . . Characters from literature and history appear and merge and disappear as "the intermisunderstanding minds of the anticollaborators" dream on. On another level, the protagonists are the city of Dublin and the River Liffey which flows through the pages, "leaning with the sloothering slide of her, giddygaddy, grannyma, gossipaceous Anna Livia." And throughout the book James Joyce himself is present, joking, mocking his critics, defending his theories, remembering his father, enjoying himself.[18]

Finnegans Wake contains universal history dreamed in the course of one night, with one man, Humphrey Chimpden Earwicker (HCE), and his mythic predecessors as particular symbols of universal man, hero, and creator-father, within the universe's cyclical pattern of history. No wonder, then, that Joyce, as man and artist, was so obsessed with the "Myth of Shakespeare, the particular hero in whose story may be found the universal laws that hold for all his type, in whose deeds may be found a universal wisdom."[19]

On the Nature of Shakespearean Allusions

Adaline Glasheen writes: "To my mind, Shakespeare (man, works) is the matrix of *Finnegans Wake:* a matrix is the womb or mold in which something is shaped or cast."[20] We have grown quite familiar with the ways in which Joyce uses such matrixes or molds: in *Ulysses*, Homer, Shakespeare, and Joyce's own life; in the *Portrait*, the Daedalus-Icarus myth. These are scaffolds and skeletons which Joyce adopts in order to flesh out his own creation. By Glasheen's own definition of "matrix," then, the scaffolding in *Finnegans Wake* is in fact multiplex (as one would expect in a work dealing with universal history). Glasheen herself has composed thirteen pages of charts (entitled "Who Is Who When Everybody Is Somebody Else") which schematize the many scaffoldings analogous to the archetypal family of HCE, ALP (Anna Livia Plurabelle), Shaun, Shem, and Issy. Nevertheless, she may be basically correct; I have come to believe that Shakespeare provides some of the central (perhaps the most central) matrixes in the *Wake*, and certainly the most important ones in terms of Shem-Joyce's vision of himself as an artist.

Foremost among these Shakespearean matrixes is that of *Hamlet*, which is undoubtedly one of the "books at the *Wake*." It is structurally and analogically important. There are by far more allusions to *Hamlet* than to any other play (Shakespearean or otherwise); and the parallels are more frequent, precise, and insistent: HCE as King Hamlet, Shem as the Prince, Issy as Ophelia, Shaun as Laertes-Polonius. References to *Hamlet* are ubiquitous; and, as in the case of *Ulysses*, the themes and motifs in *Hamlet* are structural counterparts to those in *Finnegans Wake*. The other Shakespearean plays most alluded to are *Macbeth* and *Julius Caesar*, both for similar reasons: as parallels to the filial (Cad, Hosty, Shem-Shaun, Buckley, and so forth) overthrow and replacement of the father figure (HCE, Russian General, and so on). In *Macbeth*, the murder of a father figure (Duncan) by a filial figure results in a power struggle between two filial figures (Macbeth and Macduff); in *Julius Caesar* (à la Ernest Jones, Freudian Shakespeare critic), the murder of Caesar by two "sons" (one, Brutus, a real son) results in a power struggle between three "sons" (Brutus, Cassius, and Antony). *A Midsummer Night's Dream* is important to the *Wake* largely because of the notions of the drama as a dream, the play as Bottom's dream, and the *Wake* as both the drama and the dream of all mankind. Finally, perhaps Shakespeare's own life as a man and an artist provides the most important matrix of all, for the pattern and model which Shakespeare provides becomes that which Shem-Joyce must emulate and reproduce (similarly enduring the charges of plagiarism, forgery, and madness), as well as ultimately overthrow and supplant—a filial rival replacing the patriarch at the start of a new Viconian cycle.

As we might expect, many of the Shakespearean allusions occur in clusters, fitted to the nature or theme of the particular passage in the *Wake*. Some *Wake* chapters lend themselves to Shakespearean themes more than others, and therefore have a heavier concentration of Shakespearean allusions.[21] Thus, for example, the first few pages of chapter 1 of book II—on *The Mime of Mick, Nick and the Maggies* (a mime acted out by the archetypal family)—resound with allusions to Shakespeare, Elizabethan theatres, the dramatic metaphor, and Shakespearean stage history. Later in the same chapter (in pages 248 to 251), Chuff-Shaun prepares to return and wreak vengeance on Glugg-Shem; here we have a host of explicit *Macbeth* allusions, culminating in the arrival of Chuff-Macduff to overthrow his rival and exact vengeance—like Birnam Wood coming to Dunsinane: "For a burning would is come to dance inane. . . . Lack breath must leap no more" (250.16–18).

Hodgart writes: "It is difficult to say just how many such allusions there are in *Finnegans Wake* because one cannot decide what is a 'unit' allusion."[22] Numbers and units aside, however, the question "Just what constitutes a Shakespearean allusion?" is even more difficult to answer. Peery touches this issue when he speaks about "the problem of how elusive allusion can be and remain allusion."[23] I have tried to feel my way through the jungle of allusions in the *Wake* with an open mind, avoiding preconceived ideas of what constitutes a Shakespearean allusion. As a result, I have found that Joyce's playful and clever mind has produced a great variety of Shakespearean references—many of which, I'm sure, have yet to be discovered. I will, however, try to identify and give examples of some general (and inevitably arbitrary) categories.

Peery, in his study of "fifty-five passages having close Shakespearean associations," found the following groups: variants on the name of Shakespeare, of which there were eight; variants on titles of Shakespearean plays (10 titles), of which there were eleven; and quotations, parodies, and other allusions, of which there were thirty-six.[24]

These three categories are simple, but they provide a point of departure and a general system of classification.

Variants on the Name of Shakespeare. There are many of these variants, such as "Shikespower" (47.19), "Chickspeer" (145.24), "Scheekspair" (191.02), "Great Shapesphere" (295.04), and "Will Breakfast" (575.29). However, there are numerous additional references to Shakespeare without mention of the name itself (such as 576.24, "mirrorminded"), to legends or sayings about Shakespeare (such as 125.15, "little laughings and some less of cheeks"), and to known facts about Shakespeare's life (such as 121.32, "secondbest buns"). Furthermore, there are a host of references to Shakespeare's contemporaries, relatives, and acquaintances (such as Robert Greene or Letitia Greene), and especially to the would-be Shakespeares, the "claimants"—Francis Bacon is foremost among these. There are also a number of allusions to Shakespearean actors (such as David Garrick in 55.35, "garrickson") and Shakespearean stage history (such as in 491.30, "drary lane"), including references to the Dublin theatre-world.

Variants on Titles of Shakespearean Plays. There are allusions to many of the titles: these, such as "Miss Somer's nice dream" (502.28) and "two genitalmen of Veruno" (569.31), are usually quite amusing; as well, they are the most direct and easily found among the different kinds of Shakespearean allusions. Many of the characters in the plays are also named, whether directly (such as in 228.11, "coriolano," or in 290.06, "MacBeth") or indirectly (such as in 77.14, "Dane to pfife" for Macduff, or in 289.28–29, "Liv's lonely daughter" for Cordelia).

Quotations, Parodies, and Allusions. These constitute the largest category of Shakespearean references, yielding many variants and types. First, there are direct, obvious echoes or quotes from the *Plays:* "me ken or no me ken Zot is the Quiztune" (110.13–14), "Lead on, Macadam, and danked be he who first sights Halt Linduff!" (469.20–21), and so on. Some references in this category are well-known expressions or clichés, such as "John a'Dream's" (61.04) and "in my mines's I" (425.25), echoes of Hamlet's "John-a-dreams" (II. ii. 553) and "In my mind's eye" (I. ii. 185).

Joyce repeatedly demonstrates in the *Wake*, as he does in *Ulysses* (in which Bloom and others—not only Stephen—quote Shakespeare frequently, if not always accurately), how literary language enters the vernacular in the form of popular expressions.

Much harder to find are the many indirect, lesser-known, and less obvious echoes and quotations from the plays, such as "burning body to aiger air" (132.07—King Hamlet in purgatory and Horatio's "nipping and an eager air" in I. iv. 2) or "I heard . . . midnight's chimes" (403.19–21—Falstaff's "We have heard the chimes at midnight, Master Shallow" in *2H4* III. ii. 203). Even direct, syllable-by-syllable echoes can easily elude the reader: "Now eats the vintner over these contents" (318.20) is phonetically the opening line of *Richard III*. It is even more likely, then, that the unguided *Wake* reader—trying to read the text and keep in mind at once Shakespeare, Swift, Vico, Bruno, the Koran, the Book of the Dead, and so on, along with a score of foreign languages—will overlook a hidden echo of Hamlet's famous soliloquy in "Soons to come. To pausse" (256.14–15) or will not realize that "when the ritehand seizes what the lovearm knows" (27.04) echoes a line from *Venus and Adonis*.[25]

Occasionally, a Shakespearean allusion becomes a leitmotif by which the reader can identify the presence of a character or a recurrent theme. "Cap-a-pe," for example, signals the presence of HCE; just as pansies and thoughts (from *Ham*. IV. v. 175–76: "there is pansies, that's for thoughts") identifies Issy-Ophelia, as in "loveliest pansiful thoughts" (446.03), "Pensée! The most beautiful of woman" (403.14), and so on. Similarly, references to the porter in *Macbeth* and the knocking at the gate (see, for example, the Part II entries for 63.18–36 and 69.15 ff.) underline the encounter between father and son, between HCE and the Cad.

There are, of course, questionable allusions that could be references to Shakespeare or to something else. A major subtype of these are the allusions to Shakespearean characters who were also real historical figures. How, for example, can one be sure that references to Caesar, Brutus, and Cassius have necessarily anything to do with Shakespeare? Included in Part II are only those allusions which I believe Joyce associated with Shakespeare, along with corresponding explanations. The Caesar-Brutus-Cassius references are adopted by Joyce in light of Ernest Jones's Oedipal theories on Shakespeare (and are discussed in chapter 5 of this study); thus, these are likely to be references to *Julius Caesar*. Similarly, the question might arise of whether a reference to Othello is an allusion to the play or to Verdi's opera. Often the answer is both; context and a general knowledge of the *Wake* are the best guides.

Sometimes questionable references become likely Shakespearean allusions by context. For example, 327.12–13 reads "all the Lavinias of ester yours and pleding for them to herself in the periglus glatsch." Is this Lavinia, the daughter of Titus Andronicus, and is "periglus" a reference to *Pericles?* Both counts may seem doubtful without examining the context of page 327 in the *Wake:* this passage, part of "The Norwegian Captain" episode (pp. 311–32), has to do with two suitors (a sailor and a tailor) of the daughter of an Irish innkeeper (HCE), who has incestuous desires himself. Both *Titus* and *Pericles* are plays involving suitors for the hand of a regent's daughter, and the latter play also includes an incestuous relationship between father and daughter; thus, the likelihood of Shakespearean associations in this line becomes now much more real.[26]

In some instances, a questionable allusion becomes a likely reference by attraction. I have mentioned that Shakespearean allusions often come in clusters. Consequently, in the *Macbeth* cluster of pages 248–51, "Dunckle Dalton of matching wools" (248.22) becomes a reference to Duncan and to marching woods (and to woolen Scotch plaids) simply because Joyce clearly had *Macbeth* in mind while writing these pages.

Often an allusion may be somewhat less obvious or less convincing because it is a "multiplex" allusion—that is, a conflation of many allusions, of which the Shakespearean portion may be secondary or tertiary (as with "in vanessy, were sosie sesthers wroth" in 3.11–12). For example, "Juletide" (97.03) reminds one first of Yuletide, then of July; only afterwards, remembering the many other allusions in the *Wake* to the Ides of March, does one see here "Julius's time" and the "thides or marse" (366.29–30). Similarly, in "windblasted tree of the knowledge of beautiful andevil" (194.15) the primary allusion is clearly to Eden (the Tree of Knowledge, the Tree of Good and Evil, and the devil); but the secondary allusion is Shakespearean, the "blasted heath" (I. iii. 77) of *Macbeth.*

Secondary, or "shared" allusions pose a particular problem. In "My fault, his fault, a kingship through a fault" (193.31–32), for example, there is a coupling of two verbal echoes: the Catholic confession ("through my fault, through my fault, through my most grievous fault": the *Confiteor*'s *mea culpa, mea culpa, mea maxima culpa*) and Richard III's "A horse! a horse! my kingdom for a horse!" (*R3* V. v. 7) Thus, in 238.21, "May he colp, may he colp her, may he mixandmass colp her," we may hear, in addition to the *culpas,* a faint echo of *Richard III.* As always, however, context provides the best clue; a Shakespearean reference in this example seems rather doubtful.

Finally, there are a few very obscure, indirect, and oblique allusions; these are difficult to find, but, once found, usually seem likely. Some are references to obscure lines from Shakespeare; others are difficult because they require the apprehension of a clever pun or a witty twist. To realize, for example, that "Pensée! The most beautiful of woman" (403.14–15) refers to Issy-Ophelia, one must keep in mind that *pensée* is French for thought (and is a feminine noun), as well as an echo of "pansy," and that "pansy" + "thought" = Ophelia, who said, "And there is pansies, that's for thoughts" (IV. v. 175–76). In addition, "to begin properly SPQueaRking" (455.28) may seem undecipherable (as well as unpronounceable) within the context of page 455, which deals with the Apocalypse and the Last Day. However, the capital letters form *SPQR*, the initials for the Senate and People of Rome; and, along with the echo of "squeaking," the reader who is well acquainted with *Hamlet* may recall Horatio's "The graves stood tenantless and the sheeted dead / Did squeak and gibber in the Roman streets" (I. i. 115–16)—a good description, perhaps, of the Last Day.[27]

In fact, then, the Shakespearean allusions in the *Wake* are not bright apples hanging from low boughs, ripe for easy plucking. Joyce's methods are often obscure and elusive, but there *is* a "metheg in [his] midness" (32.04–5). It is encouraging to remember that, while Joyce's methods may be labyrinthine, his model is Daedalus, not Schopenhauer or Spinoza: the allusions, symbols, and puns may be difficult, but the thought expressed is usually simple. We have learned from *Ulysses* that the elaborate, allusive, and difficult scaffolds usually house the same direct and recurrent ideas which obsessed Joyce; the same is true of the *Wake*. Joyce admitted as much when he told Frank Budgen: "If there is any difficulty in reading what I write it is because of the material I use. In my case the thought is always simple."[28]

Nor must we worry that the scaffoldings of allusion will be difficult because of what they allude to: Joyce's simplicity derives partly from the fact that, even when he alludes to other writers, he is always speaking of himself and of the thoughts that obsess him; as Stephen Dedalus says, "*If Socrates leave his house today he will find the sage seated on his doorstep. . . . We walk through ourselves . . . always meeting ourselves*" (*U*, 213). Joyce always returns to his obsession—Joyce. Very rarely does an allusion to another work involve interpreting the material alluded to; most times it involves interpreting Joyce. When Joyce asked a friend to read *Huckleberry Finn* and tell him about it (so that *Finn* might be incorporated into *Finnegan*—the connection is, first and foremost, of the simplest sort: verbal echo), he wrote to the friend: "I have never read it. . . . I shall try to use whatever bears upon what I am doing."[29] Such is the case with Shakespeare, though Joyce had certainly read the master and knew him better than most scholars ever will. Thus, for example, "in my baron gentilhomme to the manhor bourne" (365.04–15) offers an allusion both to Macduff (as in 55.10, "manorwombanborn") and to Hamlet's "though I am native here / And to the manner born, it is a custom / More honored in the breach than the observance" (I. iv. 14–16). We need not worry, however, about all the meanings and implications of the Shakespearean lines themselves, nor about how Joyce might be reflecting on or commenting on them—for he is not. He is merely picking up the verbal echo of "to the manhor bourne" to fashion a pun which suits his own context: in this passage, the taverner HCE, defending himself against accusations leveled at him, is claiming to be a gentleman and a nobleman, one not only born to the manner and customs of the nobility, but, literally, born in a baronial manor. The reader doesn't learn about Shakespeare in Joyce's allusions to Shakespeare; he learns about Joyce. As Harry Levin noted, "When a self-effacing parodist—a Max Beerbohm—takes off a writer, the result is acute criticism. When Joyce is dealing with others, he lacks this insight and precision. His parodies reveal himself."[30]

Still, while the essential thought behind the allusion may be simple, the allusion itself is often elaborate. Joyce is clever; and in order to decode the *Wake*, we must be clever. Consequently, a potential pitfall in a study of the *Wake* is the ever-present possibility of overreading. How clever can we assume Joyce to be? How elaborate can an allusion be and still be considered an intentional allusion? We must be aware of both the Scylla and Charybdis pitfalls of Joycean study: the hard and inflexible espousal of a few preconceived Joycean tenets, and the obsessive whirlpool of Joyce's encyclopedic mind. The latter is particularly dangerous, as it leads one to free association and to seeing allusions everywhere; I have tried to steer a middle course, leaving my mind open to possiblity, but not getting drawn into attempting to associate everything with everything.[31] Still, there is no doubt that I have at times been either too arbitrary or too obscure in my interpretations and in my choices of Shakespearean allusions; to such occurrences I can only mention the difficulty of obtaining a full perspective and understanding of a book like the *Wake* and recall the observation by the Englishman Haines in *Ulysses:* "Shakespeare is the happy hunting ground of all minds that have lost their balance" (*U*, 248).

I wish to acknowledge my debt to, and to laud, the dedication of those *Wake* commentators and scholars who have, in spite of the raised eyebrows and the scorn of solemn academicians, persevered and contributed to our growing understanding of this book.[32] Their efforts have often been brilliant illuminations for *Wake* readers. This study dares not be as ambitious or comprehensive as theirs have been. All our endeavors to clarify *Finnegans Wake* are bound to be, for the time being, nearsighted attempts to clarify a book too obscure for us as yet. Perhaps, however, some new light shed by our clumsy efforts shall guide future readers and scholars, allowing them eventually to see face to face: "And if he sung dumb in his glass darkly speech lit face to face on allaround" (355.08–9).

PART I

2
History and Possibility

> "It is for western man to realize that [Hamlet] is posing questions about truth itself, about the glorious but also terrifying lack of simplicity that truth shows. . . . Here, I would say, is the Hamlet problem of Hamlet problems . . .—the theme of unsimple truth. It may be said that Hamlet is indeed about the pursuit of revenge but most deeply about the pursuit of truth."
>
> Willard Farnham[1]

James Joyce's mind is that of the essential poet: it works by analogy. A defecator, a lover, a father, a poet, and God are all, by analogy, equivalent—because they each create, or produce, something. Therefore, those somethings are also, by analogy, equivalent; *Finnegans Wake*, like the letter unearthed by Biddy the Hen, is a *creatio ex* shitpile, a "letter from litter" (615.01). Joyce—who, unlike his predecessor and fellow creator-defecator-poet Shakespeare, knew much Latin and some Greek ("he had have only had some little laughings and some less of cheeks" in 125.14–15)—was aware that the Latin word for, at once, letters of the alphabet, epistolary letters, and belles-lettres, was *litterae*, a felicitous correspondence to the English word "litter" and its connotations of shit and birth. Thus, to the Joycean mind, poetic creations in English "litterature" are at once bilabial speech, biological offspring, and biodegradable waste. Each implies the others; the part reflects the whole. A poet is the god and creator of his own worlds—"After God, Shakespeare has created most" (*U*, 212)—while God is but a very major poet, "the playwright who wrote the folio of this world" (*U*, 213). HCE, the archetypal father who "Haveth Childers Everywhere" (535.34–35) and who thus also creates and populates a world, is but another version of both poet and god—of "Great Shapesphere," as Joyce "puns it" (295.04). Joyce himself, of course, is all of these things: like Stephen Dedalus's Shakespeare, he is "all in all" (*U*, 212). As a god and an artist, a poet triumphs over confining reality by creating worlds through the imagination—and each of his works is an exploration into the possible "history" of such worlds.

Let us go back for a moment. For a clear and thorough understanding of the nature of history in *Finnegans Wake* as explorations of the possible, it is helpful first to survey carefully what Joyce had written earlier in *Ulysses*.

> —History, Stephen said, is a nightmare from which I am trying to awake. . . .
> —The ways of the Creator are not our ways, Mr Deasy said. All history moves towards one great goal, the manifestation of God. (*U*, 34)

Every schoolboy learns that there are two major ways of viewing time and history: the linear way and the mythic-cyclic way. We live in a Judeo-Christian world of Garrett Deasys, believing that in the beginning was the Word, in the middle came Christ, and in the end shall be the Last Judgment and the manifestation of God. The western Christian tradition has generally (though not exclusively) assumed a linear, unwavering, progressive view of history; Vico and Joyce, however, believed otherwise. In the "Nestor" episode of *Ulysses*, Stephen Dedalus, moments before meeting Deasy, thinks: "As it *was* in the beginning, *is* now . . . and ever *shall be* . . . world without end" (*U*, 29; my italics). Joyce centered *Ulysses* not on Deasy's orthodox Christianity,[2] but on a pre-Christian myth—for myths are cyclic in nature. Bloomsday is a modern reenactment of an ancient myth—the Odyssey. Homer's *Odyssey*, however, is not reenacted precisely, nor linearly, but in more modern variations; in the typical terms of everyman Leopold Bloom, reflecting on a quasi déjà vu: "history repeating itself with a difference" (*U*, 655). Bloom's comment could easily serve as a subtitle for *Finnegans Wake*.

The acceptance and treatment of a mythical/cyclical view of time produced a revolutionary change in the thought and literature of Joyce's time. When *Ulysses* was published in 1922, T.S. Eliot called it "the most important expression which the present age has found. . . . Mr. Joyce's parallel use of the Odyssey has [the] great importance . . . of a scientific discovery. . . . Instead of narrative method, we may now use the mythical method."[3] Eliot himself employed various myths in *The Waste Land* (published that same year). Understandably, the notion of cyclical history was appealing to Eliot amid the spiritual bankruptcy of the modern wasteland: if history is linear, we can only assume that we are, to paraphrase Tennyson, moving upwards toward angels, working out the beast[4]—we are clearly doing no such thing. If, however, history is cyclic, then the world has perhaps reached the end of another cycle; and it is high time to pray for rain and renewal (or Viconian *ricorso*). Eliot observed that *Ulysses* provided a way of "giving a shape and a significance to the immense panorama of futility which is contemporary history."[5] He exhibited in his *Four Quartets* a complex awareness of the interpenetration of past, present, and future, arguing that "Time present and time past / Are both perhaps present in time future. . . ." Or, as Eliot wrote further about *Ulysses*, one has the sense "of everything happening at once."⁶ "Everything happening at once" is another possible subtitle for the *Wake*.

Joyce carried the exploration of this general notion of history furthest—in *Finnegans Wake*—with the construct of a dream, the perfect vehicle for repeated motifs and variations, for everything happening at once, for all possibilities and all history in the course of a night's dream. Earlier, in the "Nestor" chapter of *Ulysses*—a chapter whose "Art" (in Joyce's own designation) was history—Joyce had previewed Wakean history with a clear hint: "Vico Road, Dalkey" (*U*, 24). He made *Finnegans Wake* into a Viconian river. Vico argued in his *Principia d'una Scienza Nuova* that history is cyclic and that each cycle is divided into four periods: the theocratic age, the aristocratic age, the democratic age, and the *ricorso*, the return to the beginning. Thus, *Finnegans Wake* has four books, one for each age; and, like a river, the entire book runs into the sea—"A way a lone a last a loved a long the"—only eventually to return to its source: "riverrun, past Eve and Adam's, from swerve of shore to bend of bay, brings us by a commodius vicus of recirculation back to Howth Castle and Environs" (628.15–16, 3.01–3; "vicus" and "recirculation" recall Vico's *ricorso*). The beginning links up with the end. *Finnegans Wake* is a model of Joyce/Vico's view of history; it is, as Joyce calls it in the text, "the book of Doublends Jined" (20.15–16)—both of Dublin's Giant, Finn MacCool (or Tim Finnegan, HCE, and so on), and of doubleends joined. It is a "Continuarration!" (205.14)—a continuous narration.

The Nightmare of History

Why was linear history such a nightmare for Stephen Dedalus, the aspiring artist? In the opening lines of the "Nestor" episode, Stephen thinks of history as a linear concept, of time as having a beginning and an apocalyptic, catastrophic end: "I hear the ruin of all space, shattered glass and toppling masonry, and time one livid final flame. What is left us then?"⁷ (*U*, 24). "Actual," linear history has, through all ages, been acknowledged to be Time the Destroyer—or what Shakespeare called "Devouring Time."⁸ History is a destroyer, an ouster of possibilities. This theme is introduced when Stephen comments on the "pier," which a student in his class has referred to in his confusion over the name of Pyrrhus: "Kingstown pier, Stephen said. Yes, a disappointed bridge" (*U*, 25). "How sir?" a student asks. A disappointed bridge, perhaps, simply because it *is* a pier—therefore severely limited in scope, the possibility of its being a bridge having been ousted by its clearly being a pier. Actual, factual history makes it so. Stephen Dedalus is himself remorseful because of the memory of his dead mother and the hurt he gave her. Her death is fact, and history makes it so; thus, his "agenbite of inwit" cannot be absolved—for she is dead, and nothing can change that absolute fact of history. This is why, to the aspiring artist, history is such a nightmare—because of its destructive qualities:

> Had Pyrrhus not fallen by a beldam's hand in Argos or Julius Caesar not been knifed to death? They are not to be thought away. Time has branded them and fettered they are lodged in the room of infinite possibilities they have ousted. But can those have been possible seeing that they never were? Or was that only possible which came to pass? (*U*, 25)

In these crucial lines, Stephen is referring to Aristotle's theory ("Aristotle's phrase" in *U*, 25) that there is a room of infinite possibilities—if Caesar had not been knifed to death, he might have lived to a ripe old age, might have developed cancer, might even have come to America—but history limits, and chooses from that room one possibility (which is that Caesar gets knifed to death), thus destroying all others. History, then, is seen by Stephen as a usurper and a destroyer of creative potential, a restrictive force which limits other, perhaps more interesting, possibilities. Stephen goes on to quote Milton:

> *Weep no more, woful shepherd, weep no more*
> *For Lycidas, your sorrow, is not dead,*
> *Sunk though he be beneath the watery floor.* . . .
>   It must be a movement then, an actuality of the possible as possible. (*U*, 25)

To Stephen, the conflict lies between history and poetry: Lycidas's death is a historical fact; other possibilities are ousted by that certainty. The poet Milton, however, asserts that Lycidas is *not* dead; whereas factual history eliminates possibilities, poetry forges and creates new and other possibilities. Thus the poet, his poetry, and his imagination are placed in the role of revivifiers, re-creators, constructive counters to history's destructiveness: "It must be a movement then, an actuality of the possible as possible."

Joyce celebrates the alternatives; for young Stephen, those imaginative possibilities are a liberating force. The question is one of control—who is in the driver's seat, history or man? Does history control us by limiting our possibilities; or do we control history by creating new and different ones, by interpreting history in light of our own creative viewpoints? Does the father create the son; or the son, the father? Without the son, there would be no father; in the *Metamorphoses*, when Icarus dies, Daedalus (Ovid tells us) is a "father no more."[9] Thus, if Stephen Dedalus can just as easily create Simon Dedalus, then, as he observes later in the library, "Paternity may be a legal fiction" (*U*, 207). He is free to explore Aristotle's room; and, once history is banished in favor of imagination, Leopold Bloom may as easily be Stephen's father as Simon Dedalus. Imagination neutralizes history.

Thus concluding, Stephen walks along Sandymount Strand, closes his eyes, and imagines all the possibilities inherent in the Protean tide of creative imagination. He tests those possibilities against "sensible matter"—those things actually apprehensible by the physical senses, according to Stephen's Thomistic notions of art in the *Portrait*.[10] The modalities of the visible and audible may be ineluctable; the "diaphane" and "what you damn well have to see" (*U*, 186) may be "there all the time without you" (*U*, 37); but, in "Proteus," the power of the "inward eye" of imagination triumphs over the limitations of actual history. Stephen immediately gives us an example of this alternative to factual history, proceeding, on page 38, to his Aunt Sara's house. For two pages he seems to have a conversation with his Uncle Richie: it is not until another two pages have passed that the reader suddenly realizes—"He halted. I have passed the way to aunt Sara's. Am I not going there? Seems not. No-one about. He turned northeast" (*U*, 41)—that the conversation never occurred, that Stephen has never left the strand, that he didn't go to his aunt and uncle's house—he only imagined that scenario. As readers, though, we had accepted it; for us it was the same as if he *had* gone. Thus, creative imagination and art overcome the destructive powers of history.

This same nightmare of linear history—that is, that it excludes other possibilities—is also faced by Leopold Bloom, as expressed by Joyce in the incisive, cathechismic latinity of the "Ithaca" episode: "What rendered problematic for Bloom the realisation of these mutually selfexcluding propositions? [Answer:] The irreparability of the past . . . The impredivibility of the future" (*U*, 696). Bloom is unable to exorcise history from its linear, one-tracked sequence of realities (specifically, Molly's unfaithfulness to him) in order to realize mutually self-excluding propositions; but artists Stephen and Joyce can—by creating other possibilities, by bringing to life all the dead chances ousted and destroyed by linear history. Through artistic creation, Joyce counters the death-dealing destructiveness of history and fact. It is a great and moving moment in *Finnegans Wake*, when Shem-Joyce, reviled and ridiculed by his brother Shaun, gets up to defend himself, lifting his only weapon—the life wand, the phallic pen-knife of the artistic imagination: "He lifts the lifewand and the dumb speak" (195.05).

The dead and the dumb can now speak through the power of the creative, regenerative act; through the imagination are history and the past conquered. History, no longer a nightmare, is a dream vision, a resurrection of dead possibilities, a wake. Its destructive elements are exorcised through an exploration of myriad possibilities in the room of infinite ones.

Stephen has created and realized an imaginary possibility in "Proteus" in his mental voyage to his aunt and uncle's house. A little later, and a lot drunker, Stephen tries to pull off a trick of a greater order: in the library scene ("Scylla and Charybdis"), he once more unsheathes his Thomistic Aristotle—"Horseness is the whatness of allhorse. . . . Space: what you damn well have to see. . . . Hold to the now, the here, through which all future plunges to the past" (*U*, 186). He urges himself to keep to "the now, the here," to stick to the Scylla of "hard facts" and not be swept away by the Charydbic "speculation of schoolboys" (*U*, 185). Still, despite A.E.'s warning that "all these questions are purely academic" (*U*, 185), Stephen cannot avoid letting go of known history and speculating about Shakespeare. He devises a thorough and elaborate theory of Shakespeare's life and works—again, exploring Aristotle's room of infinite possibilities.

The fact that Stephen chooses Shakespeare as the subject of his speculative theories is significant. In *Ulysses*, history is composed of the hard facts of the external, material world—Bloom's world. In "Scylla and Charybdis," Stephen tries to break away from the nightmare of history; in *Finnegans Wake*, Joyce does so—and the nightmare becomes the dream of history, in which all possibilities, including actual reality, can be realized and explored—for history is ultimately uncertain and indeterminate, the subject of much gossip and varying interpretation. That is why Shakespeare is chosen: our knowledge of the Bard's personal life and history is so scant and meager—based on a few Stratford documents and a host of unverifiable legends—that it invites interpretation, fabrication, and the speculation of schoolboys (as well as scholars). It is ripe ground for Stephen's exercises in the artistic imagination and the exploration of possibilities.[11] Significantly, this paucity of fact and specific detail may be precisely why Joyce finds it so easy, in the *Wake* as well, to use Shakespeare as a universal analogy, as man-father-creator-artist-god; for our knowledge of the Bard is apocryphal and neomythical, not actual nor linearly determinate: Shakespeare's little-known life, with its still possible possibilities, allows for the universalization and fecundity of Viconian history. Again, as Goldberg writes, his is the "Myth of Shakespeare, the particular hero in whose story may be found the universal laws that hold for all his type, in whose deeds may be found a universal wisdom."[12] Shakespeare is as myriad-minded and faceted as HCE.

Imaginative Possibilities: *Finnegans Wake*

And so Joyce's notions in *Ulysses* about the "room of infinite possibilities" are carried out in the *Wake*, in which all history and literature are seen as uncertainty and gossip, the exploration of practically every possibility, and in which the study of the past is as uncertain as our knowledge of Shakespeare—his life, loves, plays (and their authorship), manuscripts, and so forth.

All of *Finnegans Wake* could be considered an attempt to answer the question, "What happened to HCE?" Like Hamlet, we want to know the truth. Finding the "truth"—if there is one—is a matter of digging through the countless possibilities, variations, and interpretations accumulated by the middenpile of time. Art and creation (and thus also shitpile and letter) are, for the Joyce of the *Wake* as well as for Stephen Dedalus and Aristotle, a "movement, an actuality of the possible as possible," an exploration of potential actualities from the room of infinite possibilities. The problem is the same with the story of HCE: we try to choose one version. But which one? Unfortunately, "Zot is the Quiztune" (110.14), and Joyce, like Hamlet (who faced the dilemma of "unsimple truth") and Aristotle before him, knew it:

> . . . me ken or no me ken Zot is the Quiztune. . . . we are in for a sequentiality of improbable possibles though possibly nobody after having grubbed up a lock of cwold cworn aboove his subject probably in Harrystotalies [Aristotle] or the vivle [the Bible] will go out of his way to applaud him on the onboiassed back of his remark for utterly impossible as are all these events they are probably as like those which may have taken place as any others which never took person at all are ever likely to be. (110.14–21)

In describing the *Wake*'s explorations as "a sequentiality of improbable possibles," Joyce appeals to the dean of the Department of Possibilities and Probabilities, Aristotle. Joyce explains in this passage that the book explores a history of resonant uncertainty and indeterminate sequentiality, a sequentiality of improbable possibles that are as possible as anything, or as much so as the sequentiality put out by linear "history": "for utterly impossible as are all these events they are probably as like those which may have taken place as any others which never took person at all are ever likely to be." Nor, as we well know, is fact or history ever certain. The present age has given us relativity and quantum mechanics; but historians and novelists have known for centuries that no event ever happens in a known or exclusively certain way, for what "happens" is ultimately determined by the beholder (in the forms of gossip, criticism, history books, and so on), and nothing is ever conclusive: every generation reinterprets history, just as each generation of critics reinterprets Shakespeare. Modern physics has given us a new terminology for this literary and historical resonance, which has been explored by such books as *Tristram Shandy, Clarissa, The Good Soldier,* and *Absalom, Absalom!;* we are dealing with the Uncertainty Principle in literature—or, what I like to call the Rashomon effect.[13] *Finnegans Wake* studies this effect by exploring all possibilities and all viewpoints which "are probably as like those which may have taken place."[14]

In a sense, all of *Finnegans Wake* deals with the basic question, "What *did* happen to HCE?" What happened in the Park by the Magazine Wall? What was the crime? *Was* there a crime? What took place in the encounter with the Cad? Nothing is certain, though there are many versions of stories being bantered about: "aither he cursed and recursed and was everseen doing what your fourfootlers saw or he was never done seeing what you coolpigeons know" (29.09–11). Like the question that worries Hamlet, the question of *Finnegans Wake* centers about the fact that we are dealing with unsimple truth, that we are in the dark ("as any camelot prince of dinmurk" in 143.07) and do not quite know what happened. As with some of Shakespeare's plays, this "drauma" (115.32), the gossip about HCE, is a tale of dubious accuracy and questionable authorship that has a great need for scholarship and critical interpretation; one way of looking at the *Wake* is to see it as a scholarly casebook on the HCE tale, including all the variant versions and interpretations thereof.

What *did* happen to HCE? The research done on the original manuscripts and early folios on HCE's small folly ("his wee follyo!" in 197.18, the "trifolium librotto" in 425.20) is inconclusive—all we know is that "the great fact emerges that after that historic date all holographs so far exhumed initialled by Haromphrey bear the sigla H.C.E." (32.12–14). As with the few documents we have about Shakespeare, little else is known for certain about HCE aside from his signature. Presumably, on the "historic date," he went out and committed a crime for which he probably suffered a fall of some sort; and subsequently, he had an encounter with a younger man. Little else is known for certain, including the "historic date" itself.[15] Much of the book explores possible variations of those events from the room of infinite possibilities.

Whatever it is that actually happens on that historic date, news of HCE's crime immediately spreads around town, "bruited" (33.16) about and noised from ear to ear, until the poet Hosty collects the rumours and composes "The Ballad of Persse O'Reilly"; this signals the downfall of Earwicker. The Cad's wife whispers poisonous gossip about this profane story into the ear of her confessor: "the gossiple delivered in his epistolear" (38.23); so also the news "hushly pierce[s] the rubiend aurellum of one Philly Thurnston" (38.34–35), and goes on and on. Pouring poison into one's ear was an image that fascinated Joyce. An earwig, namesake of H.C. Earwicker, is, according to the *Oxford English Dictionary*, a verb meaning to whisper or to insinuate: it is also "an insect . . . that poisons the brain by penetrating the head through the ear"; an ear-whisperer, gossiper, or parasite; and a madman who has a maggot or a craze in the brain—appropriate, as we shall later see, with "the mad dane" (385.16).

Joyce associated the motif of the spread of gossip by pouring slanderous poison in one's ear with *Hamlet*—for the Ghost recounts that King Hamlet was killed in this manner while he slept: "And in the porches of my ears [Claudius] did pour / The leperous distilment. . . ." (I. v. 63–64). This drama, reenacted and recoursed in Hamlet's staged dumb show, obsessed Joyce. In *Ulysses*, Stephen Dedalus recalls the words of King Hamlet's ghost to the prince:

> *List! List! O List!*
> My flesh hears him; creeping, hears.
> *If thou didst ever . . .*
> —What is a ghost? Stephen said with tingling energy. . . .
> *Hamlet, I am thy father's spirit*
>
> (*U*, 188)[16]

Stephen has King Hamlet's death by poisoning on his mind all day, but especially while he is in the library, where he pours the poison of his own Shakespearean speculations (from the room of infinite possibilities) into the ears of his listeners: "They list. And in the porches of their ears I pour" (*U*, 196). As with Hamlet *père*, HCE's demise as the father figure is caused by the poison poured into people's ears. That ear-piercing gossip is aptly titled "The Ballad of Persse O'Reilly," the ear-piercing (*perce-oreille*, or earwig) ballad of H.C. Earwicker; thus it is appropriate that HCE is repeatedly associated with King Hamlet. Like Hosty and like the Cad, Stephen Dedalus, a poet and a son, spreads rumours about Shakespeare, one of his own acknowledged father figures. Joyce also does this: in *Finnegans Wake* he anthologizes all sad stories and variations of the death of kings and fathers. "List! List!" becomes a call to listen to such poison, a call repeated throughout the *Wake ad nauseum* in every conceivable variation.[17] The *Wake* is a collection of all the poisonous and "gossipaceous" (195.04) variations of the HCE tale. King Hamlet's death by poison poured in his ear; the tales told about Hamlet and Shakespeare by Stephen Dedalus; every scholar's reading or retelling of *Hamlet*; H.C. Earwicker and earwigs; the rumours and gossip that bring about HCE's downfall; the various and variant versions and interpretations of HCE's tale; the stories at the *Wake* to which we, as guests and auditors, are called to list; the *Wake* itself; and, finally, every past, present, and future reading or interpretation of *Finnegans Wake—all* are related by analogy, by equating poison in the ear with gossip or speculation.

Chapter 3 of book I, a second retelling of the "humphriad of that fall and rise" (53.09—involving Humphrey Chimpden and the Cad), contains various versions of the story of HCE's fall and his subsequent encounter with the Cad, including several which involve a drunken Cad and a porter, like that in *Macbeth*, at a gate.[18] This "play" is constantly subject to new interpretations by the human race and by the sons of Garrick ("this new reading of the part . . . the new garrickson" in 55.33–35),[19] for "the unfacts, did we possess them, are too imprecisely few to warrant our certitude" (57.16–17). All is slander and gossip, poison poured in the porches of one's ears. Thus, this chapter is about gossip and uncertainty, about incommunicability and the impossibility of learning the truth, about the attempts of literature, scholarship, and history to state truth by fabricating varying accounts or interpretations of every incident. The chapter pursues the Rashomon effect, interviewing the men on the street ("evidencegivers by legpoll" in 57.17), a host of them—three soldiers, an English actress, an "entychologist," Shaun-Kevin, a jaunting car driver, the great cook Escoffier, a tennis player, a barmaid, a Board of Trade official, a girl detective, and so forth (pages 58–61)—and each one espouses his or her own view of the HCE tale. Though each evidence-giver has his own interpretation, nothing can be proved; and they are all probably "meer marchant taylor's fablings" (61.28)—mere lies and fables about a sailor and a tailor. All this Irish gossip is erroneous misunderstanding, and, Joyce tells us, HCE, "the Man . . . [was] subjected to the horrors of the premier terror of Errorland. (perorhaps!)"—*perhaps*, for even that is uncertain (62.23–25).

Similarly, Joyce begins chapter 8 of book I by trying to investigate HCE's crime: "or whatever it was they threed to make out he thried to two in the Fiendish park" (196.09–11)—whatever it was the three soldiers tried to make out that he tried to do to the two girls in Phoenix Park. Once again, we attempt "to make his private linen public" (196.16), for "It was put in the newses what he did . . . exploits and all" (196.20–22). Still, what *was* the crime? "What was it he did a tail at all on Animal Sendai? And how long was he under loch and neagh [lock and key]?" (196.19–20). As always, nothing is certain, "But toms will till" (196.22)—time will tell. All is uncertainty and misunderstanding, as is often pointed out in the *Wake:* "No, no, the dear heaven knows, and the farther the from it, if the whole stole stale mis betold, whoever the gulpable, and whatever the pulpous was" (396.21–24)—heaven knows, and far from it, if the whole stolen, stale tale must be told (or mistold), who was culpable (and gulping from guilt) and where the faults ("culpas") lie. We can only listen to (or read) the *Wake*'s compilation of all the gossipy possibilities and speculative misunderstandings of history and the Ballad of Persse O'Reilly. Thus, we are called to "List, list!" to a review of human history: "*Hirp! Hirp! for their Missed Understandings! chirps the Ballat of Perce-Oreille*" (175.27–28). As such a compilation, the *Wake* is thus an exploration of the "Notpossible!" (175.05).

The Letter From Litter

"Learned scholarch[s]" (31.21) also engage in such explorations. Scholarship and artistic creation, connected by the role of language (*litterae* as "litterature" and letters), are both concerned with finding, if possible, the right interpretation from the dungheap of infinite possibilities. Joyce was clearly aware of the similarity between reading the *Wake* and researching purple passages of literature; a twentieth-century foliowright, he describes his own "problem passion play" (32.32) as "the purchypatch of hamlock" (31.23–24),[20] the "patchpurple of the massacre" (111.02), "theirs porpor patches!" (200.04), "paupers patch" (316.23), and a "puling sample jungle of woods" (112.04)—a pure and simple jumble of words.[21] Joyce further emphasizes this similarity by his repeated references to holographs, folios, librettos, original manuscripts, and Shakespearean scholars and ghosters.

Finnegans Wake is Joyce's attempt to compile these error-possibilities of HCE's comedy of errors—in other words, all history. A problem play has purple passages which engender much critical speculation and scholarly research; in this sense, *Finnegans Wake* is, like the letter unearthed by Biddy the hen, an attempt to dig into the middenheap and find the "gossiple" truth. Resonant with the pun of *litterae*, the "letter from litter" (615.01) is broadly symbolic; as Tindall puts it, "Plainly more than life from Alpha to Omega, the letter represents all literature as well, especially *Finnegans Wake*."[22] This letter first appears in the opening chapter, along with Biddy the hen, a bird scrabbling at the middenheap, pecking and unearthing knickknacks (to put into her bag or "nabsack"), components of this letter from Boston: "Here, and it goes on to appear now, she comes, a peacefugle [*fugel*, Old English for bird], a parody's bird, a peri potmother . . . with peewee and powwows in beggybaggy on her bickybacky . . . picking here, pecking there, pussypussy plunderpussy. . . . She's burrowed the coacher's headlight the better to pry . . . and all spoiled goods go into her nabsack: curtrages and rattlin buttins, nappy spattees and flasks of all nations, clavicures and scampulars . . . boaston [Boston] nightgarters and masses of shoesets [Massachusetts] and nickelly nacks" (11.08–23).²³ The hen's act of digging for knickknacks is symbolic of scholarship and historical investigation: the digging and the misreadings never end. There will always be new Shakespeares and new scholars, for there are always *ricorsos*, breakfasts, and wakes: "even if Humpty shall fall frumpty times as awkward again . . . there'll be iggs for the brekkers come to mournhim, sunny side up with care" (12.12–15)—even if Humpty Dumpty (HCE) shall fall umpteen times, there'll be eggs for the breakfast come morning, and for the breakfasters come to mourn him.²⁴

This middenheap of history, from which Joyce and the hen are scrabbling, is the scene where Mutt and Jute and many others had their confrontations: "Countlessness of livestories have netherfallen by this plage, flick as flowflakes, litters from aloft, like a waast wizzard all of whirlworlds" (17.26–29)—thick as snowflakes, countless life stories have fallen by this place (and shore—*plage*), litters and letters from the sky, to form a waste, vast vision of the whole world—or of all "litterature." Now they are all entombed in this middenmound, reminding us of our inevitable fall (ashes to ashes, earth from earth): "Now are all tombed to the mound, isges to isges, erde from erde" (17.29–30). If we read Vico and listen to Mutt, however, we will understand the history of this ancestral mound of death (Thanatos) and rebirth: "And thanacestross mound have swollup them all. This ourth of years [earth of ours] is not [naught] save brickdust and being humus the same roturns [being humus and human, the same rotates and returns]. He who runes may rede it on all fours. O'c'stle, n'wc'stle, tr'c'stle, crumbling" (18.03–7). If we read the runes of the *Wake* and the litterheap, we will "rede" and understand the ruins of history as a four-part Viconian cycle, capped by crumbling castles and toppling masonry.²⁵ For in this "litterature" are all the letters of the Word and the world, the alphabet and key to history: "(Stoop) if you are abcedminded, to this claybook, what curios of signs (please stoop), in this allaphbed! Can you rede . . . its world?" (18.17–19). If you stoop to this clay bookmound, you will find the key *(clé)*, signs, and alphabet by which to read and understand the Word and the world, for it contains the old stories and all the handwriting on the wall: "It is the same told of all. Many. Miscegenations on miscegenations. Tieckle. They lived und laughed ant loved end left. Forsin" (18.19–21—*Mene Tekel Upharsin*). Many generations of incest and miscegenation lived through the Viconian cycle of living, laughing, loving, and leaving—for sin. They ensured the continuation of existence; and their stories are the letters and litters on our "allforabit" (19.02) mound: "What a mnice old mness it all mnakes! A middenhide hoard of objects! Olives, beets, kimmels, dollies, alfrids, beatties, cormacks and daltons" (19.07–9—the "abcd" in Hebrew, and also in Irish nomenclature). Their contributions to our mound of "litterature" are the origins of our books on every Tom, Dick, and Harry (or Alfred, Beatty, and Cormack): "For that . . . is what papyr is meed of, made of, hides and hints and misses in prints" (20.10–11)—all the errors and missed understandings of the Ballad of Persse O'Reilly. Therefore, you hardly need to ask if every story in the bound book of history has a score of versions and possible interpretations: "So you need hardly spell me how every word will be bound over to carry three score and ten toptypsical readings throughout the book of Doublends Jined" (20.13–16). Here Joyce is commenting on the interminable fecundity of the past and of literature, both subject to endless interpretation, by using the *Wake* as a symbol of both world and word.

Throughout the *Wake*, Biddy the Hen scrabbles for evidence in the littermound, keeping her "kiribis pouch filled with litterish fragments" (66.25–26). As chapter 8 of book I opens ("Anna Livia Plurabelle"), Biddy sifts through all the possibilities of HCE's crime: "What was it he did a tail at all? . . . How elster is he a called at all? Qu'appelle?. . . . Or where was he born or how was he found?" (196.18–197.09). This is the tale of "Don Dom Dombdomb and his wee follyo" (197.18): HCE's folly in the park is made equivalent (history = literature) to Shakespearean folios. Joyce's works are like Shakespeare's; and HCE himself is like Shakespeare the man, for little is known for certain about the lives and histories of either.

The problem play of *Finnegans Wake* is, like the letter unearthed by Biddy the hen, an attempt to dig the truth out of the middenheap of possibilities. Like the hen, Joyce faces in chapter 4 of book I the question of whether or not to attempt wading through all the muddy misinterpretations, like some Shakespearean scholar, to find the original manuscript and learn the truth. The issue is, Hamlet-like, to dig or not to dig: "Fact, any human inyon you liked any erenoon or efter would take her bare godkin out, or an even pair of hem" (79.19–21); "bare godkin" echoes Hamlet's "bare bodkin," with which a man might his quietus make. The "fact" is that any human would dig in the middenheap (with his bodkin) for those clues, the letters: "Arbour, bucket, caravan, ditch . . ." (79.25). The question for Joyce is whether or not to dig, like the gravedigger in *Hamlet*, into the graveyard of past literature and history for his style and his subject matter; Joyce describes his technique as the "mating of a grand stylish gravedigging with secondbest buns" (121.32). Digging for old skulls, like that of Yorick (see Part II, entry for 190.19), is like the scholarly digging that unearthed Shakespeare's will, which left Anne Hathaway his "secondbest bed."[26] Similarly, Biddy the hen digs out of the graveyard of "litterature" alphabetical letters, *belles-lettres*, and postal letters; thus, it is only appropriate that Biddy's discovery from the litterpile is a letter, literally a "letter from litter" (615.01).

Chapter 5 of book I concerns the letter, scholarship, and textual studies. Here again, Joyce tries to equate his works (the letter as the *Wake* and as all of literature) with those of Shakespeare, especially *Hamlet*.[27]

The chapter begins with a catalogue of possible names for the letter (on pages 104–7), an exploration into the many possibilities for titling the "untitled mamafesta" (104.04). The speaker then begins a lecture on the letter and on scholarship about the letter. He raises the question of textual scholarship, as with Shakespeare: "Say, baron lousadoor, who in hallhagal wrote the durn thing anyhow?" (107.36). As with Shakespeare, some plays may have been written by forgers, "claimants," or collaborators. The chapter pursues several of the many possibilities.

On page 110 the speaker launches into a sort of "Proteus" episode, quoting Hamlet's famed soliloquy, referring to Aristotle's room of infinite possibilities, and wondering whether the possibilities explored in the letter were likely ones. "About that original hen" (110.22), he continues, referring to HCE's original sin. The speaker begins to talk about the bird and the object at which she is scratching, "a goodish-sized sheet of letterpaper originating by transhipt from Boston (Mass.)" (111.08–10).[28] The hen has uncovered the celebrated letter, and the rest of the paragraph records its contents: a talky letter, its contents are commonplace and it sports a large teastain. The speaker now discusses the condition of the manuscript, flavoring his words with Stephen's Aristotelian-Thomistic aesthetics ("Horseness is the whatness of allhorse" in *U*, 186, and so on). He admits that the letter is a jumble of words ("It is a puling sample jungle of woods" in 112.04); that he hasn't "the poultriest notions" (112.05) of what it is about; and that, actually, it is fair game for Gypsy scholars ("Zingari schoolerm" in 112.07).

He therefore calls for us, as literary scholars, to make inspection of the letter—just as on the day when "Biddy Doran looked at literature" (112.27)[29]—and to study the hearsay of literature: "a hear or say of some anomorous letter" (112.29). The speaker launches into a textual study of the missive, noting that the characters slide up and down on the page in a pattern of fall and *ricorso*, and that the letter resembles the problem play of *Hamlet* ("tham Let" and "Hum Lit"): "But by writing thithaways end to end and turning, turning and end to end hithaways writing and with lines of litters slittering up and louds of latters slettering down, the old semetomyplace and jupetbackagain from tham Let Rise till Hum Lit" (114.16–19; "thithaways" and "hithaways" may refer to Anne Hathaway). In these lines, Joyce predicts that the *Wake* will eventually attain a literary prominence like that of *Hamlet;* this very important passage will be returned to in chapter 6, in the conclusion of this study.[30]

Because there are an infinite number of possible meanings for the letter's sequentiality of improbables, scholarly study of this work arrives at different interpretations in differing schools of criticism. The speaker follows with an imitation of psychoanalytic criticism (page 115), like that of Freud or Shakespearean critic Ernest Jones, and then one of Marxist criticism (page 116). The message (and language) of this Viconian letter (the *Wake*) could be "anythongue athall" (117.15–16); yet, while we "may have our irremovable doubts as to the whole sense of the lot, the interpretation of any phrase in the whole, the meaning of every word . . . we must vaunt no idle dubiosity as to its genuine authorship and holus-bolus authoritativeness" (117.35–118.04). The speaker then argues—as some Shakespearean scholars have done on the issue of authorship—that the fact is that the affair was done once and for all, and someone wrote it down, regardless of subjective phenomenology; he goes on to compare the letter with the Bible and the Book of Kells, admitting that it looks pretty blurred and stained. Equated with Joyce's works, the letter is similar to great literature, and specifically to Shakespeare's *Hamlet*. The professor, in his textual study of the Wakean letter, concludes about this "dummpshow" (120.07)—the dumb show on the middendump: it is a "prepronominal *funferal* [the *Wake* as a funeral and fun-for-all], engraved and retouched and edgewiped and pudden-padded, very like a whale's egg farced with pemmican as were it sentenced to be nuzzled over a full trillion times for ever and a night till his noddle sink or swim by that ideal reader suffering from an ideal insomnia" (120.09–14). This work, like Shakespeare's, has been retouched and worked over; and, like the plays or the *Wake*, it is meant to be puzzled over for a trillion nights by that ideal dreambook and insomniac reader. Finally, the passage describes the *Wake*'s Protean qualities as an exploration of infinite possibilities, which, like the cloud observed by Hamlet and Polonius, takes on many shapes, "Very like a whale" (Polonius, III. ii. 367)—this line has been quoted before, by Stephen, in, appropriately, the "Proteus" episode (*U*, 40), *Ulysses*'s exploration of infinite possibilities.[31]

Like Shakespearean folios, then, or like littermounds, works of literature are comedies of errors, compilations of misunderstandings. The "purchypatch of hamlock" is like the purple-patched *Wake*. In *Finnegans Wake*, Joyce's lifewand makes the dumb speak, exploring the infinite possibilities neglected by both history and devouring time, those imaginative alternatives that allow a cloud to become a whale.

3
All the World's a Stage

> "Art necessarily divides itself into three forms progressing from one to the next. These forms are: the lyrical form . . . the epical form . . . the dramatic form."
>
> A Portrait of the Artist as a Young Man

It is the intention of this chapter to show how Joyce conceived of *Finnegans Wake* as essentially dramatic, a Shakespearean play acted out on the "worldstage" (33.03) by the archetypal family members of a dramatic company. The "dramatic metaphor"—that is, that all the world is a stage and all the figures of history merely players—underlies all the "action" in *Finnegans Wake*, Joyce's chronicle of Viconian history. Joycean history, as we have seen, is an exploration into many possibilities; in the *Wake* these possibilities take on the forms of various plays, particularly Shakespearean plays, each re-creating a different view of the possibilities of history. Chapters 4 through 6 of this study will analyze some of these specific Shakespearean matrixes; the present chapter serves as a foundation for those analyses by showing that Joyce sets his dream of all-history in the context of the dramatic milieu: the dream as drama.

There are thousands of allusions to drama in *Finnegans Wake*—from the works of Henrik Ibsen to W.G. Wills's *A Royal Divorce*, from the plays of John Synge to those of Gilbert and Sullivan. Shakespeare is only one dramatist (albeit the major one) in this company; any attempt to deal with the "drama" in *Finnegans Wake* merely through Shakespearean references is, necessarily, like a home without Plumtree's Potted Meat—incomplete. However, we can learn much about the *Wake* and begin a detailed study of Shakespearean allusions by investigating the role of drama in the *Wake*, with particular attention given to Shakespeare.

A good starting point will be a discussion of Joyce's notion of the artist-god as playwright, and consequently, of his creations as plays.

The Playwright as God

Joycean commentators have often pointed out that the form of *A Portrait of the Artist as a Young Man* follows Stephen Dedalus's statement (*P*, 214) about the qualitative progression of art: from lyrical to epical to dramatic; from personal to impersonal, refined out of existence—as in "that old English ballad *Turpin Hero*, which begins in the first person and ends in the third person" (*P*, 215). Whether or not Joyce himself actually considered drama to be, as Stephen argues, the highest literary art form, the writer was unquestionably very fond of the genre. And, although not a playwright himself,[1] Joyce in a vague sense followed the progression of art forms he had outlined through the words of Stephen Dedalus: after the lyrical and personal qualities of *Chamber Music* and *Portrait*, he progressed to the epical form in *Ulysses*, depicting his own Odysseus in mediate relation to the city of Dublin; finally, in his last work, Joyce presented his hero against the backdrop of all the world and universal history, in a form which Joyce conceived of as essentially dramatic.[2]

As a fledgling author, Joyce's model and inspiration had been Ibsen; but in *Ulysses* and *Finnegans Wake* he became increasingly obsessed with Shakespeare as both his artistic predecessor and his rival. S.L. Goldberg has argued that Joyce's artistic imagination is dramatic in nature: "The classical temper is essentially dramatic. . . . He trusted to his dramatic imagination."[3] The dramatic qualities of such passages as the Christmas dinner scene in the *Portrait* or the library (the discussion on Shakespeare) and the brothel scenes in *Ulysses* are indisputable. Many passages in *Finnegans Wake*, and especially in chapter 1 of book II, are dramatic in form and quality. Plays of some sort or another repeatedly provide the structures and parameters of the *Wake*. Most of Shakespeare's plays are alluded to; almost all of Ibsen's dramatic pieces appear in the *Wake*, especially *The Master Builder*. Two more plays, as Atherton and others have shown, are structural pillars in the *Wake:* Dion Boucicault's *Arrah-na-Pogue* (having, among other things, a character named Sean the Post), and W.G. Wills's popular play about Napoleon's domestic affairs, *A Royal Divorce*. Most importantly, though, Joyce, like Shakespeare before him, had increasingly come to think of an artist as a playwright and a creator-god, and of the artist's works as a stage peopled by his creations, "all the charictures in the drame" (302.31–32).

In the *Portrait* Stephen Dedalus had proclaimed that in the dramatic form, "the artist, like the God of the creation, remains within or behind or beyond or above his handiwork, invisible, refined out of existence, indifferent, paring his fingernails" (*P*, 215). Whereas after the *Portrait* Joyce no longer tried to refine himself out of his own works, he was obsessed with the metaphors of the artist as both playwright and god. Creating his own worlds, a poet is a god and a father; God is the playwright who penned "the folio of the world"; Shakespeare, God, HCE, and Joyce, are all, like Hamlet's father (with whom, according to Stephen, Shakespeare identifies), "all in all" (*U*, 212).[4]

The metaphor of playwright as god becomes even more recurrent and insistent in the *Wake*, Joyce's chronicle of the world and world history. The prime mover behind the force of destiny is a playwright, "the compositor of the farce of dustiny" (162.02–3);[5] this production of the play about Viconian history is presented by "the producer (Mr John Baptister Vickar)"—Joyce as the author of the *Wake* and God as the author of history, alias Giambattista Vico and John the Baptist (255.27). God-Shakespeare-Joyce-HCE is a "worldwright" (14.19) and a "puppetry producer" (219.07–08); like Prospero, he is a "pageantmaster" (237.13) and the "god of all machineries" (253.33). In the *Wake*, the most recurrent symbol for the creator-father-god figure is, however, Michael Gunn, manager of Dublin's Gaiety Theatre, and father of Joyce's friend Selskar Gunn;[6] repeatedly HCE is referred to as, or compared with, Michael Gunn, in the role of manager of his worldstage. In chapter 1 of book II, that most "dramatic" of *Wake* chapters, HCE is introduced as "HUMP (Mr Makeall Gone)"; as stage managers, Michael Gunn and God can both make all things come or go. At the end of the same chapter, after loud applause, the exiting HCE is described as "Gonn the gawds, Gunnar's gustspells" (257.34); Gunn as god is gone; the play, Gunn's and God's gospels, is over. In line 19 of page 481 Joyce describes HCE as a builder of cities, a populator and a patriarch: "We speak of Gun, the farther"—HCE as Gunn and God the Father. So also he is described in lines 8 to 10 of page 434 as "the big gun," waiting "for Bessy Sudlow" (Michael Gunn's real wife, and an actress in his troupe) to serve him his dinner. In keeping with the theme of Viconian *ricorso*, HCE will also become, in a felicitous coinage, "the cropse of our seedfather" (55.08)—the corpse will become the earth-laden seed and father of future crops and generations. Thus, finally, in the "worldwright" metaphor, HCE is a "gunnfodder" (242.10): at once, Brecht's cannonfodder; a phallic gun; Michael Gunn, a father and a creator, a grandfather, and the fodder for future Gunns, guns, and generations. Even after death, after Makeall Gone has made all gone, himself being but cannonfodder, even then will there be the "Herewe-areagain Gaieties of the Afterpiece"—a joyous play *(pièce)* at the Gaiety in our afterlife. This will be supervised by this new Gaiety's manager, Michael Gunn, "the Royal Revolver of these real globoes" (455.25–26), the god and gun who makes this world turn, the stage manager of "these real globoes"—the Globe Theatre and the global world. As "Makeall Gone," "Gun, the farther," "gunnfodder," and "the big gun," Joyce is a playwright-god whose real life phallic gun is the creative pen of Shem the Penman.[7]

The Dream as Shakespearean Drama

If Joyce conceived of the artist-creator as a playwright, he may well have come to think of his own creations as plays. So he seems to have in the *Wake*. In pages 179 and 180, for example, Joyce describes *Ulysses*—"his usylessly unreadable Blue Book of Eccles" (179.26–27)—as an S.R.O. hit and a Christmas pantomime at the Gaiety Theatre: "an entire operahouse (there was to be stamping room only in the prompter's box and everthemore his queue kept swelling) . . . in their gaiety pantheomime" (179.35–180.04). More importantly, Joyce thought of the *Wake* itself as a drama.

Stephen Dedalus saw history as a nightmare; in the *Wake* Joyce presents history as a dream, the story of "Allmen" (419.10). This dream unrolls the drama of universal history, "a dromo of todos" (598.02)—a dream and drama of everything (Spanish *todos*), of today and of everyday. In the book itself, the word "dream" rarely appears unaccompanied by a pun on the word "drama"; this equation between dream and drama is enforced throughout. "In the drema" (69.14) of the *Wake*, "We drames our dreams" (277.17) of universal history, peopled with all the characters and caricatures of the past, "All the charictures in the drame" (302.31–32); in the *Wake*, dreams are history, and one might say, "Me drames . . . has come through!" (49.32–33)—my dreams have come true! In our own world of modern psychoanalysis, the drama of our dreams reveals our (and the world's) traumas (from *Traum*, German for dream); and so the *Wake* is, in the words of Shakespearean-Freudian critic Professor Shaun = (Ernest) Jones, "a prepossessing drauma" (115.32). It may at times be depicted as *Hamlet*, "the drame of Drainophilias" (110.11)—a dream and drama of Ophelia's; or as Bottom's eerie dream in a midsummer night's drama, "This eeridreme . . . From Topphole to Bottom" (342.30–32); or as Stephen's nightmare of history, "a lane picture for us in a dreariodreama" (79.27–28), a dreary Shakespearean drama at Drury Lane. However, behind the dream there is always the drama of cause and effect, of history-becoming-fact: "His dream monologue was over, of cause, but his drama parapolylogic had yet to be, affact" (474.04–5).

"In this drury world of ours" (600.02), the Drury Lane counterpart to this dream-drama of the *Wake* is Shakespeare's "Miss Somer's nice dream" (502.29). Whatever it is that Miss Somer or HCE or Yawn or mankind (or whoever) dreams, it is equated in the *Wake* with Bottom's dream in *A Midsummer Night's Dream*. There are many references to "bully Bottom" (III. i. 7 and IV. ii. 18), such as "bully bluedomer" (319.06), throughout the *Wake* (see the *Midsummer Night's Dream* section of Appendix 2); this equation may partially explain the ubiquitous presence of the Ass of the Four Old Men.[8]

The language of medieval and Elizabethan dream visions appears often in the *Wake*. The "methinks" and "meseems" spouted by Shakespearean dreamers appears in the dream vision of the *Wake* as "Me seemeth" (15.34), "Me drames" (49.32), "Methanks" (239.22), "medsdreams" (366.14–15), "methought" (403.18), "mescemed" (404.09), "mesaw mestreamed" (407.11), "methinks" (556.13), and so on. The greatest concentration of such terms is found in a dense cluster of Shakespearean allusions at the beginning of chapter 1 of book III, on pages 403 to 405, in a passage that I believe is modeled on Bottom's dream vision (*MND* IV. i). The connection is first hinted at on page 403, where "dhove's suckling" echoes Bottom's "I will roar you as gently as any sucking dove" (*MND* I. ii. 75). In act 4 Bottom wakes up from his dream and his state of being an "ass" to say:

> I have had a most rare vision. I have had a dream, past the wit of any man to say what dream it was. Man is but an ass if he go about to expound this dream. Methought I was—there is no man can tell what. Methought I was, and methought I had—But man is but a patched fool if he will offer to say what methought I had. The eye of man hath not heard, the ear of man hath not seen, man's hand is not able to taste, his tongue to conceive, nor his heart to report what my dream was. I will get Peter Quince to write a ballet of this dream. It shall be called "Bottom's Dream," because it hath no bottom. (*MND* IV. i. 203–13)

The dream vision described on pages 403 through 405 is also that of an ass, the Donkey who accompanies the Four Old Men ("but I, poor ass, am but as their fourpart tinckler's dunkey" in 405.06), and is similarly couched in Elizabethan dream language: "Methought as I was dropping asleep somepart in nonland. . . . And as I was jogging along in a dream as dozing I was dawdling, arrah, methought. . . . And lo, mescemed somewhat came of the noise . . . whom we dreamt was a shaddo . . . Yet methought . . ." Like the dream action (of "we shadows" in Puck's epilogue) in *A Midsummer Night's Dream*'s faeryland, this vision occurs at midnight: "Methought as I was dropping asleep somepart in nonland . . . I heard at zero hour as 'twere the peal of vixen's laughter among midnight's chimes" (403.18–21).[9] From this point onward in the *Wake*, the Ass appears very frequently (see the *Midsummer Night's Dream* section of Appendix 2), as if to remind us that the *Wake* is his dream vision. We know, for example, that we are still dealing with the Ass's dream from "somepart in nonland" when we read on page 481: "—Dream. On a nonday I sleep. I dreamt of a somday. Of a wonday I shall wake." This dream vision, "This nonday diary, this allnights newseryreel" (489.35) is none other than the *Wake* itself, the nighttime dreambook of all history.

The ass's vision, whether the dream of history or Bottom's dream, is perhaps incomprehensible, resisting rational analysis or decoding: "Man is but an ass if he go about to expound this dream," for "the eye of man hath not heard, the ear of man hath not seen. . . ." Shakespeare based his lines on I *Corinthians* 2:9: "But, as it is written, 'What no eye has seen, nor ear heard, nor the heart of man conceived, what God has prepared for those who love him'"; they are, in turn, echoed in *Finnegans Wake:* "What can't be coded can be decorded if an ear aye sieze what no eye ere grieved for" (482.34–36). Robert Boyle has argued that both Shakespeare and Joyce use St. Paul's text to make the point that "literature like Scripture deals with visions (which may be had by asses as well as Magi), and that the miraculous and inspired expression of them may not be totally subject to the rational dissection of nonpoets."[10]

This is perhaps one reason why *A Midsummer Night's Dream* and Bottom's dream inhabit the *Wake;* as Boyle concludes, "Shakespeare . . . stands with Bottom and with Joyce in accepting the chaos of the cosmos and yet in supposing that the artist's miracle will have might enough to express the inexpressible in black ink."[11] The world (and the dream of history) may not be decodable or logically comprehensible ("Man is but an ass . . .") but the artist—Shakespeare, Joyce, or Peter Quince—can depict and express the "chaosmos" (118.21).

Furthermore, in pointing out the scriptural background of the Ass's dream, Boyle helps to explain the biblical language of the passage ("And lo. . . . when lo. . . .") as well as the echoes of *A Midsummer Night's Dream.* One part of the Ass's dream reenacts the Nativity on "a particular lukesummer night" (501.18) when "the isles is Thymes" (501.21); Boyle notes that the book of *Luke* alone has the Nativity scene.[12] This reenactment, however, is also Bottom's dream on a midsummer night, by a bank "where the wild thyme blows" (*MND* II. i. 249; see also "wild thyme" in 430.29). The dream is at once a midsummer night's dream and all dreams, both "Miss Somer's nice dream" (502.29) and "Mad Winthrop's delugium stramens" (502.30). As such, it can be female ("Miss Somer") or male ("Mad Winthrop"), dream ("nice dream") or nightmare (delirium tremens),[13] midsummer or midwinter ("Mad Winthrop"). It is all history.

If one would ask Bottom or the Ass, "Do you remember a particular lukesummer night?" (501.18), he might answer: "I dhink I sawn to remumb or sumbsuch. A kind of thinglike . . ." (608.22; compare both

Bottom's "Methought I was—there is no man can tell what" and the Ass's previous "Methought as I was dropping asleep. . . . And lo, mescemed somewhat came of the noise"). The Ass remembers his dream of allhistory on a "lukesummer night"; and since the *Wake* is both dream and drama, the Ass's dream vision thus finds a parallel in Bottom's dream from *A Midsummer Night's Dream*.

The Dramatic Metaphor

The "prepossessing drauma," then, is both a traumatic dream sequence, the nightmare of history, and the archetypal family drama, *The Mime of Mick, Nick and the Maggies*. *Finnegans Wake* consists of the dream visions of the poet Joyce, representative of "Allmen"; so also the minor poet "Osti-Fosti" (48.19), Hosty, speaks in the language of Shakespearean dream visions, using verbs like "Me drames" (49.32)— medreamt my drama. A poet-playwright—by analogy, HCE and all men—dreams the nightmare of all time, the "drema" (69.14) of the world. The metaphor of the world as stage, the dramatic metaphor, is suggested recurrently in *Finnegans Wake*, and most insistently in pages 30 to 33 and 219 to 221, the two passages in which Dublin's Gaiety Theatre is aptly transformed into the Globe.

Atherton has observed that "one of Joyce's favourite images for the world, or the *Wake*, is the stage—although the famous quotation is never made."[14] Of course, few direct quotations are made in *Finnegans Wake* without being refracted through puns and double meanings. Pages 30 to 33, however, contain a cluster of allusions to Shakespeare and to the stage, most conspicuous of which is the description of HCE as "our worldstage's practical jokepiece" (33.02–3). Clearly, this is a direct reference to Jaques (the "jokepiece"?), who said, "All the world's a stage, / And all the men and women merely players . . ." (*AYL* II. vii. 139–40). As a drama on the worldstage, HCE's story is a nightly reenactment, to which the public is invited, of an archetypal story, a "druriodrama" (50.06) in this Drury Lane world of ours.

The reader first sees HCE, like the "old gardener" Adam in his "prefall paradise," sitting about in his garden, "saving daylight under his redwood tree" (30.13–15) as the king approaches. These lines again echo *As You Like It* and "Under the greenwood tree" (II. v. 1), in a context which informs that the world has been a stage from the beginning of time, and that the Green World of the Forest of Arden (in which Jaques makes his "worldstage" metaphor), Shakespeare's correlative for the world of dramatic romance, is none other than Eden and all gardens.[15] "Under the greenwood tree," a song sung by Jaques and Amiens (549.31 "amiens"), is Shakespeare's invitation to this Green World:

> Under the greenwood tree,
> Who loves to lie with me. . . .
> Come hither, come hither, come hither. . . .
> Ducdame, ducdame, ducdame.
>
> (*AYL* II. v. 1ff.)

So here also, at the beginning of chapter 2 in book I of *Finnegans Wake*, is Joyce's own "come hither," his invitation to attend the play about HCE, a production to be "staged by Madame Sudlow" (32.10) at the King Street Theatre ("king's treat house" in 32.26),[16] in a "command performance . . . of the problem passion play of the millentury" (32.30–32). Bessy Sudlow (so named in 434.08) and Michael Gunn managed the Gaiety Theatre—on King Street in Dublin—where Christmas pantomimes were annually produced.[17] This particular "pantalime," (32.11) to be staged by the proprietress, bears certain resemblances to Shakespearean plays performed at the Globe, particularly *Hamlet*. Admission to sit in the "pit stalls and early amphitheatre" (33.10) is two bits ("a two pitts paythronosed"—patronized, and paid through the nose; 32.11–12). The seating choices are "Pit, prommer [promenoir lounge] and parterre [floor behind the orchestra; parquet circle], standing room only" (33.12). The habitual theatregoers are all out tonight to see our "worldstage's practical jokepiece," HCE: "*H*abituels conspicuously *e*mergent" (33.13; my italics). Like *Hamlet*, this piece is a "problem passion play" (32.32): *Hamlet* is one of the "problem plays"—and the *Wake* is a "passion play" since, as Joyce said, book III was written in the form of the fourteen stations of the Cross; *Hamlet*'s presence is strong in these pages—there are references to Ophelia ("Offaly" in 31.18), Hamlet ("hamlock" in 31.24), and even a direct echo from the play in "you have metheg in your midness" (32.05), the observation made by Polonius about Hamlet.[18] It seems that this pantomime or problem play at the Gaiety-Globe may be "the purchypatch of hamlock" (31.23–24)—the purple patch of *Hamlet*. In any event, history is seen as a play or pantomime presented on a worldstage.

This pantomime of the *Wake* is the drama of history, in its "homedromed and enliventh performance . . . of the millentury, running strong since creation" (32.31–33). As with *Hamlet* or with the plays of the "House of Atreox" (55.03), the pantomime is an archetypal family drama: it is the tragedy of HCE's fall and his falling-out with his wife ("*A Royal Divorce*" and "Napoleon the Nth" in 32.33 and 33.02) and his daughters

("*The Bo Girl*" and "*The Lily*" in 32.35). Brothers ("our red brother" in 31.25) and sisters ("his inseparable sisters, uncontrollable nighttalkers, Skertsiraizde with Donyahzade" in 32.07–8—Scheherazade and Dunyazade, skirt-raised sisters from the *Arabian Nights*) are also here, as is the Holy Trinity, the "triptychal religious family symbolizing puritas of doctrina, business per usuals, and the purchypatch of hamlock" (31.22–23).[19]

The World as Family Drama and Stage Company

The drama is a family affair. Joyce pursues this analogy in the *Wake* by frequently referring to the characters in the drama of the *Wake* as both family members and actors in a stage company. The drama on this worldstage is "real life"—or history—and the roles are played by a theatre company (whether the Gunns, Porters, Bonapartes, Hamlets, or Holy Trinity) whose cast members are the archetypal family itself: "Real life behind the floodlights as shown by the best exponents of a royal divorce" (260.F3). The cast members are, as we know by now, the members of HCE-Porter-Gunn's household, and their Gaiety Theatre globe-stage is none other than the publican's inn and residence in Chapelizod; thus, the word "house" is used throughout the *Wake* in three senses: domestic, tavernal, and theatrical (e.g., "the whole stock company of the old house of the Leaking Barrel" in 510.17). The cast is first introduced on page 13 of the *Wake:*

> And here now they are. . . . A bulbenboss surmounted upon an alderman. . . . A shoe on a puir old wobban. . . . An auburn mayde, o'brine, to be desarted. . . . A penn no weightier nor a polepost. And so. And all. (13.23–28)

The family members are an "older man" with a hump (bulbenboss) and a stutter (Balbus), or Humphrey-HCE; his wife, ALP, a poor old woman; his daughter, Issy, an auburn maiden; and his twin sons, the Pen and the Post, Shem and Shaun. There are five so far in the cast, and yet that is not all. This household troupe is actually a "howthold of nummer seven" (242.05), having two additional, nonfamily members in the household: a male servant (Sickerson, Sanderson, etc.) and a female servant (Kate). At the start of chapter 1 of book II, the performance of *The Mime of Mick, Nick and the Maggies* is prefaced by the proper theatrical introductions of the cast; this reads: "featuring: GLUGG (Mr Seumas McQuillad). . . . IZOD (Miss Butys Pott). . . . CHUFF (Mr Sean

O'Mailey). . . . ANN (Miss Corrie Corriendo). . . . HUMP (Mr Makeall Gone). . . . SAUNDERSON. . . . KATE" (219.21–221.12)—that is, Shem the Penquill, Issy the Beauty Spot, Shaun the Post, Anna Livia (the running—*corriendo*—waters of the Liffey), HCE-Michael Gunn, Saunderson, and Kate. These are the elements of our domestic drama; and we are now ready for "The family umbroglia" (284.04).

In an acting troupe of only seven members, each actor or actress must be able to assume a number of roles on call, depending on the particular family imbroglio being performed that evening; thus, each member is symbolic of a family "type," able to be recast into almost any old play or version of a royal divorce. "Like the newcasters in their old plyable of *A Royenne Devours*" (388.07), they must be ready to take over history's old plays, each actor performing the role assigned to him by the "worldwright" and puppetry producer. This concept is important and fundamental. The notion of an archetypal cast performing different plays, or interpretations of an archetypal play, corresponds marvelously with Joyce's concept of history as a resonant exploration of different possibilities. As the *Wake* is about history, the different variations (and possibilities) of reality and history become the different plays in the repertoire performed by the acting troupe and family, "the whole stock company of the old house" (510.17), where each member is able to act the part for his "type" in each new play. The *Wake* is full of references to stock companies and acting troupes, with the same basic "types" playing different roles under each character "type." There could be no better model for Wakean history and Viconian *ricorso*. HCE can be the same basic actor under the various historical guises of Adam, Tim Finnegan, Finn MacCool, Shakespeare, and so forth; the filial usurper (Cad, Hosty, Paul Horan, etc.), "Under the name of Orani . . . may have been the utility man of the troupe capable of sustaining long parts at short notice" (49.19–21). The family is a house troupe, which performs "with nightly redistribution of parts and players by the puppetry producer and daily dubbing of ghosters" (219.06–8).

Pages 323 and 324 provide an excellent illustration of how *Finnegans Wake* is presented as a stage drama played by "the whole stock company of the house":

> tummelumpsk . . . that bunch of palers. . . . Toni Lampi. . . . ghustorily spoeking, gen and gang, dane and dare, like the dud spuk of his first foetotype. . . . And ere he could catch a hook or line to suit their saussyskins, the lumpenpack. . . . Sot!. . . . change all that whole set. Shut down and shet up. Our set, our set's allohn. (323.28–324.16)

Fritz Senn has pointed out that this passage (quoted in part) refers to a particular stage performance of *Hamlet* in Dublin at the Crow Street Theatre.[20] Referring to "the versatility of the Dublin stock companies" (and quoting from Samuel Fitzpatrick's *Dublin: A Historical and Topographical Account of the City* [1907], one of Joyce's source books for the *Wake*), Senn writes:

> "At Crow Street Digges ('Digges' in 313.26) was playing 'Hamlet' and ruptured a blood vessel. The play was immediately stopped and *She Stoops to Conquer* substituted for it. The manager's apologies having been accepted, the performers, who were all in the house, hastily dressed and went on. A gentleman in the pit had left the building immediately before the accident to Digges, for the purposes of buying oranges. He was delayed for some little time, and having left 'Hamlet' in conversation with the 'Ghost,' found on his return the stage occupied by 'Tony Lumpkin' and his companions at the Three Jolly Pigeons. He at first thought he had mistaken the theatre, but an explanation showed him the real state of affairs" (Fitzpatrick, 256–57). In *FW*, all actors play multiple parts, often simultaneously, and we [readers] all think, again and again, that we have mistaken the theatre. In particular, Joyce used the incident in the paragraph beginning 323.25, where *She Stoops* and *Hamlet* are among the things that go on at the same time.[21]

With much going on at once, the passage on pages 323 and 324 of *Finnegans Wake* is a murky one at best; in context, it seems that HCE, in the role of the Norwegian Captain, has momentarily left the tavern for the outhouse (much as the spectator at Crow Street goes out to buy oranges), and returns to find the set (tavern = theatre, of course), completely changed, as happened with *She Stoops to Conquer* and *Hamlet*. This historic worldstage seems to be constantly changing sets, exploring new and different variations and possibilities. The drinkers at the tavern have suddenly become "that bunch of palers" (a bunch of players); Tony Lumpkin appears as "tummelumpsk" and "Toni Lampi." The first play concerned Danish ghosts: both the ghost of King Hamlet, King of Denmark, ("ghustorily spoeking . . . dane and dare") daring his son on (a father spooking and speaking, "like the dud spuk," to his firstborn, "his first foetotype"); and Ibsen's *Ghosts* (*Gengangere* in Dano-Norwegian; here, "gen and gang"). However, "ere he could catch or hook or line," the set has changed back to Tony Lumpkin and the Three Jolly Pigeons—back to the "lumpenpack" accompanied by the shout: "Sot!. . . . change all that whole set. Shut down and shet up. Our set, our set's allohn"—our set's all one in the versatile drama of all-history. (The prop men, crying to shut down and set up, seem to be Sinn Feinners: ourselves, ourselves alone.) Change the set, but the show (and history) must go on, "like the newcasters in the old plyable" (388.07). The archetypal family drama is a tale renewed and reenacted nightly on the worldstage, a daily dubbing of *Hamlet* (and all family dramas) at the Globe.

The World as Shakespearean Stage History

If all the world's a stage, then all stages are the world. Thus Joyce casts his worldplay on many stages and, in writing the *Wake* drama, immerses it in the contexts of stage history.

In Joyce's dream chronicle of world history, his favorite worldstages are those associated with Shakespearean stage history, both Elizabethan and Irish. Joyce, as the "worldwright" who wrote the folio of his world and makes his Globe turn, is "the Royal Revolver of these real globoes" (455.26). The plays of Shakespeare, however, whether staged at the Globe in Bankside or at "The Blackfriars" (48.03) in Blackfriars, enjoyed more popular success than Joyce's *Wake* ever did in its author's lifetime. Joyce pleads on page 201: *"By earth and the cloudy but I badly want a brandnew bankside, bedamp and I do, and a plumper at that!"* Atherton correctly interprets this line as Joyce's complaint of his inability to find a suitable audience, like that at the Bankside, to appreciate his work: "What Joyce is saying is that he wishes the Liffey had a South Bank where literature was appreciated as it was by Shakespeare's Thames."[22] So dependent on verbal correspondences as he was, Joyce may have found that the most suitable correlative of his worldstage was not a theatre on the Bankside, but another Elizabethan playhouse, the Phoenix (or Cockpit) Theatre, in St.-Giles-in-the-Fields adjoining Drury Lane. The name Phoenix corresponds to HCE's pub in Chapelizod by the Phoenix Park (referred to in 205.25 as "Phoenix Tavern"), to the Elizabethan playhouse, and to the phoenix rising from its ashes, Joyce's symbol for Viconian *ricorso* and "the newcasters in the old plyable." Thus, he stages the *Wake's* dream-drama "by night in the Phoenix! Music. And old lotts have funn at Flammagen's ball" (321.16–17) and "out there in Cockpit" (427.34).[23] In chapter 1 of book II, *The Mime of Mick, Nick and the Maggies* is announced as being played at the Phoenix: "Every evening at lighting up o'clock sharp and until further notice in Feenichts Playhouse" (219.01–2).

However, the theatre district best known for its Shakespearean productions has been the area around Drury Lane; this region was dominated by the Drury Lane Theatre (King's House, Theatre Royal), probably the most famous playhouse in English stage history. Thus, Drury Lane, with its "druriodrama" (50.06), becomes another of Joyce's favorite metaphors for "this drury world of ours" (600.02). The author depicts for us the dream-drama of the *Wake*—he "pulls a lane picture for us, in a dreariodreama setting" (79.27–28). Like Yawn, he is a theatre buff, "He loves a drary lane" (491.29–30), and he presents the *Wake* as a pantomime of history at Drury Lane, "our Theoatre Regal's drolleries puntomine" (587.08).[24]

On these Shakespearean stages played some very well-known actors. Perhaps the most famous Shakespearean actor was Drury Lane's own David Garrick. Playing such characters as Hamlet, Richard III, and Macbeth, he was, like Finnegan or Finn MacCool, an earlier version of the HCE "type." Each Viconian cycle provides for the same roles its own interpretations, new readings of the same basic part by sons of Garrick: "hearing in this new reading of the part whereby . . . the new garrickson's grimacing . . . of that once grand old elrington" (55.33–36).[25] The same part—that, say, of Richard Crookback—may be played at different times by different men, by any Tom, Dick, or Harry, and still be Richard III: "Crookback by the even more titulars, Rick, Dave, and Barry" (134.11); Rick, Dave, and Barry refer, I believe, to perhaps the three most famous "Richards" in Shakespearean theatrical history, Richard Burbage, David Garrick, and Barry Sullivan.[26] In Shakespeare's own day the players of the worldstage, the stock companies of the old house, were troupes such as "the king's men" (47.26; also 567.17) at the Globe or "the Queen's Mum" (219.16) at the Phoenix.[27] The *Wake* is also filled with references to Shakespearean actors of other periods: Ellen Terry (and her famous debut at the age of eight as Puck) in "Terry the Puckaun" (210.34–35), Marie Ney as Ophelia in "Neya" (203.14; see part II entry), perhaps John Barrymore ("garrymore" in 583.11), and others.

The more persistent references to Shakespearean actors, however, are to those most familiar to Joyce—those on the Dublin stage. The writer centered his family troupe and stock company around Dublin's Gaiety Theatre on King Street, managed by Michael Gunn and Bessy Sudlow; the Gaiety is Joyce's "Globe," his most important symbolic worldstage. The *Wake* abounds with references to Gunn, Sudlow, and the Gaiety,[28] but other members of the theatre's troupe are also mentioned, such as Valentine Vousden (in 50.15, "volunteer Vousden," and in 439.17, "Venerable Val Vousdem") and E.W. Royce (in 205.29, "royss in his turgos the turrible"; *U*, 10 recalls "old Royce . . . in the pantomime of Turko the terrible"). Most importantly, however, the *Wake* is repeatedly referred to as a Christmas pantomime at the Gaiety: "a pantalime . . . in that king's treat house" (32.11–26), a "gaiety pantheomime" (180.04), "the Hereweareagain Gaieties . . . for the chrisman's pandemon" (455.25–26),

"Edwin Hamilton's Christmas pantaloonade . . . at the Gaiety" (513.21–22), and so forth. In pages 31 to 33, as we've seen, the family drama is introduced around "Madame Sudlow" (32.10) in the "king's treat house"; in that other most important statement of the dramatic metaphor, found on pages 219 to 221, *The Mime* itself takes place at the Gaiety with Michael Gunn in the lead role.

The Gaiety is hardly the only Dublin theatre named in the *Wake*. Mentioned are the Adelphi Theatre (later the Queen's), where *The Mime* seems to have previously played—"As played to the Adelphi" (219.14)—and Dublin's own Theatre Royal, renowned for a particularly forgettable performance of *Richard III* in which an amateur named Luke Plunkett appeared as Richard Crookback and was roundly booed and jeered at for his performance:[29] "Dook Hookbackcrook upsits his ass booseworthies jeer and junket but they boos him oos and baas his ass when he lukes like Hunkett Plunkett" (127.17–19). Still, perhaps the most famous of Dublin theatres—at least in terms of Shakespearean productions—were the Smock Alley Theatre and the Crow Street Theatre. The former is alluded to in "S. S. Smack and Olley's" (60.32) and "Smock Alley the first night" (147.32); and a detailed reference (in 323.28–324.16) has already been included to a particular performance of *Hamlet-alias-She Stoops to Conquer* at the Crow. These two theatres are more often referred to jointly in the *Wake*, since they were great rivals for Dublin's theatregoing crowd: "*From Abbeygate to Crowalley Through a Lift in the Lude, Smocks for their Graces*" (105.26–27, with perhaps also a reference to Dublin's Gate Theatre).[30] A parallel rivalry is manifested in the *Wake* by a pairing of Dublin's two major Shakespearean leads, Henry Mossop and Spranger Barry, who were always competing for theatregoing audiences; these two great Shakespearean actors were famous performers in both Dublin and London. In the *Wake* rival actors Mossop and Barry become versions of the archetypal and competing twins, Shem and Shaun[31]; they are paired on page 184 in "Carrageen moss and blaster of Barry's." As rivals, they are like the protagonists from *The Two Gentlemen of Verona*, competing for the love of Issy-Sylvia—this analogy does not bypass Joyce's wonderfully punning mind: "Play actors by us ever have crash to their gate. Mr Messop and Mr Borry will produce of themselves, as they're two genitalmen of Veruno" (569.29–31). *Two Gentlemen*, a story of male friendship, is appropriately "two genitalmen" and "Such a boyplay!" (569.34).

Joyce revels in notably fouled-up Shakespearean performances. He alludes to one of *Hamlet* played at the Crow, and one of *Richard III* staged at the Theatre Royal; the Smock Alley is not spared either. Senn has pointed out that in "But if this could see with its backsight he'd be the grand old greeneyed lobster" (249.02–3) Joyce is referring to a particular famous performance of *Othello* at the Smock Alley. In this staging, actor-manager Thomas Sheridan (184.24—"Sharadan's *Art of Panning*") played Othello, while an actor named Layfield was Iago. "When he [Layfield] came to the lines: 'Oh, my Lord! beware of jealousy; / It is a green-eyed monster,'—he gave the latter as 'It is a green-eyed lobster.' He was at that moment struck with incurable madness, and died somewhat in the manner of Nat Lee the tragic poet."[32] This fatal slip may also be the source of "And how did the greeneyed mister arrive at the B.A.?" (88.15–16) and "one old obster" (94.17).

While Henry Mossop seems to be continually associated with Spranger Barry, Thomas Sheridan is similarly linked with another famous member of the Smock Alley, Shakespearean actress Peg Woffington. Glasheen points out that "Peg and Tom seems also to form a minor motif which I cannot identify."[33] I will hazard a guess: they are Peg Woffington (1714–60) and Thomas Sheridan (1719–88), two of the most famous Shakespearean actors of their day, both of whom were members of the Smock Alley. Peg Woffington (mentioned also in *U*, 296) first became known in Dublin in 1737 in the role of Ophelia; the lover of David Garrick, she was considered the most handsome actress of her time. Sheridan, an actor and an author (and the father of Richard Brinsley Sheridan), was famed for his portrayals of Richard III, Hamlet, Brutus, Macbeth, and Othello. There are five instances in which "peg" and "tom" are linked in the *Wake;* clearly Joyce saw them as a tandem. This suggests that, just as Joyce used Mossop and Barry to signify Shem and Shaun, he uses Woffington and Sheridan to indicate illicit love, perhaps between Shem and Issy. For example, on page 436 we read: "kosenkissing . . . like Population Peg or a hint or twim clandestinely does be doing to Temptation Tom"; in context, Shaun-Laertes is lecturing Issy-Ophelia and warning her about temptation and about clandestine flirting with other boys, even with kissing "cousins" (like his "twim" Shem-Hamlet?), because Temptation may result in Population. Woffington would provide a good example for Shaun's lecture, since she and Garrick were known lovers, and, as *The Reader's Encyclopedia of Shakespeare* kindly puts it, "her morals were not above reproach."[34] That Woffington and Sheridan might have been lovers is again implied in "Regies Producer with screendoll Vedette, peg of his claim and pride of her heart" (577.15–16): the line occurs within a bedtime prayer that HCE and ALP may have good sexual relations in bed, "that he may dishcover her, that she may uncouple him" (577.18). As manager of the Smock Alley, Sheridan would be the "Regies Producer," and Woffington one of his stars; she would be the peg of his claim, and he the pride of her heart. Thus, "playing peg and pom" (586.12) means not only playing roles in a Shakespearean play, but having illicit sexual relations.

Whether at the Smock Alley or the Crow, whether staged by Sheridan and Woffington or by Mossop and Barry, the performance itself seems to be some sort of a pantomime. The world of the *Wake* is a stage on which a play of complete history, a Christmas pantomime, is repeatedly being played. "Pantomime" is one of the most frequent terms in the *Wake;* it appears at least eleven times in various guises and puns—for example, "pamtomomiom" (285.15–16, with pandemonium), "flea pantamine" (531.20), "pulltomine" (615.24), and "pantymammy" (626.27). "And this pattern pootsch punnermine . . . went on, hog and minne, a whole whake, your night after larry's night" (519.03–5): there is a "pattern" to the plot of this pantomime, for it goes on, night after night, for not only a whole week, but for the entire *Wake* ("a whole whake"). In short, it is the pantomime of history—and thus is *Finnegans Wake* itself, a mine of puns (a "punnermine"). That, perhaps, is "the gist of the pantomime . . . in this drury world of ours" (599.36–600.02). Once more the world of Drury Lane (Theatre Royal) is the stage for the drama of history, "our Theoatre Regal's drolleries puntomine" (587.08).[35]

As we might expect, however, the central site of the pantomime version of the dramatic metaphor is the Gaiety Theatre. We've seen how "Madame Sudlow" (32.10) staged the "pantalime" (32.11) of the archetypal family drama in "that king's treat house"; the drama of the *Wake* is a "gaiety pantheomime" (180.04). On pages 510 to 513, the play which "the whole stock company of the old house" (510.17) puts on appears to be "Edwin Hamilton's Christmas pantaloonade, *Oropos Roxy and Pantharhea* at the Gaiety" (513.21–22). HCE (here EHC), or Michael Gunn, is staging a Christmas pantomime by Edwin Hamilton, who, according to Glasheen, was a "Dubliner who wrote libretti for several pantomimes, including Turko the Terrible."[36] A "pantaloon" is the buffoon figure in pantomimes; the pantomime being performed appears to involve *Oedipus Rex (Oropos Roxy)* and a true "pantaloonade," *Pantharhea*. It is probably the story of HCE's crime in the park, where our hero and buffoon supposedly dropped his pants (or pantaloons) either to defecate or to expose himself to the two girls (and, as with the Russian General, may have been shot by Buckley for the act). In any case, *Finnegans Wake* appears to be symbolically set as a play, a Christmas pantomime at the Gaiety.[37]

If the play is the *Wake*, the play is all-history, and the stage metaphor pervades the plot of the book. Any *Wake* reader will soon be aware that the dream-drama of the *Wake* text is laced with stage directions, regardless of the particular context. A scene might start, as in a Shakespearean play, with "On. Sennet" (219.13); a character might leave like Polonius would: "Exeunc throw a darras . . . Enterest attawonder" (388.01–3). The folio of the *Wake* progresses as the effort of a self-conscious playwright–turned–novelist, a "worldwright" directing the movement of his world-stage, calling for the drop of the curtain or the brightening of footlights:

"Lights, pageboy, lights! Brights we'll be brights" (245.04–5); "Act drop. Stand by! Blinders! Curtain up. Juice, please! Foots!" (501.07); and so on. In a chronicle of history, all the activities of life are sooner or later portrayed in dramatic terms, whether the context is a wedding (as in 330.12), the sexual act (a "wineact come" in 587.35), or whatever.

The drama of the *Wake* is not, however, limited to past history. In one of the loveliest and most resonant passages of the *Wake*, Joyce foresees the joy of the Christmas pantomime of the afterworld.

> Postmartem is the goods. . . . Toborrow and toburrow and tobarrow! That's our crass, hairy and evergrim life, till one finel howdiedow. . . . Ah, sure . . . what a humpty daum earth looks our miseryme heretoday as compared beside the Hereweareagain Gaieties of the Afterpiece when the Royal Revolver of these real globoes lets regally fire of his *mio colpo* for the chrisman's pandemon to give over and the Harlequinade to begin properly SPQueaRking Mark Time's Finist Joke. Putting Allspace in a Notshall. (455.11–29)

In this passage, Jaun-Christ-Bottom is having an apocalyptical vision, and warns Issy that death in the only certainty—post-mortem is the goods. Our life is only a Viconian series of tomorrows (spent borrowing and burrowing for survival), ending in burial under the sod ("tobarrow"): that's the crass and grim life (of yesterday, today and tomorrow—Latin *heri, hodie, cras*) for HCE ("*c*rass, *h*airy and *e*vergrim") and for all of us in the theatre of life (W. W. Kelly's Evergreen Touring Company). Jaun is echoing Macbeth's most famous speech ("To-morrow, and to-morrow, and to-morrow . . ." in V. v. 19 ff.) on the same subject. In that address, Macbeth forged his famous equation of life as a brief stage play; the entire passage here works off of that metaphor: "Life's but a walking shadow, a poor player / That struts and frets his hour upon the stage / And then is heard no more" (V. v. 24–26).

Jaun, however, argues: what a dump seems this "humpty daum earth" with its woes ("miseryme") and its brevity ("heretoday"—gone tomorrow), "as compared beside" the joyfulness of the Second Coming ("the Hereweareagain Gaieties"). For after our brief interlude on earth, we join the unending Gaiety Theatre of heaven ("Gaities of the Afterpiece"—*pièce*, play) when the real (*real* is Spanish for "royal") stage manager—the Man who really makes the world turn ("the Royal Revolver of these real globoes," the God and gun of the Gaiety, Mr. Makeall Gone), God the Father himself, the proprietor of our heavenly worldstage (Globe Theatre and "globoes")—lets loose the blows (*mio colpo*, "my blow" in

Italian) of his chastising *(mea culpa)* thunderbolts, *then* is it time for the Christmas pantomime, for the Christ-predicted pandemonium ("chrisman's pandemon") of Hell and the Judgment Day, and for the "Harlequinade" (a pantomime in which Harlequin [the Devil] has a leading role) all to begin—which is, properly speaking, the final chapter of Time ("Mark Time's Finist Joke," Mark Twain's Finest Joke, and Time's final joke). "SPQueaRking" cleverly describes the pandemonium of the Last Day, like the day in Rome (SPQR) when Julius Caesar fell (on the Ides of March), when "The graves stood tenantless and the sheeted dead / Did *squeak* and gibber in the Roman streets" (*Ham.* I. i. 115–16; my italics).[38] Jaun finally summarizes the Judgment Day with another echo from *Hamlet:* "Putting Allspace in a Notshall" could only happen on the Last Day; doing so would please the spatialist Jaun-Shaun-Bottom, who might, like Hamlet or Brutus, say, "O God, I could be bounded in a nutshell and count myself a king of infinite space, were it not that I have bad dreams" (*Ham.* II. ii. 250; see also *"Omnitudes in a knutshedell"* in 276.L2). It is a lovely passage.[39]

The Mime of Mick, Nick and the Maggies

Finnegans Wake is most explicitly a play in chapter 1 of book II, on page 219 and following, where *The Mime of Mick, Nick and the Maggies* is presented. This mime, put on by Michael Gunn's troupe, is a microcosm of the *Wake* dream-drama. *The Mimic of Meg Neg and the Mackeys* (as it is called in 106.10) is a play given by the children before their parents—a family drama; it is a pantomime of temptation and frustration (in which Izod-Issy is frustrated in her sexual temptations of Glugg-Shem). The story reenacts some of the old themes of the story of the parents, and is thus a "daily dubbing." The Viconian play comes, like the *Wake*, in four acts.

To Joyce, always punning, a "play" is also a game—and the plot of the children's mime is literally a game, the children at play. The game that the girls ("the Maggies," led by Izod) are playing, Joyce said, is one called "Angels and Devils or colours."[40] Shaun-Chuff is Mick, or Michael the Archangel; Shem-Glugg is Nick, which is a common nickname of the Devil; and the Maggies—rainbow girls or flower girls—are the "colours." Their sport is a guessing game in which Shem-Glugg is the victim: Izod poses a riddle to him three separate times, and thrice he is baffled and disgraced; the Maggies meanwhile dance rings around Shaun-Chuff, for the answer to their riddle is "heliotrope,"[41] and the heliotropic Floras find their sunshine in Shaun. HCE then returns to commence the fourth act, in which he ends the children's hour of game and sends them upstairs to bed. At this point the play is over, the curtain falls, and the chapter ends.

The introduction and conclusion to *The Mime* are important to this study, for they form the *Wake*'s key statement of the dramatic metaphor, equating the action of the novel (here, *The Mime*) with a stage performance. Chapter 1 of book II opens with a playbill announcing the performance of *The Mime* (pages 219–22):[42]

> Every evening at lighting up o'clock sharp and until further notice in Feenichts Playhouse. (Bar and conveniences always open, Diddlem Club douncestears.) Entrancings: gads, a scrab; the quality, one large shilling. Newly billed for each wickeday perfumance. Somndoze massinees. By arraignment, childream's hours, expercatered. Jampots, rinsed porters, taken in token. With nightly redistribution of parts and players by the puppetry producer and daily dubbing of ghosters, with the benediction of the Holy Genesius Archimimus and under the distinguished patronage of their Elderships . . . while the Caesar-in-Chief looks. On. Sennet. As played to the Adelphi by the Brothers Bratislavoff (Hyrcan and Haristobulus) after humpteen dumpteen revivals. Before all the King's Hoarsers with all the Queen's Mum. And wordloosed over seven seas crowdblast in cellelleneteutoslavzendlatinsoundscript. In four tubbloids. . . . *The Mime of Mick, Nick and the Maggies*, adopted from the Ballymooney Bloodriddon Murther by Bluechin Blackdillain (authorways 'Big Storey'), featuring:
>
> GLUGG (Mr Seumas McQuillad. . . .)
> THE FLORAS. . . .
> IZOD (Miss Butys Pott . . . .)
> CHUFF (Mr Sean O'Mailey. . . .)
> ANN (Miss Corrie Corriendo. . . .)
> HUMP (Mr Makeall Gone. . . .)
> THE CUSTOMERS. . . .
> SAUNDERSON. . . .
> KATE. . . .
> . . . the show must go on.
> Time: the pressant. (219.01–221.17)

An explication for the playbill announcement reads thus:
Performed every evening at lighting up time and until further notice in the Phoenix Playhouse. (Bar and conveniences always open, a club downstairs for "diddling," or passing the time.) Entrance fee: for vagabonds, a crab-apple; for the quality, one large shilling. Newly billed for each week-

day performance. And Sunday matinees (for somnolent ones who doze through Sunday mass). By arrangement, there can be special children's hours, expurgated, and expertly catered, with jampots and rinsed porters taken in token. The play will be performed by the whole stock company, with nightly redistribution of parts and players by the puppetry producer (Michael Gunn, stage manager) and daily dubbing of ghosts with the blessing of the Holy Genesius Arch-Mime himself (St. Genesius, patron saint of actors; Greek archimimos, chief actor) and under the patronage of their Elderships . . . while the Caesar-in-Chief (God) looks on. Trumpets, please; begin the play. As previously performed at the Adelphi Theatre by the Brothers Bratislavoff (*brat* is Slavic for brother; Greek *adelphoi*, brothers) after humpteen revivals (and revivals-ricorsos of HCE = Humpty-Dumpty). Played before all the King's Horses (Chamberlain's Men) and the Queen's Men. Wirelessed and broadcast over the seven seas in Celtic-Hellenic-Teutonic-Slavic-Zend-Latin-Sanskrit soundscript. In four tableaux. . . . Called *The Mime of Mick, Nick and the Maggies*, adopted from a Senecan tragedy of blood (*Hamlet*, as we shall see) by Bluechin Blackdillain (otherwise known as the author of "Big Story"),[43] featuring: Glugg (Shem the Penman); The Flower (heliotrope) Girls; Izod (Miss Beauty Spot); Chuff (Sean the Postman); Anna Livia (the running waters of the Liffey); Hump (Michael Gunn); The Customers; Saunderson, the manservant; Kate, the maid. . . . The show must go on. Time: the present, urgent (French, *pressant*) and pressing ever onwards.

The playbill continues with a list of props used in "the Pageant of Past History" (221.18–19)—masks, lighting, pipes, hats, bags, trees, rocks, venetian blinds, doorposts, gladstone bags, and so on. Credits are given for a musical score ("Accidental music providentially arranged by L'Archet and Laccorde"—John F. Larchet was the Abbey Theatre's orchestra leader), and singers are mentioned (including "Joan MockComic"—John McCormack). Next, "the whole thugogmagog . . . to be wound up for an after-enactment by a Magnificent Transformation Scene showing the Radium Wedding of Neid and Moorning and the Dawn of Peace, Pure, Perfect and Perpetual, Waking the Weary of the World" (222. 14–20)—the whole thingamajig is then to be wound up for an after-enactment in a Magnificent Transformation Scene showing the Radiant Wedding of Night and Morning, the Dawn of Peace, the Wake, and Ricorso. (Here, too, is found another play, Congreve's *Way of the World;* and, as in the Gaiety pantomimes, there is a "transformation scene."[44]) These lines provide an apt description of book IV of the *Wake*, and, thus, the four acts of *The Mime* appear to be a microcosm of the *Wake* itself.

Once again we have learned that the *Wake* family drama is being staged at the Gaiety, with "Makeall Gone" taking the lead role of Hump (HCE). "Every evening at lighting up o'clock sharp and until further notice in Feenichts Playhouse. . . . Newly billed for each wickeday perfumance": the nightly performance reminds us that HCE's story is an archetypal "drema," dreamt, performed, and reenacted during all times; and, like a reborn phoenix, Gunn-Hump rises each morning in order to replay a tragic fall in the evening's performance. The stage thus becomes a precise, concrete, and practical application of Viconian *ricorso*. *The Mime* is, then, a "nightly redistribution of parts and players by the puppetry producer and daily dubbing of ghosters."

"Ghosters" may refer to Ibsen's *Ghosts,* to God and the Holy Ghost, to stand-ins ("redistribution of parts and players"), to ghostwriters and forgers, to the spirit of Hamlet's father, to HCE as father, and so on. It is most likely, in this context of "daily dubbing," that all of these are referred to. The playwright Ibsen, like King Hamlet and the invading Norseman, HCE, was from "Scandiknavery" (47.21); and playwrights, kings, gods, fathers, and stage managers are all rulers of sorts. "King's Hoarsers" and "Queen's Mum" (219.15–16) set the stage for the hoarse clamor for vengeance by King Hamlet and the silent guilt of Hamlet's mother, Queen Gertrude.

The Mime opens ("On. Sennet.") as does *Hamlet,* with Hump walking onstage like old King Hamlet of Denmark ("King Ericus of Schweden" in 220.25) in "his magical helmet, cap-a-pipe with watch and topper, coat, crest and supporters" (220.26–27); the ghost of Hamlet's father enters wearing a helmet, and, in Horatio's words, "Armèd at point exactly, cap-a-pe [head to foot]" (I. ii. 200).[45] The play begins to unfold and the playbill ends with Joyce again reminding us that this Norse drama is a continuing and ever-recurring saga, a "Continuarration" (205.14).

The Mime itself has much to do with *Hamlet* and *Macbeth;* these clusters of Shakespearean allusions shall be discussed later in this study. Presently we will skip to the end of the "play," to act 4 of the Children's Hour. At this point, after the children have played their game for three acts, the father (Hump-HCE-Gunn) reappears. As the stage manager of their world, he is their *deus ex machina* ("god of all machineries" in 253.33); as the shaper of their family history, "the producer (Mr John Baptister Vickar)" is "pluterpromptly brought on the scene" (255.27–29), along with his wife, to restore order. Gathering his children together, he decides it's time to go home: "Home all go. Halome" (256.11).[46] ALP tells the kids a bedtime story in the bedroom and, on this domestic scene, the curtain now falls, along with a hundred letter thunderword. "Byfall. / Upploud!" (257.29–30; *Beifall* is German for applause, and the crowd obliges). HCE-Gunn then announces that "The play thou schouwburgst,

Game, here endeth. The curtain drops by deep request" (257.31–32). The "play"—the game, *The Mime*—is over; his announcement is followed by applause again, this time louder, and capped by a final amen: "Uplouderamain!" (257.33). As always, history is theatre (*schouwburg* is Dutch for "theatre").

Thus ends *The Mime of Mick, Nick and the Maggies*.

4

The Purchypatch of Hamlock: *Hamlet* and the *Wake*

"camelot prince of dinmurk"
Finnegans Wake

Hamlet is a structural matrix in *Finnegans Wake,* a central and symbolic framework for the action on the worldstage. Its thematic relevance to the book is comprehensive and manifold; thus, *Hamlet* allusions are discovered throughout the *Wake,* not merely in occasional "clusters" built around single themes (as with the allusions to *Macbeth, Julius Caesar,* and *A Midsummer Night's Dream*). Because *Hamlet* is associated with a number of major themes in the *Wake,* much of the discussion of this play has been parceled out to chapters dealing with specific themes: "Fathers and Sons," "History and Possibility," and "The Strife Between Brothers." The present chapter will introduce and outline the basic correspondences between *Hamlet* and *Finnegans Wake.*

The State of Penmark

The title of perhaps Shakespeare's best-known play is *Hamlet, Prince of Denmark*—or, in Wake-ese, "camelot prince of dinmurk" (143.07) and "Tamstar Ham of Tenman" (187.22). Denmark had always been important to Joyce's artistic consciousness; and, indeed, the Scandinavian elements in the *Wake* have been authoritatively documented.[1] Joyce admired Henrik Ibsen above all other writers, and had learned Dano-Norwegian in order to read the playwright's original works. Joyce had already used *Hamlet,* a play set in Denmark, as one of the structural foundations of *Ulysses,* especially important in the mind of Stephen Dedalus; the play is the major topic of the library chapter, in which Stephen explicates his theory that "Hamlet's grandson is Shakespeare's grandfather and that he himself is the ghost of his own father" (*U,* 18).[2] Denmark, the home of the Danish invaders of Ireland and all that "Scandiknavery" (47.21), was the root of half of Ireland's historical tradition;[3] it was the fatherland of our archetypal foreigner-in-Dublin, the *Wake*'s HCE. Therefore it is appropriate that HCE is associated throughout the *Wake* with King Hamlet and that *Hamlet, Prince of Denmark* is a central source of allusion for the *Wake*.

Denmark is equated first with Ireland; the land of *Hamlet* is the land of the *Wake*. Scandinavia was also the worldstage of Joyce's favorite "worldwright," Ibsen. As such, it becomes transformed, through a pun, into the metaphorical world of the artist-creator-god, Joyce the Penman: just as Hamlet detects something rotten and troubling in the state of Denmark, the writer Shem-Joyce finds "small peace in ppenmark" (189.06). Writing and Denmark are repeatedly connected: "Very glad you are going to Penmark. Write to the corner" (301.F5). The readers might ask Joyce (as is asked of Shaun in chapter 1 of book III), concerning "the views of Denmark" (421.29), if it is not true that his "millions of moods used up slanguage tun times as words as the penmarks used out in sinscript? . ." (421.17–18)—that his millions of moods used slang words and language ten times worse than the penmarks used in Sanskrit, and in evil or obscene language? After reading the ink and penmarks of the *Wake*, one might question the extent to which the linguistic distortion of pen and ink will go: "What will not arky paper, anticidingly inked with penmark, push?" (606.25). In any case, Denmark and the land of *Hamlet* become associated with the world of the "worldwright" and his imagination; Scandinavia becomes "Skaldignavia" (254.33; *skald* means "poet" in Danish).

Denmark, the fatherland of the *Wake*'s archetypal father, HCE, is thus also the land of the *Wake*—Ireland. Chilly Elsinore, site of *Hamlet*, becomes Dublin, locale of the *Wake* and "Ebblinn's chilled hamlet" (*Eblanna*-Ireland's chilled village in 41.18). The "cliff / That beetles o'er his base into the sea" (I. iv. 70–71) also "beetles backwards" under "the cope of heaven" (248.18, 25) in the *Wake*.[4] Just as the creator of Dublin is metaphorically converted into the creator of the *Wake* and of the universe, and into all creators, so also the metaphor of Denmark becomes universal: Dublin, the *Wake*, the poet's imagination, the world—even the heavens. Copenhagen becomes "the cope of heaven" (248.25). Hamlet's fear of "The undiscovered country, from whose bourn / No traveller returns" (III. i. 79–80) is balanced by his hope for a safe haven in a Danish heaven, in "old hopeinhaven" (143.10; see Part II, entry for 143.03–28); "lead us to hopenhaven" (478.16), as Joyce's puts it.[5] Denmark is at once the world of *Hamlet*, of the poet and his "penmarks," of the *Wake*, of Dublin, Ireland, of the heavens, and of the entire universe.

Hamlet and *Finnegans Wake*

Because the land of *Hamlet* becomes the world of the *Wake*, the reader might expect the play itself to be equated with Joyce's story. *The Mime*, a microcosm for the *Wake* itself, is thus shown to have numerous similarities to *Hamlet*. Like *The Mime*'s "daily dubbing of ghosters" (219.08), *Hamlet* involves actors dubbing as the Ghost (as Shakespeare the actor had done himself). In the family drama at the Gaiety, the Holy Ghost was referred to as "the purchypatch of hamlock" (31.23)—the purple passage of *Hamlet*. The *Plays* in fact abound with difficult purple patches, as do Joyce's writings, with their "porpor patches" (200.04) and their "paupers patch" (316.23). Joyce refers to the production at the Gaiety as both "the purchypatch of hamlock" (31.23) and "the problem passion play of the millentury" (32.32); and *Hamlet* is one of the four "problem plays," as designated by F.S. Boas. Furthermore, *The Mime*, as symbolic of the *Wake* and the "patchpurple of the massacre,"[6] is described on page 219 as being "adopted from the Ballymooney Bloodriddon Murther." *Hamlet*, a blood-ridden tragedy in the Senecan tradition, likewise concerns revenge and murder; like other revenge plays of the period (such as Kyd's *The Spanish Tragedy* and the *Ur-Hamlet*, the prototypes for *Hamlet*), it ends in a bloody massacre. Stephen Dedalus remarks about the play: "Nine lives are taken off for his [Hamlet's] father's one, Our Father who art in purgatory. Khaki Hamlets don't hesitate to shoot. The bloodboltered shambles in act five is a forecast of the concentration camp sung by Mr Swinburne" (*U*, 187). Finally, *The Mime* is, of course, a "mime", a play without words; *Hamlet* also has its play without words: "the play's the thing, / Wherein I'll catch the conscience of the king" (II. ii. 590).[7] The motif of the *Wake* as a "dumb show" occurs several times: "the dumb scene" (88.25), "dummpshow . . . mute commoner" (120.07–8), "we'll dumb weel soon show him" (442.22), and so on. The dumb show is explicitly equated with the drama of the *Wake* in the stage directions for the HCE-ALP bedroom drama:

A time.
Act: dumbshow.
Closeup. Leads.
Man with nightcap, in bed, fore. Woman, with curlpins, hind. . . .
(559.17–20)

Again, the equation is made between the stage, the world, *Hamlet*, and the *Wake*.

The "dubbing of ghosters" (219.08) suggests other ways that *Finnegans Wake* is like *Hamlet* and other Shakespearean plays. Were there ghostwriters? Which manuscript is accurate? What was the original version? What actually happened? What does it really mean? *The Mime* is referred to as a "problem passion play"; Shakespeare's own problem plays have presented mysteries for which scholars have unearthed many answers from the middenheap of literary possibilities; these plays, like "the purchypatch of hamlock," abound with their "porpor patches" and "patchpurples."

Hamlet and the *Wake* both involve central mysteries and questions. Chapter 2 has shown how *Finnegans Wake* is an exploration of the many possible answers to the question, "What *did* happen to HCE?" Though there are many versions of the story, there appears to be no simple and verifiable truth. The question of *Finnegans Wake* is, in a sense, very much related to the question of *Hamlet*—to what Ernest Jones called "The Problem of *Hamlet*": "The central mystery in [the play]—namely, the cause of Hamlet's hesitancy [a central word in both *Hamlet* and the *Wake*] in seeking to obtain revenge for his father's murder—has well been called the Sphinx of modern Literature."[8] What worries Hamlet and makes him hesitate is that he is in the dark (a "prince of dinmurk"). Unable to get at the truth, he does not know for sure what exactly happened and thus cannot act and avenge himself. As Willard Farnham has remarked, the theme of *Hamlet* is "the theme of unsimple truth";[9] the same might be said of the "jungle of woods" (112.04) in the *Wake*'s jumble of words. The task of looking for the pure truth of the death of Hamlet's father and of HCE's crime in the park is like those of *Hamlet* scholarship: what was the real, original, reliable story in, say, Kyd's *Ur-Hamlet*? What actually goes on in Hamlet's mind? Are the truths to any of these uncertainties "getatable" (169.02)? As with some of Shakespeare's plays, the present "drauma" of HCE has dubious accuracy, questionable authorship, and a continuing need for scholarship and critical interpretation.

Little is certain in the folio about HCE's "weefollyo." HCE's fall appears to involve one or two young ladies and two or three young men; it is almost certainly brought about directly by a filial figure, whether in the form of the Cad, or of Buckley shooting the Russian General (HCE), or of Hosty composing "The Ballad of Persse O'Reilly," or of Shem. Going about his business as usual, the Cad is, like Hamlet *fils*, "a sensible ham" (37.04)—full of sensibility, an actor, a ham, a sham, Shem, Joyce. Like both the author and the reader of *Finnegans Wake*, Hamlet would like to find out what happened to his father; like the Cad, he will bring about the fall of a father figure.[10] In *Ulysses* Stephen Dedalus, a poet and a son, spreads rumors about Shakespeare, one of his acknowledged father figures; Shem-Hosty-Cad does the same to his father in the *Wake*. His "penmarks," symbols of the *Wake* itself, form a repeated call to "List! List!" to the poisonous rumors about HCE. As with Hamlet *père*, HCE's demise as the father figure is similarly caused by poison poured into the porches of our ears; it is therefore appropriate that HCE is repeatedly associated with King Hamlet.

King Hamlet and HCE

HCE is of Scandinavian ancestry and is associated with the Danish invaders; his "fall" in Phoenix Park corresponds (through the call to "List!") to the fall of Danish King Hamlet. This correspondence between HCE and *Hamlet*'s Ghost is iterated continually in the *Wake*, so that allusions to Hamlet *père* signal the presence of HCE.

As kings or fathers, both are creator-gods, worldwrights of a sort, summations of a race or a nation, gods of their creations. As the Ghost, HCE is referred to as a Great Dane: "Gaunt grey ghostly gossips . . . Cur one beast, even Dane the Great" (594.25–27). Dane the Great is HCE as King Hamlet; but a Great Dane is, of course, a cur, a beast, a dog—or, by Joycean equivalence, God.[11] Thus, father-creators are again, ingeniously, equated with gods. As the author of a family world, the father-god *is* that world. Hamlet said of his father, "'A was a man, take him for all in all, / I shall not look upon his like again" (*Ham*. I. ii. 187–88); HCE, a father-patriarch and "Here Comes Everybody" (32.18), is referred to in the *Wake* as "allinall" (242.31) and "allsall allinall" (154.05). Shakespeare, too, asserts John Eglinton in the library scene of *Ulysses*, "is the ghost and the prince. He is all in all" (*U*, 212). Stephen agrees that "the playwright who wrote the folio of this world . . . is doubtless all in all in all of us, ostler and butcher, and would be bawd and cuckold too but that in the economy of heaven, foretold by Hamlet, there are no more marriages, glorified man, an androgynous angel, being a wife unto himself" (*U*, 213). It is to Stephen's words (and to Buck Mulligan's farce based on these words, *Everyman His Own Wife*[12]) that the description on page 392 refers: "in her beaver bonnet [King Hamlet "wore his beaver up" (I. ii. 230)], the King of the Caucuses, a family all to himself."

Both HCE and King Hamlet, as we've seen, suffer a fall or demise that Joyce associates with the spread of poison in one's ears. The second and third chapters of book I of the *Wake* concern HCE's "crime" in the park, the encounter and overthrow of HCE by the Cad, and the spread of Hosty's poisonous ballad; chapter 4 details HCE's fall and burial.[13] HCE, the fallen leader, is compared a number of times in this chapter (especially in pages 78 to 84) to the fallen King Hamlet. On page 79 the reader learns that widow Kate Strong, like the hen in the middenheap, is scavenging from the remains of HCE's golden days: "Widow Strong, then, as her weaker had turned him to the wall (Tiptiptip!), did most all the scavenging from good King Hamlaugh's gulden dayne."[14] The golden days of good King Hamlet, the Golden Dane (and once a "joky" ham, like Shem or Joyce, literally a "Festy King" in 85.23), are gone; "Hamlaugh" recalls "the purchypatch of hamlock." As a fallen King Hamlet, HCE is "that thuddysickend Hamlaugh" (84.32): the dying (the thud of his sick ending, falling at "thirty-second" feet per second per second) King Hamlet.[15] After the fall, ALP's *old Dane* (201.08) is buried (on pages 76–79): the event seems to take place at "Dane to pfife" (77.14—at ten to five; also, the Dane to his wife, his "liddle phifie Annie" in 4.28), after which HCE is "from grosskopp to megapod, embalmed, of grand age, rich in death anticipated" (78.05–6). "From grosskopp to megapod" is one of the many references that connects HCE with King Hamlet's Ghost (since HCE is now "dead"), who was, in Horatio's words, "Armèd at point exactly, cap-a-pe [head to foot]": *gross Kopf* is "big head" in German, and the line means "from big head to big feet."[16] As with the buried mythical Dublin giant and HCE's predecessor, Finn MacCool, HCE's big head and feet are Howth Head and Castle Knock Gate (by Phoenix Park). In any event, now dead and buried, he is no longer King Hamlet, but the king's ghost.

The description of the Ghost as being armed *cap-a-pe* becomes a leitmotif for HCE in the *Wake*. HCE first appears on stage as the Ghost in "From grosskopp to megapod." In *The Mime of Mick, Nick and the Maggies*, he is literally introduced on stage as "HUMP (Mr Makeall Gone . . . in the programme about King Ericus of Schweden and the spirit's whispers in his magical helmet), cap-a-pipe with watch and topper, coat, crest . . ." (220.24–27). This part of *The Mime* resembles that in *Hamlet* in which the ghost ("the spirit") of King Hamlet of Denmark (like King Eric of Sweden) walks onstage, and whispers ("List, list, o list!") through his helmet ("He wore his beaver up"), armed "cap-a-pe" ("cap-a-pipe").[17] As a king who wears his beaver up, he is "in her beaver bonnet, the king of the Caucuses" (392.23–24); the Ghost's helmet is like HCE's wide beaver cap, "The first Humphrey's latitudinous baver" (52.24).

And so HCE-MacCool was laid out, head to foot, "from grosskopp to megapod" (78.05), the giant from Howth Head to Castle Knock Gate, covering the expanse of Dublin. In a celebrated passage in chapter 3 of the third book, HCE defends himself against his accusers by describing the wonders of Dublin, the city he built and personifies: "here which ye see, yea reste [also *j'y suis et j'y reste*]. On me, your sleeping giant. . . . From the hold of my capt in altitude till the mortification that's my fate" (540.16–18). Whether or not HCE's fate is to be mortified, he is none other than Dublin's sleeping giant, whom his accusers see and on whom they rest, from head ("capt") to foot ("fate"). He is the archetypal father and ruler of Dublin; perhaps this is why, when he later makes love to his wife in bed, his rubber condom,[18] which holds his seed, is referred to as his "waxened capapee" (583.29).

In the book's final chapter, ALP as the River Liffey addresses HCE as Dublin's giant, who is "Reclined from cape to pede" (619.27); she exhorts him to "Rise up, man of the hooths" (619.25—man of Howth Head), as it is time for ricorso. After so many references to King Hamlet and "cap-a-pe," the reader is hardly surprised when, near the end of the book, ALP addresses HCE ("evers the Carlton hart" in 622.29) by the direct handle of "cap-a-pe": "And you needn't hoist out with your duck and your duty, capapole, while they reach him . . ." (622.29–30)

"Cap-a-pe" is certainly not the only functional connection between King Hamlet and HCE. Act I, scene v of *Hamlet* provides some clear links; in this scene the Ghost speaks to Hamlet:

> I am thy father's spirit,
> Doomed for a certain term to walk the night,
> And for the day confined to fast in fires,
> Till the foul crimes done in my days of nature
> Are burnt and purged away.
> (*Ham.* I. v. 9–13)

With these words the ghost of the king tells his son of his death and of his present state in Purgatory, and urges Hamlet to gain revenge. HCE as the fallen father is also a ghost in purgatory who returns in the night: "a *h*unnibal in *ex*haustive conflict, an otho to return; burning body to aiger air" (132.06–7; my italics). Arising from the flames of purgatory, his "burning body" meets the "aiger air" of the Danish night—Horatio has observed that "It is a nipping and an eager air" (I. iv. 2). Stephen Dedalus, associating fathers with purgatory and *Hamlet*, remarks that "Nine lives are taken off for his [Hamlet's] father's one, Our Father who art in purgatory" (*U*, 187). It is the scene in which the Ghost incites Hamlet to seek revenge that is alluded to in reference to the production of *Hamlet*-alias-*She Stoops to Conquer* at the Crow Street Theatre: "Toni Lampi . . . ghustorily spoeking, gen and gang, dane and dare, like the dud spuk of his first foetotype" (323.36). The Danish ghost ("ghustorily," Danish *gengangere*) speaking is a dad speaking to his firstborn. What the Ghost says to Hamlet becomes a bad dream which drives Hamlet to his wits' end; the same happens to Shem: "his pawdry's purgatory was more than a nigger bloke could bear" (177.04). As does Hamlet ("Bethgelert" in 177.22; see Part II entry), Shem finds the story of his *padre* in purgatory more than he can bear. The nightmare little Jerry-Shem has on page 565, similar to the vision Hamlet has on the turrets of Elsinore's castle, concerns a father as a ghost. His mother consoles him thus: "You were dreamend, dear. The pawdrag? The fawthrig? Shoe! Hear are no phantares in the room at all, avikkeen. No bad bold faathern, dear one" (565.18–20)—You were dreaming, dear. The *padre?* The father? Shoo! There are no phantoms in the room at all, dear, no bad bold fathers. Despite ALP's consolatory words, the nightmare of history, of the past, and of the father is a vision and presence which will not lie quietly in its grave; it seems to have haunted Joyce-Jerry-Shem all his life and to have appeared in all his works. The nightmare is recalled by the Ghost's parting words to Hamlet—"Adieu, adieu, adieu. Remember me"—and Hamlet's reply: "Remember thee? / Yea, from the table of my memory. . . . Thy commandment all alone shall live / Within the book and volume of my brain" (I. v. 97–104). Practically the last words of the *Wake*, spoken by ALP, are an important echo of that final mandate: "mememormee!" (628.14).[19]

With those words, the dawn comes again and once more the Ghost "faded on the crowing of the cock" (I. i. 157); or, in Joyce's words, "the cockcock crows for Danmark" (192.21). So also the long night of the *Wake* draws to a close in book IV, the last book and chapter, as dawn returns to Dublin: "Gaunt grey ghostly gossips growing grubber in the glow. Past now pulls. Cur one beast, even Dane the Great. . . . Let shrill their duan Gallus" (594.25–27). The Ghost's words ("ghostly gossips") grow dimmer with the coming of dawn, pulled back by the past; the Great Dane, or King Hamlet, fades on the crowing of the cock (the shrill Gallus).[20] But, while *Hamlet*'s Ghost may fade at dawn, dawn in the *Wake* signals ricorso: at once, the fading of an old ghost and his resurrection in a new embodiment. This new embodiment shall be presented by the symbolic, matutinal renewal of breakfast—a form of *ricorso* that Joyce conceived of in Shakespearean terms.

Late in the book two calls are heard for the ghost of H.C. Earwicker to arise from his ashes: "Arise, sir ghostus! As long as you've lived there'll be no other" (532.04); and "Arise, sir Pompkey Dompkey! Ear! Ear! Weakear!" (568.25). Accompanying the new dawn is a clear signal for ricorso: "Calling all daynes. Calling all daynes to dawn" (593.11)—calling all the days to dawn, and calling all Danes to rise. In this call for resurrection and ricorso, HCE-King Hamlet's reincarnation for the next Viconian cycle, his son Shaun, is going to rise like a phoenix (like the "Phoenican wakes" from the "Ashias" in 608.31–32) when "the cockcock crows for Danmark" (192.21); meanwhile, the progenitor himself fades away with the end of the night of dream, just as the Ghost "faded on the crowing of the cock." Or, as Joyce writes on page 598, "The has goning at gone, the is coming to come. Greets to ghastern, hie to morgning": this is the moment ("at gone," or dawn) when the new greets the old, as the old is departing and the new is arriving—when the dawn greets the "Ghost" of yesterday, hastening tomorrow and the morning. It is through such reincarnations and ricorsos that generations fulfill their parents' pleas to "mememormee!"

Hamlet and Shem

Goldberg has written that *"Hamlet* is a portrait of the artist as a young man" and that "both Stephen and Hamlet are introspective, *lisant au livre de lui-même*, but trying mainly to understand themselves before the time is ripe."[21] Joyce found a Shakespearean counterpart for Stephen Dedalus, his artist as a young man, in Hamlet; it is therefore hardly surprising that he often associates the semiautobiographical Shem, his portrait of the artist in the *Wake*, with Hamlet. Hodgart has observed: "Hamlet is a 'type' of Shem, who is the 'wicked' twin brother, the writer, and corresponds to Joyce himself. This follows the pattern of *Ulysses*, where Stephen Dedalus is Hamlet. . . . Shem, who is the mother's boy of the twins, represents the workings of the Oedipus-complex: in fantasy he kills his father Earwicker."[22] Thus, as these early commentators have noted, there are two major similarities between Hamlet and Shem: first, each is a portrait of the artist (*à la* Mallarmé), a man of great sensibility; second, like Ernest Jones's Hamlet, Shem is a filial figure with Oedipal designs on his father figure—as the Cad-Hosty-Buckley, he will bring about the overthrow of HCE-Russian General.

Pages 36 through 38 of the *Wake* provide the first portrait of the Cad, the filial figure who "went about his business . . . as a metter of corse" (37.09–10; see endnote 19 to chapter 3). He is described, like Hamlet, as "a sensible ham" and is full of sensibility, like Shem and Joyce. (That he is also Joyce is affirmed in 37.13: "I have met with you, bird, too late"— these are young Joyce's words to Yeats.) In the following pages, the Cad tells the story he has just learned about HCE's crime to his wife; and she spreads the poison to her confessor, who then pours it into the porches of Philly Thurnston's ear and into other ears, until the whole city is aware of it. At this point, Hosty, a poet and another like Shem, composes "The Ballad of Persse O'Reilly." Like Hamlet, Hosty is a moody and melancholy sort, who also considers suicide: "on the verge of selfabyss, most starved, with melancholia over everything in general . . . devising . . . where he could throw true and go and blow the sibicidal napper off himself for two bits to boldywell baltitude in the peace and quitybus of a one sure shot bottle" (40.23–32). Hodgart points out that Joyce's earlier draft read "quietus" instead of "quitybus";[23] we recall that Hamlet contemplated suicide by making his quietus with a bare bodkin (III. i. 75–76). Hosty writes "The Ballad of Persse O'Reilly" about how HCE-King

Hamlet "fell with a roll and a rumble . . . Hump, helmet, and all" (45.02–6). The poet Shem-Hosty sings the demise of the displaced father figures of Penmark and all their "Scandiknavery," be they Sophocles, Shakespeare, Dante, Moses, or Danish HCE:

> Suffoclose! Shikespower! Seudodanto! Anonymoses!
> Then we'll have a free trade Gaels' band and mass meeting
> For to sod the brave son of Scandiknavery.
> And we'll bury him down in Oxmanstown
> Along with the devil and Danes,
>   (Chorus) With the deaf and dumb Danes,
>   And all their remains.
>
> (47.19–25)

In chapter 7 of book I, the celebrated "Shem" chapter, Shem-Joyce is described as "this hambone dogpoet who pseudoed himself under the hangname he gave himself of Bethgelert" (177.21–22). Ham and bacon (*jambon* is French for ham)[24] are disguised in this line under a pseudonym-agnomen ("pseudoed" and "hangname"). Shem-Shakespeare is a "dogpoet" because he is "the artist, like the God [dog] of the creation" (*P*, 215). At the same time he is Hamlet, who also had a pseudonym-agnomen; Glasheen has mentioned that "according to Saxo Grammaticus, Hamlet was brought up under a dog's name to save him from his uncle, Feng [Claudius]. . . . Gelert was a faithful dog, wrongly slain in a Welsh story. His grave is called Bethgelert."[25] Thus, "this hambone dogpoet" with the agnomen of Bethgelert is Shem-Joyce as Hamlet-Shakespeare. He is an "excommunicated Drumcondriac, nate Hamis" (181.35–36), whom his twin, Shaun, addresses as "hammet" (193.11). Just as Hamlet is uneasy in Denmark, Shem the artist feels troubled in his world; while something is in fact rotten in the state of Denmark, so also Shem the Penman finds "small peace in ppenmark" (189.06), where fame is slow in coming and where one is continually and on all sides assailed by Shaun types of every sort. These Shaun types condemn Shem's writings as evil, obscene (and indecipherable), "words as the penmarks used out in sinscript . . . as to the views of Denmark" (421.18, 29). Disconsolate and discouraged by such attacks, and feeling estranged and exiled, Shem-Hosty contemplates suicide. This "Woful Dane" (503.21) might join Hamlet in saying: "The time is out of joint. O cursèd spite, / That ever I was born to set it right!" (I. v. 188–89). He does in fact say that; in these "disjointed times" (104.05), "Jymes" (Joyce)-Shem advertises (according to Shaun in 181.29–30): "His jymes is out of job, would sit and write." While the times are out of joint, "Jymes" *is* out of a job and out of patience (like Job); to set these disjointed times right again, he "would sit and write." Some of the things Shem sits and writes sound suspiciously like *Hamlet;* for example, in the Children's Study Period in chapter 2, book II, Shem's marginal notes contain (among other Shakespearean echoes) the comment *"Omnitudes in a knutshedell"* (276.L2) as a note to "What's Hiccupper to hem or her to Hagaba?" (276.09). Both lines echo Hamlet himself: "What's Hecuba to him, or he to Hecuba?" (II. ii. 543) and "O God! I could be bounded in a nut-shell, and count myself a king of infinite space, were it not that I have bad dreams" (II. ii. 250).[26] One wonders about this "mad dane" (385.16), "if so be you have metheg in your midness" (32.05).[27] In any case, "by the beerlitz in his mathness" (182.07; metheglin-mead-beer, the Berlitz Method, and Joyce's multilingual Madness), Shem wrote ("scrabbled and scratched and scriobbled and skrevened" in 182.13) his "inartistic portraits of himself [*Portrait of the Artist as a Young Man*] in the act of reciting old Nichiabelli's monolook interyerear [the *monologue intérieur,* or *Ulysses,* poured into the porches of your ear] Hanno, o Nonanno, acce'l brubblemm'as, ser Autore, q.e.d." (182.19–21). The third work listed by our Author is *Hamlet,* since the line is an Italianate version of "To be or not to be, that is the question" (III. i. 56; literally, "They have or do not have, that is the problem").

Hamlet's "To be or not to be" speech is the Shakespearean passage most alluded to in the *Wake,* with many of the speech's lines echoed therein. These allusions are all listed in the *Hamlet* section of Appendix 2, under III. i. 56 to III. i. 82, and are discussed individually in Part II; there are at least five echoes of the speech's first line alone. While references to Hamlet's fourth soliloquy are spread throughout the *Wake,* two clusters of them deserve special attention. Page 319 contains three separate echoes of the speech, leading one to suspect that Hamlet's soliloquy is thematically connected with the context: "at weare or not at weare" (319.28) is "To be or not to be," since *At vaere* is Norwegian for "to be"; "a satuation, debauchly to be watched for" (319.35) echoes "Tis a consummation / Devoutly to be wished" (III. i. 63–64); "and thus plinary indulgence makes columellas of us all" (319.07) recalls "Thus conscience does make cowards of us all" (III. i. 82). An explanation for this cluster of allusions to Hamlet's soliloquy lies in the third allusion here listed. On page 319 the Norwegian Captain admits his guilt ("—I shot be shoddied, throttle me . . ." in 319.02ff.); guilt implies conscience—thus Hamlet's corresponding line. A plenary indulgence has to do with guilt; it is a remission of a sinner's entire temporal punishment, absolving one of all previous sentences incurred, and thus of the dread of that "undiscovered country from whose bourn / No traveller returns" (III. i. 79–80). Thus, the Norwegian Captain's struggle with guilt and conscience attracts, and is framed in, echoes of Hamlet's own struggle with conscience.

The other cluster is identified in question number nine in the Twelve Questions passage of chapter 6 in book I. The question involves the choices open to the artist (Shem-Joyce) in his situation, and what that "fargazer" (143.26) would see and write. "Answer: A collideorscape!" (143.28). What is at issue is whether to escape or not, to be or not to be. This puzzling paragraph subtly parallels Hamlet's fourth soliloquy: "Now, to be [or not to be] on anew . . . if a human being duly fatigued by his dayety in the sooty [the commuter returning from a day in the dirty city, having suffered "the slings and arrows of outrageous fortune"] having plenxty off time . . . at his sleepish feet and as hapless behind the dreams of accuracy ["to sleep, perchance to dream"] as any camelot prince of dinmurk [Hamlet, prince of Denmark], were . . . in the states of suspensive exanimation [Hamlet's suspended and indecisive self-examination, and suspended animation] . . . accorded . . . with an ear-sighted view of old hopeinhaven ["But that the dread of something after death, / The undiscovered country from whose bourn / No traveller returns"— Hope-in-Heaven and Copenhagen, a haven for the hopeful] with all . . . his persistence the course of his tory [perhaps "the whips and scorns of time" and history] will have been having recourses, the reverberration of knotcracking awes, the reconjugation of nodebinding ayes, the redissolusingness of mindmouldered ease and the thereby hang of the Hoel of it ["the whips and scorns of time" are described as a Viconian cycle of history and ricorso ("recourses"): birth ("reverberration"), marriage ("reconjugation"), death ("redissolusingness") and *ricorso*— echoing, perhaps, Hamlet's own catalog of the "whips and scorns of time": "Th'oppressor's wrong, the proud man's contumely, / The pangs of despised love, the law's delay . . ."] could such a none, while even led comesilencers to comeliewithhers and till intempestuous Nox . . ." (143.02 ff.) and so forth. Note the references to "Shakeagain" (143.21), "shakealose" (143.22), and "the signs of Ham" (143.23). Signs of *Hamlet* and Shakespeare are certainly present in this passage.[28] "And the thereby hang of the Hoel of it" (143.14) echoes Touchstone's "And thereby hangs a tale" (*AYL* II. vii. 28), while "comeliewithhers" (143.16) may refer to Hamlet's "our withers are unwrung" (III. ii. 234; see also 550.26, "wring her withers"). Hamlet's "Seems madam? Nay, it is. I know not 'seems'" (I. ii. 76) is here in "seem to seemself to seem seeming of." Ophelia's death is here in "Violet's dyed!" (143.26): Ophelia, before her death, said, "I would give you some violets, but they withered all when my father died. They say 'a made a good end . . ." (IV. v. 182–84). Her death spurs Shem-Joyce-Hamlet ("the fargazer") to try seeing into the "dinmurk" and coming to grips with that dim and dark undiscovered country: "Violet's dyed! then *what* would that fargazer seem to seemself to seem seeming of, dimm it all?" (143.26–27).[29] When all is dimmed, the rest is silence; the passage is itself quite dark and murky—but sense can be made of it by the light of Hamlet's soliloquy.

Ophelia and Issy

If King Hamlet is a "type" for HCE and Hamlet is one for Shem, then, by analogy, Issy, the daughter figure whose love is sought by both Shaun and Shem, should be typified by Ophelia, and so she is. In the *Wake* Ophelia's flowers become a motif for Issy.

Ophelia's name appears several times in *Finnegans Wake*. In the second chapter of book III, Jaun-Shaun urges his sister Issy and his brother Shem-Hamlet to exercise their sexual urges together: "Be offalia. Be hamlet" (465.32). (Thus perhaps "Offaly" in 31.18 also refers to Issy-Ophelia.) *Hamlet* is the "drame of Drainophilias" (110.11: the drama and bad dream of Ophelia's), at least for Joyce, who follows this line with the quintessential quotation from *Hamlet:* "me ken or no me ken Zot is the Quiztune" (110.13–14). HCE-Adam's sin in Phoenix Park, for which he suffers a fall, has something to do with his incestuous desires for his daughter Issy, or Ophelia. Thus, his happy fault *(O felix culpa!)* becomes, through a series of puns, "O happy fault!" (202.34), "Poor Felix Culapert" (536.08), "O foenix culprit" (23.16—HCE as the culprit in Phoenix Park), *"O'Phelim's Cutprice"* (72.04), and *"Ophelia's Culpreints"* (105.18).[30] Furthermore, Issy's words in the *Wake* echo Ophelia's a number of times. For example, on page 461 the sex-starved Issy invites her brother Jaun-Laertes to initiate her sexually: "Coach me how to tumble" (461.30). "Tumble" is used by the spurned Ophelia in one of her songs: "Young men will do't if they come to't. / By Cock, they are to blame. / Quoth she, 'Before you tumbled me, / You promised me to wed.'" (*Ham.* IV. v. 60–63).[31] One of Issy's footnotes in the Study Hour chapter has her saying: "Eh, Monsieur? Où, Monsieur? Eu, Monsieur? Nenni No, Monsieur" (307.F8), echoing Ophelia's other song: "Hey non nony, nony, hey nony" (IV. v. 165; see also "Neya, narev, nen, nonni, nos!" in 203.14).[32]

The main connections made between Issy and Ophelia are of two sorts, both perhaps symbolized by the term "Flura's way" (623.21): "Flura," describing ALP as the Liffey, is a combination of *fleuve* and *fleur*, of river and flower. Issy, as Nuvoletta and a younger version of ALP the river woman, is the leader of the Floras, the flower girls in the *Wake;* Ophelia is both a river maiden (having drowned in a river) and a flower girl, having named and handed out many flowers (in IV. v. 174 ff.) before her watery death.

In chapter 6 of book I, Issy as Nuvoletta, the love-starved cloud girl, tries to distract the Mookse and the Gripes from their battle so that they will pay attention to her. Her efforts, however, are wasted; and so it was all "Love's labor's lost"—or, in cloudy terms, "mild's vapour moist" (157.23). The heartbroken Nuvoletta sheds tears, and then melts into the river and dies: "Then Nuvoletta reflected for the last time in her little long life and she made up all her myriads of drifting minds in one [a hint at "myriad-minded" Shakespeare]. . . . She climbed over the bannistars [like Juliet[33]]; she gave a childy cloudy cry: *Nuée! Nuée!* A lightdress fluttered. She was gone. And into that river that had been a stream . . . there fell a tear, a singult tear. . . . But the river tripped on her by and by, lapping as though her heart was brook" (159.06–17). This lovely passage brings to mind Juliet and Ophelia, both "suicides" caused by love. The brokenhearted Ophelia is especially a parallel to Nuvoletta here, for she, too, was rejected by men and she, too, drowned in a river. The description of her death has certain parallels with that of Nuvoletta: "Clamb'ring to hang. . . . When down her weedy trophies and herself / Fell in the weeping brook. Her clothes spread wide, / And mermaid-like awhile they bore her up, / Which time she chanted snatches of old lauds. . . . Till that her garments, heavy with their drink, / Pulled the poor wretch from her melodious lay / To muddy death" (IV. vii. 172–82).

Issy, of course, is a younger ALP; and in chapter 8 of Book I ("Anna Livia Plurabelle") appear a few references to Ophelia in connection with rivers and flowers. In "Neya, narev, nen, nonni, nos!" (203.14), negatives and names of rivers are mixed in with Ophelia's song ("Hey non nony, nony, hey nony") just before her drowning in the river.[34] A few lines later, there is a catalog of flowers: "Afrothdizzying galbs . . . vierge violetian . . . throw those laurals now on her daphdaph teasesong" (203.27–30). These references to flowers strewn on a river maiden and to a song recall Ophelia's silly song, her death by water, and the flowers she herself strews: "There's fennel for you, and columbines. There's rue for you. . . . There's a daisy. I would give you some violets, but they withered all when my father died" (IV. v. 179–83). This *Wake* passage, between pages 202 and 205, concerns ALP as the Liffey water woman ("Are you in the swim or are you out?" in 204.27), and so references to Ophelia and to flowers are appropriate. As evening falls, the Liffey-ALP reaches the sea and dies; this recalls Nuvoletta's suicide and Ophelia's death: "Die eve, little eve, die! . . . Forgivemequick, I'm going! Bubye! And you, pluck your watch, forgetmenot" (215.04–8). Here, too, are flowers ("forgetmenot"); ALP's final word is similar to her farewell in the last lines of the *Wake:* "mememormee!"

Ophelia's flower passage is important in that Issy becomes Ophelia most often through the medium of flowers.

> There's rosemary, that's for remembrance. Pray you, love, remember [or "forgetmenot"?]. And there is pansies, that's for

thoughts.... There's fennel for you, and columbines. There's rue for you, and here's some for me. We may call it herb of grace o' Sundays. O, you must wear your rue with a difference. There's a daisy. I would give you some violets, but they withered all when my father died. (*Ham.* IV. v. 174–83)

In chapter 4 of book III, HCE's family is introduced as "The Porters": "Mr Porter" and "Mrs Porter" and the "little Porter babes" (560.22–561.03). When the roll comes to Issy-Nuvoletta ("A pussy . . . in all the noveletta" in 561.09–11), Issy Porter is introduced as Ophelia by a catalog of flowers: "Here's newyearspray, the posquiflor, a windaborne and heliotrope; there miriamsweet and amaranth and marygold to crown" (561.20–21). The syntactical construction here parallels that of Ophelia's catalog ("There's rue for you, and here's some for me . . . ").

Pages 225 to 227 contain a dense cluster of allusions to Ophelia. This passage occurs within *The Mime* chapter, in which, as part of "The Game" ("Angels and Devils or colours"), Issy and the Floras (the heliotrope girls) are once again trying to catch the attention of the two boys. Again the boys flee ("Jerry for jauntings. Alabye! Fled! in 225.34); and Issy, like Nuvoletta and Ophelia, finds herself rejected by men, by Shem-Jerry-Hamlet. The Floras and Issy are referred to as wilted flowers: "The flossies all and mossies all they drooped upon her draped brimfall . . ." (225.35) and "Poor Isa sits a glooming . . . in the gloaming . . . awound her swan's" (226.03–4; the "swan's" may be another hint at Shakespeare). Poor, depressed Isa seems to be strewn with Ophelia's flowers and to be dying: "Bring tansy, throw myrtle, strew rue, rue, rue. She is fading out like Journee's clothes so you can't see her now" (226.10–12). The second line—as Issy fades out at the close of day (*journée*'s "clothes," and journey's end)—echoes both Ophelia's death and Nuvoletta's in her "lightdress." As they proceed to their rainbow dance, the seven rainbow girls (colours) are introduced as flowers: ". . . W waters the fleurettes of novembrance" (226.32; Ophelia had also handed out flowers for remembrance). One of the group is called "Rue" (227.14): "for they are the florals, from foncey and pansey to papavere's blush, foresake-menought . . . all the flowers of the ancelles' garden" (227.15–18). Again there are pansies, forget-me-nots, and other flowers mentioned and alluded to. Issy, whenever rejected by men, turns her thoughts to depression, suicide, flowers, and Ophelia; thus, when in the Study Hour she is once more rejected by the twins, she contemplates suicide and thinks about "rue" in a long footnote: ". . . I was thinking fairly killing times of putting an end to myself and my malody. . . . With love ay loved. . . . You are me severe? Then rue. . . . This isabella I'm on knows the ruelles of the rut" (279.F1).

The major Ophelian flower, the pansy ("And there is pansies, that's for thoughts"), is used as a leitmotif for Issy: "for they are the florals, from foncey and pansey" (227.15–16) and "brood our pansies" (271.20). In the Study Hour, Issy-Ophelia, sitting on a stool in the corner, is designated: "With a pansy for the pussy in the corner" (278.05–6).[35] Finally, in the first and second chapters of book III, the references to Issy-Ophelia as "pansy" repeatedly turn on a bilingual pun: Ophelia said, "And there is pansies, that's for thoughts"; *pensée* is French for thought (a feminine noun), or, in Joycean equivalences, pansy. Thoughts of Issy-Ophelia are pansies (thus, "brood our pansies"). On page 403 Shaun thinks of his sister as "Pensée! The most beautiful of woman of the veilch veilchen veilde"; he later wonders what she is thinking: "what the eldest daughter she was panseying" (408.31–32). In the following chapter, Shaun as Jaun-Laertes swears that Shem-Hamlet will get his due payments if that brother has any thoughts about loving Issy-Ophelia: "He'll have pansements then for his pensamientos, howling for peace. Pretty knocks, I promise him . . ." (443.14–15). Jaun himself, of course, thinks about Issy all the time and promises to send her, even while he is away, all his "loveliest pansiful thoughts" (446.03) about her.

Laertes and Shaun

Shaun-Jaun is a Laertes "type"; being Issy-Ophelia's protective brother, we might expect as much. Chapter 2 of book III consists mainly of a lecture Jaun-Shaun gives to his sister Issy and to the Floras. He renders sententious advice to Issy about maintaining her virtue; he warns her about the advances of Dave-Shem-Hamlet and then, typically, he declares his own love for her. Jaun's sermon to his sister depends heavily on Laertes's address to Ophelia.[36]

There are indeed quite a few parallels between Jaun's lecture—especially on page 431—and Laertes's speech. Perhaps Jaun's warnings to the girls (top of page 431) about a dress code and about keeping the hems of their skirts low enough to cover the hams of their legs—"to drop a few stray remarks anent their personal appearances . . . gently reproving one that the ham of her hom could be seen below her hem" (431.01–6)—should clue us that the warning about hems and hams is really about Hamlet. There are similarities between Laertes's sermon (in I. iii. 1–43) and Jaun's speech (beginning with, on 431.21, "—Sister, dearest . . ."). Both are lectures from a brother to a sister—Laertes to Ophelia, Jaun to Issy. Both are speeches of parting and farewell: Laertes opens, "My necessities are embarked. Farewell" (I. iii. 1); Jaun-Christ, on the last leg of his *Via Crucis*, bids farewell several times—"So for e'er fare thee welt!

Parting's fun" (454.01–2), "farewell awhile . . . ware the wail" (469.19–21), and so on.

Both Jaun and Laertes are embarking on sea journeys: Laertes says, ". . . as the winds give benefit / And convoy is assistant" (I. iii. 3); and Jaun relates, "We would shove off to stray on our long last journey" (431.26–27), "and would ireturn o'er see" (445.26), and "waved instead a handacross the sea" (470.35). The brothers ask their sisters to write: Laertes advises, "Farewell. / And sister . . . do not sleep, / But let me hear from you" (I. iii. 1–4); and Jaun requests, "We honestly believe you sorely will miss us. . . . You, sis, that used to write to us the exceeding nice letters. . . . Write me your essayes" (431.24–29, 447.06–7). Both lecture on, among other things, feminine honor, virtue, chastity, love, desire, and the pitfalls of lust.

The brothers both use a sententious tone, full of imperatives. Laertes says, "Hold it a fashion. . . . Fear it, Ophelia, fear it, my dear sister. . . . Be wary, then; best safety lies in fear". Jaun's many imperatives are much more amusing: "Never lose your heart away till you win his diamond back. . . . Never park your brief stays in the men's convenience. . . . Look before you leak, dears" (433.14–34). The two lectures contain prime warnings about another's love—that of Hamlet-Shem—and both brothers warn their sisters to distrust it: Laertes cautions, "For Hamlet, and the trifling of his favor, / Hold it a fashion and a toy in blood. . . . Forward, not permanent, sweet, not lasting"; and Shaun alerts, "Mistro Melosious MacShine MacShane may soon prove your undoing and bane" (437.33–34; see also 433.36 ff.). The sisters both accept the advice, but reply by returning it in kind: Ophelia remarks, ". . . Himself the primrose path of dalliance treads / And recks not his own rede" (*Ham.* I. iii. 50–51); while Issy says, "And, since levret bounds and larks is soaring, don't be all the night" (458.12–13). Indeed, many direct references to *Hamlet*, to Ernest Jones's *Hamlet and Oedipus*, and especially to Ophelia are to be found in this chapter and in Jaun's words.

Jaun-Laertes begins his advice-giving by providing an alternative to the primrose path of dalliance: "Now. During our brief apsence . . . adhere to as many as probable of the ten commandments . . . and in the long run they will prove for your better guidance along your path of right of way" (432.25–28). At the same time he hints that he is really talking about Dave-Hamlet, echoing in "a consommation" (432.14) and "where the fate's to be wished for" (432.32–33) Hamlet's famous soliloquy: "'Tis a consummation / Devoutly to be wished" (III. i. 63–64). Jaun's warnings to Issy about promiscuity remind us that "rue" is one of the flowers associated with Ophelia: "Wet your thistle where a weed is and you'll rue it" (433.35–36) and "Rue the Day!" (444.12–13). Jaun continues: "Especially beware please of being at a party to any demoralizing home life. . . .

Where it is nobler in the main to supper than the boys and errors of outrager's virtue" (433.36–434.05). He warns Issy about Shem: if she loses her virtue to Shem, her own brother, her "errors" and outrageous virtue would be a party to demoralizing the home life of herself and the "boys." That Shem-Hamlet is the "outrager" being referred to is clear, for here again is Hamlet's soliloquy: "Whether 'tis nobler in the mind to suffer / The slings and arrows of outrageous fortune . . ." (III. i. 57–58).[37] In "Autist Algy . . . the dallytaunties . . . taking you to the playguehouse to see the *Smirching of Venus*" (434.35–435.03), Jaun seems to be warning Issy (as he did in 434.08–10; see Part II entry) about the corrupting influence of drama and literature: Algy (Shem as Algernon Swinburne— or Wilde's Algernon Moncrieff—the dilettantish literati) would only take you to a corrupt playhouse, to see a play about fornication (the *Smirching*—or *Birching*—*of Venus*) and disease ("playguehouse"), or to see Shakespeare's *Merchant of Venice*. Jaun says of the arts: "All blah! Viper's vapid vilest!" (435.16).

Jaun continues to warn Issy about illicit love with his twin brother Shem: "kosenkissing . . . like Population Peg on a hint or twim clandestinely does be doing to Temptation Tom" (436.09–11)—a reference, as we have seen, to the illicit loves of Peg Woffington and Thomas Sheridan. Kissing twins or cousins, Jaun argues, will result in population. "Once and for all," he remarks, "I'll have no college swankies" (438.32), such as Dave-Shem, or Stephen's Hamlet, that "beardless undergraduate from Wittenberg" (*U*, 207). He goes on to say that if Shem should ever have thoughts *(pensées)* about and intentions toward Issy-Ophelia ("pansy"), "He'll have pansements then for his pensamientos, howling for peace. Pretty knocks, I promise him . . ." (443.14–15). Shaun then declares his own love for Issy-Ophelia and sues for her favors: "sending uym loveliest pansiful thoughts touching me dash in-you through wee dots Hyphen, the so pretty arched godkin of beddingnights" (446.03–5). In these lines he promises while he is away to send his thoughts about Pansy-Ophelia and his love via telegrams: with dashes, dots, and hyphens. He seems to propose marriage (Hymen and wedding nights) to this pretty goddess of the bedroom and the wedding night: "godkin" is a conflated shorthand for Hamlet's "God's bodkin, man!" (II. ii. 516). It means "God's little body," a term Jaun uses here to describe Issy-Ophelia's celestial little body.

The sermon continues in this vein until page 462, when Dave-Shem suddenly arrives. To the reader's surprise, Jaun-Shaun (always a hypocrite) now turns and declares his love and admiration for his artist brother ("He has novel ideas. . . . I love him. I love his old portugal's nose" in 463.12–19), and then he points to Issy-Ophelia and says: "There's the nasturtium for ye now that saved manny a poor sinker from water on the grave" (463.20—Ophelia's "There's fennel for you . . ." and her death as a "poor sinker" in a watery grave). He shakes hands with Shem and (as happens in the *Two Gentlemen of Verona*) hands his love over to his rival: "Be offalia. Be hamlet. Be the property plot. Be Yorick and Lankystare. Be cool. Be mackinamucks of yourselves . . ." (465.32–33). Jaun-Laertes here seems to urge Issy and Dave to go ahead and play around, reversing his earlier advice. In effect Shaun says: "Go ahead, do anything and be anyone you want to. Be a flirt, an awful piece of offal, a failure, a trashy Ophelia. Be Hamlet. Be Yorick, or even York and Lancaster, for all I care. Be cool. Go ahead and make a mucky mess of yourselves." (In his advice Jaun appears to be using Shakespeare's words for authority: "As the curly bard said" in 465.28 and "Watch the swansway" in 465.35.)

There are numerous allusions or echoes from *Hamlet* which have not been dealt with in this chapter. Again, this survey was not meant to be comprehensive; my intent was only to lay out the basic matrix of *Hamlet* in the *Wake* and to identify the ensuing correspondences—HCE as the Ghost, Shem as Hamlet, Issy as Ophelia, Shaun as Laertes.[38] Many of the remaining allusions are arranged and discussed according to thematic content in the chapters following; thematic significances and functions of the correspondences between *Hamlet* and the *Wake* are dealt with in individual chapters.

Joyce found in *Hamlet* an all-encompassing matrix for his purposes in *Finnegans Wake:* the sheer number, matrical comprehensiveness, and precise correspondences of the *Hamlet* allusions to HCE's family drama prove *Hamlet* to be one of the structural "books at the *Wake*."

5

Fathers and Sons: Shakespeare and Joyce

"Am I father? If I were?"

Ulysses

In *Finnegans Wake* young men as filial figures repeatedly encounter and "overthrow" old men who are father figures: all of these encounters are retellings of the basic encounter between HCE and the Cad in Phoenix Park, presented in the tales of Buckley and the Russian General at Sevastopol, the Irish publican and the Norwegian sailor, and so forth. What does it mean, though, in Joycean terms to "overthrow" a father? To Joyce, the influence of "fathers" was at once indelibly shaping and insufferably suffocating. All his life he struggled with the paternal powers in himself: John Joyce, Dublin and fatherland, the Church Fathers, the Jesuits, God the Father, and his literary masters, such as Ibsen, Dante, and Shakespeare. In his works Joyce sees himself as a filial figure, a disciple to an old master, an Icarus to a Daedalus; but he always has that desire to shake off the wings and the guiding influence of the parent, and to fly on his own—he himself aspires to be the creator-father figure.

Stephen Dedalus, in order to assert his own creative independence, feels the need to deny the paternal link: "A father, Stephen said . . . is a necessary evil. . . . The church is founded and founded irrevocably because founded, like the world, macro- and microcosm, upon the void. Upon incertitude, upon unlikelihood. . . . Paternity may be a legal fiction. Who is the father of any son that any son should love him or he any son?" (*U*, 207). Stephen argues that the son creates the father just as much as the father engenders the son; for without the existence of the son, the "father" himself would not exist. This paradox is pointed out in the Daedalus-Icarus myth: at the moment of Icarus's death, Daedalus, Ovid tells us, is *nec iam pater*—father no longer.[1] Using Shakespeare (whose own father had died just before he wrote *Hamlet*) as an example, Stephen maintains that, similarly, when the son is deprived of his father, he is no longer a son and can then become the father and creator of an entire race:

"—Well: if the father who has not a son be not a father can the son who has not a father be a son? When Rutlandbaconsouthamptonshakespeare or another poet of the same name in the comedy of errors wrote *Hamlet* he was not the father of his own son merely but, being no more a son, he was and felt himself the father of all his race" (*U*, 208).[2]

Thus, before the young artist can become a real creator ("Am I father? If I were?" in *U*, 208), Stephen believes, he must dispose of his "father," so that he is no longer a son. Goldberg explains the overthrow of the father: "To be 'no more a son,' as Shakespeare was when he wrote *Hamlet*, means not merely that his own father was dead but that he no longer stood in spiritual dependence on another. He was himself a father, spiritually mature, handing that power, embodied in the art itself, on to his son."[3] Whereas the link between father and son is no more than "An instant of blind rut" (*U*, 208), their relationship is one of competitive rivalry for the position of father, the son continually seeking to ascend and replace his progenitor—in Stephen's words: "The sun [sic] unborn mars beauty: born, he brings pain, divides affection, increases care. He is a male: his growth is his father's decline, his youth his father's envy, his friend his father's enemy" (*U*, 207–8). The relationship between Joycean fathers and sons is one which we have learned to call "Oedipal."[4]

The Archetypal Parricide

Such a father-son relationship is behind the encounter between the younger man and the father figure in the *Wake*, and it falls right into place in the Joycean-Viconian scheme of things. The Cad (Hosty, Shem, Joyce, Buckley, and so on) will rise to encounter and then oust HCE to replace him as father, just as the young HCE overthrew old Finnegan, who had himself displaced Finn MacCool or some other father figure, and so on backwards into history. "The fall . . . of a once wallstrait oldparr is retaled early in bed and later on life down through all christian minstrelsy" (3.15–18). Every fall is followed by the ricorso of the new father; every martyrdom produces a resurrection.

The archetypal encounter between father and son in the *Wake* is that between HCE and the Cad in Phoenix Park, related in chapter 2 of book I, in which the Cad asks HCE what time it is; Joyce wrote, "The encounter between my father and a tramp (the basis of my book) actually took place in that part of the Park."[5] In a Brunonian synthesis of opposites, Shem and Shaun combine into a filial figure who overthrows and replaces HCE in the *Wake:* as early as page 14 we learn that "These sons called themselves Caddy and Primas. Primas was a santryman and drilled all decent people. Caddy went to Winehouse and wrote o peace a farce. Blotty words for Dublin" (14.11–15). Glasheen observes: "On the assumption . . . that Joyce took the epithet 'cad' to his younger self, Shem is cad-caddy-cadet or younger son, and Shaun is Primas or first born. . . . I read *FW* 14.11–15 this way: Primas shot ('drilled') all decent people, i.e., shot his father, HCE, who is [Here Comes] Everybody; Caddy wrote a farce about his father, i.e., committed patricide with words. Primas goes on to be Buckley, who shoots his father dead with a gun; Caddy goes on to be Hosty, who kills his father dead in and by 'The Ballad of Persse O'Reilly,' using not a gun but slander and satire, as ancient Irish poets did."[6] Whichever brother Caddy or Primas may in fact be, all the filial figures in the *Wake* compose one basic, usurping son. All encounters between old men and young ones in the *Wake* are variants of the archetypal parricide.[7]

Commentators have long noted that Joyce regarded Shakespeare as a literary father and as a shaping influence. Levin holds that "the thwarted filial impulse prompted Joyce to look up to some intellectual godfather. . . . Joyce seeks . . . a father in Shakespeare";[8] while Goldberg comments: "When we look for real artistic affinities . . . above all there is Shakespeare."[9] As a young man, Joyce claimed to "have written the most perfect lyric since Shakespeare";[10] by the time he was writing the *Wake*, the artist was acutely aware of the Oedipal struggle between himself and the great playwright.[11] Whereas he acknowledges Shakespeare as his intellectual and artistic master—as "Great Shapesphere" (295.04)— Joyce, as always, strikes the note of rebellion: Stephen must overthrow Simon Dedalus; Hamlet must oust Claudius and replace King Hamlet; Cad must usurp HCE.[12] In Freudian terms, the son emulates the father and becomes his rival. The same relationship was in play between Joyce and Shakespeare; in the *Wake* Joyce tries to throw off the overbearing parental influence of the "Shikespower" (47.19). The influence of Shakespeare on Joyce in *Finnegans Wake* is that of a father on a son, of a master on a disciple; and, as a son, Joyce believes himself a rival of the father and tries to overthrow and replace Shakespeare as an artistic master.

Ernest Jones: Shakespearean "Fathers and Sons"

In Joyce's works the relationship of son to father results in rebellion and parricide. It is not surprising, therefore, to find that Shakespearean allusions in passages which deal with father-son encounters are taken mainly from *Hamlet, Macbeth,* and *Julius Caesar,* for all three of these plays involve rebellions against father figures of some sort. For this reason alone, before any attempt is made to trace and interpret these allusions, it is important to review the interpretation of Shakespeare by psychoanalytic critic Ernest Jones. Although Joyce made fun of Jones and his mentor Freud in the *Wake*, his Viconian schema in many ways parallels Freud's notions of the Oedipal complex.[13]

Whereas Joyce's ideas in the *Wake* about father-son rivalries did not necessarily derive from Jones or Freud (but rather from Vico), he undoubtedly had read Jones or was aware of Jones's Oedipal interpretations of *Hamlet* and *Julius Caesar*, for Ernest Jones appears as a character several times in the *Wake*.[14] While Joyce creates "Professor Jones" as a comically overbearing version of Shaun, he still uses Jones's notions of Shakespeare—which parallel Joyce's own ideas of Viconian fathers and sons—in the *Wake;* critics have pointed out, for example, that the discussion of Burrus and Caseous by "Professor Jones" (*FW*, 161–62) depends on Ernest Jones's reading of *Julius Caesar* in *Hamlet and Oedipus*.[15] Therefore, an awareness of Jones's ideas on *Hamlet* and *Julius Caesar* helps to clarify Shakespearean allusions relating to the encounter between father and son in the *Wake* and aids in understanding the nature of the encounter itself.

In *Hamlet and Oedipus* Ernest Jones, M.D., explains his psychoanalytic reading of *Hamlet* based on the Oedipus complex as described by his teacher, Sigmund Freud. He discusses "the central mystery in [*Hamlet*]—namely, the cause of Hamlet's hesitancy in seeking to obtain revenge for his father's murder."[16] The author argues that Hamlet's vacillation reflects the fact that at heart he does not want to carry out the task; his state of mind resembles a certain form of Freudian hysteria: "if Hamlet had been plunged into this abnormal state by the news of his mother's second marriage, it must be because the news has awakened into activity some slumbering memory . . . which is so painful that it may not become conscious."[17] What he remembers is his suppressed Oedipal feelings: perhaps "Hamlet had in years gone by, as a child, bitterly resented having had to share his mother's affection even with his own father, had regarded him as a rival, and had secretly wished him out of the way."[18] The prince wishes to kill his father so that the son, "taking over the sexual role of the father, should then espouse the mother."[19] Thus, Jones argues, Hamlet "has all the makings of as great a criminal as was Claudius".[20] He continues: "*his* [Hamlet's] *moral fate is bound up with his uncle's for good or ill.* In reality his uncle incorporates the deepest and most buried part of his own personality, so that he cannot kill him without also killing himself." Jones carries this reasoning to its logical Freudian conclusion: "In the last analysis Hamlet deals himself the punishment of death because death represents the most absolute form of castration."[21]

Jones goes on to argue that in Hamlet's miseries, Shakespeare was recording his own plight and emotional struggle. According to Freud, a father's death is "an event which is usually the turning point in the mental life of a man."[22] Jones points out that in 1601, just before the popularly accepted date of *Hamlet*'s composition, two of Shakespeare's own father figures died: the Earl of Essex and John Shakespeare, William's father.[23] Freud and Jones believed that the death of a father could revive the forbidden wishes of infancy, resulting in a mental conflict like that dramatized in *Hamlet*. These forbidden desires in the son are the repressed Oedipal instincts against the father and the ensuing feelings of rivalry. "To this source," writes Jones, "many social revolutionaries—perhaps all—owe the original impetus of their rebelliousness against authority. . . . In Shakespeare the family tragedy is placed in the foreground. The origin of all revolutions is the revolution in the family."[24]

Jones applies his theory of the Oedipus complex to *Julius Caesar*, another play which involves the theme of revolution. A ruler, he argues, is a father figure: "Psycho-analytic work has shown that a ruler, whether king, emperor, president, or what not, is in the unconscious mind a typical father symbol, and in actual life he tends to draw on to himself the ambivalent attitude characteristic of the son's feelings for the father. On the one hand, a ruler may be piously revered, respected, and loved as the wise and tender parent; on the other, he may be hated as the tyrannical authority against whom all rebellion is justified."[25] Caesar is "the original father, both loved and hated at once, even by his murderer."[26] After illustrating similarities between Caesar and the father figures in *Hamlet*, and between Hamlet and Brutus (including the fact that the name "Hamlet" has the same etymological significance as that of Brutus, both words meaning "doltish" or "stupid"), he maintains that Shakespeare's *Julius Caesar* reflects the same primal rebellion as *Hamlet*. The attitudes of the "son" toward the "father" are shown in three different sons: "Brutus represents the son's rebelliousness, Cassius his remorsefulness, and Antony his natural piety, the 'father' remaining the same person."[27] "A highly significant confirmation" for Jones of the Oedipal root of the play's composition "is the circumstance that Shakespeare in composing his tragedy entirely suppressed the fact that Brutus was the actual, though illegitimate, son of Caesar; this fact is plainly mentioned in Plutarch, the source of Shakespeare's plot, one which he almost literally followed otherwise. Even Caesar's famous death cry 'Et tu, mi fili, Brute!' appears in Shakespeare only in the weakened form 'Et tu, Brute!' "[28] Shakespeare must have repressed the primordial filial-rebellious instincts into the background of *Julius Caesar*, and yet these Oedipal instincts surface "to kill the Father [Caesar] who is thought to be ill-treating and tyrannizing over the mother [Rome]." Jones believes that this is the meaning of Brutus's explanation of the regicide-parricide: "Not that I loved Caesar less, but that I loved Rome more."[29]

This may seem like vulgar Freudianism, but Joyce's application of these theories was just as basic. In *Finnegans Wake* the father, HCE, is frequently referred to as Caesar; he is the victim of the archetypal parricide. Burrus and Caseous (Brutus and Cassius) represent two facets of the "son," Shaun and Shem. The "son" now appears to have three facets, for to Burrus and Caseous is added Antonius, in that "Antonius-Burrus-Caseous grouptriad" (167.04). It is for these reasons that references to Caesar, Brutus, and Cassius in the *Wake* are parallel to, and most likely refer to, Ernest Jones's reading of Shakespeare's *Julius Caesar*.

Finnegans Wake: The Overthrow of the Father

The second chapter of book I relates the encounter in Phoenix Park between HCE and the Cad (pages 31–36): one morning as H.C. Earwicker "was billowing across the wide expanse of our greatest park" (35.08), dressed in "his rubberised inverness, he met a cad with a pipe" (35.11).[30] The latter asks him for the time, a query which elicits from HCE a guilty defense of his character; from this the Cad gathers that HCE has committed some crime. The possession of this knowledge by the Cad and other "sons" brings about HCE's downfall.

Little is known for certain about HCE's fall, though in the *Wake* Joyce explores a great host of possibilities. The "historic date" (32.13) of the fall itself is a mystery that is fun to speculate upon. While critics have made various guesses, the Shakespearean references point to April 15 (or, conceivably, March 15) of some indeterminate year. This Caesar about to be deposed by his "sons" Brutus and Cassius walks out on "one happygogusty Ides-of-April morning (the anniversary, as it fell out, of his first assumption of his mirthday suit)" (35.03–5). This suggests that HCE committed his *felix culpa* and suffered his fall (like Caesar, on the Ides) on April 15, which, coincidentally, is his own birthday; "assumption" evokes yet another Ides, since the liturgical feast of the Assumption of the Blessed Virgin Mary is celebrated every year on August 15. That HCE's fall is accompanied by a number of references to Caesar's descent and that the day of the fall is later referred to as the "roman easter" (43.12) reminds us not only of the Roman Ides of March (the "eyots of martas" in 40.10), but even more appropriately of another Irish fall: the defeat of the Easter Rebellion on April 15, 1916. "Ides" (or the "murdhering idies" in 354.25) becomes a term associated throughout the rest of the book with the murder of paternal figures in the *Wake*, for "thit thides or marse makes a good dayle to be shattat" (366.29–30)—the Ides of March makes a good day to be shot at.[31]

Whatever it is that HCE actually did in the park, the news of his crime spreads quickly around town. This suffusion from ear to ear signals the downfall of Earwicker: the Cad goes home and tells his wife, who whispers the poisonous gossip to her confessor, who passes it on to "one Philly Thurnston" (38.35), and so on and so on. The news spreads until, on that "eyots of martas" (40.10), it reaches the ears of one Hosty, "an illstarred beachbusker" (40.21). His state of mind is much like that of another "son," Hamlet; the melancholy Hosty also considers suicide: "he could throw true and go and blow the sibicidal napper off himself for two bits to boldywell baltitude in the peace and quitybus" (40.30–32). Ophelia sang that she might know her true love "By his cockle hat and staff" (IV. v. 23); Hosty could similarly be identified "through Sant Iago by his cocklehat" (41.02). Like Shem and Joyce, this filial figure is a poet; he writes a song about HCE's fall, which sweeps "across *E*bblinn's chilled *h*amlet" (41.18; my italics; Elsinore and Dublin-*Eblanna*) and which "caressed the ears of the subjects" (41.24). This "Ballad of Persse O'Reilly" is the "rann that Hosty made" (44.07); it has to do with HCE's fall "on the roman easter" (43.12); and, printed on pages 45 through 47, it brings chapter 2 to a close.

The ballad celebrates the overthrow of fathers by sons, like the regicide of Caesar by Brutus and Cassius on the Ides: "He was a fafafather of all schemes for to bother us" (45.13), a "fine dairyman" among his "butter" and "bull of the Cassidys" (45.20–22; butter and cheese, Burrus and Caseous, Brutus and Cassius). It strikes the note of revolution; just as Brutus and Cassius overthrew Julius Caesar, as Hamlet ousted his pseudofather, King Claudius (and had secretly wished to displace his own father), as Hosty the poet (Shem, Cad, and so on) overthrows HCE, so Joyce himself rebels against and throws off the suffocating parental influence of his pseudofathers: "Suffoclose! Shikespower! Seudodanto! Anonymoses!" (47.19).[32] Joyce is the new Shakespeare, just as Hosty-Hamlet is the new king of Denmark-Penmark; as father-creators, they can now "makeall gone" and bury all the "Scandiknavery," all the trappings of the displaced rivals, whether Shakespeare, King Hamlet, or HCE: "Then we'll have a free trade Gaels' band and mass meeting / For to sod the brave son of Scandiknavery. . . . with the deaf and dumb Danes, / And all their remains." (47.20–25).

The next chapter (book I, chapter 3) records the spread of the ballad, "a poisonous volume of cloud barrage indeed" (48.05), and offers various versions of this now legendary encounter between HCE and the Cad. Levin, among other critics, has pointed out that now "as the son becomes a father, he ceases to be a disciple and becomes a rival. Like 'Great Shapesphere,' he [Joyce] emulates God and rivals nature."[33] He in fact simply replaces the father figure. Like God, the usurping son is a creator, a "worldwright" in his own right;[34] Hosty writes songs. HCE, the former bard and "retired cecelticocommediant" (33.03), amid "that family of bards" (48.06–7), has been reduced from his former Adamic grandeur to the level of "some lazy skald or maundering pote" (56.22—*skald* is Danish for and "pote" is an anagram for "poet"). Hosty, who caused HCE's demise, is elevated to the laureate and Joycean stature of "a musical genius" who is "the owner of an exceedingly niced ear, with tenorist voice to match, not alone, but a very major poet" (48.20–22).

While the second telling in chapter 3 of the "humphriad of that fall and rise" (53.09, involving Humphrey Chimpden and the Cad—or here, the Archicadenus) concerns different details, the Shakespearean allusions are similar to those in the first telling. *Hamlet* is here in "poleaxe your sonson's grandson" (53.32—King Hamlet and "the sledded polacks" in I. i. 63, and Stephen's theory of *Hamlet*), as is *Macbeth*, in "manorwomban-born" (55.10—Macduff was, as Joyce writes in 79.08-9, "no man of woman born"; Lady Macbeth is echoed in 52.05–6—see Part II entry). Just as Lewis Theobald and others dubbed and ghosted Shakespearean plays, and just as Joyce rewrites and reinterprets the Ancients, the "Archicadenus" presents to the audience, "craving their auriculars to recepticle particulars," his revolutionary version (55.30–32). In "this new reading of the part," in 55.33–36, the "new garrickson" (son-usurper replacement for David Garrick, famed Shakespearean actor) replaces by apostasy and substitutes by Father-Son consubstantiation ("hypostasised by substintuation") the "orerotundity" of HCE, "that once grand old elrington" (perhaps Thomas Elrington, another famous actor). The son-as-rival displaces the father; the disciple replaces the master; Joyce writes a purple patch of his own.

Nothing is certain about this encounter: "Thus the unfacts, did we possess them, are too imprecisely few to warrant our certitude" (57.16–17); but the version retold here is like that of Caesar's and Parnell's ("ivy") rise and fall: "ulvy came, envy saw, ivy conquered" (58.06). From page 58 until the end of the chapter, a number of versions of the encounter are authored by a number of people.

Whatever it is that actually happened, a group of references seem to center around one version in which the drunken Cad was trying to enter HCE's pub after closing time.[35] The encounter took place at "A stone-hinged gate" (69.15), which "was triplepatlockt on him on purpose by his faithful poorters" (69.25). This particular version appears to be underlined by a Shakespearean motif. There are in these pages many and recurrent references to the gate and to porters. Hodgart suggests that "the name of the hero [of the *Wake*] . . . is probably Porter."[36] Publican HCE is appropriately known as Porter; in chapter 4 of book III, HCE and his family are identified as "The Porters . . . Mr Porter . . . Mrs Porter . . .

little Porter babes" (pp. 560–61). Furthermore, among the dream symbols of the *Wake*, the gate to HCE's pub, his home, and his castle in Chapelizod is metamorphosed into Castle Knock Gate ("Thus come to castle. Knock." in 262.05–6), the gate to the western end of Phoenix Park, which sits on Castle Knock, a hill by Chapelizod. In "outandin brown candlestock" (50.05) there may be an echo of Castle Knock; connection between Castle Knock Gate and *Macbeth* is also suggested here, since the line also echoes Macbeth's "Out, out, brief candle!" (V. v. 23). Thus, all references in the subsequent (or earlier) pages to porters, to the gate, and to Castle Knock are woven into the story of the encounter through the medium of *Macbeth* and its drunken porter scene. This scene in *Macbeth* takes place on the night that Macbeth murders Duncan, his king and father figure, and thus replaces his rival. A similar encounter in the *Wake* at the Porters's gate is attended by allusions to *Macbeth*'s porter at the gate.

Pages 63 to 72 recall this encounter at the pub's gate one evening between HCE (the keeper of this alehouse in Chapelizod) and the Cad (the fender). The details seem to run as follows: The Cad explains that he was drunk, "a most decisive bottle of single in his possession, seized after dark," and that he found himself "at temperance gateway . . . in a gate's way" (63.17–20). He tried to open a bottle of stout (porter is a kind of stout) by hammering his head against the bloody gate, calling for the porter (HCE-Porter, the innkeeper): "trying to open zozimus a bottlop stoub by mortially hammering his *magnum bonum* . . . against the bludgey gate for the boots about the swan" (63.32–35; "the swan" hints at Shakespeare). "This battering babel allower the door and sideposts . . . was not in the very remotest like the belzey babble of a bottle of boose" (64.09–11): the Cad's drunken battering and knocking all over the door and sideposts of the gate creates quite a disturbance, and is, like the *Wake* itself, a hellish and drunken mixture of tongues (tower of Babel), a Luciferian (Beelzebub) "belzey babble." "Battering babel" and "belzey babble" recall the words of *Macbeth*'s drunken porter, who walks out to the gate saying, "Here's a knocking indeed. . . . Who's there, i'th'name of Belzebub? . . . . I'll devil-porter it no further." (*Mac.* II. iii. 1 ff.)

The presence of "the fender [Cad] and the bottle at the gate" (65.35) results in an encounter—the battle at the gate. Still knocking, the Cad "hickicked at the dun and dorass" (67.19)—kicked at the gate of the Dun and Dorass Inn.[37] The porter (Porter-HCE), however, had locked the stone-hinged iron gate ("gape") to keep the invader out: "A stonehinged gate . . . applegate . . . the iron gape, by old custom left open to prevent the cats [or Cads] from getting at the gout [or gate], was triplepatlockt on him on purpose by his faithful poorters" (69.15–26). Undaunted, "Humphrey's unsolicited visitor . . . bleated through the gale outside which the tairor of his clothes was hogcallering . . . that he would break his bulsheywigger's head for him . . . that he would break the gage over his lankyduckling head . . . and went on at a wicked rate" (70.13–32): the iron gate is now metamorphosed into a wicket gate, and Humphrey Chimpden's visitor, the drunken Cad, shouts through the gate outside, threatening to break the gate ("gage") over HCE's Bolshevik (Danish, really) head. He unloads his verbal artillery "at a wicked rate" at the wicket gate (c.f. "at the wicket" in 72.28). The Cad is depicted as "the tairor of his clothes": a tailor of clothes and a terror, tearing his clothes and screaming ("hogcallering") at HCE. *Macbeth*'s drunken porter would have let the Cad in: "Faith, here's an English tailor come hither for stealing out of a French hose. Come in, tailor. Here you may roast your goose" (II. iii. 12–14).[38] Foiled by "Sublime Porter" (72.02–3) and his locked gate, the Cad stands at the wicket gate and throws a few rocks at the wicket gate to HCE's inn to support his verbal artillery before leaving: "That more than considerably unpleasant bullocky before he rang off drunkishly pegged a few glatt stones, all of a wise . . . at the wicket in support of his words" (72.25–28; "wicket" may refer to cricket as well). Thus ends this second version of the encounter between HCE and the Cad.[39]

The fallen HCE is given a burial at sea in chapter 4 of book I. In the opening pages (75–90) of this section can be identified another such pattern of allusions to the three plays of regicide-parricide, *Hamlet, Macbeth* and *Julius Caesar*. HCE's coffin is buried at sea at ten minutes to five o'clock: "by their Oorlog [*horloge*, watch] . . . it was Dane to pfife" (77.13–14); later, reincarnated as Shaun, HCE will be the Thane of Fife—Macduff. The "Dane" is HCE-King Hamlet. Like the ghost of King Hamlet of Denmark, the buried HCE is laid out "from grosskopp to megapod, embalmed" from head to foot (78.05–6; "cap-a-pe"): the big head *(gross Kopf)* and megafeet of this archetypal father are Howth Head and the hill of Castle Knock, the two extremities of Dublin.[40] Or, if HCE was buried at sea, his flesh has "the multitudinous seas incarnadine[d]" (*Mac.* II. ii. 60–61): "the first old wugger of himself in the flesh, whiggissimus incarnadined" (79.02–3). HCE is thought to be hibernating, like a salmon, feeding himself secretly for the ricorso and the rise of a new cycle: this future HCE is described as "no man of woman born" (79.08–9)—that is, Shaun-Macduff, for Macduff was "none of woman born" (*Mac.* IV. i. 80) and would become Duncan-HCE's avenger and replacement in a new Viconian cycle.

Widow Kate Strong now paints "a lane picture for us, in a dreariodreama setting" (79.27–28)—a Drury Lane dramatic retelling of HCE's story—with her "bare godkin" (79.20; Hamlet's "bare bodkin," with which a man might his quietus make); she scavenges "from good King

Hamlaugh's gulden dayne" (79.34–35) for details about the fall of "that thuddysickend Hamlaugh" (84.32). The day of the fall recalls the Ides and *Julius Caesar*, for here we have the "nobiloroman" (84.15; Brutus was "the noblest Roman of them all" in *JC* V. v. 68). Once again we attempt "solving the wasnottobe crime cunundrum" (85.22) of the "historic date" of the crime in the park. This investigation takes place in court "at the Old Bailey on the calends of Mars" (85.26–27)—a date very much like the Ides of March (the calends of the ancient Roman month is its first day, from which the days are counted backward to the ides)—and is heralded by a judicial version of "List, list!": "Oyeh! Oyeh!" (85.31, or the Old Bailey's "Oyez! Oyez!"). The court investigates the encounter between HCE and the filial figure(s) in the park on "the ephemerides of profane history" (87.07)—the Ides, ephemeral periods (times of falls and falling) of history. Questions are asked about the lecherous all-father: "And how did the greeneyed mister arrive at the B.A.?" (88.15; *Othello*'s "greeneyed monster" of jealousy), for example. HCE appears to defend himself at this trial, but it is no longer clear whether this is "Father ourder" (89.25)—our father—or his successor and son. The conflict now seems to be between the twins, "Peeler and Pole" (86.12)—Peter and Paul—or "Mickmichael . . . and neckanicholas" (90.10–11)—Mick and Nick. Shakespeare's twins are also here, in "Two dreamyums in one dromium? Yes and no error" (89.03): two Dromios (the twins of *Comedy of Errors*) in one dromedary hump (or HCE). They are like two peas from the same pod: "And both as like as a duel of lentils? Peacisely" (89.04). Just as Ernest Jones had forecasted, the death of Julius Caesar on the Ides (the "Juletide" of 97.03) precipitates a rivalry between his "sons," both struggling to be the new Caesar: "Let there be fight? And there was. Foght" (90.12–13). Thus, Brutus and Cassius ("bullycassidy" in 87.15) are present, as is the prize that they always fight over in the *Wake*, Cleopatra-Margareen ("Cliopatrick" in 91.06).

The Rivalry of the Sons

The struggle between the "sons" is a primary theme of the next few chapters. On page 124 is the first description of Shaun as "à grave Brofèsor" (124.09)—a grave professor; in the following chapter (book II, chapter 6), he assumes the title of "Professor Jones" and answers twelve questions at length in professorial-lectorial fashion, making many references to *Hamlet* and *Julius Caesar*. Question eleven particularly concerns the relationship between the brothers: Shaun, addressed directly as Jones, is asked if he might be willing to help his impoverished, starving brother by lending him some money: "we don't think, Jones, we'd care to this evening, would you? / Answer: No, blank ye!" (149.09–10). Shaun-Jones launches off on a digressive lecture to his student, "Schott" (149.19, 24; also in 161.23); his sermon deals with, among other things, spatialism, the dime-cash problem, and the struggle between rivals in the tale of the Mookse and the Gripes. His final digression (on pages 161–68) is about this competition and is spoken in Jonesian-Shakespearean terms: the strife of the "sons" after Caesar's death.[41] These pages concern "Burrus and Caseous" (161.12; Brutus and Cassius), Margareen (Cleopatra), and the deposed king, Caesar—or, in dairymen's terms, butter (French *beurre*), cheese (Latin *caseus*), and margarine. Brutus, Caesar's regicide, is "Burrus . . . yet unbeaten as a risicide" (161.17), and his opposite rival is "Caseous . . . obversely the revise of him" (161.18; obviously the obverse and reverse of him). That we are touching on Shakespeare (breakfast—butter, margarine, etc.) is hinted at in the description of the twins as "shakespill and eggs" (161.31).

Ernest Jones says that Brutus, Cassius, and Anthony, as aspects of the son with Oedipal instincts, must annihilate Caesar—thus, we have "Caesar outnullused" (161.36)—annihilated.[42] The lines on page 162 seem to refer specifically to Shakespeare's *Julius Caesar:* "The older sisars (Tyrants, regicide is too good for you!) become unbeurrable from age, (the compositor of the farce of dustiny however makes a thunpledrum mistake by letting off this pienofarte effect as his furst act as that is where the juke comes in) having been sort-of-nineknived and chewly removed . . .": the old Caesar is a victim of tyrannicide (but not regicide), having become a "tyrant" but not yet a king and "unbeurrable" (unbearable and unbutterable). The "compositor" of this particular "farce of dustiny" (farce of destiny, of a man's fall into dust, and Verdi's *La Forza del Destino*) is William Shakespeare, who, however, has often been accused by critics of creating an anticlimax, of letting out the crowning pianoforte effect ("pienofarte effect," as that is where the joke comes in) too early ("as his furst act," though it's not in the first act but in the third): Caesar's (or "Juke" Humphrey's) death, in which he is stabbed by a Cad-of-nine-lives who is "sort-of-nine-knived"—in which, that is, he is knifed by the nine conspirators (and "duly removed").[43]

Professor Jones goes on to describe the struggle between the Cavalier Cassius and the Roundhead Brutus ("Caseous . . . a caviller but Brutus has the reachly roundered head" in 162.21–22). The two brothers are edible twins, like Butterbread and ham sandwiches: *"Der Haensli ist ein Butterbrot, mein Butterbrot!* [Butterbread and my brother] *Und Koebi iss dein Schtinkenkot!"* [*Schinkenbrot* is "ham sandwich" in German] (163.06). As butter and cheese, these rival dairymen are descendants of

Caesar—or "Cheesugh!" (163.10). However, a new element is now introduced into the competition: "on this stage there plainly appears the cowrymaid M." (164.07–8). The readers "meet Margareen" (164.14) and learn that this dairymaid ("cowrymaid") is none other than Cleopatra: "A cleopatrician in her own right" (166.34). While "Margareena she's very fond of Burrus . . . and she velly fond of chee" (166.30–31), this "eastasian import" (166.32) goes on and "complicates the position . . . by implicating herself with an elusive Antonius, a wop" (166.35–167.01), "while Burrus and Caseous are contending for her misstery" (166.36)—that is, she takes up with the elusive Mark Antony, an Italian in Egypt, while Brutus and Cassius are contending for her mastery and maidenhood (miss-tery).

Ernest Jones's triangle of the three "sons" following the fall of the father is now complete; and we have "This Antonius-Burrus-Caseous grouptriad" (167.04). As Brutus, Shaun-Jones ends his lecture by threatening to do to Shem-Caseous what he did to Caesar: "Merus Genius to Careous Caseous! *Moriture, te salutat!*" (167.23–24). This is a message from Pure Genius to decaying Cheese: "O, you who are about to die, he salutes you!"[44]

Another facet of the rivalry between the sons after the fall of the father is reflected in allusions to *Macbeth*. King Duncan's murder eventually results in a power struggle between Macbeth and Macduff. As has been shown, *The Mime* is about a competition between Mick-Chuff and Nick-Glugg for the love of the Maggies, led by Issy-Izod. Much of that chapter involves Issy's flirtations with Glugg-Shem; later in the chapter Chuff returns to battle Glugg over Izod. These pages (248–52) contain a dense cluster of allusions to *Macbeth*, with the returning Chuff pictured in the culminating scene as Macduff come to wreak vengeance on Macbeth, just as Birnam Wood came to Dunsinane. The coming of Macduff is first prophesied by "the witch on the heath" (468.35): "Ansighosa pokes in her potstill to souse at the sop be sodden enow and to hear to all the bubbles besaying: the coming man, the future woman" (246.10–12)—And she goes and pokes in her pot and in her still to see if the soup be hot enough to hear all the bubbles prophesying the coming man. In *Macbeth* the witches stirring their cauldron prophesy both the coming of Macbeth to the throne and the coming of the man born of no woman, Macduff, to victory at Dunsinane. The next seven pages of *Finnegans Wake* teem with references to *Macbeth*. "Dunckle Dalton of matching wools. Shake hands through the thicketloch! Sweet swanwater!" (248.22–23) hints at Shakespeare ("Shake hands" and "swan"), and especially at *Macbeth* (Duncan and the marching woods). The marching thickets of Birnam Wood again hide Macduff's business: "Underwoods spells bushment's business. So if you sprig poplar you're bound to twig this" (248.28–29). Macduff's soldiers are "bushmen" because their business is to be "under woods"; Macbeth did not speak ("sprig") the "poplar" tree language (of the witches' "spells") and did not understand ("twig") this.

Finally, the big event arrives—Chuff returns on page 250 to claim Izod, and Birnam Wood is come to Dunsinane: "Yet's the time for being now, now, now. For a burning would is come to dance inane. Glamours hath moidered's lieb and herefore Coldours must leap no more. Lack breath must leap no more" (250.16–18). At last Macduff-Chuff is come to avenge the usurpation of Macbeth-Glugg and to stop the inane dance of flirtation between Glugg and Issy. In *Macbeth*, to "leap" is to usurp[45]—so Macbeth is the "Leapermann" (250.21), who, short of breath ("Lack breath"), must leap (and dance) no more. The lines are a *Macbeth* gold mine. The first sentence echoes Macbeth's words just before the battle: "There would have been a time for such a word. / Tomorrow, and tomorrow, and tomorrow . . ." (V. iv. 18–19). Following this are echoes of "Though Birnam Wood be come to Dunsinane" (V. viii. 30) and of the voice Macbeth heard as he murdered Duncan: "Methought I heard a voice cry 'Sleep no more! / Macbeth does murder sleep. . . . Glamis hath murdered sleep, and therefore Cawdor / Shall sleep no more, Macbeth shall sleep no more'" (*Mac*. II. ii. 34–42).

So Macduff brings his marching woods to Macbeth's Dunsinane: "Led by Lignifer, in four hops of the happiest, ach beth cac duff, a marrer of the sward incoronate. . . . Will any dubble dabble on the bay?" (250.34–36). Led by marching woods, Macduff reaches Dunsinane as simply as a, b, c, d. "Lignifer" recalls both Lucifer, and tree and stone—Shem and Shaun, lignostone wood and *fer* (French iron and sword), swords hidden (literally and verbally) amid woods and words, Birnam Wood marching to Dunsinane.[46] Macbeth ("ach beth") and Macduff ("cac duff") are both regicides (marrers of coronated swords and of the Word Incarnate). These events follow the "Double, bubble" predictions of the babbling witches ("dubble dabble"), for "most anysing maybefallhim from a song of a witch" (251.11); this was certainly true for Macbeth, since most anything *did* befall the poor son of a bitch from the song of a witch. For Macbeth, "The specks on his lapspan are his foul deed thougths, wishmarks of mad imogenation. Take they off! Make the off!" (251.16–17). While Cymbeline's daughter, Imogen, may be here, we are primarily in the mad, guilt-ridden imaginations of Macbeth and his lady, who were unable to wash the specks of their foul deed out of their thoughts, which "rather / The multitudinous seas incarnadine" (*Mac*. II. ii. 61). As he prepares to fight Macduff, Glugg-Macbeth is saying, like his wife, "Out, damned spot! Out, I say!" (V. i. 31). The duel between the two "crown pretenders" (252.15) finally occurs in the swordplay of "Come, thrust! Go, parry! . . . Exchange, reverse" (252.04, 10). These stage directions could well have applied to Macbeth's final fight: "Lay on, Macduff, / And damned be him that first cries, 'Hold, enough!'" (V. viii. 33–34).[47]

The children maintain this same behavior pattern in the Study Hour chapter—that is, the boys contend with each other and Issy awaits the victor. Sometimes the boys are Brutus and Cassius, as when Shem again asks his brother to make him a loan: "Dear Brotus, land me arrears" (278.L3). Shem's plea cleverly combines two well-known passages from *Julius Caesar:* Cassius's "The fault, dear Brutus, is not in our stars, / But in ourselves, that we are underlings" (I. ii. 140–41); and, of course, Mark Antony's "Friends, Romans, countrymen, lend me your ears . . ." (III. ii. 72). The setting, however, is both Rome and Inverness ("on the Ides of Valentino's, at Idleness" in 289.27–28); and the sons are Macbeth ("poor MacBeth" in 290.06) and Macduff at times, as when Issy remarks that "I loved to see the Macbeths Jerseys knacking spots of the Plumpduffs Pants" (302.F1).

A brief cluster of *Julius Caesar* allusions appears on pages 281 and 282; the children are again "Margaritomancy . . . Bruto and Cassio" (281.14–15). As Cleopatra, Margareen can't decide whom she loves better: "What if she love Sieger [German for "victor"] less though she leave Ruhm moan?" (281.22–23). She echoes Brutus's motive: "Not that I loved Caesar less, but that I loved Rome more" (III. ii. 21–22). The echo of Brutus's speech is continued a few lines later: "With sobs for his job, with tears for his toil, with horror for his squalor, but with pep for his perdition" (282.01–3)—". . . There is tears for his [Caesar's] love; joy for his fortune; honor for his valor; and death for his ambition" (III. ii. 26–28).

In chapter 3 of book III the encounter between HCE and the Cad on the Ides is rehearsed in the story of how Buckley shot the Russian General (HCE). Once again, therefore, we recall the decline of Caesar, "when booboob brutals and cautiouses only aims at the oggog hogs in the humand, then . . . blows the gaff off mombition and thit thides or marse makes a good dayle to be shattat. Fall stuff" (366.25–30). In this passage HCE-Russian General, having admitted his piglike sins, concludes that if his accusers can only see the swinish side of a human being, then he deserves to be shot at. Buckley and the accusers are represented by Brutus and Cassius ("brutals and cautiouses"), who *do* only view the swinish side of a human ("only aims at the oggog hogs in the humand"). Consequently, Caesar is killed on the Ides of March ("thides or marse") for his "mombition" ("But Brutus says he was ambitious, and Brutus is an honorable man"). Thus, HCE is the Russian General defecating at ("shattat") Sevastopol on the Ides, a good day to be shot at: "thides or marse makes a good dayle to be shattat." *Et tu, Brutè?*—then fall Caesar. Fallen, HCE-Caesar is "Fall stuff"—or Shakespeare's Falstaff.

The struggle between the surviving filial figures rages on. For example, in the second chapter of book III Jaun-Shaun lectures Issy about flirting with Shem-Macbeth and reminds her of *Macbeth*: "And remember this, a chorines, there's the witch on the heath, sistra" (468.34–35). The witches had predicted that whatever happened, Shaun-Macduff would return to wreak vengeance. Jaun then bids farewell (his "last fireless words of postludium" in 469.20–29) with a battle cry that echoes Macbeth's final words: "Lead on, Macadam, and danked be he who first sights Halt Linduff!" (469.20–21)—"Lead on, Macduff, / And damned be him that first cries, 'Hold, enough!'" (V. vii. 33–34). (Shaun, however, is Macduff; so the roles are reversed, and the line seems to be addressed by Macduff—"Linduff"—to Macbeth—"Macadam," or son of Adam.) This filial struggle continues for the rest of the *Wake* under various guises.[48]

Will this "tale told of Shaun and Shem" (215.35) go on forever?[49] Hardly—for we know, that the book will end and begin again in *ricorso*, and that HCE will rise again in a new cycle, his two aspects (featured in the sons) remerged and reamalgamated by a Brunonian synthesis of opposites into a new phoenix and a new Finnegan, waking and rising from the ashes ("equals of opposites, evolved by a onesame power of nature or of spirit . . . and polarised for reunion by the symphysis of their antipathies" in 92.08–11). The Shakespearean references tell us much about the presence and the meaning of Bruno's ideas in the *Wake*, for, late in the book, Joyce informs us that "Britus and Gothius shall no more joustle for that sonneplace but mark one autonement" (568.08–9). In other words, at dawn Ernest Jones's Brutus and Cassius, the competing "sons," shall be no longer jostling for the place vacated by Caesar, the father ("joustle" for that son's place and for a place in the sun). The one who will in the end rise to take that place, however, will be—literally and historically—neither of them, but their Brunonian synthesis, whom they shall observe ("mark") as the at-one-ment ("one autonement"). "Mark one autonement" is Marcus Antonius, the new ricoursing Caesar (and winner of Cleopatra's love).[50]

This passage is important because it shows how the Shakespearean allusions (here the *Julius Caesar* matrix à la Ernest Jones) can contribute to the greater philosophical meanings of the *Wake* as a whole, illuminating and complementing Vico and Bruno in a crucial Joycean concept: the replacement of the "father" in a Viconian cycle through a Brunonian union of Jonesian-Shakespearean "sons."

Joyce's vision, thus, of fathers and sons is that of a Viconian cycle, in which the son becomes a rival to his father, overthrows him, and rises to replace him. Joyce himself, like Stephen Dedalus, wishes to deny and throw over the paternal influence; specifically, he feels himself to be in a father-son relationship with Shakespeare. Although he repeatedly acknowledges Shakespeare as his master, as "Great Shapesphere," he still wishes, like Robert Greene's Shakespeare, to be the only Shake-scene around.[51] By having Shaun accuse Shem-Joyce of wishing to be the top bard and of lacking respect for the memory of his masters, however, Joyce repeatedly levels a charge of ambition at himself. As Shaun puts it, Shem "was in his bardic memory low" (172.28), for "Maistre Sheames de la Plume . . . was . . . aware of no other shaggspick, other Shakhisbeard . . . as he was himself" (177.30–35). After all, Shaun asks, what has Shem-Joyce actually created? "Inartistic portraits of himself" (182.19); an "usylessly unreadable Blue Book of Eccles," (179.27; *Ulysses* of Eccles St., the blue cover, first edition) written in "monolook interyerear" (182.20; *monologue intérieur);* a set of "fermented words" (184.26) full of "quashed quotatoes" and "messes of mottage" (183.22). How can Joyce expect to rival or overthrow his master? Perhaps Joyce does so by writing the *Wake:* how better to slay the father than, as Hosty does to HCE in "The Ballad of Persse O'Reilly," to make out of his most famous tragedies a cosmic farce?

What, then, does a disciple do with the old master? Does one reject his influence and leave him? Or does one merely imitate him? The "quiztune" —the choice between stifling death (at the hands of the "Shikespower") and escape—echoes Hamlet's famous soliloquy; as it was for Hamlet, the choice here is "collideorscape!" (143.28). Joyce provides the word itself as the answer to the question—"Answer: A collideorscape!" —for in the question lies the solution. In the kaleidoscope of *Finnegans Wake*, Joyce chooses escape: divorce from his fatherland and from the examples of his literary masters, particularly Shakespeare, as well as from his real parents, country, religion, and language. He is left physically, spiritually, and artistically exiled. He must now go to new lands, mock his masters, invent his own literary techniques, and explore the undiscovered country.

6
The Strife Between Brothers

"Maistre Sheames de la Plume . . . aware of no other shaggspick, other Shakhisbeard."

Finnegans Wake

In the Wakean scheme of things, a father is overthrown in an encounter with one or more filial figures, and then (as is outlined in Ernest Jones's reading of *Julius Caesar)* the "brothers" contend for the position vacated by the fallen father. This strife between brothers (eventually resulting in a Brunonian union of opposites) is repeatedly reenacted in the *Wake*, though under many guises: Burrus and Caseous, Macbeth and Macduff, the Mookse and the Gripes, Chuff and Glugg, Kev and Dolph, Kevin and Jerry, the Ondt and the Gracehoper, and the tree and the stone, to name a few. Those sections most densely concerned with this rivalry are chapters 6 and 7 of book I (particularly the latter), the points of confrontation between Shaun (Professor Jones) and Shem. This struggle between the twins reveals to us, through Shakespearean references, much about Joyce's own feelings towards his work, and especially towards *Finnegans Wake*.

In number eleven of the "Twelve Questions," Shaun as Professor Jones is asked if he might be willing to help his impoverished, drunken, starving, exiled brother ("on the binge a poor acheseyeld from Ailing," 148.33—an exile from Erin with ailing eyes) by lending him some money: "we don't think, Jones, we'd care to this evening, would you?" (149.10). Shaun-Jones launches into a spatialist-vorticist-Freudian-Shakespearean lecture to pupil "Schott" (149.19,24; 161.23,33) on the strife between opposites[1]—space versus time, eye versus ear, stone versus tree, Mookse versus Gripes, Burrus versus Caseous—spiced with allusions to Shakespeare and to Ernest Jones's Freudian-Oedipal readings ("eatupus complex" in 128.36) of Shakespearean plays. Finally, very late in the chapter, he returns to the request for a loan and, by appealing to the Mosaic Law, identifies himself with Shylock and Justice (prefiguring the confrontation between Justius and Mercius in the following chapter): "No! . . . My unchanging Word is sacred. . . . That mon that hoth no moses in his sole nor is not awed by conquists of word's law . . . were he my own breastbrother . . . though it broke my heart to pray it, still I'd fear I'd hate to say!" (167.18–168.12). Shaun is appealing to the legalistic, Mosaic value of the Word and is saying that the man who has no "moses" in his soul—were he Shaun's own brother—would be turned down. His words echo Shakespeare's *Merchant of Venice:* "The man that hath no music in himself / Nor is not moved with concord of sweet sounds . . . " (V. i. 83–84). The accuser here, however, is Shylock-Shaun-Justius (whereas in that play the line accuses and refers to Shylock), who defends the Mosaic letter-of-the-law over the spirit, accusing Shem-Mercius-Portia of having "no moses" in his soul. Actually, it will be Shem-Mercius who will display the quality of mercy in this strife between brothers.

"Shem"

The greatest confrontation between the brothers occurs in the "Shem" section of *Finnegans Wake*, chapter 7 of book I, pages 169 to 195. This passage involves a series of vituperative accusations leveled at Shem by his brother, Shaun; Joyce puts into Shaun's mouth all of the great accusations that previous (and subsequent) critics made against Joyce himself. Thus, the strife between the brothers here takes on the overtones of the encounter between Joyce and his unsympathetic critics, between Shem-Joyce and the Shauns of the world.

Shaun begins his tirade with an attack on Shem's "lowness": his brother is an eater of wrong foods and a scoundrel with ugly features; he is unclean, unwashed, and smelly, a drug addict and a drunk; he is satanic; he has an underwear fetish; he is not a regular guy; he is someone who won't enter into a good argument; he is many other low things. Some of Shaun's charges do seem more penetrating than others; these are the ones that deal with Shem-Joyce's role as a poet.

Shaun says that the profession of an artist and a writer is a disrespectful and shiftless one: "His jymes is out of job, would sit and write" (181.29–30). Here is drawn "Jymes" Joyce-Shem, unemployed ("out of job") and lacking the patience (of Job) for regular work, choosing instead to try setting the world right by just sitting and writing; the line, again, echoes Hamlet's "The time is out of joint. O cursèd spite, / That ever I was born to set it right" (I. v. 188–89).

Furthermore, while choosing to be a bard, Shem "was in his bardic memory low" (172.28). Not only are his own memories despicable, but, according to Shaun, his lack of respect for Shakespeare and his memory of the Bard are "low." Like Hosty or the Cad, this "sham" wishes to overthrow the paternal "Shikespower": "his pawdry's purgatory was more than a nigger bloke could bear.... How is that for low, laities and gentlenuns?" (177.04–8). The shade of his father's purgatory was more than Shem-Hamlet could bear;[2] like Ernest Jones's Hamlet, he now must overthrow his father. Shaun attacks Shem for his artistic hubris, for his lack of filial respect for the holy writings of his master, for his view of himself as Shakespeare's rival: "Shem always blaspheming, so holy writ, Billy ... his Ballade Imaginaire ... by Maistre Sheames de la Plume ... that he was ... aware of no other shaggspick, other Shakhisbeard, either prexactly unlike his polar anthisishis [either exactly unlike his polar antithesis] or procisely the seem [precisely the same] ... as he was himself" (177.23–34). Shaun here accuses Shem of blasphemously trying to play Master Will the Penman with such artistic egotism as to dare shake the Bard's beard and brook no other Shakespeare as his rival. The accusation "that he was ... aware of no other shaggspick, other Shakhisbeard" brings to mind Robert Greene's similar charge in the *Groatsworth of Wit* (which may have been referred to in these pages in "for four testers one groat," 170.03) that Shakespeare considered himself "in his owne conceit the onely Shake-scene in a countrie." What right has Shem to shake the beard of Shakespeare? What has Shem-Joyce in fact created, that he should believe himself such a shake-scene? He has produced only "inartistic portraits of himself" (182.19), a "usylessly unreadable Blue Book of Eccles" (179.27) in "monolook interyerear" (182.20), and a set of "fermented words" (184.26), full of "quashed quotatoes" and "messes of mottage" (183.22).

Shaun goes on to say that "Shem was a sham and a low sham" (170.25). Just as Robert Greene charged Shakespeare with being an imitator "beautified with our feathers," Shaun accuses Shem of being a sham—a fake, a forger, and a plagiarist. Shem has to put on an act, like Hamlet, and go under a penname: "this hambone dogpoet pseudoed himself under the hangname he gave himself of Bethgelert" (177.21–22).[3] Greene accused Shakespeare of copying other English playwrights and of touching up their works and staging them under his own name; he warned that "there is an upstart Crow, beautified with our feathers, that ... with his *Tygers heart wrapt in a Players hide*, supposes he is well able to bumbast out a blanke verse as the best of you: and being an absolute *Iohannes fac totum*, is in his owne conceit the onely Shake-scene in a countrie."[4] Similarly, Shaun accuses Shem of "trying to copy the stage Englesemen"; thus "he broughts their house down" (181.01). This charge had been leveled at Joyce: "what do you think Vulgariano [Shem] did but study with stolen fruit how cutely to copy all their various styles of signature so as one day to utter an epical forged cheque on the public for his own private profit" (181.14–17)—and brings to mind the Shakespearean forgers, especially William Henry Ireland (see "Vortigern" in 565.12), who also tried to copy various styles of Shakespearean signature for his own profit. The "epical forged cheque" is the epic *Ulysses*, for which Joyce, trying to "forge . . . the uncreated conscience of [his] race" (*P*, 253), was accused of pillaging Homer's and Shakespeare's creations for his own profit. Both Greene's Shakespeare and Shem-Joyce produced "artstouch-ups" (171.27), touchup jobs of others' works. Shaun calls his cowardly brother a "fraid born fraud" (172.21), who "faked O'Ryan's, the indelible ink" (185.25). Just as Greene might have wondered how many "artstouch-ups," how many beautified feathers hiding a tiger's heart, had been inflicted upon the public by a sham and plagiarist, so also Shaun asks about Shem: "Who can say how many pseudostylic shamiana, how few or how many of the most venerated public impostures, how very many piously forged palimpsests slipped in the first place by this morbid process from his pelagiarist pen?" (181.36–182.03).

Shem-Joyce's work is not only fakery, but also an egotistical, exhibitionist sort of literature, "inartistic portraits of himself" (182.19), a "wetbed confession" (188.01) probing "the mystery of himsel" (184.09). It is agnostic and luciferian in its pride and conceit: "Do you hold yourself then for some god in the manger, Shehohem, that you will neither serve not let serve, pray nor let pray?" (188.18–19). After all, Shem-Joyce's literature, despite all its perversness, is not even original; it is, rather, a set of plagiaristic fakeries, and he is a scavenger, a "sniffer of carrion, premature gravedigger" (189.28), feeding off the opuses of dead authors or off "any boskop of Yorek" (190.19). Gravedigging recalls the gravedigger of *Hamlet*, present in this chapter as Shem the "premature gravedigger," who is nourished by his memories of any skull of Yorick. "Any boskop of Yorek" refers both to the ecclesiast (bishop?) Yorick in *Tristram Shandy* and to the gravedigger in *Hamlet*, digging up the old skull of Yorick, the "tragic jester" (171.15—which also refers to Shem). According to *Webster's*, "Boskop man" (named after a locale in the Transvaal, like Peking or Piltdown Man) was "a late Pleistocene southern African man, [probably] ancestral to modern Bushmen and Hottentots." In German *Böse* means "devil" or "fiend," and *Kopf* means "head." "Boskop," then, can represent either a prehistoric skull or an ancestor; it is likely that "boskop of Yorek" means skull of Yorick and ancestors (or devils) of yore.[5] Thus, Shem-Hamlet is being accused of gravedigging from and cannibalizing the materials of dead authors.

Finally, Shaun accuses Shem of not only sustaining himself on the works of others, but—in writing "inartistic portraits" and a "wetbed confession" of "the mystery of himsel"—of ultimately feeding upon his own body, life, and works: "by blind poring upon your many scalds and burns and blisters, impetiginous sore and pustules . . . but it never stphruck your mudhead's obtundity . . . that the more carrots you chop, the more turnips you slit, the more murphies you peel, the more onions you cry over, the more bullbeef you butch, the more mutton you crackerhack, the more potherbs you pound, the fiercer the fire and the longer your spoon and the harder you gruel with more grease to your elbow the merrier fumes your new Irish stew" (189.31–190.08).[6]

This is rather frank and unsettling self-questioning on Joyce's part. The chapter itself is a Catholic confession-inquisition of sorts, with Shaun playing the confessor-interrogator: "Let us pry. [Let us pray.] We thought, would and did ["I have sinned in thought, word and deed" from the standard Catholic confession]. *Cur, quicquid, ubi, quando, quomodo, quoties, quibus auxiliis?* [like questions in a Catholic examination of conscience: Why, what, where, when, in what way, how often, with whose help?]" (188.08–9). Shaun proceeds, prying Shem's conscience with penetrating charges, some of which Joyce must have been acutely conscious himself: "anarch, egoarch, hiresiarch, you have reared your disunited kingdom on the vaccuum of your own most intensely doubtful soul. Do you hold yourself then for some god in the manger, Shehohem, that you will neither serve not let serve, pray nor let pray?" (188.16–19). This examination of Shem's conscience ("Examen of conscience" in 240.07) is searing enough to spur Shem (as Mercius) into confessing, gulping out his *mea culpa, mea culpa, mea maxima culpa* in an echo of *Richard III*: "**MERCIUS** (of hisself): *Domine vopiscus!* My fault, his fault, a kingship through a fault!" (193.31–32).[7]

The greatest unanswerable charge that Shaun repeatedly thrusts at Shem is that which Joyce perhaps felt most closely and acutely: "Shem, you are. Sh! You are mad!" (193.28). Polonius plied the same charge at Hamlet, questioning the "metheg in your midness" (32.05).[8] In chapter 6 of book I, Shaun had accused Shem of having a "fine artful disorder" (126.09). "Metheg in your midness" and "fine artful disorder" are both, perhaps, apt descriptions of the *Wake*—at least by Shaun-sympathizers. In chapter 6 Shaun compared Shem's cleverness to his own officious, Polonius-like methodiousness: "baileycliaver though he's a nawful curillass and I must slav to methodiousness. I want him to go and live like a theabild in charge of the night brigade" (159.30–32); Shem is "baileycliaver" (very clever, and town wise—Irish *baile;* also Balaclava) while Shaun slaves at his methodiousness.[9] It is in the present chapter (chapter 7 of book I), however, that Shaun-Polonius repeatedly calls Shem-Hamlet's method mad. He questions whether the verbiage and "his semantics" (173.32—and shem-antics) of *Finnegans Wake*, so full of "a meticulosity bordering on the insane" (173.34), could possibly be understood by any sane person: "But would anyone, short of a madhouse, believe it?" (177.13). Shaun titles Shem's "Ballade Imaginaire" (177.27), among other things, *"When He Is Going Batty"* (177.29). The accusation of "metheg in your midness" (32.05) is repeated here as "the beerlitz in his mathness" (182.07; method = metheg = mead = beer; and the Berlitz Method), the madness of a polylingual Berlitz Method.[10] Shem-Joyce writing *Ulysses* is described by Shaun as "the shuddersome spectacle of this semidemented zany" (179.24). Later in the *Wake*, Jaun introduces Dave-Shem as "A jollytan fine demented brick" (463.35–36). The greatest lowness Shaun can accuse Shem of is "lowquacity" (424.34), the low quackness of Shem, "you with your dislocated reason" (189.30). Shaun calls Shem an "unfrillfrocked quackfriar" (191.01). Shem seems to acknowledge and admit to this charge, for, when at the chapter's end he, as Mercius, lifts his lifewand, a series of quacking sounds follows: "—Quoiquoiquoiquoiquoiquoiquoiq!" (195.06).[11]

The accusation might be irreparably damaging if not for the miracle of creation: mad or not, "he [Shem] lifts the lifewand and the dumb speak" (195.05). As we have already discussed in this study, the pen of the artistic imagination neutralizes the death and destructiveness of history; through an exploration of its protean possibilities, the dumb can now speak. The pen of the poet, the phallus of the lover, the lifewand of the mad Shem: all can create. Joyce implies that artistic creation and history are, in their very essences, nonlogical and nonrational; they cannot be made logical and cannot be analyzed or interpreted logically. There is no single, clear version of a tale—we can only understand through the madness of analogy, coincidence, and dream vision. As a "drema," the *Wake* is both the historic dream of a night ("Miss Somer's nice dream," 502.29) and the nightmare ("Mad Winthrop's delugium stramens" in 502.30) of history. In his own *Midsummer Night's Dream*, Shakespeare wrote that "The lunatic, the lover, and the poet / Are of imagination all compact" (V. i. 7–8). By such analogies does the poetic mind work; and Joyce was all three—lunatic, lover, and poet.

The chapter ends with the confrontation between Shaun-Justius and Shem-Mercius. In chapter 6 Shaun, in turning down Shem's request for a loan, had stood for the justice of Shylock and the Mosaic code; Shem represented the mercy of Portia. In chapter 7 Shem once again is broke ("spluched" and "fireless") and is begging Shaun for a groatsworth to help him out; Shaun (Jonathan) answers Shem-David's wireless ("fireless") cable with another negative: "[Shem-Dave] cabled . . . to his jonathan for a brother: Here tokay, gone tomory, we're spluched, do something, Fireless. And had answer: Inconvenient, David!" (172.22–25). We are reminded, as the confrontation is beginning on page 187, that we are dealing "in mercy or justice" (187.21). Justius then proceeds to level his searing accusations. Having refused "to give you [Mercius-Shem] your pound of platinum" (192.17), Justius, like Shylock, now demands his "pound of flesh": "will you for the laugh of Scheekspair just help mine with the epithet?" (191.01–2). Justius is asking Mercius (all the while calling Mercius names like "unfrillfrocked quackfriar" in 191.01) for help in finding the right words for something that he is composing, help him as only a bard could, "for the laugh of Scheekspair"—for the humor (and life) of Shakespeare, and for the love of Jesus. Jesus is particularly appropriate here since, the spokesman of mercy, he advocated the turning of the other cheek (thus "cheeks pair")—which is just what Mercius does, in spite of all of Justius's verbal slaps.[12]

On the following page Joyce-Mercius is again compared to Jesus, "excruciated, in honor bound to the cross of your own cruelfiction" (192.17–18—Jesus' crucifixion and Joyce's fiction), while Shaun, "just a little judas tonic" (193.09), continues verbally to scourge and crucify his brother. Mercius finally answers, acknowledging his *culpa* ("My fault . . .") and the fact that he is "cannibal Cain" (193.32); he accepts his brother: "the days of youyouth are evermixed mimine" (194.04). He then "lifts the lifewand and the dumb speak," for, having been crucified, Mercius-Jesus-Portia effects a Wake and a Resurrection. What "the dumb speak" is "—Quoiquoiquoiquoiquoiquoiquoiq!"—the mad, quacky, babbling of a brook. Chapter 8 ("Anna Livia Plurabelle") follows swiftly on the tail of this babbling, for, in that chapter, the mercy of mad Shem is vindicated by Anna Livia and her aqueous flow of humanity, mercy, and ricorso.

The Charge of Forgery

We have seen that in the strife between the brothers, one of the repeated charges made about Shem-Joyce by Shaun is that Shem is a sham, a fake, and a forger, or plagiarist. In fact, this accusation is a (or perhaps the) major theme of the strife. Both Joyce and Shakespeare suffered the charge of questionable authorship; this fact must have heightened Joyce's sense of a bond between his own works and those of Shakespeare. Joyce himself was accused (and self-accused) of simply cannibalizing the past and its great works of literature, of sometimes lifting entire passages from other works and placing them in his own books;[13] furthermore, the author admitted his own lack of originality.[14] Shakespeare had first been accused by Robert Greene of being a plagiarist; later, his authorship was questioned by the proponents of various "claimants," who argued that Francis Bacon, or the Earl of Rutland, or Southampton, or others—and not Shakespeare—had written the plays. As "shakespill and eggs" (161.31), Joyce allows Bacon throughout the *Wake* to double for Ham-Hamlet-Shakespeare. Joyce would have agreed that he was a plagiarist and a "gravedigger" because he consciously gathered his materials from the middenheap of the past, in order to record the "drema" of history; and because he was wont to compare his own work to Shakespeare's, he was willing to acknowledge in the *Wake* that Wakean history was also written by Shakespeare's doubles, by the Bacons and the Southamptons and the Rutlands, or even by the forgers, of this world. Like Stephen Dedalus, all we know is that Shakespeare's plays (and history) were written by "Rutlandbaconsouthamptonshakespeare or another poet of the same name in the comedy of errors" (*U*, 208). In the *Wake* there are a number of references to Francis Bacon, the Baconians, Delia Bacon, Ignatius Donnelly, and some other "claimants"; we also find a number of references to famous forgers.[15] Forgery, theft, and plagiarism appear to be givens in Joyce's concept of the literary world.

Atherton first noted numerous references to literary manuscripts, including Shakespearean ones, in *The Books at the Wake*, on pages 67 through 70. Manuscripts can also, however, be forgeries. While Bacon and Rutland were both believed by some to have written the plays, Lewis Theobald, William Henry Ireland, and others tried to pass off forgeries as Shakespearean manuscripts. The truth, as in the HCE tale, is barely "getatable." Such problems of scholarship and authorship may be what the recurrent breakfast items—such as ham, bacon, and eggs—refer to; as Atherton maintains: "This is the reason . . . for the presence of Bacon, even though he is often disguised as 'shakespill and eggs' (161.31) and the like. Shakespeare, like Joyce himself, is being accused of being a forger."[16] Indeed, Shakespeare and Joyce are no exceptions from the "forgers" who shaped their works-in-progress by stealing material from the middenheap of history. Shem's title of "Shem the Penman" was based on Jim the Penman, a notorious forger; Joyce referred to himself as "James the Punman."[17]

A number of famous forgers are thus frequently introduced into the *Wake*, flavoring the texture of Shaun's repeated accusation against Shem of forgery. Scottish poet and forger James Macpherson and his "translations" of Ossian are alluded to in *From MacPerson's Oshean Round by the Tides of Jason's Cruise* (123.25), "MacFearsome" (227.32), "Makefearsome's Ocean" (294.13), and "jameymock farceson" (423.01).[18] "Vortigern, ah Gortigern!" (565.12) might refer to William Henry Ireland's *Vortigern and Rowena*, which Ireland ("Mister Ireland" in 608.14) tried in 1796 to pass off as a lost play of Shakespeare's.

The forger most alluded to in the *Wake* is Lewis Theobald (Pope's "Tibbald" in the *Dunciad*), who was also suspected of forging and tampering with Shakespearean plays (Theobald maintained that a play entitled *Double Falsehood* was a lost Shakespearean drama). In "Theabild" (159.31) Shaun implies that Shem's cleverness ("baileycliaver") results in forgery. Theobald is also mentioned in "theobalder" (263.05), "Boald Tib"

(28.05), "tell Tibbs has eve" (117.19), "Saint Tibble's Day" (236.08), and "till tibbes grey eves" (424.29). Atherton believes that the most convincing proof that "Tibbs" is Theobald the forger is in the last allusion, "till tibbes grey eves," because it is followed by a direct accusation of forgery: "Every dimmed litter in it is a copy and not a few of the silbils and wholly words I can show you in my Kingdom of Heaven. The lowquacity of him!"

In the fifth chapter of the first book of the *Wake*, a passage concerning the letter, scholarship, and textual studies, Joyce attempts to equate his works (the letter is the *Wake* as well as all literature) with Shakespeare's. Professor Shaun-Jones asks in his lecture: "who in hallhagal wrote the durn thing anyhow?" (107.36). Though he states that "we must vaunt no idle dubiosity as to its genuine authorship and holusbolus authoritativeness" (118.03–4), he goes on to make a number of references to Shakespearean forgers and imitators (e.g., Theobald in "tell Tibbs has eve" in 117.19) and to Shakespearean manuscripts (such as "those four-legged ems" in 123.01). Shaun discusses the manuscript and versions of the letter, and decides that it is "a grand stylish gravedigging with secondbest buns" (121.32)—a gravedigging of the past, uncovering stale and secondhand chestnuts. The secondhand sources for this letter include the *Odyssey* of Homer's "ulykkhean" (123.16—Ulysses), the "wretched mariner" (123.23), and the plays of Shakespeare ("pattern shapekeeper" in 123.24), from which patterns the shape of Shem-Joyce's tales are forged. Still, who was the scribe who penned the letter? It was not Shaun the Post, playing at being Shakespeare ("Hans the Curier" with "some little laughings and some less of cheeks" in 125.14–15), but the odious one himself, a forger like Jim the Penman: "Shem the Penman" (125.23).

The next chapter contains several more references to Shakespearean forgers or claimants. In two instances Bacon is used as an interchangeable double for Shakespeare: in "be bacon or stable hand" (141.21; legend tells that young Shakespeare held horses for London theatregoers) and in "shakespill and eggs" (161.31).[19] Besides Bacon and the Earl of Rutland (148.08), there are references here to a couple of outlandish "claimants": to the theories that Elizabeth I wrote the plays in "More poestries from Chickspeer's . . . by the Lady who Pays the Rates" (145.24–31) and, possibly, to the Society of Jesus in "our once in only Bragspear" (152.33–34).[20]

In chapter 7, as we've seen, one of the main accusations that Shaun levels at his brother is that "Shem was a sham and a low sham" (170.25) for fantasizing about success as a playwright in the "gaiety pantheomime" (180.04) while being, in fact, a forger like Greene's Shakespeare, writing an "epical forged cheque" (181.16) forged from the matter of Homer's epic.[21] Shaun calls Shem a plagiarist (see also "Pelagiarist" in 525.07) and asks: "Who can say how many pseudostylic shamiana, how few or how many ... forged palimpsests slipped in the first place by this morbid process from his pelagiarist pen?" (181.36–182.03).

The topic of forgery recurs occasionally for the rest of the book and is often couched in Shakespearean terms. Chapter 2 (the Children's Study Hour) of book II contains a number of these references. Theobald reappears in "theobalder" (263.05); there are references to Ignatius Donnelly, a leading Baconian and the author of *The Great Cryptogram*, in "cryptogam" (261.27) and "daredevil donnelly" (281.F3); and Delia Bacon, the first Baconian, appears in "Belisha beacon" (267.12).[22] During the geometry lesson, there is a confrontation between brothers reminiscent of that in the "Shem" chapter. Both boys try their hand at lewd geometry, drawing the deltaic genitals. Dolph-Shem shows Kev-Shaun "figuratleavely the whome of your eternal geomater" (296.31–297.01,—the figurative figleaf womb/home of their mother) and the implications of "her safety vulve" (297.27). Introduced to the wonders of sex, Kev has a reaction similar to that of Shaun-Stannie on page 190; he asks Shem why he didn't work for the Guinness Brewery or become a priest, and then accuses him of being a "baileycliaver" forger: "Ever thought about Guinness's? And the regrettable Parson Rome's advice? . . . You know, you were always one of the bright ones, since a foot made you an unmentionable, fakes! You know, you're the divver's own smart gossoon . . . so you are, hoax!" (299.30–300.06). Jealous of his brother's "creactive mind" (300.21; Issy comments, "Picking on Nickagain, Pikey Mikey?" in 300.F1), Shaun cries out, "thur him no quartos!" (300.30). Kev-Shaun is about to hit his brother, thus, "Show him no quarter"; but quarter is transformed into Shakespearean quartos, since Shaun's complaint is that his brother is a forger of manuscripts. Issy and Dolph try to appease Kev-Shaun by telling him that he can write just as well as Dolph-Shem. Kevin starts composing a letter (the letter "for bosthoon, late for Mass" in 301.05), but once again Dolph must show him how, teaching Kev how to write "All the charictures in the drame" (302.32). The ungrateful Kev then slugs his brother. Once again they are Justius and Mercius: having again asked his brother for a loan (in 302.02–7), and after helping his brother write a letter (symbol for the *Wake* and for literature), Dolph is knocked out by a punch from Kev-Justius—to which "mercystroke" (303.27) Dolph-Mercius again turns the other cheek and thanks his brother: "Thanks eversore much, Pointcarried!" (304.05) and "MERCI BUCKUP" (304.R1). He refuses to condemn his accuser, who meanwhile, goes on accusing Shem of forgery: "Forge away, Sunny Sim!" (305.04–5; Joyce was familiarly known as "Sunny Jim").

The clearest and most direct accusation of forgery takes place in chapter 1 of book III. Once more Shaun proposes (on page 413) to compose a letter or play, which finally seems to be a Swift-like will, leaving his possessions for his "dears" (Esther and Vanessa): "This, my tears, is my last will intesticle wrote off in the strutforit about their absent female assauciations" (413.17–18). Composition is again described in Shakespearean terms; the lines bring to mind the controversy over Shakespeare's will. We recall Stephen Dedalus's discussion of Shakespeare's female associations in London while absent from Anne Hathaway, his "Penelope stayathome" (*U*, 201) at Stratford ("strutforit"), to whom he left his secondbest bed in his last will and testament ("my last will intesticle"). Shem-Joyce's own letter (here, *Ulysses*: "theodicy"—*The Odyssey*—in 419.30) is described by Shaun as trash: ". . . it is not a nice production. It is a pinch of scribble, not wortha bottle of cabbis. Overdrawn! Puffedly offal tosh! [Perfectly awful nonsense (tosh), puffed-up offal]" (419.32–33). Then, illogically, he claims the letter as his own and, on pages 422 through 425, launches into a massive accusation of Shem, attacking him for plagiarism and forgery, amid references to Shakespearean claimants and forgers. The accusations here remind one of those in chapter 7 of the first book.

Shaun hints that Shem's letter (i.e., Joyce's works) was actually plagiarized from himself: "—Well it is partly my own, isn't it?" (422.23). (Perhaps because he is lying, Shaun now eats his hat in 422.24–25, "taking at the same time . . . a hearty bite out of . . . his hat.") Then, rather illogically, Shaun claims that Shem's letter was first borrowed from Shakespeare, from "Old Knoll and his borrowing" (422.32).[23] The vilification continues, with references to Shem as an "imitator" (423.10) and an "eggschicker" (423.19—shakespill, bacon, eggs, and imitation). Mention is made of James Macpherson ("jameymock farceson" in 423.01), of Lewis Theobald again ("till tibbes grey eve" in 424.29), and of Delia Bacon ("till that hag of the coombe rapes the pad off his lock" in 423.25).[24] Immediately after the reference to Theobald, Shaun finally makes the clear and direct charge that Shem, ever "low," stole the letter from him: "Every dimmed letter in it is a copy and not a few of the silbils and wholly words I can show you in my Kingdom of Heaven. The lowquacity of him! . . . Thaw! The last word in stolentelling! And what's more right-down lowbrown schisthematic robblemint! Yes. . . . He store the tale of me shur. Like yup. How's that for Shemese?" (424.32–425.03)—Every damned letter in it is copied, and many of the syllables and holy words I can show you to be mine. The loquacity and madness of him! The last word in stolen storytelling! And what's more, it's downright, low-down, lowbrow, systematic and thematic robbery of my mint, of my own *Day of the Rabblement*. He stole the tale from me, sure. Shaun goes on to claim that "my trifolium librotto, the authordux Book of Lief, would, if given to daylight . . . far exceed what that bogus bolshy of a shame, my soamheis brother . . . is conversant with in audible black and prink. Outragedy of poetscalds! Acomedy of letters! I have them all, tame, deep, and harried, in my mine's I" (425.20–25). Shaun affirms that he has just as much bardic talent as Shem, and he could write a work that would make his brother's look feeble by comparison; he says that his own libretto, in three folios, would, if it ever is allowed to come to light, be the real, orthodox and authorial Book of Life (unlike Joyce's *Ulysses*), and would far exceed what that shameful forger of bogus greatness (*bolshoi* is Russian for "great"), Shem ("shame"), my Siamese ("soamheis" verbally suggests "as I am, he is") twin, is able to do in black and white, in print, in ink. He is an outrageous tragedy as a poet *(skald)*! His work is a literary Comedy of Errors! I have all the fictional characters, every Tom, Dick and Harry, deep in my mind's eye (Hamlet's "In my mind's eye, Horatio" in I. ii. 185).

Probably few critics could have subjected Joyce to a more thorough and intense literary examination of conscience than that to which he subjected himself in *Finnegans Wake*.

The connection between Shem-Joyce's forgery and Shakespeare should be sketched out. To begin with, Shakespeare has also often been accused of fakery, either by plagiarizing other authors (according to Greene) or by not actually authoring the plays, which were supposedly written instead by Francis Bacon or others. Therefore, the charges of forgery in *Finnegans Wake* are repeatedly couched in Shakespearean terms: Shaun accuses Shem of being a Theobald, or of copying "stage Englesemen," as Shakespeare purportedly did. On the other hand, the rivalry between brothers-authors is expressed in terms of breakfast foods. Of course, "Francis Bacon" lends itself to such word play. Bacon and Shakespeare become in the *Wake* a literary version of the warring twins, Shaun and Shem, competing for the genuine authorship of the letter, the love of Issy, and other such prizes. We have seen that a Jones-Shakespeare version of the strife between brothers was presented in terms of dairy foodstuffs: butter, cheese, and margarine. These staples of the breakfast table become, in another version of the filial struggle, shakespill and eggs: Hamlet and eggs, or Bacon and eggs. Thus, the repeated references in the *Wake* to breakfast foods report the sibling rivalry, forgery, Shakespeare, and, of course, *ricorso*, since breakfast comes with each new day.

Shakespearean Breakfasts

Joyce found Shakespearean names wonderfully suited to his related themes of the rivalry of the brothers, and of the ensuing breakfast and *ricorso*. Eggs are a fine symbol for *ricorso*, for they are the source of new life and they are eaten at dawn, at breakfast.

A traditional model for the artistic sensibility, Hamlet represents the Shem-Shakespearean half of the breakfast table—both ham and eggs ("Ham's cribcracking yeggs" in 76.05–6) and an omelet: *"Mon foie,* you wish to ave some homelette, yes, lady! Good, mein leber! Your hegg he must break himself" (59.30–32) and "Here is a homelet" (586.18). However, the rival, Shaun-Bacon, claims that Shem-Shakespeare is a fake, and that the true Bard is not ham but bacon: this explains all the references in the *Wake* to ham and bacon. Bacon is an alternative for Shakespeare (and ham), as in "bacon or stable hand" (141.21). The twins are "twinsome bibs but hansome ates, like shakespill and eggs!" (161.31). For the porcine vagueness of "shakespill" we could substitute either ham or bacon and still have a satisfactory breakfast plate.

"Shakespill and eggs" appears within the Burrus and Caseous digression in Professor Jones's lecture, in which the twins are seen as butter and cheese, as Brutus and Cassius, striving for dominance in the world of Roman breakfasts. Burrus and Caseous are thus also described by the professor in terms of breakfast foods: "This, of course, also explains why we were taught to play in the childhood: *Der Haensli ist ein Butterbrot, mein Butterbrot! Und Koebi iss dein Schtinkenkot! Ja! Ja! Ja!"* (163.04–7). One brother ("brot") is a slice of bread with butter *(Butterbrot,* German)—or Burrus-Brutus; the other, Caseous-Cassius, is a ham sandwich *(Schinkenbrot,* German)—perhaps with cheese. Eggs, on the other hand, represent Humpty-Dumpty-HCE, whose fall by the Magazine Wall sets both sons striving to become the new top egg: "whiles eggs will fall cheapened all over the walled the Bure [butter, *beurre,* Burrus] will be dear on the Brie [brie cheese, or Cassius]" (163.27–28). Thus, the "eggs" component of "shakespill and eggs" is the HCE side of both Shem and Shaun, striving and battling to be the new top egg, or the new, re-coursed HCE-Humpty: "With harm and aches till farther alters!" (229.01)—with ham and eggs till father changes *(ricorso).*

Ham and bacon are thus associated with the twins fighting for the top spot at the upcoming breakfast of *ricorso.* In chapter 8 of book I, ALP serves the crestfallen—and fallen—HCE a Shakespearean breakfast, including "her meddery eygs, yayis, and a staynish beacons on toasc and a cupenhave so weeshywashy of Greenland's tay or a dzoupgan of Kaffue mokau an sable . . . and a shinkobread (hamjambo, bana?) for to plaise that man hog" (199.16–20). Trying to please her man-hog, she serves him a breakfast which includes eggs ("eygs" and *yayi,* Kiswahili for "egg"), Danish bacon on toast, a cup and a half (or Copenhagen) of wishy-washy green tea, a *soupçon* of cafe mocha, and so on—and, again, a ham sandwich *(Schinkenbrot* and French *jambon).* Perhaps ALP is dishing out a choice—between Ham or Bacon—for HCE's future successor. Later, HCE eats his dinner thus: "Now eats the vintner over these contents oft with his sad slow munch for backonham" (318.20–21). The vintner is, certainly, HCE the publican; the line is a Joycean re-creation of the opening of *Richard III:* "Now is the winter of our discontent / Made glorious summer by this son of York." Shakespeare's "son of York" becomes transformed, in Joyce's mind, into York ham. "These contents," which HCE munches sadly and slowly, form a sort of ham sandwich, combining both his "sons" of York, ham and bacon, in "backonham." Although the Earl of Sandwich is not here, Francis Bacon and the Duke of Buckingham are, sandwiched into this marvelous portmanteau word—a real BLT.[25]

The twins may be thus but poles in a Brunonian union of opposites and versions of the same union that results in the whole father-creator-god, just as Shem and Shaun will combine to form the new HCE. Shem-Dave, for example, is "one Davy Browne-Nolan, his heavenlaid twin, (this hambone dogpoet pseudoed himself under the hangname he gave himself of Bethgelert)" (177.20–22); again, ham ("hambone," *jambon)* is here. Ham-Shakespeare and Bacon are the same (so the Baconians claimed) or are Brunonian (Browne-Nolan, and Bruno the Nolan) twins, disguised under the pseudonym-agnomen of Saxo's Hamlet-Bethgelert, both claiming to be a "dogpoet," "the artist, like the God of the creation" (*P*, 215).

Breakfasts feature bacon, ham, and eggs: "go make bakenbeggfuss . . . and a shinkhams topmorning withis his coexes" (41.13–15)—top-of-the-morning with bacon-breakfast, ham *(schinken,* German), and two eggs. Ham and bacon—or Shem and Shaun—are twins and products of one egg (HCE), as Yawn-Shaun says about his twin brother and himself: "I remember ham to me, when we were like bro and sis over our castor and porridge. . . . We were in one class of age like to two clots of egg" (489.15–19; see Part II entry). Yawn recalls childhood days (of porridge and castor oil) with his twin, (Castor and Pollux) Shem, or "ham," when they were like brother and sister, as alike as two clots in one egg. Now they are striving against each other to become the new top egg, or HCE.

Which of the twins will be re-coursed as the new HCE is the question. The answer—which explains much of Joyce's use of Bacon and Shakespeare (and Bruno) in the *Wake*—is, of course, both of them, in a Brunonian union of opposites: the new HCE will be a synthesis of Siamese opposites. "How frilled one shall be as at taledold of Formio and Cigalette! What folly innocents! Theirs whet pep of puppyhood! Both barmhearts shall become yeastcake by their brackfest. I will to leave a my copperwise blessing between the pair of them, for rosengorge, for greenafang" (563.27–31). This passage describes the twins, Jerry and Kevin, in bed; thus, again, it is a "taletold" of Shem and Shaun, the Macbethian ("a tale told by an idiot") motif of the strife between twins—Ant and Grasshopper (Formio and Cigalette, or *Romeo and Juliet),*

Rosencrantz and Guildenstern ("rosengorge" and "greenafang"). Standing over them, HCE wills his blessing to both, for they shall be united at dawn: "both barmhearts shall become yeastcake by their brackfest"; or—in terms recalling the strife between Brutus and Cassius to be the new Caesar—after the long nightmare of history, at dawn "Britus and Gothius shall no more joustle for that sonneplace but mark one autonement" (568.08–9). Brutus and Cassius shall no longer jostle for the place vacated by Caesar (the son's place, and a place in the sun); rather, they shall observe ("mark") an atonement, or a Brunonian at-one-ment. In other words, they shall be united into the new Caesar—that is, Marcus Antonius ("mark one autonement").

Dawn and *ricorso* shall bring the morning and a break to the long night's fast and wake: "there'll be iggs for the brekkers come to mournhim, sunny side up with care" (12.15)—come morning, there'll be eggs for breakfast, and for the breakfasters come to mourn him (HCE-Finnegan). There has been a long night of dream and darkness, but the dawn shall bring the light of day and a wake; it is thus a "lightbreakfastbringer": "The silent cock shall crow at last. The west shall shake the east awake. Walk while ye have the night for morn, lightbreakfastbringer, morroweth whereon every past shall full fost sleep. Amain" (473.22–25). This connection between breakfast and the ricorso-marked union of opposites is a key to the use of Shakespeare and Bacon in the *Wake*. For, although Bacon and Shakespeare struggle as rival twins, in the end there are still the plays; though Shem and Shaun compete for the authorship of the letter, a new HCE will rise between them, forged from both their images, to claim the letter. While either Shakespeare or Bacon may have authored the plays and the letters of literature, the new, ricorsed Shakespeare will be a plagiarist, rewriting in a Viconian *Wake* the letter, forged out of all the letters in the middenheap written by the Shems, Shauns, and Shakespeares of the past. The *Wake* breakfast he will serve may be "a grand stylish gravedigging with secondbest buns" (121.32), but, since he forges from and explores all history and all the possibilities in the room of infinite historical possibilities, he is no longer the disciple of Shakespeare but the usurping son as father-creator himself, speculating about and re-creating the father and the past, defeating history through the powers of the imagination.

As dawn approaches late in the book, we expect (and so do find) a growing number of references in the *Wake* to the upcoming breakfast. Late in the book, HCE, "Mr Brakeforth" (575.11—breakfast, and dawn breaking forth), dreams of himself as "under the new style of Will Breakfast" (575.29).[26] This "Will Breakfast" is clearly both Will Shakespeare—connected in the *Wake* with ham, bacon and eggs—and the new, *ricorso* HCE, who at dawn will breakfast. Here is the clearest statement of the connection between Shakespeare and the Wakean breakfasts: both are "Will Breakfast" because both imply the undergoing of *ricorso*—new Shakespeares and new Bacons synthesized in a Joycean middenheap, or wake. When daybreak finally arrives in book IV ("Calling all downs. Calling all downs to dayne" in 593.02)—the Book of *Ricorso* and renewal—it is accompanied by a call to breakfast, the symbol of waking and morning. References to "Shakespearean" breakfasts abound in this final book. The *Wake* is now "a story about brid and breakfedes" (597.16)—about bed (dreams) and breakfast (wakes), and the bird (phoenix) rising from the ashes. Breakfast is for everyone, ham and eggs all around, with little eggs scrambled together in a big pan: "And let every crisscouple be so crosscomplimentary, little eggons, youlk and meelk, in a farbiger pancosmos. With a hottyhammyum all round. Gudstruce!" (613.10–12). Let the crisscrossed couple of striving twins, the little eggs (you and me, yolk and milk; or butter and cheese) be scrambled together in a far bigger pan and cosmos—and mark an atonement in a Brunonian-Viconian *ricorso*, or God's truce. It is a charming call to "brarkfarsts" (613.23).

The importance of scrambling the eggs of the past is clarified in a major statement of Joyce's Viconian theory, especially in its application to literature:

> Our wholemole millwheeling vicociclometer ... (... be he Matty, Marky, Lukey or John-a-Donk), autokinatonetically preprovided with a clappercoupling smeltingworks exprogressive process (... known as eggburst, eggblend, eggburial and hatch-as-hatch can) receives through a portal vein the dialytically separated elements ... type by tope, letter from litter, word at ward ... in fact, the sameold gamebold adomic structure of our Finnius the old One, as *h*ighly *c*harged with *e*lectrons as *h*ophazards can *e*ffective it ... Cockalooralooraloomenos, when cup, platter and pot come piping hot, as sure as herself pits hen to paper and there's scribings scrawled on eggs. (614.27–615.10; my italics)

We have come to the moment of *ricorso*, of hatching a repetition of the Viconian cycle (the "vicociclometer"). The cycle has four parts, whether we call them Matthew, Mark, Luke and John-a-Donk (the Donkey-Bottom, who is Hamlet's "John-a-Dreams"—or, perhaps, the "woful Dane Bottom" in 503.20) or eggburst, eggblend, eggburial, and hatch-as-hatch-can (i.e., birth, marriage, death, and *ricorso*); it is a continuous "process," like a "smeltingworks exprogressive process." The *Wake*, too, is a *Work in Progress;* Joyce knew that his "clappercoupling" work in progress, like Shakespeare's *Troilus and Cressida,* would be "clapper-clawed with the palms of the vulgar"[27] and would be condemned by misunderstanding critics. The dawn, however, brings a new HCE, a new lifetree, a new author-father-creator, receiving through its portal veins the fresh elements—type by type, letter by letter, word by word. But, like the letter from the litterheap (and like all "litterature"), the new cycle is the same ("letter from litter") as the old, with the same atomic and Adamic structure as was in the original middenheap of Eden: old HCE-Adam is reincarnated as a new HCE and all new works of scholarship on the *Wake* (like the hen scrabbling for the letter) are only retellings of the old letter itself, new plagiarized versions of Shakespeare and Joyce. When the morning comes, the cock shall still crow ("Cockalooralooraloo") and breakfast (piping hot—cup, platter, pot, and eggs) shall still be served, regardless of who is presently penning the letter—regardless of who "pits hen to paper," still "there's scribings scrawled on eggs."[28] All letters and all scholarship are basic recombinations and reworkings of the same forged letter; so also the *Wake* and all of Joyce's works are reworkings of other people's odysseys and dramas. The dawn rises only to serve up new breakfasts and newly forged Shakespeares.

Conclusion

Joyce, however, was a realist; he knew that it would be a long time before his *Wake* would pass through the dark night and be resurrected, before it would be breakfasted on eagerly by readers scrabbling through the middenheap for the great classics of "litterature." In the text of *Finnegans Wake* itself he predicted the crises and eventual triumph of his last book. He wished that one would "look at this prepronominal *funferal*, engraved and retouched and edgewiped and puddenpadded, very like a whale's egg farced with pemmican, as were it sentenced to be nuzzled over a full trillion times for ever and a night till his noddle sink or swim by that ideal reader suffering from an ideal insomnia" (120.09–14)—that is, that this book (the "funeral" or wake), engraved and retouched and padded from all the fragments of the middenheap, protean in its nature and in its exploration of possibilities, might become a fun-for-all and find ideal readers with ideal insomnias, who would be willing to nuzzle over this dreambook of all-history for ever and a night.[29] Although Joyce may have wanted this, he nevertheless knew well that "You'll have loss of fame from Wimmegame's fake" (375.16–17). While the literary reputation of *Ulysses* was finally beginning to rise, *Finnegans Wake* would bring the author infamy again. Foreseeing that the literary world would relegate to his great work of sixteen years the status of the eccentric forgeries of a madman, Joyce could only regard enviously the luck of Shakespeare and exclaim: *"By earth and the cloudy but I badly want a brandnew bankside, bedamp and I do, and a plumper at that!"* (201.05–6).[30]

Joyce did know there would be a time for him, too, when his literary reputation would, like the Phoenix of *ricorso*, rise from the ashes:

> But, boy, you did your strong nine furlong mile in slick and slapstick record time and a farfetched deed it was . . . and your feat of passage will be contested with you and through you, for centuries to come. The phaynix rose a sun before Erebia sank his smother! Shoot up on that, bright Bennu bird! . . . Eftsoon so too will our own sphoenix spark spirt his spyre and sunward stride the rampante flambe. Ay, already the sombrer opacities of the gloom are sphanished! Brave footsore Haun! Work your progress! Hold to! Now! Win out, ye divil ye! The silent cock shall crow at last. The west shall shake the east awake. Walk while ye have the night for morn, lightbreakfastbringer, morroweth whereon every past shall full fost sleep. Amain. (473.12–25)

Tindall relates the context surrounding this important passage: "As an exile, Shaun is Shem. Returning in triumph to Irish applause, Shem will be Shaun. . . . He is Haun or Shem and Shaun, who will enjoy their Easter rising together. All this on page 473, the last and most important page of the chapter."[31] Thus, Haun is Joyce himself as a union of Shem and Shaun. Joyce compares his writing to Stephen Dedalus-like racing around a track (in the *Portrait*), but his "feat [or feet] of passage" (Joyce's works) will be contested for centuries to come. However, Joyce predicts that his phoenix ("phaynix," the Bennu bird of the Book of the Dead) will finally, eventually rise, and "eftsoon" will the "sphoenix" spark its spirit out, rise from its pyre in Phoenix Park ("sphoenix spark spirt his spyre"), and stride upward toward the flaming sun; already the gloom is vanishing. We can picture the weary-eyed "acheseyeld from Ailing," or the "Brave and footsore Haun," encouraging himself during those sixteen lonely years working on *Work in Progress*. Joyce prays that the Luciferian devil, Shem-Nick or Stephen Dedalus the artist, may win out at last, when the "lightbreakfastbringer" shall bring about a wake and a *ricorso*, after centuries of disputation, when the silent cock shall finally crow for *Finnegans Wake*. Joyce ends his passage with an Amen ("Amain").

Joyce knew that, while the *Wake* might be his literary calvary "for centuries to come," his fame would eventually undergo a resurrection: "(O, you were excruciated, in honour bound to the cross of your own cruelfiction!) to let you have your Sarday spree and holinight sleep (fame would come to you twixt a sleep and a wake) and leave to lie till Paraskivee and the cockcock crows for Danmark" (192.17–21). Joyce is at once Jesus and Hamlet, both of whom had to learn to wait for vindication. Joyce, like Jesus, was crucified ("excruciated") to the cross of his own "cruelfiction" (*Ulysses* and the *Wake* as his crucifixion), was a martyr for his art, passing up a Saturday spree in order to wait for an Easter Sunday. Whereas Joyce knew that he would suffer a loss of fame from *Finnegans Wake*, he still predicts that "fame would come to you twixt a sleep and a wake"—that between a sleep (Molly and Bloom's sleep at the close of *Ulysses* or HCE's sleeping dream) and a wake *(Finnegans Wake)*, fame will ultimately come to Joyce. He will be resurrected on the third day (when also the cock crowed thrice for Peter between Christ's own sleep and wake). The cock crows also in Denmark (King Hamlet's ghost "faded on the crowing of the cock" in I. i. 157), where Hamlet, too, struggled with the notions of death, sleep, wakes, and dreams. Fame would eventually come twixt a sleep and a wake.[32]

Nevertheless, Joyce, foreseeing the way critics would mock and misrepresent the *Wake*, must have wondered (like Anna Livia): "A hundred cares, a tithe of troubles and is there one who understands me?" (627.15). Would such madness as *Finnegans Wake* ever be appreciated or understood? Perhaps the loveliest answer to the question appears in a passage in which Joyce made a prediction about *Finnegans Wake* and his own techniques:

> But by writing thithaways end to end and turning, turning and end to end hithaways writing and with lines of litters slittering up and louds of latters slettering down, the old semetomyplace and jupetbackagain from tham Let Rise till Hum Lit. Sleep, where in the waste is the wisdom? (114.16–20)

That is to say: literature (or letters) also has its *ricorso*s and falls, its litters (as in births and risings) slittering up and its latters (later in life, and falling ladders) slettering down. Literary reputations might rise and fall in a seesaw fashion, shifting now to Shem ("see me to my place"), now to Ham ("tham"), and now to Japhet ("jap it back again"). Hamlet ("tham Let"), watching the fluctuations in the state of Denmark, soliloquizes on the meaning of life and death: "Sleep, where in the waste is the wisdom?" (Where in the wait is the wisdom?—Hamlet's recurrent dilemma; also, perhaps an echo of "Death, where is thy sting?"). Joyce-Hamlet philosophically questions his own folios and their chances for acceptance in the literary world, knowing that the immediate rewards in the writing profession are few: there is "small peace in ppenmark" (189.06). He must wait for eventual recognition; but, he asks himself, where in such a wait does wisdom lie? It lies in the "waste," in the middenheap; for the letter/

litter *(Finnegans Wake)* is sleeping, resting in wait and in waste ("twixt a sleep and a wake"), listening until "the cock crows for Danmark" (192.21) and the time to be unearthed by some scratching scholar-hen (some "Misthress of Arths," like Biddy in 112.29) is arrived, waiting until *Finnegans Wake* can rise from the ashes of the middenpile and be truly appreciated. Perhaps Joyce will eventually, like Shakespeare, have an appreciative Bankside audience.[33] He shares, though, the question posed by Hamlet: to wait or not to wait, to be or not to be—is there wisdom in the waste of eternal sleep? Sleep, dreams, wakes, Hamlet, and *Finnegans Wake* are all thematically and inextricably interwoven here.

Finnegans Wake did not find acceptance in Joyce's lifetime; but like Hamlet, Joyce learned to wait, believing his *Wake* to be a real sleeper: "From tham Let Rise till Hum Lit." Joyce must have often told himself to let the *Wake* sleep ("Let sleepth," 555.01), until, like a ricorsing Phoenix, it will rise from its mound of ashes and be accepted, be recognized as a new *Hamlet* in the new Viconian cycle. Then it will, at long last, become Hum Lit: it will be read, enjoyed, and appreciated by lovers of the humanities and of literature.

PART II

Shakespearean Allusions in *Finnegans Wake*

Entries are by page and line numbers.

Book I, Chapter 1

3.04 *violer d'amores:* Glasheen argues, in *AWN*, II, 6 (Dec. 1965): 17–18, that "violer d'amores" refers to *Twelfth Night*'s Viola, and that "rory end" a few lines later (3.13–14) refers to *As You Like It*'s Rosalind, as part of the transvestite and "boywoman" theme in the passage.

3.11–12 *all's fair in vanessy, were sosie sesthers wroth:* echoes of Macbeth's castle Inverness, the three "weird sisters" who undid him, and their "fair is foul and foul is fair" address. Swift's Esther and Vanessa, and the Biblical trio of Susanna, Esther and Ruth, are also here. Atherton, p. 163.

5.05 *Of the first was he to bare arms and a name:* the reference is to Adam, and echoes *Hamlet:* "CLOWN: There is no ancient gentlemen but gard'ners, ditchers, and grave-makers. They hold up Adam's profession. / OTHER CLOWN: Was he a gentleman? / CLOWN: 'A was the first that ever bore arms. / OTHER CLOWN: Why, he had none. / CLOWN: What, art a heathen? How dost thou understand the Scripture? The Scripture says Adam digged. Could he dig without arms?" (V. i. 27–35) See Glasheen, *AWN*, I, 4 (Aug. 1964): 5.

5.27 *Heed! Heed!:* first instance (among many) of "List, List!" (*Ham.* I. v. 22). See also chapter 4 of this study.

6.25 *dusty fidelios:* Hodgart notes (p. 752) this as a *Cymbeline* reference; it is also a pun on *Adeste Fideles* and a reference to Beethoven's *Fidelio*.
   Imogen disguised herself as a boy named Fidele. There is a further hint of the famous lines from the song in *Cymbeline:* "Golden lads and girls all must, / As chimney-sweepers, come to dust" (IV. ii. 262–63). See entries for 20.30 and 256.11 ff.

7.09–10 *Finfoefom the Fush:* Edgar, in *King Lear* (III. iv. 174–75): "His word was still, 'Fie, foh, and fum, / I smell the blood of a British man.'" See McHugh, p. 7. This line is echoed at least ten times in the *Wake*; see *Lear* section of Appendix 2.

7.12–14 *But, lo, as you would quaffoff his fraudstuff and sink teeth through that* *pyth of a flowerwhite bodey behold of him:* the first of a number of associations between Falstaff ("fraudstuff") and the activities of eating and drinking. Sir Toby Belch appears in a similar capacity in the *Wake.* The "flowerwhite bodey" is the Communion wafer, the body of Christ; "behold of him" recalls *Ecce homo.* Joyce refers to such foodstuff as a fraud. Like Christ, Falstaff rose from the "dead" in *Henry IV, Part 1,* as Glasheen notes (p. 89). Cf. entries for 456.20–24 and 423.11, 13, 33.

10.28 *Downadown, High Downadown:* the mad Ophelia says, "You must sing 'A-down a-down, and you call him a-down-a.'" (*Ham.* IV. v. 170). The twenty-nine girls (led by Issy) are being discussed—a proper context for a reference to the daughter-figure. See entry for 593.02.

10.34 *A verytableland of bleakbardfields!:* an echo of the controversial line describing the dying Falstaff: "and 'a babbled of green fields" (*H5* II. iii. 16), originally accepted as "a table of green fields." "Bard" (here as elsewhere) is a clue that the reference is Shakespearean. *RES,* p. 327: "One line in the Folio text was subjected to the most famous emendation in Shakespeare's works. It occurs in the Hostess' description of the death of Falstaff. The Folio reading is 'and a Table of green fields' (II. iii. 17). Lewis Theobald, one of Shakespeare's earliest editors, emended this phrase to 'and 'a babbled of green fields.' Theobald's alteration was ridiculed by later 17th-century editors, but it has come to be generally accepted by modern editors. Recently, however, there have been some attempts to discredit the emendation, and reinterpret the Folio reading."

As elsewhere in the *Wake,* Joyce shows an intense interest in manuscripts, textual controversies, forgeries, misreadings, and so forth. Lewis Theobald is alluded to a number of times, as in 159.32, "theabild," and in 263.05, "theobalder."

11.04–5 *when Thon's blowing toomcracks:* Macbeth asks, "What, will the line stretch out to th' crack of doom?" (IV. i. 117).

13.16–17 *List! Wheatstone's magic lyer:* List! to the magic lyre and songs of King Lear's ("lyer") fool ("Whetstone"). "GHOST: List, list, O list!" (*Ham.* I. v. 22). See entry for 13.27.

13.27 *Adear, adear!:* O dear; and adieu. In *Hamlet,* the Ghost begins unfolding his tale with "List, list, O list!" (I. v. 22), and ends with the words, "Adieu, adieu, adieu. Remember me" (I. v. 91). All three statements occur frequently in the *Wake,* in many variations. ("Mememormee!" is one of the last lines of the book.) Hamlet sets them down in the tables of his memory: "It is 'Adieu, adieu, remember me.' / I have sworn't" (I. v. 111–12).

15.08–9 *Year! Year!:* List! List! (*Ham.* I. v. 22) Hear! Hear!

15.17 *duncledames: dunkel Damen* ("dark ladies" in German) and the Dark Lady of the sonnets. Or possibly from "Come hither, come hither, come hither.... Ducdame, ducdame, ducdame" (*AYL* II. v. 37, 48). Aimens asks, "What's that 'ducdame'?" to which Jaques replies: "'Tis a Greek invocation to call fools into a circle." In any case, calling fools into a circle seems to fit this context in the *Wake,* in which the dark ladies are answering back to the not-so-bright fellows: "Who ails tongue coddeau, aspace of dumbsilly?" (15.18), or

Où est ton cadeau, espèce d'imbécile? ("Cad" is for Shem, and "space" is for Shaun.)

16.07 *You phonio saxo? Nnnn.*: Mutt and Jute try to find a common language: Do you speak Saxon? Possibly also a reference to Saxo Grammaticus, source of the Hamlet tale; see entries for 304.18 and 388.31.

16.36 *He was poached on in that eggtentical spot*: ham and poached eggs, the Shakespearean breakfast theme (see chapter 6). The passage has Mutt identifying Jute as Sitric, king of the Danes (Denmark and *Hamlet*), invader in Dublin. Shakespearean legend has it that the Bard was arrested for deer-poaching as a youth.

18.06 *O'c'stle*: Sir John Oldcastle? Oldcastle, soldier and friend of Henry V, was Shakespeare's model (and original name) for Falstaff; Shakespeare changed the name to Falstaff at the protest of Oldcastle's descendants. In *Henry IV, Part I* (I. ii. 47) Hal addresses Falstaff as "my old lad of the castle."

18.22–24 *The meandertale, aloss and again, of our old Heidenburgh in the days when Head-in-Clouds walked the earth*: L.A.G. Strong, (in *The Sacred River*, p. 68), names this line as a Shakespearean allusion. Perhaps "walked the earth" is an echo of *Hamlet's* Ghost, "Doomed for a certain term to walk the night" (I. v. 10). Bloom quotes it as "walk the earth" (*U*, 152). Cf. entry for 19.25.

19.25 *What a meanderthalltale to unfurl . . .*: an echo of the Ghost's "I could a tale unfold whose lightest word / Would harrow up thy soul . . ." (*Ham.* I. v. 15).

20.03 *has still to moor before the tomb of his cousin charmian*: Othello the Moor. Charmian was Cleopatra's Egyptian attendant, who, like her mistress, commits suicide at the end of *Antony and Cleopatra*.

20.30 *golden youths:* recalls the song from *Cymbeline:* "Golden lads and girls all must, / Like chimney–sweepers, come to dust" (IV. ii. 262–63); song also referred to in 256.11 ff. See entries for 6.25, and 256.11 ff.

20.34 *Veil, volantine, valentine eyes:* Valentine was one of the *Two Gentlemen of Verona*. See also entries for 249.03–4 and 569.28–35.

20.35 *She's the very besch Winnie blows Nay on good:* see entries for 448.20 and 28.09.

21.02 *Lissom! lissom!:* List, list! (*Ham.* I. v. 22).

27.04 *when the ritehand seizes what the lovearm knows:* from *Venus and Adonis*, l. 158: "Can thy right hand seize love upon thy left?" See Glasheen, in *AWN*, I, 4 (Aug. 1964): 5.

27.08 *his olde by his ide:* Ides of March. See chapter 5 of this study.

28.04 *Shakeshands:* Shakespeare, and *La ci darem la mano*. This passage, like *La ci darem* and *Ulysses*, concerns adultery. Cf. *Ulysses*, p. 63 and passim. See also entry 535.11, "handshakey," in which "shakey" is clearly Shakespeare. Cf. entry for 96.23.

28.05 *Boald Tib:* bold Lewis Theobald (Pope's "Tibbald"), Shakespearean forger. See Atherton, p. 70, and chapter 6 of this study.

28.06 *Pollockses:* Hamlet-*père* "smote the sledded Polacks on the ice" (I. i. 63). See entry for 53.32.

28.09 *It's an allavalonche that blows nopussy good:* see entries for 448.20 and 20.35.

29.26 *fishmummer:* Polonius, whom Hamlet calls a "fishmonger" in II. ii. 174. Cf. entries 144.30 and 408.36.

Book I, Chapter 2

30.13–14 *the grand old gardener was saving daylight under his redwood tree:* from Amiens's and Jaques's song in *As You Like It* (II. v. 1 ff.): "Under the greenwood tree, / Who loves to lie with me. . . . Come hither, come hither, come hither. . . ." Cf. entries for 74.10 and 15.17. The grand old gardener was Adam in Eden; Adam was also a character in the green world of *As You Like It.* Cf. entry for 549.31 for another reference to both Amiens and Adam.

31.18 *Offaly:* Ophelia. Cf. 465.32, "Be Offalia. Be hamlet."

31.23–24 *the purchypatch of hamlock:* the purple passage of *Hamlet;* see also 200.04, "porpor patches." Purple passages are also commonly known as purple patches.

"Hamlock" is perhaps a conflation of Hamlet and Havelok ("Watchman Havelok" in 556.23). Glasheen's entry on Havelok (p. 120): "Havelok the Dane—hero of a 14th-century verse romance which has much in common with the early Hamlet story . . . Havelok is a watcher like Hamlet and brings a malefactor to justice." See also entries for 79.33–35 and 84.32.

Possibly the line also refers to Socrates ("hemlock").

31.32 *I've mies outs ide Bourn:* Ides of March and *Julius Caesar* (see chapter 5 of this study). "Bourn" is perhaps Hamlet's "undiscovered country, from whose bourn / No traveller returns" (III. ii. 79–80). See also entries for 190.21 and 365.04–5.

32.05 *if so be you have metheg in your midness:* mead (metheglin) in your belly and Polonius's "Though this be madness, yet there is method in't" (II. ii. 203). Cf. "fine artful disorder" in 126.09; see also chapter 6 of this study.

32.32 *performance of the problem passion play:* "problem plays" is used to describe those Shakespeare plays containing great problems of interpretation. The term was first used by F.S. Boas in reference to *Hamlet, All's Well that Ends Well, Troilus and Cressida,* and *Measure for Measure.*

"Passion play": Joyce said that book III is composed in the form of the fourteen stations of the Cross and across those stations moves a carrier (Shaun the Post) of the Word (*Letters,* I, p. 214).

33.03 *our worldstage's practical jokepiece:* the practical jokepiece is perhaps Jaques, who said, "All the world's a stage, / And all the men and women merely players" (*AYL* II. vii. 139). This worldstage's creator is a "worldwright" (14.19).

35.03–4 *one happygogusty Ides-of-April morning (the anniversary, as it fell out, of his first assumption of his mirthday suit):* Julius Caesar and the Ides of March. April 15, 1916 was the date of the Easter Rebellion in Ireland: thus both Ides of April and Ides of March are revolutionary references (in a page full of such references, since the Cad is overthrowing HCE).

"Assumption": August 15, the Ides of August, in the Catholic liturgical calendar, is also the Feast of the Assumption of the Blessed Virgin Mary (into Heaven). Cf. also 43.18, "roman easter" and chapter 5 of this study. In *Finnegans Wake* HCE = Julius Caesar; his sons, who overthrow him, are Brutus and Cassius.

37.04 *a sensible ham:* possibly Hamlet.

38.26 *Mr Browne, disguised as a vincentian:* Bruno the Nolan is described in this passage as going around disguised as a Paulist priest (named after St. Vincent de Paul). "Vincentian," however, is even more apt since, in *Measure for Measure*, Duke Vincentio is, during most of the play, also disguised as a priest (Friar Lodowick). The allusion may include G.K. Chesterton's detective, Father Brown.

40.01 *All Swell that Aimswell: All's Well That Ends Well.*

40.10 *eyots of martas:* Ides of March and *Julius Caesar.*

40.11 *lavinias:* Lavinia, daughter of Titus in *Titus Andronicus*, who faces that most challenging of Shakespearean stage directions: "Enter Lavinia, her hands cut off, and her tongue cut out, and ravished" (II. iv). See also entry for 327.12–13.

40.23–32 *on the verge of selfabyss, most starved, with melancholia over everything in general . . . had been towhead tossing on his shakedown . . . where he could throw true and go and blow the sibicidal napper off himself for two bits to boldywell baltitude in the peace and quitybus:* the melancholy Hosty (the Cad-Son figure) considers suicide. The description of Hosty's state seems much like that of Hamlet's, who also seeks to make his "quietus." Hodgart points out (p. 740) that Joyce's earlier draft read "quietus"; thus, "the quotation has been thrown under a bus." (But Hayman's *A First-Draft Version* reads "quietness"; and Hosty is described as "feeling suicidal"). "Shakedown" is a hint to look for Shakespeare here.

41.02 *Sant Iago by his cocklehat: Othello's* villain is joined with Ophelia's true love: "How should I your true love know / From another one? / By his cockle hat and staff / And his sandal shoon" (IV. v. 23–26). Stephen says in *Ulysses*, p. 50: "My cockle hat and staff." The shrine of Santiago de Compostela was a favorite destination of European pilgrims, carrying the emblem of a cockleshell. Cf. entry for 81.10.

41.18 *Ebblinn's chilled hamlet:* Dublin *(Eblanna)* and *Hamlet's* Elsinore.

42.36 *Rutland heath:* perhaps the Earl of Rutland, one of the "claimants" to the authorship of Shakespeare's plays. In "Scylla and Charybdis," John Eglinton says that "Herr Bleibtreu . . . who is working up that Rutland theory, believes that the secret is hidden in the Stratford monument" (*U*, 214). See "Rutland" in entries for 148.08 and 437.05.

47.19 *Shikespower!:* Shakespeare, in the language of the revolutionary and outlaw. Also present in this line are Sophocles, Dante, and Moses.

47.26 *And not all the king's men nor his horses / Will resurrect his corpus:* from the Humpty Dumpty nursery rhyme: "All the king's horses and all the king's men, / Couldn't put Humpty Dumpty [HCE] together again." Shakespeare was a member of the King's Men, an acting company. See also entries for 567.17, 219.15–16, and 285.L2.

Book I, Chapter 3

48.03 *The Blackfriars:* famed Elizabethan theatre.

50.02 *but at this poingt though the iron thrust of his cockspurt start might have prepared us we are wellnigh stinkpotthered by the mustardpunge in the tailend:* Hodgart (pp. 747–48) argues that these lines refer to Falstaff: "Although, as the critics say, Hal's earlier words *might have prepared us* for the rejection of Falstaff in *Henry IV, Part 2*, yet we are finally bothered by the sting in the play's tail." The presence of Poins ("poingt") and Hotspur ("cockspurt") might support such a reading.

50.05 *outandin brown candlestock:* an echo, as Hodgart notes (p. 748), of Macbeth's "Out, out, brief candle!" (V. v. 23). Castle Knock may be here, too. Castle Knock Gate and *Macbeth* combine in this chapter in a number of allusions to the porter scene and the knocking at the gate. See entry for 51.24.

50.06 *druriodrama:* a play about fairies (druries)—like *A Midsummer Night's Dream*. See entry for 52.20. Drury Lane drama; see also entry for 79.27–28 and 600.02.

51.09 *(lust!):* Hamlet's "List!" (I. v. 22) with a twist.

51.24 *the porty:* HCE-Porter is referred to here as a porter, like *Macbeth*'s porter at the gate. See references to drunken porters at gates in the rest of this chapter—e.g., entries for 63.17–19, 63.32–35, 64.09–11, etc. See also the *Macbeth* section of Appendix 2 (under II. iii. 1–20) and chapter 5 of this study.

52.05–6 *but all the bottles in sodemd histry will not soften your bloodathirst:* another *Macbeth* echo in this chapter's cluster. Lady Macbeth: "Here's the smell of the blood still. All the perfumes of Arabia will not sweeten this little hand" (*Mac.* V. i. 47–48). See McHugh, p. 52; see also entry for 627.28–30.

52.20 *Mary Nothing:* cf. *A Midsummer Night's Dream* V. i. 16–17: "the poet's pen / Turns them to shapes, and gives to airy nothing / A local habitation and a name."

52.24 *The first Humphrey's latitudinous baver with puggaree behind:* this is one of many descriptions connecting HCE with the Ghost in *Hamlet*, who "wore his beaver up" (I. ii. 230). See chapter 4 of this study; see also Hodgart, p. 740.

53.32 *poleaxe your sonson's grandson:* a parody of Stephen Dedalus's Shakespeare theory in *Ulysses*. "He [King Hamlet] smote the sledded Polacks on the ice" in *Hamlet* I. i. 63 results in Stephen's "sledded poleaxe" (*U*, 187) and Bloom's "poleaxe" (*U*, 171); "sonson's grandson" echoes Buck Mulligan's parody of Stephen's theory that "Hamlet's grandson is Shakespeare's grandfather and that he himself is the ghost of his own father" (*U*, 18). See entry for 28.06.

55.10 *manorwombanborn:* unlike Macduff, who was "none of woman born" (*Mac.* IV. i. 80). See also entries for 79.08–9 and 365.04–5, and Hodgart, p. 743.

55.25 *pursue the bare:* famous stage direction for Antigonus, in *The Winter's Tale:* "Exit, pursued by a bear" (III. iii. 57). See Hodgart, p. 750.

55.31   *craving their auriculars to receptacle particulars:* Antony's "Lend me your ears"—and "List, list!"

55.33–36   *hearing in this new reading of the part . . . the new garrickson's grimacing . . . of that once grand old elrington bawl:* the world as stage, parts being taken by famous Shakespearean actors David Garrick and Thomas Elrington (also F. Elrington Ball, editor of Swift's *Correspondence*). Whereas Garrick became most famous in the role of Hamlet, he at first had played the Ghost. Thus "garrickson" might refer to Hamlet himself. McHugh notes (p. 55) that Reverend S. Hughes's *Pre-Victorian Drama in Dublin* refers to "Garrick's school of grimace."
   See entries for 121.02–8 and 134.10–11.

58.06   *Lou! Lou!:* List! List! (*Ham.* I. v. 22).

58.18   *lo! lo!:* List!

58.25   *cappapee:* Horatio's description of the ghost of Hamlet's father was "A figure like your father, / Armèd at point exactly, cap-a-pe [head to foot]" (I. ii. 199–200). "Cap-a-pe" seems to be a leitmotif for HCE. See chapter 4; and Hodgart, p. 739. Compare "cap-a-pipe" in 220.26, "from grosskopp to megapod" in 78.05, "capapee" in 583.29, "Reclined from cape to pede" in 619.27, etc.
   In context, the three soldiers in 58.24 are referred to as "cappapee"—armed from head to foot.

58.29   *the first woman, they said, souped him . . . Lili Coninghams, by suggesting him they go in a field:* here, woman is the seductress. "The first woman" (Eve) was Adam's temptation and downfall; so also Bloom was seduced by Molly, who tumbled him in a rye field on Howth, and Shakespeare (according to Stephen), by Anne Hathaway: "By cock, she was to blame. She put the comether on him . . . a boldfaced Stratford wench who tumbles in a cornfield a lover younger than herself" (*U*, 191). Best amends "cornfield" to "Ryefield." Lili Cunningham is perhaps the alcoholic wife (mentioned in *Dubliners* and *Ulysses*) of Martin Cunningham; and in *Ulysses* Cunningham is equated with Shakespeare. In "Hades" Bloom thinks Martin's face is "Like Shakespeare's face" (*U*, 96); and in "Circe" Stephen sees the Cunninghams in his hallucination: "The face of Martin Cunningham, bearded, refeatures Shakespeare's beardless face" (*U*, 568). Thus, "Lili Coninghams" may here refer to Shakespeare's wife, Anne Hathaway, who souped him and tumbled him in a cornfield-ryefield. Furthermore, since in the *Wake* young ALP is a "lilith," thus Anne Hathaway = Issy-ALP and all women; and Shakespeare = HCE or "Allmen" (419.10). "Lilith" Cunningham is alluded to in 75.05–10, 205.11, 241.04, 366.24, 391.22 ff., and 422.32. Martin Cunningham is alluded to in 387.27, 388.13, 391.22 ff., 392.03, 393.05, and 467.33.

59.10   *while it is odrous comparisoning to the sprangflowers:* Dogberry's famous "Comparisons are odorous" (*Ado* III. v. 15). In the context of fragrant "sprangflowers," the comparison is no doubt "odorous" in nature. See also entry for 163.26.

59.30–32   *Mon foie, you wish to ave some homelette, yes, lady! Good, mein leber! Your hegg he must break himself:* the opinion of the continental chef Eiskaffier concerns breakfast: ham and eggs ("hegg") and omelettes, or Hamlet ("homelette"); see also "omulette" (230.07) and "homelet" (586.18).

61.04 *John a'Dream's:* Hamlet calls himself "A dull and muddy-mettled rascal . . . / Like John-a-dreams, unpregnant of my cause" (II. ii. 552–53). See Hodgart, p. 742.

62.06 *the old vic:* famous Shakespearean theatre in London.

63.17–19 *a most decisive bottle of single in his possession, seized after dark . . . temperance gateway was there in a gate's way:* the following few pages seem to elaborate a version of the encounter between HCE and the Cad, one (or both) of them drunk and knocking at a gate (perhaps Castle Knock Gate, near Chapelizod). HCE-Porter is the keeper of an alehouse in Chapelizod. This brings to mind the drunken porter at the gate in *Macbeth*. Cf. 69.26, "faithful poorters," and 72.02, "Sublime Porter." See chapter 5 of this study.

63.32–35 *trying to open zozimus a bottlop stoub by mortially hammering his magnum bonum . . . against the bludgey gate for the boots about the swan:* the Cad is explaining that he was drunk and knocking against the stone gate ("gatestone" in 63.28), and he tried to open a bottle of stout (or "porter") by hammering his head against the bloody gate, while calling for the innkeeper. Again, the porter at the gate. "Swan" hints at Shakespeare. See chapter 5 of this study.

64.09–11 *This battering babel allower the door and sideposts . . . was not in the very remotest like the belzey babble of a bottle of boose:* Cad-Joyce's drunken battering and knocking at the gate (all over the door and the sideposts) is like the *Wake* itself—a drunken mixture of tongues, a Luciferian, (Beelzebub) "belzey babble" of tongues. *Macbeth's* porter says, "Here's a knocking indeed. . . . Who's there, i'th'name of Belzebub? . . . I'll devil-porter it no further" (II. iii. 1–16).

65.04 *Now listen, Mr Leer!:* "List!" and a lascivious King Lear. See "kingly leer" in 398.23. As Hodgart points out (p. 751), this line is followed by "a comic story of an old rip and two 'daughters.'"

65.35 *the bottle at the gate:* the porter (as in bottled beer) at the gate, and the Cad's battle and encounter at the gate (the knocking at Castle Knock Gate) with HCE-Porter.

68.25 *Hear, O hear:* List, O List!

69.05–7 *the whole of the wall . . . wallhole:* perhaps the hole in the wall between Pyramus and Thisbe in *A Midsummer Night's Dream*. In this "drema," the wall (Magazine Wall) seems to be associated with the gate (Castle Knock Gate) near the park (Phoenix), at which an encounter-confrontation takes place between a father figure and a filial figure. See Hodgart, p. 750.

69.10 *a garthen of Odin and the lost paladays when all the eddams ended with aves:* a Norse Garden of Eden, the lost paradise during the times of Adams and Eves ("eddams" and "aves"), when all the Norse eddas ended with Latin *aves*—in short, during the Danish conquests of Ireland (followed by the Roman-Latin conquests), Ireland's lost "salad days" ("lost paladays"), "when [she] was green in judgment, cold in blood" (*Ant*. I. v. 73–74). Cf. 615.25, "paladays last."

69.15 ff. *A stonehinged gate . . . applegate . . . the iron gape, by old custom left open to prevent the cats from getting at the gout, was triplepatlockt on him on purpose by his faithful poorters:* another version of the HCE-Cad encounter;

in this "drema" (69.14) of the Porters at the gate, HCE is inside and the drunken Cad is locked out by the iron gate, used to prevent Cads from getting at the gate.

70.08–9 *wider he might the same . . . other he would, with tosend and obertosend:* whether he might or might not—a possible echo of "To be or not to be," to send or not to send over.

70.13–32 *Humphrey's unsolicited visitor . . . . bleated through the gale outside which the tairor of his clothes was hogcallering . . . that he would break his bulshewigger's head for him . . . that he would break the gage over his lankyduckling head . . . and went on at a wicked rate:* another version of the encounter, in which the drunken Cad, locked out "at the gale [gate] outside," threatens to break the "the gage" over HCE-Humphrey's head, and unloads his verbal artillery "at a wicked rate" at the wicket gate (cf. "at the wicket" in 72.28).

"The tairor of his clothes": Cad is seen as a tailor of clothes, and a terror, tearing his clothes and screaming ("hogcallering") at HCE. Shakespeare's drunken porter said: "Faith, here's an English tailor come hither for stealing out of a French hose. Come in, tailor. Here you may roast your goose" (*Mac.* II. iii. 12–14). *The Taylor of the Cloth* was a collection of Irish airs by George Petrie; see McHugh, p. 70.

71.12 *York's Porker:* amid this catalog of 111 names appears an entry which, according to Glasheen (p. 314), "combines Francis Bacon, whose town residence was York House, and Richard III (York), whose crest was a boar." The reference may simply be to York ham, alluded to in 318.21 ("backonham"), a line which echoes the opening line of *Richard III*. Cf. entry for 318.20–21.

72.02–3 *Sublime Porter:* the Porter (HCE or Cad?) at the gate.

72.04 *O'Phelim's Cutprice: O felix culpa,* "O foenix culprit" (23.16), and Ophelia. See *"Ophelia's Culpreints"* (105.18). Ophelia's culprit might be Hamlet.

74.03 *(lost leaders live! the heroes return!):* Love's Labor's Lost, re-expressed as the promise of *Finnegans Wake*—the returning and the rising of the phoenix. Also, Browning's "The Lost Leader." Cf. entry for 157.23 "mild's vapour moist."

74.05 *orland:* perhaps *As You Like It*'s Orlando. See entry for 74.10.

74.10 *green woods:* "Under the greenwood tree" and the Green World of the Forest of Arden, from *As You Like It*. See entry for 30.13–14.

74.16–19 *Humph is in his doge. Words weigh no no more to him than raindrips to Rethfernhim. Which we all like. Rain. When we sleep. Drops. But wait until our sleeping. Drain. Sdops.:* Hodgart observes (p. 743) that these lines echo Macbeth's "Duncan is in his grave; / After life's fitful fever he sleeps well" (III. ii. 22–23).

Book I, Chapter 4

76.05–6 *Ham's cribcracking yeggs:* Hamlet, Bacon, eggs, and breakfast (and HCE's initials). See chapter 6 of this study.

76.11 *Now hear:* List.

76.26 *old knoll:* see entry for 422.31–32.

77.14 *it was Dane to pfife:* ten before the hour of five, and Macduff, the Thane of Fife. The Dane is also HCE-King Hamlet (see entry for 78.05) addressing his "pfife" (wife), ALP, "liddle phifie Annie" (4.28; cf. also 411.11 "never get stuck to another man's pfife"). Possibly this is the hour of HCE's burial, which is what is being described in context.

78.05 *from grosskopp to megapod:* a description of the dead HCE, postburial, from big head to big foot, "cap-a-pe," like the ghost of Hamlet's father. See also entries for 58.25, 220.25–26, 583.29, and 619.27. HCE's *gross Kopf* is no doubt Howth Head. It is also the "gross and scope of my opinion" (I. i. 68), words spoken by Horatio after seeing the ghost of King Hamlet, armed "cap-a-pe." Horatio's gross scope, or general view, was that "This bodes some strange eruption to our state" (I. i. 69).

79.02–3 *even the first old wugger of himself in the flesh, whiggissimus incarnadined:* from Macbeth's "This my hand will rather / The multitudinous seas incarnadine" (II. ii. 60–61). So also perhaps in this context HCE's flesh, buried at sea, is bloodying the multitudinous seas. Macduff is also on this page; see entries for 77.14 and 79.08–9.

79.08–9 *no man of woman born:* Macduff again, who was "none of woman born" (*Mac.* IV. i. 80). See also entry for 55.10 and Hodgart, p. 743.

79.20 *bare godkin:* Hamlet's "bare bodkin," with which a man might his quietus make; "godkin" might also be Hamlet's "God's bodkin, man!" (II. ii. 516). Cf. entries for 500.02, 578.16, and 268.15.

79.27–28 *she pulls a lane picture for us, in a dreariodreama setting:* Kate Strong presents HCE's "dreama," a dream-drama in Drury Lane ("lane" and "dreario"), London's theatre street and the name of the famous theatre associated with David Garrick. See also "druriodrama" (50.06), "Drury" (543.20), and "drury world of ours" (600.02).

The line also refers to the celebrated Lane Pictures at the Irish National Gallery.

79.33–35 *Widow Strong, then, as her weaker had turned him to the wall . . . did most all the scavenging from good King Hamlaugh's gulden dayne:* the golden days of good King Hamlet, the golden Dane. "King Hamlaugh" strikes me as equivalent to "Festy King" (85.23), at least in nomenclature.

There is also a reference here to "for the weakest goes to the wall . . . therefore women, being the weaker vessels, are ever thrust to the wall" (*Rom.* I. i. 12–15). See Peery, p. 243.

80.17–18 *the first babe of reconcilement is laid in its last cradle of hume sweet hume:* reconcilement comes through a babe. As Stephen Dedalus says about Shakespeare, "There can be no reconciliation . . . if there has not been a sundering. . . . What softens the heart of a man, Shipwrecked in storms dire, Tried, like another Ulysses, Pericles, prince of Tyre? . . .—A child, a girl placed in his arms, Marina . . . Marina, a child of storm, Miranda, a wonder, Perdita, that which was lost. What was lost is given back to him . . ." (*U*, 195). Stephen appeals to the dating of the plays by Shakespearean biographer Georg Brandes (*U*, 195); Brandes may be here in "brandihands" (80.14). According to Stephen, Shakespeare's "babe of reconcilement" was his granddaughter Elizabeth Hall (see entries for 338.31 and 411.27–28).

At life's end, one's final home-sweet-home is "hume," or humus.

81.10 *And if he's not a Romeo you may scallop your hat:* of course, Juliet's true love, as well as, perhaps, Ophelia's true love again, whom she should know by his "cockle hat" (IV. v. 25). See also entry for 41.02. Cockles and scallops are similar marine bivalve mollusks and popular seafoods.

Glasheen notes (p.247) that "Like Shakespeare, Joyce plays on 'Romeo' as a medieval pilgrim who, coming from the shrine of St. Iago, or James, wears a scallop shell."

82.11 *a different and younger him of the same ham:* like Hamlet *père* and Hamlet *fils*, the son is but a younger version of the same "refleshmeant" (82.10), flesh and blood, by consubstantiation, as with God the Father and God the Son, as in Stephen Dedalus's theory of Shakespeare.

84.15 *nobiloroman:* Brutus, "the noblest Roman of them all" *(JC* V. v. 68).

84.32 *that thuddysickend Hamlaugh:* the falling (the thud of his sick ending, falling at "thirty-second" feet/sec./sec.) Hamlet, the death of King Hamlet. See also "King Hamlaugh" in 79.35.

85.27 *calends of Mars: Julius Caesar* and Ides of March. The calends (or kalends) of the ancient Roman month is its first day, from which the days were counted backward to the ides. See entries for 27.08, 31.32, 35.03, 40.10, and 97.03 for other references to the Ides of March.

85.31 *Oyeh! Oyeh!:* Festy King "was subsequently haled up at the Old Bailey on the calends of Mars." At the Old Bailey the judiciary call to attention is "Oyez, oyez!"—another variant of "List! List!"

88.15 *And how did the greeneyed mister arrive at the B.A.?: Othello* and Iago's "the green-eyed monster" of jealousy (III. iii. 166). See entries for 249.02–3 and 184.24.

88.25 *the dumb scene:* the dumb show in *Hamlet*, possibly.

89.03 *Two dreamyums in one dromium? Yes and no error:* two twins in one hump (Shem, Shaun, and the dromedary HCE-HUMP), and the twins (Dromio of Ephesus and Dromio of Syracuse) in *The Comedy of Errors* ("no error"). They were like two peas from the same pod: "And both as like as a duel of lentils? Peacisely" (89.04).

See Hodgart, p. 750.

91.06–7 *Cliopatrick (the sow) princess of parked porkers:* an Irish Cleopatra, a real porker—the sow that eats her own farrow.

93.17–18 *he was dovetimid as the dears at Bottome:* a reference to *A Midsummer Night's Dream*'s Nick Bottom, who said that he would "roar as gently [or timidly?] as any sucking dove" (I. ii. 75). See Hodgart, "Work in Progress," p. 19; see also entries for 319.03–6, 342.30–31, and 503.21. Cf. 403.16, "dhove's suckling."

94.17 *one old obster:* HCE is one jealous old man, a "greeneyed lobster" (249.03; cf. *Oth*. III. iii. 166). See entries for 249.02–3 and 88.15.

95.33 *hist! . . . hast!:* List, list!

96.23 *shakeahand:* Shakespeare and *la ci darem.* See entries for 28.04 and 535.11.

97.03 *Juletide:* Julius's time, the Ides, as well as Yuletide and July.

99.06 *Morse nuisance noised:* the gossip about HCE's fall is telegraphed (in Morse code) around. The entire passage is about pouring poison in the porches of gossipers' ears; this particular phrase sounds like a verbal echo of *Love's Labor's Lost;* see also entries for 74.03 and 157.23.

103.10–11 *and we list, as she bibs us, by the waters of babalong:* we "list" to the preceding song, sung by ALP, about renewal and reconciliation by the arrival of babies. "Babalong" is a good description of baby talk. "By the waters of babalong" echoes Psalm 137 ("By the rivers of Babylon"), sung in Babylonian exile, and recalls Eliot's *Waste Land* ("By the waters of Lemman . . . "). Again, a child brings reconciliation after sundering (exiled HCE's fall)—as in Stephen's theory of Shakespeare. See entry for 80.17–18.

Book I, Chapter 5

104.05 *disjointed times:* as in *Hamlet,* when "The time is out of joint" (I. v. 188). Cf. entry for 181.29–30.

104.11 *Buy Birthplate for a Bite:* a union of the theme of Jacob and Esau (and the birthright), and Richard III's cry, "My kingdom for a horse!" *(R3* V. v. 7, 13). Other echoes of that line occur in 134.08, 352.09–10, and 373.15; the line is a repeated motif in the *Wake.*

104.12 *Which of your Hesterdays Mean Ye to Morra:* probably a reference to Macbeth's "To-morrow, and to-morrow, and to-morrow / Creeps in this petty pace from day to day. . . . And all our yesterdays have lighted fools / The way to dusty death" (V. v. 19–23). The past consists of memories of guilt (like Hester Prynne's)—of "Hesterdays." Cf. entry for 105.22.

104.20–22 *Cleopater's Needlework . . . on the Sahara . . . and the Parlourmaids of Aegypt:* Cleopatra combined with one of Joyce's favorite prose stylists, Walter Pater, and the fleshpots of Egypt. In the first folio edition of *Antony and Cleopatra,* Cleopatra is several times spelled as "Cleopater" *(Pelican Shakespeare,* p. 1172).

105.01 *When the Myrtles of Venice Played to Bloccus's Line: The Merchant of Venice* combined here with an entry from *The Index Manuscript* ("myrtle of Venus with Bacchus's wine"), based on a line from the song "To Anacreon in Heaven": "The myrtle of Venus with Bacchus's vine." See Rose, *James Joyce's The Index Manuscript,* p. 241.

105.18 *Ophelia's Culpreints:* "O foenix culprit" (23.16), Ophelia's culled prince (perhaps Hamlet), and Ophelia's ass prints. See also "culprines" (504.26) and "O'Phelim's cutprice" (72.04).

105.22 *Look to the Lady:* from *Macbeth,* II. iii. 115, 122.

110.11 *the drame of Drainophilias:* the dream as a drama. Drama is probably *Hamlet,* or Ophelia's dream, since "ophilias" is here and since the quintessential quote from *Hamlet* follows forthwith. See entry for 110.14.

110.14 *me ken or no me ken Z ot is the Quiztune:* Hamlet's "To be or not to be—that is the question" (III. i. 56). The question is also one which stymies Hamlet: what actually *did* happen? which among all of Aristotle's infinite possibilities? Will we ever know, for "utterly impossible as are all these events they are probably as like those which may have taken place as any others which never took person at all are ever likely to be" (110.19–21)?

111.05 *Belinda of the Dorans:* Glasheen argues (p. 71) that Biddy Doran, the hen who tries to resurrect the memory of HCE, is linked (through Delia-Artemis the goddess) to Delia Bacon (1811–59), the first Baconian and the American authoress of *The Philosophy of Shakespeare's Plays Unfolded* (1857). She believed that by breaking into Shakespeare's tomb she could prove that Bacon was the playwright Shakespeare; she never did so, but went mad instead—supporting Haines's observation that "Shakespeare is the happy hunting ground of all minds who have lost their balance" *(U,* 248). See entry for 208.29; and also Glasheen, pp. 21, 27, 71, and 76. See entry for 423.25.

112.20 *Ague will be rejuvenated:* ricorso, eternal youth, healing, and possibly a reference to King Lear, who learned that, "I am not ague-proof" *(Lr.* IV. vi. 104).

114.19–20 *from tham Let Rise till Hum Lit. Sleep, where in the waste is the wisdom?:* hidden in here is Hamlet ("tham Let" and "Hum Lit"), who also asked himself about the wisdom of eternal sleep. Joyce-Hamlet, watching the risings and falls of the rotten state of life, soliloquizes on the meaning of life, sleep, and death.

"Thithaways" and "hithaways" in 114.16–17 may refer to Anne Hathaway.

117.02 *Here, Ohere!:* a spatial version of "List, O list!" (Hear!).

117.19 *tell Tibbs has eve:* reference to Lewis Theobald (Pope's "Tibbald" in the *Dunciad),* Shakespearean scholar and forger. Atherton discusses (pp. 69–70) the Theobald allusions; see also chapter 6 of this study. As to the Shakespeare canon, "we must vaunt no idle dubiosity as to its genuine authorship and holusbolus authoritativeness" (118.03–4). Cf. 424.29, "till tibbes grey eyes." Hart *(Structure and Motif,* p. 244) writes that "till Tibb's Eve" means "never."

118.04–5 *And let us bringtheecease to beakerings on that clink:* an echo of Iago's song, "And *let me* the canakin *clink,* clink; / And let me the canakin clink" *(Oth.* II. iii. 64–65; my italics).

118.13 *Coccolanius:* Coriolanus, perhaps.

120.07–8 *dummpshow:* the dumb show in *Hamlet,* and the middendump. See entries for 88.25 and 559.18.

120.11 *very like a whale's egg:* Polonius's "Very like a whale" (III. ii. 367). This important passage on the "prepronominal *funferal*" (120.10) describes the Protean qualities of the *Wake,* which, like the cloud observed by Hamlet and Polonius, takes on many shapes. This line is also quoted, appropriately, in the "Proteus" episode, by Stephen Dedalus *(U,* 40) and in 307.F2, "Wherry liked the whaled prophet."

121.01 *his Claudian brother:* Claudius was brother to King Hamlet in *Hamlet;*

Claudio was brother to Isabella in *Measure for Measure.* See entry for 121.02–8.

121.02–8 Glasheen writes (p. 58): "Because 121.02–8 imitates Lichtenberg's description (it is in the *Variorum Shakespeare*) of Garrick acting Hamlet, I assume [Claudian brother] to be Claudius the usurping king of Denmark."

121.32 *The gypsy mating of a grand stylish gravedigging with secondbest buns (an interpolation . . .):* a wake and the *Wake* are—like *Hamlet*'s tragic jester, like Biddy scratching in the mudpile, or like Stephen Dedalus's fox, who buried his grandmother under a hollybush—gravediggings of sorts. Such scholarly research and digging into the graves of the past, even in a grand style, produces, at best, secondbest buns—like Shakespeare's will (made much of in "Scylla and Charybdis") leaving Anne Hathaway his secondbest bed.

This passage also deals with the problems of scholarship and of original manuscripts. See Atherton, p. 67, Tindall, p. 110, and Hodgart, p. 749, for discussions of this passage. In *James Joyce: A Student's Guide* (London: Routledge & Kegan Paul, 1978), p. 145, Hodgart suggests that these lines refer to the gravediggers in *Hamlet*, to Hamlet's "The funeral baked meats / Did coldly furnish forth the marriage tables" (I. ii. 180–81), and to the mixture of high and low styles which neoclassical critics found objectionable in Shakespeare.

122.36–123.01 *the toomuchness, the fartoomanyness, of all those fourlegged ems:* Atherton maintains (p. 67): "This must refer to the suggestion, made first by the MS. of the *Play of Sir Thomas More*, that putting four legs to occasional m's was Shakespeare's besetting sin as a writer." Cf. entries for 123.24 and 123.31–32.

123.24 *our plumsucked pattern shapekeeper:* in context, Joyce is admitting that his works are borrowings and plagiarisms from others: Homer's "ulykkhean" (123.16), "wretched mariner" (123.23); the shape of Joyce's tale is also patterned on Shakespeare ("pattern shapekeeper," referred to in 539.06 as "Shopkeeper"). The subsequent line compares Joyce's work to Macpherson's forgeries of Ossian: *"MacPerson's Oshean"* (123.25).

123.31–32 *The original document was in what is known as Hanno O'Nonhanno's unbrookable script:* the original script may have been from Shakespeare (whose "fourlegged ems" are mentioned in 123.01), since Shakespeare ("shapekeeper" in 123.24) wrote "To be or not to be, that is the question," rendered in 182.20 as *"Hanno o Nonanno, acce'l brubblemm'as."*

125.14–15 *Not Hans the Curier though had he had have only had some little laughings and some less of cheeks:* if only Shaun, the cheeky Postman (courier), had had, like the joking Shem and like (Ben Jonson's) Shakespeare, some little Latin and some less of Greek.

Book I, Chapter 6

126.09 *fine artful disorder:* see entry for 32.05.
127.11 *if he outharrods against barkers:* Hamlet's "It out-herods Herod" (III. ii. 13). See Hodgart, p. 742.

127.17–19 *Dook Hookbackcrook upsits his ass booseworthies jeer and junket but they boos him oos and baas his aas when he lukes like Hunkett Plunkett:* a double-crossing Duke, working by hook and by crook, like Shakespeare's hump-backed Richard the Third, known as "Crookback." See also *Ulysses*, pp. 209 and 211, in which Stephen refers to "Richard Crookback" and "Richard, a whoreson crookback." HCE, "HUMP" (220.24), has a hump on his back. See also entries for 134.10–11, 138.32–33, and 319.20.

The rest of the passage refers, as Fritz Senn has shown, to a well-remembered, 19th-century performance of *Richard III* by a stage-struck amateur named Luke Plunkett at Dublin's Theatre Royal: "Some of his readings of well-known passages were exceedingly erratic, and his death scene so amused the audience that they insisted on its repetition, with which demand the tragedian solemnly complied" (from Senn, quoting Fitzpatrick,) *AWN*, o.s. 1 (Mar. 1962).

"Booseworthies" combines the drinkers at the pub, Richard III's battle at Bosworth Field, and the amused Dublin audience jeering and laughing ("jeer," "boos," and "baas") at Plunkett's performance. He "upsits his ass" and "baas his aas" because, as Roland McHugh points out (*AWN*, XVI, 5 [Oct. 1979]: 72), the *Annals of the Theatre Royal* note that "Mr. Luke Plunkett thought himself the greatest Richard III in existence. . . . He usually rode into Bosworth Field on a donkey."

127.31–32 *plays gehamerat when he's ernst:* plays Hamlet when he's earnest. May refer to Ernest Jones ("Professor Jones" in this chapter), who wrote *Hamlet and Oedipus*. See entry for 128.36.

128.15 *Titius, Caius and Sempronius:* Caius and Sempronius were minor characters in *Titus Andronicus*, and kinsmen of Titus. In context, it means every "Tom, Dick and Harry."

128.15–17 *made the man who had no notion of shopkeepers feel he'd rather play the duke than play the gentleman:* HCE prefers the role of Richard III ("Dook Hookbackcrook" in 127.17) because he has no notion of Shakespeare. "Shopkeeper" stands for Shakespeare, as in 539.06, "Daunty, Gouty and Shopkeeper" (Dante, Goethe, and Shakespeare) and 123.24, "pattern shapekeeper"; see also 183.26, "shopkeepers' wives." England's national poet is appropriately titled "Shopkeeper," since England was, according to Napoleon, a nation of shopkeepers ("no notion of shopkeepers").

128.31–32 *three hundred sixty five idles:* 365 days in a year; ides (as in 40.10, "eyots of martas"; 35.03, "Ides-of-April"; and 83.25, "calends of mars") are once again used to signify days or time in the *Wake*.

128.36 *has an eatupus complex and a drinkthedregs kink:* Shaun-Jones's answers to the Questions in this chapter reveal the psychoanalyst side of him as Ernest Jones, who wrote *Hamlet and Oedipus*. Like Hamlet, Shem, according to Shaun-Jones, has an Oedipus complex and has "metheg in [his] midness" (32.05)—i.e., he drinks too much. Cf. entry for 127.31–32.

131.17 *god at the top of the staircase, carrion on the mat of straw:* perhaps an echo of Hamlet's words to Polonius in II. ii. 181–82: "For if the sun breeds maggots in a dead dog [god, perhaps], being a good kissing carrion. . . ." See Hodgart, p. 741.

131.30–31 *nods a nap for the nonce:* echoes such Shakespearean lines as Claudius's "A chalice for the nonce" (*Ham.* IV. vii. 159).

132.06–7 *a hunnibal in exhaustive conflict, an otho to return; burning body to aiger air:* again, Hannibal-HCE (here, h.e.c.) as King Hamlet's ghost, whose burning body (i.e., in Purgatory) returns to the "nipping and eager air" (I. iv. 2) of Elsinore on the evening he is seen by Hamlet and Horatio. See Hodgart, p. 740.

133.17 *fiefeofhome:* Edgar's "Fie, foh, and fum" again (*Lr.* III. iv. 174–75). See entry for 7.09–10.

134.04 *double trouble:* "Double, double, toil and trouble" (*Mac.* IV. i. 10). See entry for 138.02–3.

134.10–11 *in Silver on the Screen but was sequenced from the set as Crookback by the even more titulars, Rick, Dave and Barry:* who played the role of Shakespeare's Richard III (Crookback) on the Silver Screen? Not any Tom, Dick, or Harry; actually a Larry—Laurence Olivier, that is. Joyce names here three of the most famous Shakespearean actors in stage history, who played Richard III in perhaps the three most famous portrayals of Richard Crookback: in Shakespeare's day, Richard Burbage made his first hit in the part of Richard; in the 18th century, David Garrick played Richard from 1741 to 1776 at Drury Lane; and in the 19th century, Irish actor Barry Sullivan acted in the role of Richard III for over twenty years. (See *RES*, pp. 700, 833.) I believe "Barry" (a first name, like Rick and Dave) refers to Barry Sullivan, not to Spranger Barry, as Glasheen suggests (p. 24).

Perhaps "twiniceynurseys fore a drum" (134.08) is an echo of Richard's "My kingdom for a horse!" (V. v. 7, 13).

137.34 *a laughsworth of his illformation over a larmsworth of salt:* McHugh suggests (p. 137) an echo of Robert Greene's *A Groatsworth of Wit Bought with a Million of Repentance* (see also entry for 414.20); however, the line seems more clearly to echo Prince Hal's "but one halfpennyworth of bread to this intolerable deal of sack" (*1H4* II. iv. 514–15). See entry for 288.F1.

138.02–3 *his troubles may be over but his doubles have still to come:* this prediction for HCE seems based on the witches' predictions for Macbeth: "Double, double, toil and trouble. . . ." (IV. i. 10 ff.) Cf. 246.10–12, in which "still" also alludes to the witches' bubbling cauldron—or, here, the "lobster pot" (see entry for 138.03).

138.03 *the lobster pot that crabbed our keel:* possibly an echo of *Love's Labor's Lost* V. ii. 909: "While greasy Joan doth keel the pot." See McHugh, p. 138; see also entry for 138.02–3.

138.32–33 *hahnreich the althe . . . writchad the thord:* two of Shakespeare's plays and kings, *Henry VIII* and *Richard III*.

138.36–139.01 *with one touch of nature set a veiled world agrin:* "One touch of nature makes the whole world kin" (Ulysses, in *Tro.* III. iii. 174). See also "one twitch, one nature makes us oldworld kin" in 463.16; Hodgart, p. 751. The line, here, refers to HCE's crime in the park, which started the whole world snickering and gossiping. Perhaps the crime was simply a touch of nature—did HCE simply heed the call of nature and piss (or shit, like the

Russian General)? In the next line, he "went within a sheet of tissuepaper of the option . . ." (139.02).

141.21 *bacon or stable hand:* stablehelp or, perhaps, Francis Bacon and the stable hand of a forger. Legend has it that Shakespeare as a young man held horses for the London theatre audience. Thus, the phrase stands for "Bacon or Shakespeare." See chapter 6 of this study.

143.03–28 See chapter 4 of this study for a comparison of this dense passage with Hamlet's famous fourth soliloquy.

143.05 *his gouty hands:* possibly an echo of Macbeth's "And on thy blade and dudgeon gouts of blood" (II. i. 46). See *AWN*, o.s. 1 (Mar. 1962), p. 5.

143.06–7 *hapless behind the dreams of accuracy as any camelot prince of dinmurk:* Hamlet, prince of Denmark, and his fears of what dreams may come in that eternal sleep.

143.10 *old hopeinhaven:* Hamlet's hope in Heaven, a haven for lost Danish souls, like Copenhagen—as opposed to "the undiscovered country" in Hamlet's soliloquy. This page is full of references to "camelot prince of dinmurk" (143.07). See entry for 220.34.

143.12 *the course of his tory will had been having recourses:* the course of history will have Viconian ricorsos; also, perhaps, an echo of Shakespeare's sonnet 129 ("Th'expense of spirit in a waste of shame . . ."): "Had, having, and in quest to have. . . ." Coincidentally, the poem contains both "shame" and "shun" ("To shun the heaven that leads men to this hell"). *AWN*, o.s. 1 (Mar. 1962), p. 8.

143.15 *and the thereby hang of the Hoel of it:* echo of Touchstone's "And thereby hangs a tale" (*AYL* II. vii. 28); or of the Clown in *Othello*, "O, thereby hangs a tail" (III. i. 08–9).

143.16 *comeliewithhers:* comely limbs ("withers"), seducers ("Come lie with her"), and possibly a reference to Hamlet's "our withers are unwrung" (III. ii. 234). See entries for 550.26, and 143.26.

143.21–22 *all the rivals to allsea, shakeagain, O disaster! shakealose!:* Joyce, perhaps, is the rival of Shakespeare, the "greatest shake-scene in a countrie."

143.23 *the signs of Ham:* the signs of Hamlet cover this page of the *Wake*.

143.26 *Violet's dyed!:* a reference to Ophelia's and Polonius's deaths. Ophelia, before her death, said, "There's a daisy. I would give you some violets, but they withered [cf. "comeliewithhers" in entry for 143.16] all when my father died. They say 'a made a good end" (IV. v. 182–84). *AWN*, o.s. 1 (Mar. 1962), pp. 5 ff.

143.26–27 *what would that fargazer seem to seemself to seem seeming of, dimm it all?:* this emphasis on the notion of "seeming" brings to mind Hamlet's words to his mother: "Seems, madam? Nay, it is. I know not 'seems'" (I. ii. 76). *AWN*, o.s. 1 (Mar. 1962), pp. 5 ff. As Patrick A. McCarthy notes about this line, "While Hamlet knew not 'seems,' Joyce's dreamer knows little else" (*The Riddles of* Finnegans Wake, p. 76).

144.14 *Like Jolio and Romeune:* this is part of a saccharine romantic exchange between Shaun and Isabel; thus references to lovers like Romeo and Juliet are appropriate in these pages. See "juliettes" (148.13), "Antony Romeo" (152.22), and so on.

144.30 *the rubberend Mr Polkingtone, the quoniam fleshmonger:* the reverend and preachy Polonius, an erstwhile fishmonger. Hamlet to Polonius: "You are a fishmonger" (II. ii. 174). See also 29.26, "fishmummer."

"Fishmonger" means a bawd, a procurer—a "fleshmonger," precisely.

145.24 *More poestries from Chickspeer's:* more poetry from Shakespeare. Was Chickspeer's perhaps a Dublin post office (more posts) or a bakery (more pastries)? See also entries for 191.02, "Scheekspair," and 257.19–20, "the baker's booth . . . Missy Cheekspeer" (the latter argues for a bakery).

145.24–34 *More poestries from Chickspeer's. . . . O, you mean the strangle for love and the sowiveall of the prettiest? Yep, we open hap coseries in the home. And once upon a week I improve on myself I'm so keen on that New Free Woman with novel inside. I'm always as tickled as can be over Man in a Surplus by the Lady who Pays the Rates. But I'm as pie as is possible. Let's root out Brimstoker and give him the thrall of our lives. It's Dracula's nightout. For creepsake don't make a flush! Draw the shades, curfe you. . . . :* poetry from Shakespeare; struggle for love; survival of the fittest; feminism; female novels; a man dressed as a lady; curfew and curses; and Bram Stoker, the Irish author who wrote *Dracula*. Glasheen points out (p. 272) that this passage "becomes more comprehensible if you know that Stoker wrote a jesting piece, claiming Elizabeth I was really a man. The piece was taken seriously by a Mr. Titterton, who claimed in *New Witness*, 1913, that Elizabeth-the-man wrote Shakespeare's plays."

147.03 *Hearhere!:* List! List!

147.11 *Celia:* Rosalind's friend in *As You Like It*. See also entry for 608.18.

147.19–20 *Whoses wishes is the farther to my thoughts:* Issy's words echo those of Henry IV to his son: "Thy wish was father, Harry, to that thought" (*2H4* IV. v. 92). See Hart, *Structure and Motif*, p. 246.

148.08 *Rutland blue's:* see entries for 42.36 and 437.05.

148.13 *not for all the juliettes in the twinkly way:* not for all the stars in the Milky Way (Issy speaks to Shaun)—a dream image of romeos with their milky, star-crossed lovers.

148.26 *Liss, liss!:* List, list!

149.10 *we don't think, Jones, we'd care to this evening, would you?:* part of book I, chapter 6's eleventh question, in which Shaun is asked if he might be willing to help his impoverished starving brother by lending him some money. Shaun is addressed directly here as Jones—i.e., Ernest Jones, psychoanalytic critic of Shakespeare.

The appeal of the Shem figure to the Shaun figure for a loan occurs a number of times; see chapter 5.

150.30 *'by Allswill': All's Well that Ends Well*. Cf. "All Swell that Aimswell," in 40.01.

151.13–14 *the watches cunldron apan the oven, though it is astensably a case of Ket's rebollions:* what is ostensibly a case of Kate's (the Porters's cook) cooking is also the witches' cauldron in *Macbeth* (also a play about rebellion and insurrection), in which the "weird" Kates boiled their evil bouillons upon the oven.

152.15 *Audi, Joe Peters! Exaudi facts!:* Listen (Latin, *audi*) to the facts! List! Lend me your ears!

152.22 *My hood! cries Antony Romeo:* an image collapsing Antony, Romeo, and Richard III calling for his horse.

Mabel Worthington—in *AWN*, X, 6 (Dec. 1973): 93—has observed that "Antony Romeo" refers also to "Antony Rowley," in the song "The Frog's Courting" (see also McHugh, 152: "A Frog He Would A-wooing Go").

152.33–34 *our once in only Bragspear, he clanked, to my clinking, from veetoes to threetop, every inch of an immortal:* "Bragspear" is both Nicholas Breakspear (Pope Adrian IV) and Shakespeare. The description of a king in clanking armor echoes both King Hamlet (who was "Armed . . . from top to toe" in I. ii. 228; or "from veetoes to threetop") and King Lear, "every inch a king" (IV. vi. 106). (This armored king is also Arthur, "our once and future king.") Furthermore, as John Garvin notes (in *James Joyce's Disunited Kingdom*, p. 170), "our once in only Bragspear" reminds one of Robert Greene calling William Shakespeare "the only Shake-scene."

The pun of Shakespeare and Breakspear has led to another connection, of which Joyce, as a Jesuit product, was probably aware; Schoenbaum wrote (p. 595): "An equally beguiling suggestion was made by Harold Johnson in *Did the Jesuits Write Shakespeare?* (1910). Noting that the only English Pope, Adrian IV (1154–59) bore the name of Nicholas Breakspear, Johnson proposes that the pontiff inspired the pseudonym [i.e., "Shakespeare"] adopted by members of the Society of Jesus as they varied their devotions by busying themselves with *Romeo and Juliet* and *Antony and Cleopatra.*"

154.05 *allsall allinall:* again, HCE is being equated with King Hamlet. Hamlet speaks of his father thus: "'A was a man, take him for all in all, / I shall not look upon his like again" (I. ii. 187–88). In *Ulysses* "all in all" is used to describe Shakespeare: "The truth is midway, [John Eglinton] affirmed. He is the ghost and the prince. He is all in all. / —He is, Stephen said. The boy of act one is the mature man of act five. All in all" (*U*, 212). Cf. entry for 242.31.

154.18 *achilles:* Achilles, Greek hero, in Homer and in *Troilus and Cressida*.

157.08–9 *Nuvoletta in her lightdress . . . leaning over the bannistars:* Michael H. Begnal—in *AWN*, II, 4 (Aug. 1965): 4—argues that Nuvoletta is a modern Juliet—in the balcony scene—on her balcony (bannisters) on a damp evening, trying here to attract the Mookse and the Gripes. Cf. "juliettes" in 148.13, where Juliet is again associated with stars. Ophelia's suicide is also a parallel; see entry for 159.08–18.

157.23 *but it was all mild's vapour moist:* the loving but coy efforts (see entry for 157.08–9) of Nuvoletta to attract (and distract) the Mookse and the Gripes are wasted; therefore, it was all *Love's Labor's Lost*. Moist vapor is dew, so we have here also Mildew Lisa (*mild und leise*, from *Tristan and Isolde*). This Juliet's "Good night, good night! Parting is such sweet sorrow" is "Ah dew! Ah dew!" (158.20), the vaporous farewell of Nuvoletta, the cloud-girl.

157.27 *Enobarbarus:* Antony's closest Roman friend was Enobarbus, who betrayed Antony and then killed himself for his betrayal, in *Antony and Cleopatra.*

158.20 *Ah dew! Ah dew!:* Nuvoletta-Ophelia's parting words are the same as those of King Hamlet's Ghost: "Adieu, adieu, adieu. Remember me" (I. v. 91). See entry for 157.23.

159.07 *and she* [Nuvoletta] *made up all her myriads of drifting minds in one:* echoes Coleridge's "myriad-minded" Shakespeare. Cf. entry for 576.24.

159.08–18 *She climbed over the bannistars. . . . And into that river . . . :* Nuvoletta, heart broken by her rejection, sheds tears, then melts into the river. Both Juliet and Ophelia were also suicides, driven to death by love. Ophelia especially is a parallel: she, too, was rejected by men, and she, too, died by drowning in a river. See entry for 157.08–9.

159.30–32 *baileycliaver though he's a nawful curillass and I must slav to methodiousness. I want him to go and live like a theabild in charge of the night brigade:* Shaun is comparing Shem's cleverness to his own Polonius-like methodiousness (see 32.05, "metheg in your midness"). Shem's cleverness ("very clever"—"baileycliaver"; and town[*baile*]-wise) leads Shaun to make a hidden accusation of forgery, for Theobald ("theabild") was a very clever forger of Shakespearean plays. See chapter 6 of this study.

Balaclava and "The Charge of the Light Brigade" are also here.

160.18 *if I weren't a jones in myself:* Shaun identifies himself with Ernest Jones.

160.35–168.12 As part of his answer to the eleventh question, Shaun-Jones digresses into a lecture about Burrus, Caseous, Cheesugh, and Margareen (Brutus, Cassius, Caesar, and Cleopatra), based on Ernest Jones's Oedipal theories about Shakespeare's plays, and especially, here, about *Julius Caesar.* See chapter 5 of this study.

161.12 *Burrus and Caseous:* Shaun and Shem are Brutus and Cassius.

161.17 *Burrus . . . yet unbeaten as a risicide:* in *Julius Caesar* Brutus is a regicide.

161.30 *Lettucia in her greensleeves:* Glasheen claims (p. 110) this refers to Leticia (or Lettice, or Letty) Greene, who lived with her husband, Thomas Greene, in Stratford-on-Avon. The Greenes supposedly were kinsmen of Shakespeare: Thomas had referred to Shakespeare as "My cosen Shakespeare" in a famous document in which his wife is named as "Lettice" (see *RES*, 272). A reference to Shakespeare ("shakespill and eggs" in 161.31) follows immediately. The pun on lettuce and greens is obvious.

Glasheen is uncertain as to what Letty Greene has to do with Shakespeare; perhaps this concerns her husband. In 1814 a scholar named John Britton pointed out a recorded burial on March 6, 1590 of one "Thomas Green, *alias* Shakspere," whom he supposed to be a bastard born to Anne Shakespeare. Britton was early to accuse Anne of adultery; many others, including Joyce's Stephen Dedalus, followed. See Schoenbaum, p. 312.

There are numerous references to Lettucia, Letty, etc., in the *Wake*. See entry for 184.25,35. "Greensleeves" is a well-known Elizabethan tune.

161.31 *shakespill and eggs:* Shakespeare and eggs. Ham (Hamlet, Shakespeare the actor), bacon (Francis), omelette (Hamlet), and eggs reappear frequently in the *Wake;* the references are, I believe, to problems of scholarship and to forgeries of manuscripts. Atherton notes (p. 165) that in this line "Shakespeare, like Joyce himself, is being accused of being a forger." See also chapter 6.

161.36 *Caesar outnullused:* Caesar annihilated, or Caesar Borgia's *aut Caesar aut nihil* (according to Tindall, p. 122). The *Britannica* notes that Cesare Borgia (1475–1507) was a "Renaissance captain whose motto was *Aut Caesar aut nihil* ('Either Caesar or Nothing')." Borgia was Machiavelli's political idol. Borgia's motto was taken from Suetonius, *Caligula* 37: *Aut Caesar aut nullus;* see McHugh, p. 161.

The following pages contain a number of references to *Julius Caesar.*

162.01 *The older sisars (Tyrants, regicide is too good for you!):* the older Caesars, tyrants and victims of regicide.

162.02–5 *(the compositor of the farce of dustiny however makes a thunpledrum mistake by letting off this pienofarte effect as his furst act as that is where the juke comes in) having been sort-of-nineknived . . . :* Julius Caesar ("sisars"), who was "nineknived" by the nine conspirators in *Julius Caesar.* See chapter 5 (and endnote 43) for a discussion of this passage.

162.08 *who never quite got the sandhurst out of his eyes:* reference to Caesar, according to Tindall, p. 123.

163.06 *Butterbrot . . . Schtinkenkot!:* Schinkenbrot is German for ham sandwich—again, references to ham and bacon (see also entry for 199.16–20), as well as to other foods—butter, cheese, etc. The reference is to Caseous-Shem (as opposed to *Butterbrot*-Brutus). See chapter 5 of this study.

163.26 *odiose by comparison:* Dogberry's "Comparisons are odorous" (III. v. 15) in *Much Ado.* Burrus-Shaun-Jones seems to be accusing his brother, Caseous (smelly cheese—see 163.10, "Cheesugh!") of being smelly, odious, and idle (otiose). See Peery, pp. 243, 249; see also entry for 59.10.

164.07–8 *on this stage there pleasantly appears the cowrymaid M.:* the cowrymaid in this chapter, Margareen, is Cleopatra, since she rejects Burrus and Caseous, and runs off with Antony, "a wop" (167.01). See entry for 166.34.

166.34–167.03 *A cleopatrician in her own right . . . :* Margareen as a Roman Cleopatra. This "eastasian import" (166.32) goes on and "complicates the position while Burrus and Caseous are contending for her misstery by implicating herself with an elusive Antonius, a wop" (166.35–167.01). The elusive Antony is an Italian in Egypt; Brutus and Cassius are contending for her mastery and mystery.

167.04 *This Antonius-Burrus-Caseous grouptriad:* the triangle of Ernest Jones's Oedipal theory (in *Hamlet and Oedipus*) of the "three sons"— Antony, Brutus, and Cassius—overthrowing the father figure, Caesar. See chapters 5 and 6.

"Antomine" and "boor" in line 167.03 refer to Antony and Burrus.

167.23–24 *Merus Genius to Careous Caseous! Moriture, te salutat!:* the martial salute of Caesar's armies: *Ave Caesar, morituri te salutant!* ("Hail, Caesar, they who are going to die, salute you!"). See also entry for 237.12.

The line seems to be a death threat made to the decaying cheese-Cassius-

134   SHAKESPEAREAN ALLUSIONS

Shem ("Careous Caseous") by Shaun-Burrus-Brutus, the pure genius (*Merus Genius* in Latin): you who are about to die, he salutes you!

167.35–168.01   *That mon that hoth no moses in his sole nor is not awed by conquists of word's law . . . :* from *Merchant of Venice* (V. i. 83–84): "The man that hath no music in himself, / Nor is not moved with concord of sweet sounds. . . ." See Peery, p. 251. The accuser here, however, is Shylock-Shaun-Justius (whereas in the play the line accuses, and refers to, Shylock), who defends the Mosaic Law and the letter over the spirit and accuses Shem-Mercius-Portia of having "no moses" in his soul. Joyce's Mercius, however, displays the quality of mercy. Shylock-Shaun, living by the letter of the law, says in 167.28: "My unchanging word is sacred."

168.11   *jack by churl:* echoes Demetrius in *A Midsummer Night's Dream:* "Follow? Nay, I'll go with thee, cheek by jowl" (III. ii. 338). Cf. 215.19, "cheap by foul." Like Demetrius and Lysander fighting over Helena, Burrus and Caseous have been fighting over Margareen in these pages.

Book I, Chapter 7

170.03   *for four testers one groat:* as in, perhaps, Greene's *A Groatsworth of Wit.* See entries for 360.36 and 414.20–419.08.

171.15   *the tragic jester:* the gravedigger and Yorick in *Hamlet.* Shem-Joyce is here (in the "Shem" chapter) identified as the tragic jester. See 190.19, "boskop of Yorek."

172.05   *John's is a different butcher's:* Shaun is seen as the butcher (and Shem as the baker). Since Shem is Shakespeare the Bard, Shaun is identified with his father, John Shakespeare, who was reportedly a butcher. Aubrey, in his *Brief Lives,* claims John Shakespeare was a butcher; Joyce refers to John Shakespeare as such in *Ulysses* (e.g., *U*, 213).

172.28   *he was in his bardic memory low:* Shem has the memory of a poet; and he is low because he holds the memory of the Bard in disrespect (like the Cad-Joyce, trying to overthrow the "Shikespower" in 47.19). Shaun accuses Shem of being "aware of no other shaggspick, other Shakhisbeard" (177.32), of ignoring the memory of the national poet.

173.34   *with a meticulosity bordering on the insane:* as with "metheg in your midness" (32.05), Shaun accuses Shem-Joyce of madness—here, of madness in the method. Joyce's methods *were* full of medieval meticulousness. This is the first of a number of times in this chapter that Shaun charges Shem with madness. See entry for 32.05 and chapter 6 of this study. Cf. lines 177.10, 179.24, 182.07, 189.30 and 191.01.

174.09–10   *clasp shakers (the handtouch which is speech without words):* again, shaking hands and *La ci darem la mano;* see also entries for 28.04, 96.23, and 535.11.

174.28   *rival teams of slowspiers counter quicklimers:* perhaps, in the names of these football teams, a play on the name "shake-speare." In any case, this confrontation between brothers, between angels (Michael) and devils (Nick), ends with a lovely result and score: "All saints beat Belial! Mickil Goals to Nichil!" (175.05; *nihil*).

The game may be between England and Ireland, since Shakespeare is the English national poet and "quicklimers" are the Irish, who threw quicklime into Parnell's eyes. Joyce wrote, in "The Shade of Parnell," that "the citizens of Castlecomer threw quicklime in his eyes. . . . Within a year he died of a broken heart" (*Critical Writings*, pp. 227–28).

175.05–28: A new version of the earlier Ballad of Persse O'Reilly and a review of history as the "Notpossible!" (175.05)—history as gossip and speculations, the exploration of all possibilities and misunderstandings. The song concludes with a call to "list" to this poison poured in the porches of our *oreilles*. "*Hirp! Hirp!* [*Hark! List!*] *for their Missed Understandings! chirps the Ballat of Perce-Oreille.*" See also chapter 2.

175.14 *Not yet Witchywitchy of Wench struck Fire of his Heath:* Macbeth and the witches on the blasted heath, combined with "Mishe mishe" and the burning bush.

175.20 *where theirs is Will there's his Wall:* maybe a variant of the traditional Shakespearean pun which Stephen Dedalus presents as: "If others have their will Ann hath a way" (*U*, 191). Puns on "Will" occur a number of times in the sonnets (e.g., sonnets 134, 135, and 136).

177.04 *his pawdry's purgatory was more than a nigger bloke could bear:* the purgatory of Shem's "Our Father" is that of the ghost of Hamlet's own *padre*, "doomed for a certain term to walk the night" in purgatory. For Hamlet, also, this revelation was too much to bear. That Joyce associated father and purgatory with *Hamlet* is seen in Stephen Dedalus's lines: "Nine lives are taken off for his father's one, Our Father who art in purgatory. Khaki Hamlets don't hesitate to shoot" (*U*, 187).

"Paddy's Purgatory," in Irish legend, is Ireland.

177.20–22 *one Davy Browne-Nolan his heavenlaid twin (this hambone dogpoet pseudoed himself under the hangname he gave himself of Bethgelert):* ham and bacon again; "hambone" is also *jambon*, French for "ham" (see also "beacons and hamjambo" in 199.16–20). Ham and Bacon, Shakespeare-Hamlet and Francis Bacon, are the same (or so the Baconians claimed), or are Bruno-like ("Browne-Nolan," Bruno the Nolan) twins, disguised under a pseudonym-agnomen ("pseudoed" and "hangname"). Shakespeare is a "dogpoet" because he is "the artist, like the God [dog] of the creation" (*P*, 215). Hamlet also had a pseudonym-agnomen; Glasheen points out (pp. 28 and 93): "According to Saxo Grammaticus, Hamlet was brought up under a dog's name to save him from his uncle, Feng [Claudius]. . . . Gelert was a faithful dog, wrongly slain in a Welsh story. His grave is called Bethgelert." Thus, "this hambone dogpoet" with the agnomen of Bethgelert is Hamlet-Shakespeare.

Poet William Robert Spencer wrote a popular ballad about this faithful dog in Welsh legend, titled "Beth-Gelert, the Good Greyhound." "Hambone poet" and "Bethgelert" are entries in Joyce's *Read 'Em and Weep* index in *The Index Manuscript*. See Rose, *The Index Manuscript*, pp. 239, 241.

177.23–32 *Shem was always blaspheming, so holy writ, Billy . . . his Ballade Imaginaire . . . by Maistre Sheames de la Plume . . . that he was . . . aware of no other shaggspick, other Shakhisbeard:* Shaun accuses Shem of being "in his bardic memory low" (172.28), of trying to play Master Will Shakespeare, the Penman, with such artistic egotism as to dare to shake the Bard's beard and brook no other Shakespeare as his rival. The accusation brings to mind both Greene's similar charge, in the *Groatsworth,* that Shakespeare was "in his owne conceit the onely Shake-scene in a countrie," and Nora's statement that "There's only one man he [Joyce]'s got to get the better of now, and that's that Shakespeare."

Shaking one's beard as a symbol of lack of respect calls to mind two passages from *Hamlet:* Hamlet's "Who calls me villain? breaks my pate across? / Plucks off my beard and blows it in my face?" (II. ii. 557–58) and Claudius's "You must not think / That we are made of stuff so flat and dull / That we can let our beard be shook with danger, / And think it pastime" (IV. vii. 30–33).

181.01 *trying to copy the stage Englesemen he broughts their house down:* Shaun charges Shem—as Robert Greene charged Shakespeare—of plagiarizing the English dramatists. See entry for 181.14–17.

181.14–17 *What do you think Vulgariano did but study with stolen fruit how cutely to copy all their various styles of signature so as one day to utter an epical forged cheque on the public for his own private profit:* an accusation of forgery that brings to mind the Shakespearean forgers, especially William Henry Ireland (see entry for 565.12), who also tried to copy various signatures for his own profit. If the "epical forged cheque" is *Ulysses,* Joyce is being accused of pillaging Homer, Shakespeare, and others for his own profit.

The charge here (as well as the language) is, again, reminiscent of the *Groatsworth.*

181.29–30 *His jymes is out of job, would sit and write:* "Jymes" Joyce-Shem, out of patience (like Job) and out of a job, wants to be an author, but, alas, "The time is out of joint. O cursèd spite, / That ever I was born to set it right [sit and write]" (*Ham.* I. v. 188–89).

181.35 *the excommunicated Drumcondriac, nate Hamis:* Shem (an excommunicated Irishman) as Hamlet, perhaps.

182.07 *by the beerlitz in his mathness and his educandees:* the Berlitz Method (Joyce taught foreign "educandees" at Berlitz schools) in his madness. The charge by Shaun of Shem's madness echoes both Polonius's "Though this be madness, yet there's method in't" and "metheg in your midness" in the *Wake* (32.05), since "metheg," or metheglin, is mead or beer.

182.19–21 *in the act of reciting old Nichiabelli's monolook interyerear, Hanno, o Nonanno, acce'l brubblemm'as:* Shem-Nick-Machiavelli reciting this *monologue intérieur (Ulysses* perhaps) becomes Hamlet reciting his own monologue, an Italianate version of "To be or not to be [or, they have or do not have], that is the question"—*Hanno, o non anno, aqui la problema es.* Cf. entry for 123.31–32.

183.11-12 *doubtful eggshells:* perhaps a reference to Hamlet, who bemoaned his own doubtfulness and hesitancy, in contrast to Fortinbras, who dared "all that fortune, death, and danger dare, / Even for an eggshell" (IV. iv. 52–53).

183.26 *shopkeepers' wives:* Shakespeare's wives; this reading is verified in 539.06, where the Bard is again called "Shopkeeper": "Daunty, Gouty and Shopkeeper" (Dante, Goethe and Shakespeare); see also "shopkeepers" in 128.16. The line occurs within a lovely catalog describing Joyce's works (". . . upset latten tintacks [upset Latin syntax] . . . once current puns, quashed quotatoes, messes of mottage [misquoted and mashed potatoes, messes of words and pottage] . . .") and the characters in them, such as "fallen lucifers . . . washerwomen's, shopkeepers' wives, merry widows, ex nuns, vice abbess's, pro virgins, super whores," and so on.

Since England is also a "notion of shopkeepers" (128.16), the line can be generalized to mean Englishmen's wives.

184.21 *Currageen moss and blaster of Barry's:* in Joyce's plaster of Paris are included Henry Mossop and Spranger Barry, rival Shakespearean actors in Dublin's Crow Street (105.25) and Smock Alley (147.32, 105.25, 60.31) Theatres. The theaters were also fierce rivals in the Dublin worldstage. The passage seems to deal with Dublin theaters, as Thomas Sheridan, actor and manager of the Smock Alley, is mentioned in 184.24. See also 569.30, in which Messrs. Mossop and Barry assume the roles of the two gentlemen of Verona.

184.24 *Sharadan's Art of Panning:* a reference to Thomas Sheridan, actor and manager of Dublin's Smock Alley Theatre, where the famous production of *Othello* took place, in which Iago's lines about the "green-eyed monster" (III. iii. 166) were rendered instead as the "green-eyed lobster." Sheridan played Othello and an actor named Layfield was Iago. See entries for 88.15 and 249.03. Sheridan wrote a two-volume work called *The Art of Reading* (1775).

184.25, 35 *Litty fun Letty fan Leven* and *Layteacher Baudwin:* Glasheen claims that references to Leticia, Lettice, Lettuce, or Letty are to Leticia Greene, wife of Thomas Greene. See entry for 161.30.

Thomas Greene, who lived with his wife in Stratford, was the town clerk in 1614; local records suggest that Shakespeare and Greene were probably kinsmen, and that the Greenes stayed at New Place (the Shakespeares' home) in 1609. See Schoenbaum, p. 35.

There may also be an echo in 184.25 of *Cosi Fan Tutte*.

187.21–195.06 *in mercy or justice:* the following eight pages contain a confrontation between Shaun as the fixed, standard, legalistic power of Justice (Justius) and Shem as mercy (Mercius); as such, the brothers take on the roles of Shylock and Portia. See chapter 6 and entries for 191.02, 192.17, and 193.31.

187.22 *Tamstar Ham of Tenman:* Hamlet, Prince of Denmark.

188.27 *Cold caldor!:* perhaps Macbeth, thane of Glamis and of Cawdor. See also entry for 250.14–18.

The phrase is an oxymoron, since *caldor* (Latin) means heat—thus, cold heat. Cf. 189.14.

189.06 *small peace in ppenmark:* small comfort in the artist's world, where fame (the mark of the pen) is slow in coming; situation as rotten as in the state of Denmark.

189.14 *Chalwador:* perhaps Cawdor again. See entry for 188.27.

189.28 *premature gravedigger:* Shem as *Hamlet*'s clown, digging up Yorick. These pages are filled with references to clowns, jesters, and gravediggers— e.g., in 171.15, "tragic jester" and in 190.19, "boskop of Yorek."

190.19 *boskop of Yorek:* this description of Shem refers to both the ecclesiast Yorick (or perhaps the Bishop of York) in Sterne's *Tristram Shandy* and the "gravedigger" (189.28) in *Hamlet*, digging up the old skull of Yorick, the "tragic jester" (171.15). According to *Webster's*, "Boskop man" was "a late Pleistocene southern African man, [probably] ancestral to modern Bushmen and Hottentots"; in German, *Böse* = devil or fiend, while *Kopf* = head. "Boskop," therefore, can mean prehistoric skull, ancestors, or skull of the devil (the Vice, Clown, jester); I take "boskop of Yorek" to mean skull of Yorick, ancestors of yore, and mind of a devil. It is a very full and functional portmanteau word.

In *Hamlet*, the gravedigging Clown identifies this "boskop of Yorek": "Yorick's skull, the king's jester" (V. i. 169).

190.21 *your bourne of travail:* the limit of labor, the labor of birth ("born" and travail), the limits of travel, and Hamlet's "the undiscovered country, from whose bourn / No traveller returns" (III. i. 79–80). See also entries for 31.32, 365.04–5, and 379.35.

191.02 *for the laugh of Scheekspair:* for the laugh (and life) of Shakespeare; and for the love of Jesus, who turned the other cheek. This is particularly appropriate in this passage (the Justius-Mercius confrontation), since Shem as Mercius here turns the other cheek to Shaun's accusations and to the blow of his deathwand. See also entries for 145.24, 257.19–20, and 229.36–230.01.

In context, Shaun-Justius is asking Shem-Mercius to help him find the right words, as only a bard could: "Will you for the laugh of Scheekspair just help mine with the epithet?"

191.14 *that other, Immaculatus, from head to foot, sir, that pure one:* Shaun-Stanislaus Joyce is the pure one of the twins, and the one resembling HCE; thus, he also is referred to by "cap-a-pe": "from head to foot." Cf. in *Hamlet*: "[Armed] My lord, from head to foot" (I. ii. 228).

192.14 *Reynaldo:* Polonius's servant.

192.17 *to give you your pound of platinum and a thousand thongs a year:* Shylock's pound of flesh. These pages concern Justice and Mercy.

192.20–21 *(fame would come to you twixt a sleep and a wake) and leave to lie till Paraskivee and the cockcock crows for Danmark:* this refers to Joyce, Jesus, Hamlet, and Shakespeare. Fame will eventually come to Joyce between a sleep (*Ulysses*—Molly and Bloom's sleep) and the *Wake*. Like Jesus, Joyce is a martyr crucified to his art ("O, you were excruciated . . . to the cross of your own cruelfiction"), though he will be resurrected on the third day (so also thrice the cock crowed to Peter between Christ's own sleep and wake); the cock crows also in Denmark (King Hamlet's ghost "faded on the crowing of the cock" in I. i. 157), where Hamlet also struggles with the notions of death, sleep, wakes, and dreams. Also, a direct echo of Edmund's comment about his brother Edgar in *King Lear:* "Got 'tween asleep and wake" (I. ii. 15).

Joyce's prediction of the eventual wakening of his fame from the ashes is echoed elsewhere. See lines 201.11 and 114.20, and chapter 6 of this study.

In reference to "Danmark," Glasheen reminds us (p. 67) that *"Dan"* was the "eponymous ancestor of the Danes."

193.10 *to make you go green in the gazer: Othello*'s "green-eyed monster" (III. iii. 166) of jealousy. See McHugh, p. 193; see also entries for 88.15, 94.17, and 249.02–3.

193.10 *Do you hear what I'm seeing, hammet?:* Shaun addresses Shem as Hamlet-Hamnet (as well as "damn it"). Hamnet was the name of Shakespeare's only son, who died at age eleven; Stephen Dedalus links him with Prince Hamlet (*U*, 188).

193.12–28 *Come here, Herr Studiosus, till I tell you a wig in your ear. . . . It's secret! . . . I had it from Lamppost Shawe. . . . Sh! Shem, you are. Sh! You are mad!:* Shaun calls Shem to "List!" while pouring the poison of an earwig into his ear. He tells a secret started by Shaun the Post ("Lamppost Shawe") and spread from ear to ear, like Hosty's song. Shaun-Polonius at last whispers the secret in the porches of Shem's ears: "Sh! You are mad!" Here, then, is the most direct accusation of madness.

193.31 *MERCIUS: . . . My fault, his fault, a kingship through a fault:* Shem-Mercius's answer to Shaun-Justius's accusations is an acknowledgment of guilt (he calls himself Cain in the next line). This confession is a mixture of Richard III's "A horse, a horse, my kingdom for a horse!" (*R3* V. v. 7, 13) and the Catholic *Confiteor*'s *Mea culpa, mea culpa, mea maxima culpa,* translated in the English Confession as "through my fault, through my fault, through my most grievous fault." (A kingship through a fault also recalls the *felix culpa* and the Phoenix culprit.) Cf. 238.20, "May he colp, may he colp her, may he mixandmass colp her!"

Mercius and Justius in this *Wake* chapter come out of the context of *Merchant of Venice.* See chapter 6 of this study.

193.31–194.24: Hodgart argues (pp. 743–44) that this passage involves many references to *Macbeth*—most of which I find a bit obscure. However, 194.15 (see entry for that line) is possibly a reference to *Macbeth.*

194.15 *windblasted tree of the knowledge of beautiful andevil:* conflation of Eden's trees of Knowledge and of Good and Evil, and the "blasted heath" of *Macbeth* (I. iii. 77). Note also in 340.08, "bloasted tree." (A heath is also a species of tree.)

Book I, Chapter 8

197.18 *Don Dom Dombdomb and his wee follyo!:* HCE and his small sin, his wee folly. The passage speculates on what HCE's indiscretion or crime really was—"whatever it was they threed to make out he thried to two in the

Fiendish park" (whatever it was the three lipoleums tried to make out he tried to do to the two maggies in Phoenix Park). "What was it he did a tail at all on Animal Sendai?" (196.10, 19). Whatever it was, the "gossipaceous" washerwomen try "to make his private linen public" (196.16). However, the "wee follyo" is also Earwicker's small folio, equating Joycean manuscripts with Shakespearean ones. Tindall argues (p. 142) that, since "wee" is *oui*, the small folio is Joyce's yes-book, ending with Molly Bloom's great word. Thus, the "wee follyo" is *Ulysses*, and Victor Bérard's Ulysses, the "gran Phenician rover" (197.31), is HCE.

199.16–20 *her meddery eygs, yayis, and staynish beacons on toasc and a cupenhave so weeshywashy of Greenland's tay or a dzoupgan of Kaffue mokau an sable or Sikiang sukry . . . . and a shinkobread (hamjambo, bana?) for to plaise that man hog:* more Shakespearean breakfasts for HCE. Eggs, Danish bacon (Hamlet and Sir Francis) on toast, a cup and a half ("cupenhave" or Copenhagen) of wishy-washy Greenland tea, some coffee mocha (or, perhaps, sugary Sikiang tea) and a ham sandwich, a "hamjambo shinkobread." (*Schinkenbrot* = "ham sandwich" in German; *jambon* = "ham" in French.) See also entries for 161.31, 163.06, 177.20–22, and 318.20–21.

AWN, o. s. 8 (Dec. 1962), p. 3, points out that *Hajambo, bwana?* is a popular greeting in Kiswahili. See Rose, *The Index Manuscript*, p. 283. McHugh notes (p. 199) that *yayi* is Kiswahili for egg.

200.09 *Madame Delba to Romeoreszk: Romeo and Juliet*, and Gounod's opera based on it. Dame Melba was a famous Australian operatic soprano who sang Juliet to Jean de Reszke's Romeo; see Hodgart, p. 751 and Glasheen, p. 190.

200.33 *Odet! Odet!:* Oyez! Oyez! and List, list! The call to listen, from one washerwoman gossiping to another. Several lines later (201.03–4): "Listen now. Are you listening? Yes, yes! Idneed I am! Tarn your ore ouse! Essonne inne!" (Turn your *oreilles!* Listen in!).

201.05–6 *By earth and the cloudy but I badly want a brandnew bankside, bedamp and I do, and a plumper at that!: RES* observes (p. 56): "Bankside was a district within the borough of Southwark on the South Bank of the Thames, and the site of most of the Elizabethan public theatres, including the Hope, the Rose, the Globe, and the Swan. . . . In 1596 Shakespeare was living in or near the Bankside."

Atherton sees in this line a complaint by Joyce, the rival of Shakespeare, about his inability to find an audience, like that of Bankside or Blackfriars, to appreciate his work: "What Joyce is saying is that he wishes the Liffey had a South Bank where literature was appreciated as it was by Shakespeare's Thames," writes Atherton (p. 163).

201.11 *winter's doze:* possibly a reference to *The Winter's Tale*.

203.14 *Neya, narev, nen, nonni, nos!:* negatives and names of rivers are mixed here with Ophelia's song ("Hey non nony, nony, hey nony" in IV. v. 164). Ophelia is associated with rivers because she drowned in one. See also the entries for 307.F8 and 203.28–30.

In 1925 Marie Ney played Ophelia at the Old Vic, with Ernest Milton in the role of Hamlet.

203.28–30 *Afrothdizzying galbs . . . vierge violetian . . . throw those laurals now on her daphdaph teasesong:* references in this passage (on Isabel and ALP) to flowers strewn on a river maiden and to a song recall Ophelia's silly song (see entry for 203.14), her death by water, and the flowers she herself strews: "There's fennel for you, and columbines. There's rue for you. . . . There's a daisy. I would give you some violets, but they withered all when my father died" (IV. v. 179–183). See entry for 143.26. The passage between pages 202 and 205 is about ALP as the Liffey, the water woman ("Are you in the swim or are you out" in 204.27); references to Ophelia and to flowers therefore seem appropriate.

203.29 *Letty Lerck:* Letitia Greene, perhaps. See entry for 161.30.

205.18 *their dinners of cheeckin and beggin:* more Shakespearean foods: chicken and bacon, Shakespeare and Bacon. Like "shakespill and eggs," or like cheese and butter, these may be disguised variants of the same things, like Shakespeare (or 191.02, "Scheekspair") and Bacon, according to the Baconians. Cf. 257.20, "Cheekspeer.

205.25 *Phoenix Tavern:* the "Porter-House" (see in 204.09, "porter-house") inn-playhouse is also (besides being the Globe, the Gaiety, etc.) the Phoenix Theatre, an Elizabethan playhouse in Drury Lane. See also entry for 219.02.

207.24 *Leste, before Julia sees her!:* Quick (Italian, *lesto*), before Julia notices! and *Julius Caesar.*

208.16 *fancyfastened, free:* possibly Oberon's "In maiden meditation, fancy free" (*MND* II. i. 164). See McHugh, p. 208.

208.29 *the dowce little delia:* perhaps ALP as sweet little Delia Bacon. Like Biddy the Hen, ALP is carrying her "zakbag, a shammy mailsack" (206.09) and trying to vindicate her husband; so also Delia Bacon was attempting to vindicate her own HCE, her namesake Francis Bacon. See also entries for 111.05 and 423.25.

209.14–15 *I aubette my bearb it's worth while poaching on! Shake it up, do, do!:* a reference to the popular legend that Shakespeare ("Shake it up") was arrested for deer-poaching on Sir Thomas Lucy's estate in Stratford, and, as a result, had to leave Stratford for London; he was, thus, indirectly propelled into his dramatic profession. "Aubette my bearb" could contain an allusion to John Aubrey's (1626–97) *Brief Lives*, which included a brief biography of Shakespeare and was one of the early sources of Shakespearean biography and legend. See entry for 604.19.

210.25 *Magpeg Woppington:* one of the recipients of ALP's gifts is famed Dublin Shakespearean actress Peg Woffington. See entries for 413.02, 436.09–11, 577.16, 579.17, and 586.12, as well as chapter 3 of this study, for more on Woffington.

210.34–35 *a putty shovel for Terry the Puckaun:* among the presents and gifts catalogued here is one for famed Shakespearean actress Ellen Terry, who at the age of eight played Puck in Charles Kean's famous 1856 production of *A Midsummer Night's Dream* at the Princess Theatre. See *RES*, p. 546 and Glasheen, p. 280; see also entries for 212.15 and 215.19.

211.08 *Camilla, Dromilla, Ludmilla, Mamilla:* these may be female versions of male characters in Shakespeare's plays; Camillo (in *The Winter's Tale*),

Dromio (in *Comedy of Errors*), and Mamillius (in *Winter's Tale* also) seem to correspond. The closest to Ludmilla is either Lucillius (in *Timon of Athens* and also in *Julius Caesar*), or Lucullus (in *Timon*). Cf. "Capilla, Rubrilla, and Melcamomilla" in 492.13.

211.35–36 *for Who-is-silvier—Where-is-he?:* among ALP's presents is one for a character whose identity and location are unknown. He may be Shakespeare (or someone Shakespearean), since the Bard wrote the song that starts: "Who is Silvia? What is she? . . ." *(TGV* IV. ii. 39). See Hodgart, p. 749.

The reference may be to Sylvia Beach of Shakespeare and Company. See Glasheen, p. 276.

212.15 *She gave them ilcka madre's daughter a moonflower and a bloodvein:* ALP sems to have gifts for everyone, for every mother's son or, as in this case, for every mother's daugther. "Ilcka madre's daughter" may echo Peter Quince's lines, "Come, sit down, every mother's son, and rehearse your parts" (*MND* III. i. 64–65). See entry for 359.31–360.16.

214.32 *you hamble creature:* a humble Hamlet, perhaps. One of the sources for *Hamlet* was Belleforest's *Histoires Tragiques*, an English translation of which was entitled *The Hystorie of Hamblet* (1608). See J. Dover Wilson, Introduction to the *New Shakespeare Hamlet* (Cambridge: Cambridge Univ. Press, 1968), p. xvi.

215.04–8 *Die eve, little eve, die! . . . Forgivemequick, I'm going! Bubye! And you, pluck your watch, forgetmenot:* as evening falls, the Liffey-ALP reaches the sea and dies, recalling Nuvoletta's suicide in chapter 6 and Ophelia's death. Here, too, are flowers ("forgetmenot"). ALP's farewell words ("forgetmenot") are similar to those in the last lines of the *Wake*, "mememormee!" (628.14), which echo the parting words by the ghost of Hamlet's father to Hamlet: "Remember me!" (I. v. 91).

215.19 *He married his markets, cheap by foul:* the reference is to HCE (the "Etrurian Catholic heathen" in 215.20). "Cheap by foul" echoes Demetrius in *A Midsummer Night's Dream:* "Follow! Nay, I'll go with thee, cheek by jowl" (III. ii. 338). Cf. 168.11, "jack by churl."

215.35 *A tale told of Shaun or Shem:* recalls Macbeth's "a tale / Told by an idiot" (V. v. 26). See entry for 515.07; also lines 275.24, 324.05, 396.23, 563.26, and 597.08.

Book II, Chapter 1

219.02 *Feenichts Playhouse:* HCE's tavern (cf. 205.25, "Phoenix Tavern") has been transformed into a theatre, the Phoenix Playhouse. The Phoenix was a famous Elizabethan playhouse in St.-Giles-in-the-Fields, adjoining Drury Lane. See *RES*, p. 633.

The first pages of this chapter are rich with theatre terms which describe the playhouse; the form is that of a playbill announcement: opening time, bar and conveniences, entrance fee, and so on. See chapter 3 of this study for a detailed explication of the chapter's opening paragraph.

219.13 *Caesar-in-Chief:* God is here referred to as a Julius Caesar, Caesar *le chef.*

219.13 *On. Sennet.:* The *Mime of Mick, Nick and the Maggies* opens with a Shakespearean stage direction, a trumpet blast signaling a scene opening. Seemingly, Joyce has a Brechtian sense of theater, always insisting on our awareness that the fare we are witnessing is theater, a staged drama, a reenactment.

Since the central play in this chapter is *Macbeth*, here is an example of a Shakespearean stage direction (*Mac.* III. i. 2): "Sennet sounded. Enter Macbeth as King, Lady Macbeth, Lennox, Ross, Lords, and Attendants."

219.14 *As played to the Adelphi:* the Elizabethan Phoenix Playhouse (see entry for 219.02) appears to have its Irish reincarnation in Dublin's Adelphi Theatre, where the mime is being played. See Senn, p. 8. The Adelphi later became the Queen's—perhaps another reason for "Queen's Mum" two lines later.

There was, however, also an Adelphi Theatre in London, which was famous for its Shakespearean productions. See, for example, *RES*, p. 546 on its 1905 *Midsummer Night's Dream.*

219.15–16 *Before all the King's Hoarsers with all the Queen's Mum:* "humpteen dumpteen" (219.15) and his fall are here; Humpty Dumpty is HCE, and is often associated with King Hamlet and Shakespeare. "King's Hoarsers" and "Queen's Mum" might also set the stage for King Hamlet's hoarse clamor for vengeance and the silent guilt of his queen, Gertrude. More relevant to the local theatre metaphor, however, is the reference to the King's Men and the Queen's Men, two major Elizabethan theatre companies. The King's Men (also known as the Chamberlain's Men) was the company to which Shakespeare and Burbage belonged, and which owned the Globe. Shakespeare wrote his great works for this group. The Queen's Men (also, Queen Elizabeth's Men) were less enduring (1583–1603). See also 285.L2, "Arthurgink's hussies and Everguin's men."

"Queen Mum," of course, is the popular British term for the Queen Mother.

219.18–19 *The Mime of Mick, Nick and the Maggies:* Play at the Phoenix, "in four tubbloids" (219.17–18), explicated in chapter 3 of this study.

220.25–26 *(in the programme about King Ericus of Schweden and the spirit's whispers in his magical helmet), cap-a-pipe with watch and topper, coat, crest and supporters . . . :* the dramatic fare for the evening, as announced by stage manager "Mr Makeall Gone" (220.25—Michael Gunn), resembles *Hamlet*, in which the ghost (the "spirit") of King Hamlet of Denmark (like King Eric of Sweden) walks onstage and whispers ("List, list, o list!") through his helmet ("He wore his beaver up" in I. ii. 230). Horatio describes him as "A figure like your [Hamlet's] father, / Armèd at point exactly, cap-a-pe [head to foot]" (I. ii. 199–200)—thus, "cap-a-pipe." See entries for 221.29, 58.25, 78.05, 583.29, 619.27, 622.30.

"Coat, crest and supporters," Rose notes, are the "three most important components in a complete display of armorial bearings" (*The Index Manuscript*, p. 361).

220.34 *Poopinheavin:* this portmanteau word describes a ship in a storm and a heaving poop (a "quemdam supercargo" in the previous line), but also God-the-Father (Pop—or Pope—in Heaven, like Emily Dickinson's "Papa above!"), Heaven, and King Hamlet's capital, Copenhagen. This falls within a passage describing HCE as King Hamlet, who is not quite yet a "pop in heaven," but "Our Father who art in purgatory" (*U*, 187). References to *Hamlet* are often accompanied by references to Copenhagen; see, for example "old hopeinhaven" in 143.10 (hope in heaven, Copenhagen, and a hopeful harbor), "cope of heaven" in 248.25, and "hopenhaven" in 478.16.

There are many references to Copenhagen in the *Wake;* it is, for example, the name of Duke Wellington's big white horse. Noted in this study, however, are only those references to Copenhagen which seem to relate to *Hamlet.*

221.29 *Kopay pibe by Kappa Pedersen:* another reference to King Hamlet, armed "cap-a-pe" (I. ii. 200). See entries for 58.25, 78.05, 220.25–26, 583.29, 619.27, and 622.30.

Here, HCE-King Hamlet melds into the Cad with the pipe. "Kappa Pedersen" combines "cap-a-pe" with Kapp and Peterson, a firm of Dublin pipe and tobacco makers (Glasheen, p. 152); thus, "cap-a-pipe" (220. 26).

222.01 *the pit:* one of a number of references to Elizabethan theatres in this chapter. See chapter 3 of this study.

223.07 *Viola:* the heroine of *Twelfth Night.*

223.19 *Arrest thee, scaldbrother!:* Shaun-Chuff's entering words (in this scene) to his poet-brother (*skald* in Danish is poet), Shem-Glugg, echo *Macbeth's* "Aroint thee, witch!" (I. iii. 6). See also entries for 406.13 and 492.34.

224.08 *Towhere byhangs ourtales:* in *As You Like It,* Jaques notes: ". . . from hour to hour we rot and rot; / And thereby hangs a tale" (II. vii. 28). In *Othello* the clown says, "O, thereby hangs a tail," and the musician asks, "Whereby hangs a tale, sir?" (III. i. 8–9). Cf. line 143.15.

224.10 *A dire, O dire!:* "Adieu, adieu! Remember me!" (*Ham.* I. v. 91, 110).

225.35 *The flossies all and mossies all they drooped upon her draped brimfall . . . :* the Floras and Issy here—like Nuvoletta in book I, chapter 6, and like Ophelia—wilt and die because they are rejected by men. "Poor Isa" (226.04) is clearly related to Ophelia, for in the next two pages appear many references to Ophelia.

226.04–5 *Poor Isa sits a glooming . . . around her swan's:* here—in the "swan"—is Joyce's hint of Shakespearean references again, especially with Issy-Ophelia.

226.10–12 *Bring tansy, throw myrtle, strew rue, rue, rue. She is fading out like Journee's clothes so you can't see her now:* Ophelia says: "There's rosemary, that's for remembrance. . . . And there is pansies, that's for thoughts. . . . There's fennel for you, and columbines. There's rue for you, and here's some for me. . . . O, you must wear your rue with a difference" (IV. v. 174–82). The second line seems to describe Ophelia's death, which Gertrude relates: "[She] / Fell in the weeping brook. Her clothes spread wide, / And mermaid-like awhile they bore her up. . . . Till that her garments, heavy with their drink, /

Pulled the poor wretch from her melodious lay / To muddy death" (IV. vii. 174–82).

Issy-Ophelia also fades out like the close of day *(la journée):* "like Journee's clothes," at the close of her journey.

226.12 *Still we know how Day the Dyer works:* Day the Dyer would be the poet-playwright-god-creator himself. The line echoes Shakespeare's sonnet 111: "My nature is subdued / To what it works in, like the dyer's hand."

226.32 *W waters the fleurettes of novembrance:* before her death by water, Ophelia handed out flowers of remembrance: "There's rosemary, that's for remembrance. Pray you, love, remember" (IV. v. 174–75). As McHugh notes (p. 226), rosemary's purple flowers bloom in November.

227.01–2 *The many wiles of Winsure: The Merry Wives of Windsor.*

227.14 *Beatrice . . . and Rue:* among the seven rainbow girls (spelling W-O-B-N-I-A-R) are two Shakespearean heroines: Beatrice of "McAdoo about nothing" (see entry for 227.33) and *Hamlet'*s Ophelia.

227.15–16 *for they are the florals, from foncey and pansey to papavere's blush, foresake-me-nought:* the rainbow girls, or the Floras, are Ophelia's flowers, such as the pansy ("And there is pansies") and the forget-me-not ("There's rosemary, that's for remembrance. Pray you, love, remember" in IV. v. 173–74).

227.29–30 *a puck on the plexus: Midsummer Night's Dream*'s Puck, perhaps.

227.33 *McAdoo about nothing: Much Ado about Nothing.* "Beatrice" (227.14) is also here.

In the First Folio (1623), Shakespeare's play is entitled *Much Adoo about Nothing.* McAdoo is the name given in the *Wake* to one of the seven sacraments discussed in the passage—in this case Matrimony; thus, "Adoo" might stand for "I do."

228.11 *the coriolano: Coriolanus.* In illustrating "silence, exile, and cunning" by this line, "the bruce, the coriolano and the ignacio," Joyce is alluding to the silence of Bruce, the exile of Coriolanus, and the cunning of Ignatius Loyola.

229.08–9 *nation of sheepcopers:* England as a "nation of shopkeepers." This passage refers to Joyce's rejection by the English press, "the old sniggering publicking press" with its "satiety of arthurs" (Society of Authors). Instead, it is the nation of the "Shopkeeper," whose national poet is Shakespeare, referred to elsewhere in the *Wake* also as Shopkeeper; see entries for 128.15–17, 183.26, and 539.05–9.

229.14–15 *From the Mermaids' Tavern:* this phrase, occurring in an ordered list of references to episodes in *Ulysses,* refers to the "Sirens" chapter (". . . Skilly and Carubdish. A Wondering Wreck. From the Mermaids' Tavern. . ."), which takes place in a bar where the two barmaids are the "sirens," or, here, mermaids. The reference is also to the Mermaid Tavern, a 17th-century London tavern on Bread Street, Cheapside, and the most famous gathering place for actors, playwrights, and literary figures of the time. Shakespearean legend has long held that Shakespeare, Ben Jonson, Beaumont, Fletcher, Carew, Donne, and Inigo Jones used to gather there often for drink, wit, and carousing. Thomas Coryate, in *Crudities* (1611),

referred to the feastings at the Mermaid Tavern by "the right worshipfull fraternity of Sirenaical gentlemen." This verbal correspondence to *Ulysses*'s "Sirens" may have been noticed by Joyce, perhaps persuading him to refer to his episode here as "From the Mermaids' Tavern."
See *RES*, p. 531 and Schoenbaum, pp. 294–96.

229.21 *her Lettyshape, his gummer:* Letitia Green as ALP, Glugg's "gummer" (mother and grandma).

229.36–230.01 *the grusomehed's yoeureeke:* while Archimedes' *Eureka!* may be here, more likely the reference is to the skull of *Hamlet's* Yorick—thus, a "gruesome head." This head gets ambushed on the cheekside in the following line: "he was ambothed ... first on the cheekside ... and ... over on the owld jowly side" (see 191.02, "for the laugh of Scheekspair").

230.05–7 *eggspilled him out of his homety dometry ... because all his creature comfort was an omulette:* Glugg is expelled ("eggspilled") from his home, the home of HCE-Humpty-Dumpty, and feels as alienated as *Hamlet* ("omulette"). Shakespeare and King Hamlet were also displaced from their rightful places by Bacon and Claudius. See entries for 161.31 and 59.30–32.

230.35 *Remember thee, castle throwen?:* Glugg-Shem-Joyce, exiled (see entry for 230.05), feeds on the memory of his castle and throne, echoing words by Hamlet. The Ghost's parting line to Hamlet was "Remember me," to which Hamlet answered: "Remember thee? ... Remember thee? / Yea, from the table of my memory ..." (I. v. 91–98). See entry for 628.14.

According to Hodgart (p. 740), the line combines the *Hamlet* reference with a George Moore melody.

232.27–28 *Old cocker, young crowy, sifadda, sosson:* HCE is the old cocker, the usurping son is the young crow—like father, like son ("sifadda, sosson"). Joyce's usage of "crow" for the usurping son may derive from Robert Greene's accusation of Shakespeare as a usurper of other people's plays: "an upstart crow beautified with our feathers" (in the *Groatsworth of Wit*). In his notes for the 1912 *Hamlet* lecture at Trieste, Joyce misremembers the quote as "an upstart crow beautiful with our feathers" (William H. Quillan, "Composition of Place: Joyce's Notes on the English Drama," *James Joyce Quarterly* 13, no. 1 [Fall 1975]: 4–26).

233.19–21 *letting punplays pass to ernest: / —Haps thee jaoneofergs?:* perhaps "ernest ... jaoneofergs" refers to Freudian-Shakespeare critic Ernest Jones, author of *Hamlet and Oedipus* (Oedipus may be alluded to in "rex of regums" in 233.17).

234.11–12 *childfather from tonsor's tuft to almonder's toe:* a father from head to toe, and an extreme variant of "cap-a-pe," head to foot (King Hamlet was "Armed ... from top to toe" in I. ii. 227–28). See also entries for 58.25, 220.25, etc. As Joyce says elsewhere in the *Wake*, "every inch of an immortal" (152.34—echoing, of course, King Lear).

The line also recalls Lady Macbeth's "unsex me here, / And fill me from crown to the toe top-full / Of direst cruelty" (*Mac.* I. v. 39–41).

236.08 *Saint Tibble's Day:* "Tibbs Eve," Lewis Theobald, etc. See Atherton, pp. 69–70, and chapter 6 of this study.

237.12 *we herehear, aboutobloss, O coelicola, thee salutamt:* one of many references in the *Wake* to Julius Caesar or to Shakespeare's play of that name. *Ave, Caesar, morituri te salutant* was the salute with which his gladiators and his army greeted Caesar: "Hail, Caesar, we who are about to die, salute you." See entry for 167.23–24.

238.23 *List!:* List, list, O List!

242.31 *allinall:* HCE is here referred to by the same term as Shakespeare, the creator-father, was in *Ulysses:* "The truth is midway, [John Eglinton] affirmed. He is the ghost and the prince. He is all in all. / —He is, Stephen said. The boy of act one is the mature man of act five. All in all" (*U*, 212). The references originate from *Hamlet* itself, in which Hamlet speaks of his father: "'A was a man, take him for all in all, / I shall not look upon his like again" (I. ii. 187–88). Cf. line 154.05.

245.18–24 *Darkpark's acoo with sucking loves. Rosimund's by her wishing well. . . . Jacqueson's Island:* describes the dream world of the park, where lovers make romantic trysts at night. Thus, echoes of magical and romantic green worlds are appropriate—such as that of *As You Like It* (cf. 74.06 "greenwoods"), with reference here possibly to Rosalind and Jaques, or of *A Midsummer Night's Dream* (Bottom's "I will roar you as gently as any sucking dove" in I. ii. 75).

Jackson's Island is another famous literary-pastoral retreat—Huck's destination after his escape early in *Huckleberry Finn*.

246.10–12 *Ansighosa pokes in her potstill to souse at the sop be sodden enow and to hear to all the bubbles besaying: the coming man, the future woman:* and she goes and pokes in her pot and in her still to see if the soup is hot enough and to hear all the bubbles prophesying the coming man. This appears to be a reference to the witches' cauldron, especially since the next seven pages are teeming with references to *Macbeth*. The witches' "Double, double, toil and trouble" chant prophesies both the coming of the man Macbeth to the throne and the coming of the man born of no woman (Macduff) and of Birnam Wood to Dunsinane.

248.18 *when he beetles backwards:* echo of "the cliff / That beetles o'er his base into the sea" (*Ham.* I. iv. 71). Haines quotes the line on page 18 of *Ulysses*.

248.22–23 *Dunckle Dalton of matching wools. Shake hands through the thicketloch! Sweet swanwater!:* the next few pages are thick with references to Shakespeare ("Shake" and "swan") and especially to *Macbeth*, culminating in the arrival of Chuff-Macduff to wreak vengeance—like Birnam Wood to Dunsinane—on Glugg-Macbeth. See entries for 28.04 and 535.11. Duncan may also be here; and Birnam Wood is represented ("thicket" and the marching woods). See Hodgart, p. 746.

248.25 *cope of heaven:* Copenhagen and the roof of heaven. See entry for 143.10.

248.28–29 *Underwoods spells bushment's business. So if you sprig poplar you're bound to twig this:* more references to the marching woods and thickets of Birnam Wood. Macduff's soldiers are "bushmen" because their business is to be "under woods." These references culminate on page 250, when "burning would" comes to "dance inane."

249.02–3 *But if this could see with its backsight he'd be the grand old greeneyed lobster:* Othello and the "green-eyed monster" (III. iii. 166) of jealousy. Issy is implying that if Chuff-Othello could see her flirting with Glugg-Iago, he would be quite the jealous one. However, Glugg's reign is soon to end; in the guise of Macduff, Chuff will return (on page 250) to claim vengeance and reclaim his rightful place.

As Fritz Senn has pointed out (p. 5), Joyce is also referring to a particular and famous performance of *Othello* at Dublin's Smock Alley Theatre (see references to Smock Alley in 60.31, 105.25, 147.32) by Thomas Sheridan (in 184.24), actor and manager of the theatre. In this performance, Sheridan played Othello, while an actor named Layfield rendered Iago's lines about the "green-eyed monster" badly, and ended up saying, "It is a green-eyed lobster." See also entries for 88.15 and 184.24.

"If this could see with its backsight he'd be the grand old greeneyed lobster" also recalls Hamlet's line to Polonius: "if, like a crab [or lobster, perhaps], you could go backward" (II. ii. 202).

249.03–4 *He's my first viewmarc since Valentine:* Valentine was one of the *Two Gentlemen of Verona*. Cf. lines 20.34 and 569.30.

250.07 *ajew ajew:* "Adieu, adieu!" again.

250.14–18 *Yet's the time for being now, now, now. For a burning would is come to dance inane. Glamours hath moidered's lieb and herefore Coldours must leap no more. Lack breath must leap no more:* Macduff-Chuff and Birnam Wood have finally come to avenge the usurpation of Macbeth-Glugg and to stop the inane dance of Glugg and Issy. To "leap" is to usurp; and Macbeth, the "Leapermann" (250.21), short of breath, must leap no more. The lines are a *Macbeth* treasury. The first sentence echoes Macbeth's: "There would have been a time for such a word. / To-morrow, and to-morrow, and to-morrow . . ." (V. v. 18–19). Then we have "Though Birnam Wood be come to Dunsinane" (V. vii. 30), and Macbeth's vision as he murders Duncan: "Methought I heard a voice cry 'Sleep no more! / Macbeth does murder sleep.' . . . Glamis hath murdered sleep, and therefore Cawdor / Shall sleep no more, Macbeth shall sleep no more" (II. ii. 34–42).

250.34–36 *Led by Lignifer, in four hops of the happiest, ach beth cac duff, a marrer of the sward incoronate. . . . Will any dubble dabble on the bay?:* Lignifer recalls Lucifer, tree and stone (Shem and Shaun, ligneous wood, lignostone wood and *fer*—iron and sword), swords hidden amid woods—or Birnam Wood marching toward Dunsinane. (*Lignifer* is also Latin for one who carries wood, as do Macduff's troops; see McHugh, p. 250.) The "abcd" here hides Macbeth ("ach beth") and Macduff ("cac duff"), both killers of kings (marrers of coronated-incarnated swords and swards, and of the Word Incarnate). These events follow the predictions of the babbling witches—"dubble dabble": "Double, double, toil and trouble."

251.11 *most anysing maybefallhim from a song of a witch:* this was certainly true for Macbeth; most anything *did* befall him from the "dubble dabble" (250.36) song of the "weird sisters."

251.16–17 *The specks of his lapspan are his foul deed thoughts, wishmarks of* *mad imogenation. Take they off! Make the off!:* while *Cymbeline's* Imogen may be here, we are still dealing largely with *Macbeth,* with the mad, guilt-ridden imaginations of Macbeth and Lady Macbeth, whose consciences were indelibly spotted. With Lady Macbeth, Glugg-Macbeth is saying, "Out, damned spot! Out, I say!" (V. i. 32).

254.07 *Clio's:* Cleopatra's. See entries for 91.06 and 271.L2.
Clio is also the muse of history.

254.18 *to the mind's ear:* an ear-sighted (ear-Shem vs. eye-Shaun) view of Hamlet's "In my mind's eye" (I. ii. 186) and Horatio's "the mind's eye" (I. i. 112).

254.31–34 *An insodaintily she's a quine of selm ashaker while as a murder of corpse when his magot's up he's the best berrathon sanger in all the aisles of Skaldignavia:* this line refers to Queen ("quine") ALP and to her King of Scandinavia, HCE. Perhaps, considering the oblique reference to Gertrude's act of murder and to King Hamlet of Denmark, this passage is a statement by Joyce of his rivalry with Shakespeare ("ashaker"). Just as Joyce thought of his father as a rival for the best singer (tenor, not baritone) in the Irish isles, so also the prize here is for the best poet (singer of tales) in the "aisles of Skaldignavia"—or poetry-dom *à la Hamlet,* since a *skald* is Danish for "poet."

256.11–15 *—Home all go. Halome. Blare no more ramsblares . . . And cease your fumings. . . . For here the holy language. Soons to come. To pausse:* go home and hear the holy language (perhaps of the *Wake),* telling what is to come and to pass. Hodgart has ascertained that the passage contains very obscure allusions to *Hamlet* and to *Cymbeline.* The theme is, among other ideas, death and fear of death. The mime-drama draws to an end, and the great apocalyptic stage curtain is about to drop—as it literally does in 257.31, accompanied by the thunder of the Father-Producer-God. The theme is brought out in "Home all go. . . . Blare no more. . . . And cease your fumings," and in "Soons to come. To pausse." Hodgart maintains (in "Work in Progress," p. 31) that the key quotations are unspoken: 1) From the "burial" song for Imogen in *Cymbeline:* "*Fear no more* the heat o' th' sun, / Nor the furious winter's rages; / Thou thy worldly task hast done, / *Home art gone* and ta'en thy wages. / Golden lads and girls all must, / As chimney-sweepers, come to dust. . . . Fear no more the lightning flash, / Nor th'all-dreaded thunder-stone . . ." *(Cym.* IV. ii. 258–71; my italics). 2)—"For in that sleep what dreams may *come* / When we have shuffled off this mortal coil, / Must give us *pause*" *(Ham.* III. i. 66–8; my italics.)

"Halome" also contains, perhaps, *Salomé,* a play by Oscar Wilde; Samuel Beckett wrote a poem (published 1934) called "Home Olga."

256.23 *and why is limbo where is he:* "Who is Silvia? What is she . . . " *(TGV* IV. ii. 39). See also entry for 211.35–36.

257.01 *What is amaid today todo? So angelland all weeping bin that Izzy most unhappy is:* Issy as Isabella of *Measure for Measure,* who was weeping and unhappy on account of Angelo ("angelland"). What was a maid in her situation to do?

See also 556.05, "sister Isobel."

257.15,22 *his place of beacon . . . the prize of a pease of bakin:* Chuff and Glugg seem to be competing for a piece of bacon, just as some have claimed that Shakespeare has usurped the rightful place of Bacon.

257.19–20 *the baker's booth . . . Missy Cheekspeer:* Monsieur Shakespeare. See also entries for 145.24 and 191.02. Shem is the baker; Shaun is the butcher. Perhaps there was a bakery or "poestry" shop in Dublin named Chickspeer's.

257.34–35 *When the h, who the hu, how the hue, where the huer?:* perhaps an allusion to the question of the sonnets' "Mr. W. H."'s identity, a riddle which has long puzzled Shakespearean scholars. Willie Hughes was a suggested candidate.

257.35–36 *lots lives lost:* possibly another version of *Love's Labor's Lost*.

Book II, Chapter 2

261.27 *cryptogam of each nightly bridable:* Hodgart suggests (in *James Joyce: A Student's Guide*, p. 164) that this line refers to Ignatius Donnelly's *The Great Cryptogram*, the source of the Baconian heresy about the authorship of Shakespeare's plays. See entry for 281.F3.

263.05 *theobalder:* Lewis Theobald (Pope's "Tibbald"), Shakespearean scholar, adapter, and forger. In 1728 he printed a play entitled *Double Falsehood*, which he claimed to be a modernized version of a lost Shakespearean play, *Cardenio*. Nothing has ever turned up to substantiate Theobald's claim.

See chapter 6 of this study and Atherton, pp. 69–70 on the Theobald allusions.

268.04–5 *All every inch of it:* a phallic allusion, seemingly an echo of Lear's "Ay, every inch a king" (IV. vi. 106). See 252.34, "every inch of an immortal."

268.15 *And a bodikin a boss in the Thimble Theatre:* perhaps a real theatre in London or Dublin. "Bodikin" echoes Hamlet's "bare bodkin" (III. i. 76) and his "God's bodkin, man!" (II. ii. 516). Thus, what is playing at this theatre seems to be, via "bodkin," *Hamlet*.

See also "bare godkin" in 79.20, "bodkin" in 578.16, and line 500.02, in which thimbles and bodkins are reunited: "They're playing thimbles and bodkins." As Glasheen has pointed out, the "Thimble and Bodkin Army" was a "nickname of the Parliamentary Army of the [English] Civil War" *(OED)*.

269.18 *glib Ganymede:* in the Forest of Arden, *As You Like It*'s glib Rosalind took on the alias of Ganymede.

269.19–20 *To me or not to me. Satis thy quest on:* "To be or not to be, that is the question" *(Ham.* III. i. 56). Sex-starved Issy is trying to talk the brothers into coming to her and satisfying their urges on her. Cf. 110.12, "ken or no me ken Zot is the Quiztune."

271.03–6 *Sire Jeallyous Seizer, that gamely torskmester, with his duo of druidesses in ready money rompers, and the tryonforit of Oxthievious, Lapidous and Malthouse Anthemy:* Julius Caesar: the triumvirate of Octavius, Lepidus and Mark Antony. Passage is accompanied by entry 271.L2.

271.L2 *Cliopatria, thy hosies history:* Cleopatra, who had to do with all the Romans named in the entry for 271.03–6. See also entries for 91.06, 104.20,

166.34, and 254.07. Clio is the muse of history. Cleopatra's nose changed history ("thy hosies history"), for (Glasheen reminds) Pascal wrote that "had it been shorter, the whole aspect of the earth would have been altered" (in *Pensées* II. 162). Pascal's *Pensées* are thus associated with *pensée*-pansy-Ophelia-Issy-Cleopatra. See entry for 271.20, and also "Pensée! The most beautiful of woman" in 403.14–15. See Blaise Pascal, *Pensées and The Provincial Letters* (New York: Modern Library, 1941), p. 59.

271.20 *brood our pansies:* Ophelia's pansies. See *Hamlet* section of Appendix 2 (under IV. v. 174 ff.) for all "pansy" references. Since "there is pansies, that's for thoughts" (IV. v. 175), pansies (or *pensées*) are associated with thinking, or "brooding." See also chapter 4 of this study; see also Pascal's *Pensées* in entry for 271.L2.

274.L3 *till the calends of Mary:* like the Ides of March. See also entry for 85.27.

274.L4 *As Shakefork might pitch it:* as Shakespeare might put it; see also entry for 295.04.

276.L2 *Omnitudes in a knutshedell:* a reference to Hamlet's frustration at being, like Wyndham Lewis or Shaun, a spatialist: "O God! I could be bounded in a nut-shell, and count myself a king of infinite space, were it not that I have bad dreams" (II. ii. 260). See Peery, p. 254; see also line 455.29.

276.08–9 *What's Hiccupper to hem or her to Hagaba? Ough, ough, brieve kindli!:* a combination of Hamlet's "What's Hecuba to him or he to Hecuba?" (II. ii. 542) and Macbeth's "Out, out, brief candle!" (*Mac.* V. v. 23).

277.F2 *And a ripping rude rape in his lucreasious togery:* a rather lewd vision of Shakespeare's *Rape of Lucrece*.

278.05–6 *With a pansy for the pussy in the corner:* Strong claims (p. 72) that this line refers to Osric, in *Hamlet;* the line also refers to Issy-Ophelia, who is the "pussy in the corner." Sitting in a corner of the study-room, she says that she is "setting on [her] stool," and then quotes from *Hamlet* (see entry for 278.F2.) The pansy is an Ophelian flower: "And there is pansies, that's for thoughts" (IV. v. 175). This line is often referred to in the *Wake;* pansies-for-thoughts becomes a leitmotif for Ophelia. See chapter 4 of this study.

278.13 *All the world's in want:* possible echo of "All the world's a stage" (*AYL* II. vii. 139). "Puck" in the previous line (278.12) may refer to *A Midsummer Night's Dream*'s Robin Goodfellow.

278.L3 *Dear Brotus, land me arrears:* this line combines two well-known passages from *Julius Caesar:* Cassius's "The fault, dear Brutus, is not in our stars, / But in ourselves, that we are underlings" (I. ii. 140–41); and Mark Antony's "Friends, Romans, countrymen, lend me your ears . . ." (III. ii. 73). The latter is another version of "List, list!"

The line is also Shem's request for a loan: Dear Brother, lend me arrears.

278.F2 *he'd have a culious impressiom on the diminitive that chafes our ends:* Hamlet: "There is a divinity that shapes our ends" (V. ii. 10). See Hodgart, p. 742. Issy is saying, in a hilarious way, that if you were sitting on a stool as hard as the one she is sitting on, you could bet there'd be a curious impression on the diminutive behind that chafes our end and *derrière*.

278.F7 *Strutting as proud as a great turquin weggin that cuckhold:* Tarquin the

Proud was the last king of Rome. The line may echo Macbeth's "withered murder, / Alarumed by his sentinel, the wolf, / Whose howl's his watch, thus with his stealthy pace, / With Tarquin's ravishing strides, toward his design / Moves like a ghost" (II. i. 52–56). Cf. entry for 277.F2.

Shakespeare's *Rape of Lucrece* is about Tarquin's "ravishing strides" against Lucrece, wife of Collatinus, "that cuckhold."

279.05 *alls war that end war:* *All's Well that Ends Well.*

279.F1: In this long footnote, Issy contemplates committing suicide: "I was thinking fairly killing times of putting an end to myself and my malody." Her malady is rejection by the twins; thus, as in Nuvoletta's suicide, there are references to Ophelia, another rejected lover, and her "rue": "Then rue. . . . This isabella I'm on knows the ruelles of the rut." Some of the phrases, as Rose notes (p. 241), are based on songs that are lovers' laments.

"All these gelded ewes jilting about" may echo *Othello;* and "isabella" may refer to the heroine of *Measure for Measure.*

280.06–7 *tomorrows gone and yesters outcome:* tomorrows and yesterdays recall Macbeth's "Tomorrow, and tomorrow, and tomorrow. . . . And all our yesterdays have lighted fools / The way to dusty death" (V. v. 19–23). See entry for 104.12.

281.06 *la pervenche en Illyrie:* Illyria, on the east coast of the Adriatic, is the setting for *Twelfth Night.* However, as Atherton has noted (p. 34), the entire paragraph (in French) is lifted verbatim from Edgar Quinet.

281.15–6 *Bruto and Cassio:* Brutus and Cassius; however, Cassio is also Othello's lieutenant. This line is immediately followed by an allusion to *Othello* (see entry for 281.17–21).

281.17–21 *('tis demonal!) . . . (il folsoletto nel falsoletto col fazzolotto dal fuzzolezzo). . . . Sickamoor's so woful sally. Ancient's aerger:* Desdemona and the Moor in *Othello.* The Moor's action was both sick and demonic; he was woefully sorry for it, a sick amour. Sycamores are everywhere in the *Wake;* here, they are appropriately joined by willows (*salyx,* "sally"), for Desdemona sang a "willow" song about sycamores and willows: "The poor soul sat sighing by a sycamore tree, / Sing all a green willow. . . . Sing willow, willow, willow" (IV. iii. 40–43). The Moor's antient ("Ancient"; cf. 343.23, "antiants") was Iago; his previous antient, "Cassio," is also here (281.16), as is Othello's ill-fated handkerchief (or at least Verdi's *Otello's*)—*il fazzoletto.*

281.22–23 *What if she love Sieger less though she leave Ruhm moan?:* Margareen's motives may be like Brutus's in *Julius Caesar:* "Not that I loved Caesar less, but that I loved Rome more" (III. ii. 21–22). See entry for 282.01–3; see also Hodgart, p. 747.

281.F3 *You daredevil donnelly, I love your piercing lots of lies and your flashy foreign mail so here's my cowrie card, I dalgo, with all my exes, wise and sad:* the footnote to "But Bruto and Cassio are ware only of trifid tongues," in lines 281.15–16. Atherton believes (p. 246) that "donnelly" refers to Ignatius Donnelly; Donnelly, an American politician and the author of *The Great Cryptogram,* claimed that Bacon's authorship of the Shakespeare corpus could be demonstrated by discovering and studying the "cypher" planted by Bacon in the plays themselves. Perhaps the "trifid tongues" of Bruto and

Cassio, with their "exes, wise and sad" (x's, y's and zed), are a reference to the code, or "cypher." Atherton writes also that "Joyce conceals the name 'Bacon' near many of his references to Shakespeare, and there is probably a cryptogram in this section of the *Wake*." See also chapter 6 of this study. "Cryptogam" appears in 261.27.

282.01–3 *With sobs for his job, with tears for his toil, with horror for his squalor but with pep for his perdition:* still in Brutus's speech (see entry for 281.22–23) in which he defends his assassination of Caesar: ". . . There is tears for his love; joy for his fortune; honor for his valor; and death for his ambition" (*JC* III. ii. 26–28).

282.29 *caiuscounting:* Peter Toye wrote—in *AWN*, II, 4 (Aug. 1965): 27—that "'caiuscounting' (282.29) may refer to Dr. Caius [in *The Merry Wives of Windsor*]: 'Vat be all you, one, two, tree, four, come for?' [*JC* II. iii. 20] and 'If dere be one, or two, I shall make-a de turd' [III. iii. 208]—the second of these references having a particular relevance to the concerns of the chapter. A further possibility is Caius Cassius's 'The clock hath stricken three' [*JC* II. i. 192], though the allusion here would not seem to help the meaning of the text."

283.14 *tods of Yorek:* a weight unit of York, but also *Hamlet*'s Yorick; see entry for 190.19.

285.L2 *Arthurgink's hussies and Everguin's men:* King Arthur's horses and Queen Guinevere's Men, or all the King's horses and all the Queen's Men. See also King's Men and Queen's Men, Elizabethan dramatic companies, in entry for 219.15–16.

287.18 *husk, hisk, a spirit spires:* the spirit of Hamlet's father whispering, "List, list, O list!" Perhaps the next line ("meager suckling of gert stoan") refers to Prince Hamlet, suckling of Gertrude; "gert stoan" combines *Hamlet*'s queen with Gertrude Stein.

288.F1 *An ounceworth of onions for a pennyawealth of sobs:* an echo from *Henry IV, Part 1* (Prince Hal referring to Falstaff's expenditures): "O monstrous! but one halfpenny worth of bread to this intolerable deal of sack!" (II. iv. 514–15). See Hodgart, p. 750 and line 137.34. McHugh (p. 288) sees this as possibly an echo of Greene's *A Groatsworth of Wit Bought With a Million of Repentance*.

289.27–29 *(on the Ides of Valentino's, at Idleness, Floods Area, Isolade, Liv's lonely daughter . . .):* references to *Julius Caesar*'s Ides of March, *Macbeth*'s Inverness, and *King Lear*'s "Cordelia. Cordoglio. Lir's loneliest daughter" (*U*, 192).

290.06 *poor MacBeth:* Macbeth.

290.09 *MacAdoo: Much Ado.* See entry for 227.33.

291.12 *in juwelietry and kickychoses and madornments:* the baubles and jewelry seem to include Shakespeare's Juliet. "Kickychoses" echoes Toby Belch's "kickshawses" (trifles, *quelques choses*) in *Twelfth Night* I. iii. 103.

291.22 *that miching micher:* Mick-Shaun and, perhaps, Hamlet's "Marry, this is miching mallecho; it means mischief" (III. ii. 131). See entry for 468.26 and see Hodgart, p. 742.

292.21 *what stale words whilom were woven with and fitted fairly featly for:*

from Ariel's song in *The Tempest:* "The wild waves whist, / Foot it featly here and there" (I. ii. 378–79).

292.25 *hark back to lark to you symibellically:* to sing to Imogen, as in *Cymbeline* ("symibellically"): "Hark, hark, the lark at heaven's gate sings . . ." (*Cym.* II. iii. 19). See Hodgart, p. 752.

295.04 *As Great Shapesphere puns it:* Great Shakespeare, the god of his creation, as Joyce puns it. See also entry for 274.L4.

295.21 *All's fair on all fours:* possibly refers to *All's Well that Ends Well.* Cf. (among others) "alls war that end war" in 279.05.

300.L1 *Primanouriture and Ultimogeniture:* first (and last) nourishings and primogeniture. Here also is perhaps a hidden Imogen. See line 251.17 and entry for 292.25.

300.30 *(thur him no quartos!):* Kev-Shaun is angry at Dolph-Shem and about to hit him—thus, "show him no quarter!" Quarter becomes transformed into Quartos and Shakespearean manuscripts, perhaps because one of Shaun's complaints is that his brother is a forger (see lines 300.01–6).

301.F5 *Very glad you are going to Penmark:* cf. 189.06, "small peace in ppenmark."

302.F1 *I loved to see the Macbeths Jerseys knacking spots of the Plumpduffs Pants:* Issy, perhaps a fan of some Shakespearean rugby team, seems to be saying that she'd love to see the Macbeth Jerseys knock the spots off the pants of the plump Macduff squad.

A plum-duff is a "plain flour pudding with raisins or currants in it, boiled in a cloth or bag" *(OED).*

302.F2 *Lifp year fends you all and moe, fouvenirs foft as fummer fnow, fweet willings and forget-uf-knots:* Issy takes on Elizabethan calligraphy and Ophelia's flowers: leap year sends you all and more, souvenirs soft as summer snow, sweet Williams and forget-me-nots.

303.02 *And this . . . is the way Romeopullupalleaps:* one of the "charictures in the drame" (302.32) appears to be an athletic Romeo.

304.18 *By Saxon Chromaticus:* Saxo Grammaticus, Danish historian and poet. His *Gesta Danorum* or *Historicae Danicae* (c. 1185–1200) is a chronicle history of Denmark and a source of the Hamlet tale. See lines 16.07 and 388.31.

305.18–20 *Old Keane . . . where is that Quin:* possibly Edmund Kean (1787–1833) and James Quin (1693–1766), two of the greatest actors in Shakespearean stage history. See Nathan Halper, *AWN*, XII, 5 (Oct. 1975): 82.

306.L2 *Julius Caesar. Pericles . . . Ajax: Julius Caesar* and *Pericles* are plays of Shakespeare; Ajax was a Greek hero and a character in *Troilus and Cressida.*

306.L4 *Alcibiades:* possibly the Athenian captain of that name in *Timon of Athens.*

307.27 *If You Do It Do It Now:* recalls Macbeth's "If it were done when 'tis done, then 'twere well / It were done quickly" (I. vii. 1–2).

307.F2 *Wherry like the whaled prophet in a spookeerie:* a combination of the prophet Jonah in the whale, and Polonius's "Very like a whale" (*Ham.* III. ii. 367). See entry for 120.11.

307.F8 *Eu, Monsieur! Nenni No, Monsieur!:* once again, Issy plays with Ophelia's "Hey non nony, nony, hey nony" song (IV. v. 165). See entry for 203.14.

Book II, Chapter 3

313.26 *Digges:* according to Senn (p. 6), an actor in one of Dublin's stock companies, for whom he acted the role of Hamlet at the Crow Street Theatre (105.27). A particular performance of his *Hamlet* is alluded to on page 323.

Leonard Digges, an Elizabethan poet and an acquaintance of Shakespeare's, contributed a commendatory poem to the First Folio of 1623. See *RES*, p. 183.

316.16 *seven oak ages:* the Seven Ages of Man (in *As You Like It* II. vii. 142–43).

316.34 *a warry posthumour's expletion:* a weary posthumous expression. Perhaps a reference to *Cymbeline*'s Posthumus. See entries for 377.09 and 422.14.

318.20–21 *Now eats the vintner over these contents oft with his sad slow munch for backonham:* a Joycean recreation of the opening of *Richard III:* "Now is the winter of our discontent / Made glorious summer by this son of York." Food is here again; HCE is at dinner, chewing a ham sandwich, a "sad slow munch for backonham". The Earl of Sandwich is not alluded to, though Francis Bacon and the Duke of Buckingham are, sandwiched into this portmanteau word, a real B-L-T. Shakespeare's "son of York" becomes, in this line, York ham *(jambon de York).*

The Duke of Buckingham was Richard III's henchman in *Richard III.* In Shakespeare's time, George Villiers was the Duke of Buckingham. The reference to "backonham" may also be to Francis Bacon, a "pretendant" to the authorship of the plays, or to John Sheffield, Duke of Buckingham, an "adapter" and rewriter of Shakespearean plays.

See Glasheen, pp. 22, 42 (citing Fritz Senn).

319.03–6 *—I shot be shoddied, throttle me . . . for bringing briars to Bembracken and ringing rinbus round Demetrius for, as you wrinkle wryghtly, bully bluedomer:* Demetrius is one of the lovers in *A Midsummer Night's Dream,* and "bully bluedomer" is Nick Bottom, who is called by both Peter Quince and Flute "bully Bottom" (III. i. 7; IV. ii. 18). See Hodgart, p. 747.

In context, HCE as the Norwegian captain is admitting his guilt and his sense of guilt-conscience (see entry for 319.07); he appears to be, then, like Shakespeare's Puck, admitting his guilt in playing tricks on Demetrius and Bottom: I should be shot ("I shot be shoddied"), HCE is saying, "for ringing rinbus round Demetrius" and "bully bluedomer." Recall Puck's apology in the epilogue of the play: "If we shadows have offended. . . . Gentles, do not reprehend" (V. i. 412 ff.). Puck is mentioned again in line 326.03.

"Bluedomer" may also refer to the sky, the blue dome of heaven. "Bringing briars to Bembracken" has an echo of "carrying coals to Newcastle."

319.07 *and thus plinary indulgence makes columellas of us all:* Hamlet's "Thus conscience does make cowards of us all" (III. i. 83). The Norwegian Captain here admits his guilt; guilt implies conscience, and thus Hamlet's line. A plenary indulgence erases conscience and guilt, for it is a remission of a sinner's entire temporal punishment.

"Plinary" and "columellas" also refer to the Quinet motif: *comme aux jours de Pline et de Columelle.*

Pages 318–19 have a number of references to *Richard III* and *Hamlet*, including three to Hamlet's famous soliloquy.

319.20 *And be the coop of his gobbos, Reacher the Thaurd: Richard the Third.* Launcelot Gobbo is Shylock's clown and servant; he and Old Gobbo, his father, appear in *The Merchant of Venice.*

319.28 *at weare or not at weare:* to be or not to be. *At vaere* is Norwegian for "to be." See Hodgart, p. 740.

319.35 *a satuation, debauchly to be watched for:* Hamlet's "'Tis a consummation / Devoutly to be wished" (III. i. 63).

321.04 *lampthorne . . . wand:* Hodgart (p. 750) sees this line as a reference to the lantern and the wall in *A Midsummer Night's Dream* (played by Starveling and Snout), meant to represent Moonshine and Wall.

321.11 *a kiber galler:* the *Skeleton Key* (p. 206) first pointed out that this means a peasant's toe and is a reference to Hamlet's "The age is grown so picked that the toe of the peasant comes so near the heel of the courtier, he galls his kibe" (V. i. 130–32). Stephen Dedalus has this line in mind in "Scylla and Charybdis": "I gall his kibe" (*U*, 215). The *Hamlet* allusion here is probably a felicitous verbal echo, for "peasant's toe" makes little sense in context. The phrase may focus primarily on a foreigner (*ghall* in Irish) to Ireland, perhaps from the Khyber.

321.18 *by night in the Phoenix! Music. And old lotts have funn at Flammagen's ball:* lots of fun at *Finnegans Wake,* the dream-drama that will be played at the Phoenix Theatre. See entry for 219.02.

323.28–324.16 *tummelumpsk . . . that bunch of palers . . . Toni Lampi. . . . ghustorily spoeking, gen and gang, dane and dare, like the dud spuk of his first foetotype. . . . And ere he could catch or hook or line to suit their saussyskins, the lumpenpack. . . . Sot! . . . change all that whole set. Shut down and shet up. Our set, our set's allohn:* this passage provides an excellent illustration of how *Finnegans Wake* is presented as a stage drama, played by "the whole stock company of the old house" (510.17). It refers to a particular performance of *Hamlet* in Dublin, as has been pointed out by Senn (p. 6), starring "Digges" (313.26) at the Crow Street Theatre. See chapter 3 of this study for an explication and discussion of the passage.

326.03 *As puck as that Paddeus:* possibly Puck from *A Midsummer Night's Dream.* Glasheen suggests (p. 240) that Puck, who plucks a flower that alters the hearts and minds of the Athenians in the play, is being connected with St. Patrick ("Paddeus"), who does the same with his shamrock, altering the Irish mind through religion.

326.07-8 *intra trifum triforium trifoliorum:* amid this Holy Trinity there appears to be a folio reference; see lines and entries for 197.18, 300.30, and 425.20-25.
 May also echo the liturgical *Per omnia saecula saeculorum.*
327.12-13 *and all the Lavinias of ester yours and pleding for them to herself in the periglus glatsch:* and all the Lavinias of yesteryears and pleading for them to herself in the perilous glass? Here is the hapless Lavinia (who in *Titus Andronicus* has her hands cut off and her tongue cut out, and is ravished), as well as *Pericles* ("periglus"). Both references are functionally appropriate in this passage, in which the Tailor (HCE) is trying to convince the Sailor (the Norwegian Captain) to marry his daughter—which he does. Lavinia is daughter of Titus, and both the Emperor Saturninus and his brother wish to marry her. HCE has an incestuous desire for his own daughter, and so *Pericles* is particularly appropriate; in that play, King Antiochus has an incestuous relationship with his daughter, whom he has prevented from marrying by presenting to all her suitors a riddle which they must solve at the cost of their lives. Young Pericles, Prince of Tyre, arrives to solve that riddle. Thus, these two Shakespearean references reinforce the themes of incest and of betrothal to the daughter of one's adversary, which are present in the HCE-Tailor-Sailor tale.
 The Index Manuscript lists "lavimia" [sic], "gletsch," and other words on this page in the Romansch index. In Romansch, *lavinia* means "avalanche" and *glatsch* means "icicle." (Rose, *James Joyce's The Index Manuscript,* pp. 8, 12.)
328.22 *from Coxenhagen till the brottels on the Nile:* from Copenhagen to the brothels on the Nile; Shakespeare's plays had as wide a range, from *Hamlet* to *Antony and Cleopatra.*
329.04 *hip, hip, horatia!:* hurray, and possibly *Hamlet*'s Horatio. The "rover" in the tale being told is named Horace.
330.12-18 *some family fewd felt a nick in their name. Old Vickers sate down on their airs and straightened the points of their lace. Red Rowleys popped out of the lairs and asked what was wrong with the race. . . . The Burke-Lees and Coyle-Finns paid full feines for their sinns:* the marriage of the sailor-rover to HCE's daughter is being celebrated in these pages; this particular passage seems to imply, in the context that all the world's a stage performance, that this marriage of upstarts offended some of the old, theatregoing families. Some felt a nick was being made in their name and started a feud ("some family fewd felt a nick in their name"). Patrons at the Old Vic sat down in their chairs with haughty airs ("Old Vickers sate down on their airs and straightened the points of their lace"). Irate Rowleys ("Rowley" in 376.30— William Rowley, famed actor in Shakespeare's company and dramatist), stage figures since Shakespeare's time, popped out of their chairs and asked what the world was coming to ("popped out of the lairs and asked what was wrong with the race"). Old families like the Burke-Lees and Coyle-Finns had paid full fares for their seats ("paid full feines for their sinns"). The identities

of the Burke-Lees or Coyle-Finns are mysteries, though Elizabeth I's treasurer was Lord Cecil, William Burghley; they appear to be Sinn Feiners. No doubt they also represent Bishop Berkeley and Finn MacCool.

Rowley collaborated with Thomas Middleton on *The Changeling;* according to Sir Sidney Lee, he also helped to write *Pericles,* alluded to in these pages (in 327.12–13).

330.30–32 *Knock knock. War's where! Which war? The Twwinns. Knock knock. Woos without! Without what? An apple. Knock knock:* the knocking at the gate again (cf. *Macbeth* section of Appendix 2). This knocking (Who's there? Who's without?) becomes transformed into the newlyweds' sexual experiences, in which a good "knocking" results in pregnancy, producing the twins and Issy (an apple). Cf. lines 262.05–6 and 379.01, also lines 530.32, "Tipknock Castle!" and 50.05, "candlestock."

Glasheen has suggested that these lines may conceivably include another famed Shakespearean "knocking": Antipholus of Ephesus knocking and being refused admission to his own home by Dromio of Syracuse, in that mad confusion concerning two pairs of twins ("The Twwinns") and who is who ("Which war! . . . Woos without!").

331.22–23 *and so will is the littleyest, the myrioheartzed:* "Will" Shakespeare was described by Coleridge as "myriadminded"—a term Joyce refers to in *Ulysses,* p. 205 and in *Finnegans Wake,* 159.07 and 576.24. See entry for 576.24.

335.32–34 *And it was the lang in the shirt in the green of the wood, where obelisk rises when odalisks fall, major threft on the make and jollyjacques spindthrift on the merry:* the tale of the first fall in Eden is being retold in this passage; and thus, once again, there are references to the green world and green woods of the Forest of Arden-Eden. The long and the short ("lang in the shirt") of this rise and fall, which took place "in the green of the wood" (see 74.06, "greenwoods," from *AYL*), was a major theft ("major threft")—of an apple. The melancholy Jaques is present as "jollyjacques." See entries for 30.13–14, 74.10, and 450.32–33.

Glasheen points out (p. 110) that Sir George Greenwood, K.C., M.P., "believed Shakespeare the actor to be distinct from the poet and had a controversy about it with Andrew Lang ["lang in the shirt]."

336.05 *measures for messieurs: Measure for Measure.*

336.15 *his awebrume hour, her sere Sahara of sad oakleaves:* Hodgart (p. 746) identifies this line as a reference to *Macbeth.* The line refers to the "auburn hour," the hour of fall and death; so also does Macbeth: "I have lived long enough. My way of life / Is fall'n into the sear, the yellow leaf . . ." (V. iii. 22–23). "Sear," or sere, means dry and withered—as in the Sahara.

337.26 *heahear:* List!

338.11–12 *BUTT (mottledged youth . . . is supposing to motto the sorry dejester:* Butt-Shem described as a model youth dressed in motley, who is supposed to model the tragic jester of *Hamlet.* Cf. entry for 171.15.

338.31 *when the morn hath razed out limpalove:* see entry for 411.27–28. Stephen Dedalus referred to Elizabeth Hall, Shakespeare's granddaughter, as "Lizzie. Grandpa's lump of love" (*U*, 195, 213). Perhaps Anne Hathaway ("hath") is also here.

339.14 *Obriania's beromst!:* "Obriania" seems to combine *A Midsummer Night's Dream*'s Oberon and Titania, the king and queen of the fairies.

340.07–8 *The field of karhags and that bloasted tree. Forget not the felled!:* the "blasted heath" of *Macbeth* (I. iii. 77), the field on which Macbeth encounters the witches (hags). See entry for 194.15 (a heath can also be a tree).

340.09 *warful doon's bothem:* see entries for 369.12 and 503.21.

340.32–34 *strait a way.... Piping Pubwirth to Haunted Hillborough:* Glasheen wrote—in *AWN* V, 5 (Oct. 1968): 75–76—"E.K. Chambers, *William Shakespeare*, Oxford, 1930, vol. II, 292, quotes a John Jordan (1770–90) as saying that Shakespeare was fond of ale and gloried in his capacity to drink it. Two companies of yeomanry, gathered in Bidford (7 miles below Stratford), challenged Shakespeare and his friends to a drinking bout. When Shakespeare and his party went to Bidford, the soldiers were gone to Evesham Fair, so they drank against 'Sippers' and worsened them. On the way home, Shakespeare slept under a crabtree. In the morning his friends wanted him to return to Bidford and continue the contest. Shakespeare refused and said:

Piping Pebworth, Dancing Marston,
Haunted Hillborough, Hungry Grafton,
Dadgeing Exhall, Papist Wicksford,
Beggarly Broom, and Drunken Bidford.

I do not understand the anecdote, but the doggerel is quoted, in a military context, at *FW* 340.33–34: '... strait a way [Stratford] ... from Piping Pubwirth to Haunted Hillborough....'"

342.30–31 *eeridreme ... From Topphole to Bottom:* perhaps the eerie dream and drama of Bottom in *A Midsummer Night's Dream*. Bottom is also alluded to in line 340.09. "From top to bottom" also echoes the description of King Hamlet's Ghost, "Armed ... from top to toe" (I. ii. 228).

343.22–23 *in the tragedoes of those antiants their grandoper:* in the tragedies of the ancients and their great works. The Ondt ("antiants") and the Gracehoper are also here. Glasheen notes (p. 113) that this line refers to *Othello*, apparently meaning the tragedy of the "ancients." This is possible: in *Othello* first Cassio and then Iago were Othello's "ancients" (ensigns), and are referred to as such nine times in the play. "Grandoper" also calls to mind grand opera; *Othello* became an opera by Verdi.

343.36 *Flute!:* Glasheen (p. 96) reads this (and some other more obscure references) as an allusion to *A Midsummer Night's Dream*'s Francis Flute, one of the "rude mechanicals." This is not convincing, particularly since the entire line is a parody of the opening of *Paradise Lost:* "Of manifest 'tis obedience and the. Flute!"

344.05–6 *Which goatheye and sheepskeer they damnty well know:* which Goethe, Shakespeare, and Dante damn well know. See also entry for 539.05–9.

345.15 *you smugs to bagot:* "You Smoke Tobacco," an Elizabethan song. Baggot is a street in Dublin. Bagot is a minor character in *Richard II*.

347.04 *Steep Nemorn:* "Sleep no more! . . . Macbeth shall sleep no more" (*Mac.* II. ii. 34–42). Perhaps also Hamlet's "To die, to sleep / No more" (*Ham.* III. i. 60). If the reference is to *Macbeth*, then "the mount of Bekel" in the same line is appropriate, since probably the reference is to *Beth*el. We are amid a passage in which the Mideast is blended with more familiar locales—cf. "freshprosts of Eastchept" in 347.12.
 See line 250.18.

347.12 *freshprosts of Eastchept:* fleshpots of Egypt and fresh toasts *(prosit!)* from a tavern in Eastcheap, the setting for the Falstaff scenes in *Henry IV, Parts 1 and 2*. See Hodgart, p. 750.

347.26 *all feller come longa villa finish:* Longaville is a lord in King Ferdinand's court, in *Love's Labor's Lost*.

349.02 *Ist dramhead countmortial or gonorrhal stab?:* a reference to court-martials and venereal disease—perhaps also to Lear's ungrateful daughter Goneril.

350.23 *rawmeots and juliannes: Romeo and Juliet*, and raw meat with julienne vegetables.

352.09–10 *my oreland for a rolvever, sord, by the splunthers of colt and bung goes the enemay the Percy rally got me:* Butt-Buckley, green with envy and anger, shoots the Russian General, but first calls for his gun: Richard III's "My kingdom for a horse!" becomes "my Ireland for a revolver, sir." By the splendors of Buckley's Colt .45, bang goes the enemy (Russian General-HCE), who falls, saying "Persse O'Reilly got me." He might have been *Richard II*, who was brought down by a revolution of Percys (a "Percy rally"—Northumberland and his son, Hotspur), or *Henry IV*, who was almost brought down likewise.
 The popular phrase "A Roland for an Oliver" is also here (McHugh, p. 352); *Brewer's Dictionary of Phrase and Fable*, one of Joyce's sourcebooks, defines the phrase as "A blow for a blow. TIT FOR TAT . . ." (1870; reprint ed., New York: Harper and Row, 1970, p. 927).

354.24 *their murdhering idies:* the Ides of March again, the dates of murder and regicide. The line echoes the popular term "murdering Irish" (498.15; *U*, 200); among those "murdered" by the Irish was Parnell, on Ivy Day, by the "mutthering ivies" (354.23).

354.33 *corrolanes': Coriolanus.*

359.04 *under the selfhide of his bessermettle:* baser mettle, or metal, combined with the Bessemer process for making steel. This recalls Flavius's "See whe'r their basest mettle be not moved" (*JC* I. i. 61); also, perhaps, "They have all been touched and found base metal" (*Tim.* III. iii. 6).

359.31–360.16 *We are now diffusing among our lovers of this sequence (to you! to you!) the dewfolded song of the naughtingels. . . . Let everie sound of a pitch keep still in resonance, jemcrow, jackdaw, prime and secund with their terce. . . . pick out and you vowelize your name. . . . You pere Golazy, you mere Bare and you Bill Heeny, and you Smirky Dainty and, more beethoken. . . . :* Hodgart (in "Work in Progress," p. 29) has shown how this radio broadcast dealing with nightingales, music, and musicians is based on *A Midsummer Night's Dream*, though there are no direct quotes. He wrote:

"The quotation most obviously relevant to the situation is from *A Midsummer Night's Dream* (a play which is naturally a fertile source of cross-references). Nick Bottom before he is translated, talks of disguising his voice: 'I will roar you as 'twere any nightingale.' As is typical of Joyce, this quotation is not given; but the passage contains other references to the play. 'Let everie sound of a pitch keep still' ('Come, sit down, every mother's son and rehearse your parts.' *MND* III, i); 'pick out and vowelize your name. . . . You pere Golazy' ('Read the names of the actors. . . . You, Nick Bottom', I, ii; and the stumbling over the names is similar). Finally, since the passage is about music, Joyce puns on the names of many musicians."

360.36 *our groatsupper:* a Groatsworth of a Gracehoper. Perhaps "greendy" in 360.30 is Robert Greene. The connections appear more likely by virtue of the possibility that Joyce's Ondt and Gracehoper fable (on pages 414–19) may have had its source in Greene's *Groatsworth*. See entry for 414.20–419.08; see also chapter 5, endnote 48.

361.22 *before the bridge of primerose:* possibly Ophelia's "the primrose path of dalliance" (I. iii. 50). See entry for 553.05–6.

364.14 *Attonsure! Ears to hears!:* Attention! List!

365.04–5 *in my baron gentilhomme to the manhor bourne:* "to the manhor bourne" refers to both Macduff (see also entries for 55.10 and 79.08–9) and to Hamlet: "though I am native here, / And to the manner born, it is a custom / More honored in the breach than the observance" (I. iv. 14–16).

The taverner HCE is defending himself against the accusations leveled at him, and is here claiming to be a gentleman and a nobleman—not only born to the manner and customs of the nobility, but literally born in a baronial manor.

The word "bourne," from Hamlet's "undiscovered country, from whose bourn no traveller returns," occurs frequently in the *Wake*. See, for example, "bourne of travail" in 190.21, and "bourne" in 366.14, where it is again a misspelling of "born." The word appears three times in pages 365–67.

366.25–30 *when booboob brutals and cautiouses only aims at the oggog hogs in the humand, then . . . blows the gaff off mombition and thit thides or marse makes a good dayle to be shattat. Fall stuff:* Brutus, Cassius, Caesar's ambition, the Ides of March, and Falstaff. See chapter 5 for an explication of this passage about HCE-Russian General and Buckley.

"Mombition" and "Fall stuff" recall Antony's "Ambition should be made of sterner stuff" (*JC* III. ii. 92).

367.23 *fare fore forn:* "Fie, foh, and fum" again (*Lr*. III. iv. 174).

367.29 *the bounds whereinbourne our solied bodies all attomed attain arrest:* the boundaries wherein our solid bodies are at home, atoned, and can attain rest and arrest. Seems like a *Hamlet*-flavored description of death, of that "undiscovered country from whose bourn / No traveller returns" (III. i. 79–80). See entry for 365.04–5. "Solied bodies" refers to Hamlet's deathwish stated in his first soliloquy: "O that this too too sullied flesh would melt, / Thaw . . ." (I. ii. 129). Joyce's "solied" seems to be a compromise (in the "sullied flesh" controversy) between the now-accepted "sullied" ("sallied" in the 1604–5 quarto) and the "solid" of the 1623 folio.

369.12 *Woovil Doon Botham:* see entry for 503.21.

369.29 *her chilikin puck:* "Finnegans Wake"—and the character Puck.

370.13 *Fool step!:* a foolish step, a full stop, and Falstaff. See entries for 366.25, 379.17, and 595.32. Foolish steps lead to downfalls; a fall brings a full stop.

370.28 *the feof of the foef of forfummed:* once more, "Fie, foh, and fum" from *Lear* (III. iv. 174).

373.14–15 *the magreedy prince of Roger. Thuthud. Heigh hohse, heigh hohse, our kingdom from an orse!:* the greedy prince is Richard III. See entry for 319.20. Echoes of his famous cry—"A horse! a horse! my kingdom for a horse!" (V. v. 7, 13)—recur a number of times in the *Wake*.

In context, the taverners are making accusations against HCE; thus, their kingdom comes from a horse-arse-bear (HCE), an ass on his high horse.

374.06 *Still pumping on Torkenwhite:* perhaps Polonius's "Still harping on my daughter" (*Ham.* II. ii. 187). Lewis Carroll's Alice has just been referred to three lines earlier—so a reference to Ophelia, as Polonius's daughter, is not surprising. See Hodgart, p. 741.

377.09 *Postumus:* L.A.G. Strong (*The Sacred River*, p. 73) names this as a Shakespearean reference, presumably to *Cymbeline's* Posthumus Leonatus. The reference here (in view of the spelling) is more likely to Horace's famed Postumus Ode, Ode II.14 (Horatian odes are quoted a number of times in the *Wake*). The first line of the Postumus Ode is *Eheu fugaces, Postume, Postume*, which has been alluded to previously in "Eheu, for gassies!" (58.18). Other Horatian allusions include "fount Bandusian" in 280.32, "lalage" in 229.10, and "monument aerily perennious" in 57.22, referring, respectively, to Horace III.13, I.22, and III.30. See Tindall, pp. 80, 183.

379.17–18 *One bed night he had the delysiums that they were all queens mobbing him. Fell stiff.:* the taverners describe HCE's dream-nightmare in bed one bad night, in which he had delusions and deliriums about an Elysium ("delysiums"), a paradise in which all the girls were mobbing him ("queens mobbing him"). The line might refer also (and appropriately) to Mercutio's Queen Mab, the "faeries' midwife" who "gallops night by night / Through lovers' brains, and then they dream of love" (*Rom.* I. iv. 53, 70–71). The girls cause HCE to sin and fall—so it's not clear whether "Fell stiff" refers to an erection caused by the wet dream or to HCE's fall (cf. 366.30, "Fall stuff"). In any case, HCE is thus Falstaff; like the latter, he is surrounded by taverners at an inn. Falstaff, too, has delusions, in *The Merry Wives of Windsor*, about his attractiveness to women, resulting in his being "mobbed" by the ladies, dressed as fairies, at the end of the play.

"Queens mobbing" may also refer to the "mobled queen" (II. ii. 490–93) in the Player's speech in *Hamlet*. See Hodgart, p. 742.

379.35 *Beyond bournes and bowers:* again, the "undiscovered country from whose bourn no traveller returns" (*Ham.* III. i. 79–80). See entries for 190.21, 365.04–5, and 367.29.

382.02 *his charmed life:* Macbeth says, "I bear a charmèd life" (V. viii. 12). See McHugh. p. 382.

382.11 *her beaconegg:* Bacon, shakespill, and eggs.

Book II, Chapter 4

385.16 *the mad dane:* Hamlet perhaps?

388.31 *sexon grimmacticals:* Anglo-Saxon grammar books and Saxo Grammaticus, a source of the Hamlet story. See entry for 304.18.

390.04,27 *his old fellow. . . . That old fellow:* possibly references to *Othello*, whose name Joyce punned as "How my oldfellow chokit his Thursdaymomum" (*U*, 567). See entries for 410.04 and 485.17.

391.21 *from Roneo to Giliette: Romeo and Juliet.*

392.23–24 *in her beaver bonnet, the king of the Caucuses, a family all to himself:* recalls King Hamlet, whose ghost "wore his beaver up" (I. ii. 230), and who was described by Hamlet as "all in all" (I. ii. 187)—a phrase made much of in "Scylla and Charybdis" ("All in all . . . bawd and cuckold. . ." in *U*, 212), culminating in Buck Mulligan's farce, *Everyman His Own Wife*—or, as is expressed here, "a family all to himself."

394.28 *katte efter kinne:* Atherton notes—in *AWN*, IV, 2 (Apr. 1967): 41—that this phrase is based upon Touchstone's "If the cat will after kind" in *As You Like It* (III. ii. 98).

396.14–15 *What would Ewe do? With that so tiresome old milkless a ram. . . ?:* the four annalists defend the sexual act of Issy (as Eve and Ewe)—"what would you do?" The ewe and ram in a sexual context recall the imagery of *Othello*, in which "an old black ram [Othello] / Is tupping your white ewe" (I. i. 88–89).

398.23 *kingly leer: King Lear;* perhaps also the Irish King Leary.

398.29 *Hear, O hear:* List, o list!

399.34 *So, to john for a john, johnajeams, led it be!:* at the end of book II, the four old men fall asleep (let it be—or, is it the ass they are leading?) and are led, like HCE, into the world of dreams and the *Wake*. The next three chapters concern Shaun and his dream. "Johnajeams" refers to Hamlet's sleepy dawdler, "John-a-dreams" (II. ii. 553).

Joyce had a habit of ending books (here, book II of the *Wake*) with the act of falling asleep.

Book III, Chapter 1

403.14–15 *Pensée! The most beautiful of woman of the veilch veilchen veilde:* this most beautiful of women in the whole wide world is Issy-Ophelia, who is repeatedly linked with flowers, especially the pansy: "There's rosemary, that's for remembrance. Pray you, love, remember. And there is pansies, that's for thoughts" (IV. v. 174–75). Since pansies are for thoughts, they are transformed into the French word for "thought," *pensée*. The same verbal conjunction is used in other references to Ophelia: "what the eldest daughter she was panseying" in 408.32, "He'll have pansements then for his pensamientos" in 443.14, and "loveliest pansiful thoughts" in 446.03. See Hodgart, p. 741.

Ophelia is also associated with violets (German *veilchen;* see entry for 143.26); "veilch veilchen" refers to Goethe's *Das Veilchen,* in which a violet dies under the feet of a lovely shepherdess, supposedly the most beautiful woman in the whole world.

This "most beautiful of woman" is also Issy as Cleopatra, considered the most beautiful woman in the world, whose nose, according to Pascal's *Pensées* ("Pensée!"), changed history and the face of the earth. See entries for 271.L2 and 271.20 for the Pascal-*pensée*-Cleopatra-Ophelia-pansy connection.

403.16 *her aal in her dhove's suckling:* Bottom says, "I will roar you as gently as any sucking dove" (*MND,* I. ii. 75). See entries for 93.17 and 245.18. Bottom's dream predominates these pages; see also entry for 403.18–407.22.

403.18–407.22 *Methought as I was dropping asleep somepart in nonland. . . :* Bottom has appeared two lines earlier; the dream-vision described on pages 403–5 is that of an ass, the Donkey who accompanies the four old men: "but I, poor ass, am but as their fourpart tinckler's dunkey" (405.06–7; "tinckler" also refers to John Bunyan, another famous Renaissance dreamer, whose *Pilgrim's Progress* was set forth as the author's dream, and who was a tinker by profession). But this chapter is also the dream of HCE, who, having fallen asleep in the pub in the previous chapter, now dreams a vision of Shaun the Post, in which he sees himself as an ass and as Shaun, both referred to in the chapter as "I." Thus, in HCE's dream, HCE-Shaun, the HCE of the dream-future, is an ass.

The passage, as has been pointed out by Glasheen (p. 36) and others (e.g., Begnal, *Narrator and Character,* p. 58), is modeled on Nick "Bully" Bottom's dream, in which he is transformed into an ass. The passage here is full of the Elizabethan language for dream-visions: "Methought as I was dropping asleep. . . . And as I was jogging along in a dream as dozing I was dawdling, arrah, methought. . . . And lo, mescemed somewhat came of the noise . . . whom we dreamt was a shaddo. . . . Yet methought Shaun . . ." Like the dream action of *A Midsummer Night's Dream*'s faeryland and of Puck's "we shadows" (V. i. 412), this vision takes place at midnight: "Methought as I was dropping asleep somepart in nonland . . . I heard at zero hour as 'twere the peal of vixen's laughter among midnight's chimes" (see entry for 403.19–21; "vixen" recalls *MND*'s Hermia, who "was a vixen when she went to school" in III. ii. 324; "goodmantrue" two lines later may possibly conjure up Robin Goodfellow). Bottom describes his dream thus: "I have had a most rare vision. I have had a dream, past the wit of any man to say what dream it was. Man is but an ass if he go about to expound this dream. Methought I was—there is no man can tell what. Methought I was, and methought I had . . ." (IV. i. 203–7). See also chapter 3 of this study for a discussion of the significance of Bottom's dream, *A Midsummer Night's Dream,* and dream-visions in the *Wake.*

The ass in this chapter has a prophetic vision of the future HCE embodied in the "New World" man, Shaun the Post. If he is the ass of the Four Gospellers, the ass who reappears throughout *Finnegans Wake,* and if he is a prophetic ass, might not one conjecture that he is Christ himself, teaching his disciples Matthew, Mark, Luke and John? Shaun, in fact, does undergo his *Via Crucis* in this chapter: as Joyce himself explained, the fourteen questions posed to Shaun here are the fourteen Stations of the Cross *(Letters,* I, pp. 214, 216). Thus, the ass may be HCE, Shaun, Bottom, and Christ. Who or what exactly the ass is has become almost as elusive a question to *Wake* scholars as the enigma of the man in the brown macintosh has become for students of *Ulysses.*

See Boyle, *James Joyce's Pauline Vision,* pp. 32–33, 102, on the "shadow" and on Joyce as the ass.

403.19–21 *I heard . . . midnight's chimes:* refers to Falstaff, who in *Henry IV, Part II* (III. ii. 203) says, "We have heard the chimes at midnight, Master Shallow." (Orson Welles's film version of *Henry IV* was titled *The Chimes at Midnight.*)

404.09–11 *And lo, mescemed somewhat came of the noise. . . . When look, was light . . . :* Hodgart suggests (p. 740) that this is an echo of Horatio's "But look, the morn in russet mantle clad . . ." *(Ham.* I. i. 166). The echo is slight.

405.04 *Had I the concordant wiseheads . . . :* still another *A Midsummer Night's Dream* echo (Theseus: "How shall we find the concord of this discord?" in V. i. 60); see entry for 482.34–36 for explanation.

406.13 *getting his tongue arount it and Boland's broth broken:* this description of Shaun eating his soup ("broth") seems to include a reference to the witches in *Macbeth* ("Aroint thee, witch" in I. iii. 6; see also 223.19, "Arrest thee, scaldbrother"—perhaps brother, broth, and witches are related somehow). Cf. 492.34, "aroint him."

406.25 *hurrah there for tobies:* a toast to mugs of stout (tobies), and to *Twelfth Night*'s Sir Toby Belch, who is present a number of times in this chapter. Shaun's eating and drinking habits, described in this passage, resemble those of Falstaff (mentioned in 403.21) and of Belch. See also the entry for 423.11,13,33 for other references to Sir Toby, including his well-known "cakes and ale" quotation.

408.31–32 *First he was living to feel what the eldest daughter she was panseying:* Shaun, speaking, tells how Shem was wondering what their sister Issy was thinking: "pansy"-ing is Issy-Ophelia's way of cerebrating, since, as Ophelia said, "There is pansies, that's for thoughts" (IV. v. 174). See entries for 403.14–15, 443.14–15, and 446.03–5.

408.36 *Piscisvendolor!:* Shem ("Fish hands Macsorley" in 408.25) is being accused of mistreating Issy-Ophelia and (in Latin) of being, like Polonius, a fishmonger *(Ham.* II. ii. 174). Cf. "fishmummer" in 29.26 and "fleshmonger" in 144.30.

409.03 *Ear! Ear! Not ay! Eye! Eye!:* ear and eye, Shem and Shaun, and their separate versions of "List! List!" (like "Hear ohere!" and "Oyez! Oyez!"). Also, perhaps, an echo of a purple passage in *Richard II:* "Ay, no; no, ay; for I must nothing be . . ." (IV. i. 201).

410.04 *my oldfellow's orologium:* my father's watch. There may be several references to *Othello* on this page (see "Emailia" in 410.23). "Oldfellow" is a pun on Othello in the "Circe" chapter of *Ulysses*, in which "Shakespeare" crows, "Iagogo! How my Oldfellow chokit his Thursdaymomum. Iagogo!" *(U*, 567).

410.23 *Speak to us of Emailia:* a request is made to Shaun the Post about ALP's letter (the "mail"). ALP may also be Iago's wife Emilia or Aegeon's wife Aemelia (mother of the twins in *The Comedy of Errors)*. At the end of *Othello*, Emilia's revelations lead to Othello's last speech: "Speak of me as I am . . ." (V. ii. 342).

411.08–11 *Never back a woman you defend, never get quit of a friend on whom you depend, never make face to a foe till he's rife and never get stuck to another man's pfife:* these dicta of Shaun's philosophy preview book III, chapter 2, in which Shaun continues *ad nauseum* with his Laertes-like lecture. See entry for 431.21–457.24.

411.27–28 *The gloom hath rays, her lump is love:* seemingly a reference to Stephen Dedalus's theory about Shakespeare in *Ulysses*, in which he imagines that the gloom in Shakespeare's domestic life is finally dispelled by the arrival of "a child, a girl placed in his arms, Marina . . . prosperous Prospero, the good man rewarded, Lizzie, grandpa's lump of love" (*U*, 195, 213). Shakespeare's "lump of love" was Lizzie, or Elizabeth Hall, daughter of Shakespeare's daughter, Susanna Hall. See entry for 338.31; as in that line, "hath" here may stand for Anne Hathaway. See also entry for 80.17–18.

412.21 *quoth mecback:* quoth Macbeth.

413.02 *there is a peg under me and there is a tum till me:* Peg Woffington (1714–60) and Thomas Sheridan (1719–88) were the most famous Irish Shakespearean actors in their day. The *RES* (p. 386) reports that "during the 18th century the Smock Alley was the center of Irish theatrical life. . . . Members of this company who were later to win fame in London as Shakespeareans were James Quin, Peg Woffington, and Thomas Sheridan." Joyce may have seen Woffington and Sheridan as a tandem of Irish Shakespearean acting, considering the number of times "peg" and "tom" are linked in the *Wake*. See also entries for 436.09–11, 577.16, 579.17, and 586.12. The combined references to Peg and Tom in *Finnegans Wake* suggest that Joyce knew or imagined Woffington and Sheridan to be lovers: see chapter 3 of this study.

Shaun is here describing his plans to compose a play, if "my pen is upt to scratch" (412.32). His publishers will be the Dublin firm of Browne and Nolan, and, as long as his salary is properly paid, he will write a play (or an opera, like Verdi's *La Forza del Destino),* which will be published *(Nihil Obstat, Imprimatur)* as long as there is a leg under him, or as long as Woffington and Sheridan are around to take the lead roles: ". . . it is also one of my avowal's intentions . . . so apt as my pen is upt to scratch, to compound . . . for my publickers, Nolaner and Browno, Nickil Hopstout, Christcross, so long as, thanks to force of destiny, my selary as a paykelt is propaired, and there is a peg under me and there is a tum till me" (412.30–413.02).

413.17–18 *This, my tears, is my last will intesticle wrote off in the strutforit about their absent female assauciations:* Shaun is composing, Swift-like, a will leaving his possessions for his "dears," Esther and Vanessa. The lines bring to mind the controversial issue (in Shakespearean scholarship) of the Bard's will; we recall Stephen Dedalus's discussions of Shakespeare's female associations, especially in London while absent from Anne Hathaway, who was his "Penelope stayathome" (*U*, 201) at Stratford ("strutforit") and to whom he left his secondbest bed in his last will and testament ("my last will intesticle"). See "secondbest buns" in 121.32.

414.20–419.08: Shaun's fable of the Ondt and the Gracehoper derives from the fable of the Ant and the Grasshopper by La Fontaine. It seems, however, that Joyce may have modeled it more directly on Greene's *A Groatsworth of Wit*, which is mentioned in *Ulysses* (on pages 187, 190, 204, and 210.). See chapter 5, endnote 48 for a discussion and comparison of Greene's story and Joyce's version; see also chapter 6 of this study.

The connection in Joyce's mind between *Groatsworth* and Gracehoper is demonstrated in 360.36, "our groatsupper." See also chapter 5, endnote 48.

416.18 *Iomio! Iomio!:* perhaps an echo of "O Romeo, Romeo! wherefore art thou Romeo" (*Rom.* II. ii. 33).

417.31 *Never did Dorsan from Dunshanagan dance it with more devilry:* possibly Dunsinane and all that witches' devilry in *Macbeth*. Cf. "dance inane" in 250.16.

418.18 *So saida to Moyhammlet and marhaba to your Mount:* the poem concluding the fable of the Ondt and Gracehoper includes a statement to "my Hamlet," garbled by Mohammed going to the mountain.

418.35 *ail's weal: All's Well that Ends Well.* See entries for 40.01 and 279.05.

419.21–22 *I'm as afterdusk nobly Roman as pope:* Shaun claims to be as Roman as the Pope or as Brutus, "the noblest Roman of them all" (*JC* V. v. 68). See entry for 84.15.

420.15–16 *An infant sailing eggshells on the floor of a wet day would have more sabby:* Shaun's comment here about Shem is a syntactical echo of Hamlet's indictment of his mother: "O God, a beast that wants discourse of reason / Would have mourned longer" (I. ii. 150–51). "Eggshells" recalls Fortinbras, who was willing to risk "all that fortune, death, and danger dare, / Even for an eggshell" (IV. iv. 52–53). "Eggshells" may also echo *Exiles*.

421.18 *words as the penmarks used out in sinscript:* the Bard's scribbling (Sanskrit penmarks) and Hamlet's Denmark; see entry for 189.06. Perhaps because the Bard wrote *Hamlet* (in which the Ghost is referred to as Denmark, as in I. i. 48), the Bard-Shem is referred to a few lines later as Denmark: "But I would not care to be so unfruitful to my own part as to swear for the moment positively as to the views of Denmark" (421.27–29).

422.14 *Obnoximost posthumust!:* Shaun accuses Shem of being obnoxious. Strong (p. 73) sees this as a reference to Posthumus Leonatus, Imogen's husband in *Cymbeline*. See entry for 377.09.

422.18–19 *May we petition you, Shaun illustrious, then, to put his prentis' pride in your aproper's purse:* maybe an echo of Iago's advice to Roderigo: "Put money in thy purse" (*Oth.* I. iii. 338 ff.). Shaun, like the Ondt, is a hoarder, and puts much money in his purse.

422.23–425.05 —*Well it is partly my own, isn't it? . . . :* in these four pages,

Shaun makes another direct accusation that Shem is a forger and a plagiarist, and that Shem's letter was, in reality, plagiarized from Shaun. (See chapter 6 for a more complete treatment of the theme of forgery and Shakespearean scholarship). Shaun here claims the letter as his own. The next four pages contain references to: James Macpherson (423.01, "jameymock farceson"; Macpherson's Ossian created a great controversy; see lines 123.35, 227.32, and 194.13 for other references to Macpherson's Ossian); "imitator" (423.10); "eggschicker" (423.19; bacon and eggs are associated with Shakespearean forgeries); possibly Bacon and Delia Bacon (see entry for 423.25); and Lewis Theobald, the Shakespearean forger (see entry for 424.29). In 424.31–425.03, Shaun finally makes a clear and direct charge that Shem stole the letter from him.

422.31–32 *Beerman's bluff was what begun it, Old Knoll and his borrowing:* Glasheen observes (p. 157) that Old Knowell (cf. 76.26, "old knoll") was the role Shakespeare was believed to have played in Ben Jonson's *Everyman in His Humour*. Joyce is suggesting that the letter was originally written by Shakespeare, who was also accused of "borrowing" from others; the letter thus becomes a symbol for the *Wake* and for all literature. "Beerman" is HCE the publican, and Old Knoll is HCE as Howth Head (the "bluff").

423.11, 13, 33 *Does he drink because I am sorely there shall be no more Kates and Nells. . . . thank the Bench. . . . negertoby:* here is Sir Toby Belch's famous question to Malvolio: "Dost thou think, because thou art virtuous, there shall be no more cakes and ale?" (*TN* II. iii. 106). Belch is mentioned on this page in "Bench" and "negertoby." Shaun eats in Belch-like fashion. Peery has observed that Belch's famous line "is given an adroit twist when the speaker, Shaun, is the puritan, rather than the bon vivant, Sir Toby, and the antecedent of 'he' is the bon vivant instead of the puritan" (p. 250). Similar reversals occur between Shakespearean characters in 167.35–168.01, 468.03–4, and 469.20–21.

423.25 *till that hag of the coombe rapes the pad off his lock:* the reference is to Pope's "The Rape of the Lock"; however, the passage is about plagiarism and forgery, and, since Shakespeare-Shem was accused of plagiarizing Bacon-Shaun, the "hag" might be Delia Bacon, who tried to prove that Bacon was Shakespeare by raping the lock of Shakespeare's tomb. Glasheen argues (pp. 21, 27) that Biddy Doran, the hen, is associated with Delia Bacon, and is called Belinda in 111.05, after the heroine of "The Rape of the Lock." See chapter 6 of this study and entries for 111.05 and 208.29. Perhaps "sygnus the swan" (423.21) is the Swan of Avon.

424.29 *till tibbes grey eves:* a reference to Lewis Theobald (Pope's Tibbald), Shakespearean scholar and forger. The line occurs within Shaun's direct accusation of Shem's plagiarism ("Every dimmed letter in it is a copy . . ."). See chapter 6; see also entries for 28.05, 117.19, 159.30–32, 236.08, and 263.05; see also Atherton, pp. 69–70.

425.20–25 *my trifolium librotto, the authordux Book of Lief, would, if given to daylight . . . far exceed what that bogus bolshy of a shame, my soamheis brother . . . is conversant with in audible black and prink. Outragedy of* *poetscalds! Acomedy of letters! I have them all, tame, deep and harried, in my mine's I:* after accusing Shem of plagiarism, Shaun now affirms that he has just as much bardic talent as Shem, and could write a work that would make his brother's look feeble. He says that his own libretto, in three folios, would, if it were ever allowed to come to light, be the real, orthodox Book of Life (unlike Joyce's *Ulysses*), and would far exceed what that shameful bogus of a Bolshevik forger (his Siamese twin) is able to do in black and white, in print, in ink. His brother's is an outrageous tragedy of poets *(skalds)!* A literary *Comedy of Errors!* He has all the fictional characters himself, every Tom, Dick, and Harry, in his mind's eye. ("In my mind's eye, Horatio," *Ham.* I. ii. 186).

Cf. 477.23, "in their minds years."

The Academy of Letters, which Yeats invited Joyce to join (Joyce refused), is also here; see McHugh, p. 425.

425.30 *pucktricker's:* Puck (certainly a trickster) and St. Patrick.
426.20–21 *the ghost of an ocean's, the wieds of pansiful heathvens:* the ghost of a notion, the width of merciful Heaven. Hamlet's Ghost and Ophelia (pansy) may also be here.
427.34 *beminded us out there in Cockpit, poor twelve o'clock scholars:* the twelve questioners or scholars ask the departing Shaun to remember them while he is gone and at the Cockpit. The Phoenix, or Cockpit Theatre, was an Elizabethan playhouse in St.-Giles-in-the-Fields, adjoining Drury Lane. See entry for 219.02.

Book III, Chapter 2

429.18–19, 430.06–7 *restant, against a butterblond warden of the peace, one comestabulish Sigurdsen . . . the first human yellowstone landmark (the bear, the boer, the king of all boors):* the landmark in front of St. Bridget's nightschool that Jaun rests upon is the drunken HCE (where he was left two chapters ago), as a mixture of the blond constable (Lally Tompkins), Sigurson (the male servant), and Sackerson, the famed Elizabethan bear. See entries for 471.30 and 530.22. Joyce had already mentioned Sackerson in "Scylla and Charybdis": "The flag is up on the playhouse by the bankside. The bear Sackerson growls in the pit near it, Paris garden" (*U*, 188). Georg Brandes reports that "close to the Globe Theatre lay the Bear Garden for bear-baiting, the rank smell from which greeted the nostrils even before it came in sight. The famous bear Sackerson, who is mentioned in *The Merry Wives of Windsor* (I. i. 266), now and then broke his chain and put female theatregoers shrieking to flight" (Gifford and Seidman, p. 164).
430.29 *savouring of wild thyme and parsley:* Boyle (in *James Joyce's Pauline Vision*, p. 6) suggests that the "yellowstone landmark" on this page coincides with the "Woful Dane Bottom" (503.21; Bottom of *MND*) and *A Midsummer Night's Dreams*'s "bank where the wild thyme blows" (II. i. 249).
431.01–6 *to drop a few stray remarks anent their personal appearances . . .*

gently reproving one that the ham of her hom could be seen below her hem: Jaun-Laertes's sermon to his Ophelias (the 29 schoolgirls)—see entry for 431.21–457.24—starts with a dress code and warnings about hams, hems, and Hamlet.

431.21–457.24 *—Sister, dearest . . . :* Jaun's sententious sermon to his sister forms the bulk of this chapter and is perhaps indebted to Laertes's address to Ophelia where he warns her about Hamlet (I. iii. 1–43). This possibility was suggested by Hodgart (p. 741). There are quite a few parallels, especially on page 431, to Laertes's speech. See chapter 4 of this study, pages 69–72, which describe the parallels in detail.

432.25–29 *Now. During our brief apsence . . . adhere to as many as probable of the ten commandments . . . in the long run they will prove for your better guidance along your path of right of way:* Jaun-Laertes's advice provides an alternative to the "primrose path of dalliance" (I. iii. 50). See entry for 431.21–457.24.

432.32–33 *where's the fate's to be wished for:* along with "a consummation" a few lines earlier (432.14), Jaun-Laertes's sermon also seems to echo Hamlet's famous soliloquy: "'Tis a consummation / Devoutly to be wished" (III. i. 63–64). See entry for 433.36–434.05.

433.35–36 *Wet your thistle where a weed is and you'll rue it:* Jaun's warning to Issy reminds us that "rue" is one of the flowers associated with Issy-Ophelia: "There's rue for you, and here's some for me" (IV. v. 180). See entry for 444.12.

433.36–434.05 *Especially beware please of being at a party to any demoralizing home life. . . . Where it is nobler in the main to supper than the boys and errors of outrager's virtue:* Jaun-Laertes's warning to Issy is about Shem: if she loses her virtue to Shem, her own brother, she would be a party to a demoralizing home life. That Shem-Hamlet is the "outrager" being referred to is clear, for here again (see entry for 432.32–33) Jaun is echoing Hamlet's soliloquy: "Whether 'tis nobler in the mind to suffer / The slings and arrows of outrageous fortune . . ." (III. i. 57–58).

434.18 *if you can't point a lily get to henna out of here:* the passage discusses Mary Magdalen ("Marie Maudlin" in 434.16), and the line seems to say that "if you can't throw the first stone, get the hell out of here." There is also an echo of Salisbury's lines in *King John* (IV. ii. 11–16): "to paint the lily, / To throw a perfume on the violet . . . Is wasteful and ridiculous excess." See McHugh, p. 434.

434.19, 27 *Put your swell foot foremost . . . to joy a Jonas:* Tindall (pp. 240, 249) has pointed out that "Ernest Jones's *Hamlet and Oedipus* is brought to mind by 'errors of outrager's virtue' from *Hamlet* (434.04–5), 'swell foot' or Oedipus (434.19), and 'Jonas' (434.27)." Jones, a psychoanalyst and Shakespearean critic, was somewhat of an authority on incest—which is what Jaun-Laertes is proposing to Issy-Ophelia. As we've seen, Ernest Jones ("Professor Jones") is a surrogate for Shaun-Jaun.

434.35–435.03 *Autist Algy . . . the dallytaunties . . . taking you to the playguehouse to see the Smirching of Venus:* Jaun appears to be warning Issy about the corrupting influence of drama and literature, as he did also in 434.08–10. Algy (Shem as Algernon Swinburne, the dilettantish literati) would only take you to a playhouse, to see a play about fornication *(Smirching—*or *Birching— of Venus)* and disease ("playgue")—or Shakespeare's *Merchant of Venice.*

Jaun continues by condemning the appreciation of art as well; see entry for 435.16.

435.16 *All blah! Viper's vapid vilest!:* this is Jaun's opinion of the arts, with an echo of *Love's Labor's Lost.* See lines 74.03 and 157.23.

436.09–11 *kosenkissing . . . like Population Peg on a hint or twim clandestinely does be doing to Temptation Tom:* another reference to the duo of Peg Woffington and Thomas Sheridan (see entry for 413.02).

Shaun-Laertes continues his warnings to Issy-Ophelia about clandestine flirting and temptation with other boys, including being a kissing cousin, like "Population" Peg Woffington; temptation, after all, results in population. Woffington is a good example, since she and David Garrick were known lovers, and, as the *RES* (p. 957) puts it, "her morals were not above reproach." Were Peg and Tom, then, also known to be lovers? See entries for 413.02, 579.17, and 586.12.

437.05 *Rutland Rise:* the Earl of Rutland perhaps. See entries for 42.36 and 148.08.

438.31–36 *Once and for all, I'll have no college swankies. . . . that rogues' gallery of nightbirds and bitchfanciers, lucky duffs and light lindsays:* Jaun-Laertes warns Issy-Ophelia that he will not brook her flirtations with any college smoothies—like Hamlet, the "beardless undergraduate from Wittenberg" (*U*, 207). "Lucky duffs" (lucky ducks) and "lindsays" seem somehow connected with Macduff; see, for example, line 469.20: "Lead on, Macadam, and danked be he who first sights Halt Linduff!" Glasheen observes (p. 170) that "light Lindsays" may refer to the lines in "Battle of Otterbourne": "He chose the Gordons and the Graems / With the Lindsays, light and gay. . . ." If so, both the Lindsays and Macduff (in "danked be he who first sights Halt Linduff"; see entry for 469.20–21) have to do with Scottish battles.

440.18–19 *Mary Liddlelambe's flitsy tales, espicially with the scentaminted sauce:* Tindall maintains (p. 241) that fairy tales combine here with Lamb's sentimental *Tales from Shakespeare,* one of the books Jaun recommends Issy to read.

Rose notes that the line joins Mary Lamb, the nursery rhyme "Mary had a little lamb," sentiment, and "the notion of lambs' tails dished up with scented mint sauce" (*The Index Manuscript,* p. 313). Mary and Charles Lamb's *Tales from Shakespeare* (1807) were sentimentalized, fairy tale-like versions of Shakespeare's plays for young readers.

441.11 *what stuck to the Comtesse Cantilene . . . :* McHugh—in *AWN,* XVI, 5 (Oct. 1979): 68—shows that the line is taken from a story in the *Annals of the Theatre Royal, Dublin:* a "Contessa gave a thoroughly Shaksperian [sic] reading to Romeo."

441.33 *the goattanned saxopeeler upshotdown chigs peel of him:* whatever this upshot is, it again contains Goethe, Dante, and Shakespeare ("saxopeeler" and "chigs peel"). See entries for 47.19, 344.05–6, and 539.05–9 for other combinations of these three poets.

442.22 *we'll dumb well soon show him:* possibly *Hamlet*'s dumb show again. See entries for 88.25, 120.07–8, and 559. 18.

443.14–15 *He'll have pansements then for his pensamientos, howling for peace. Pretty knocks, I promise him . . . :* Jaun swears that if Shem-Hamlet has any thoughts about Issy-Ophelia, he'll get his due payments ("pretty knocks") for his Ophelian thoughts ("pensamientos") at Jaun-Laertes's hands. Thoughts about Ophelia are rendered as "pansements" and "pensamientos"; cf. lines 403.14, 408.32, and 446.03.

444.12 *Rue the Day!:* see entry for 433.35–36 and *Hamlet* IV. v. 180.

445.22 *if you think I'm so tan cupid:* Shaun may be damn stupid as well as "Dan Cupid," the name Berowne gives to the god of love in *Love's Labor's Lost* (III. i. 169). See McHugh, p. 445.

446.03–5 *sending uym loveliest pansiful thoughts touching me dash in-you through wee dots Hyphen, the so pretty arched godkin of beddingnights:* Jaun declares his love to Issy-Ophelia, and sues for her favors. He promises Ophelia to "send you my thoughts" ("uym" = you my) while he's away, and to wire his love to her by telegram: with dashes, dots, and hyphens. He seems to propose marriage (Hymen?) to this pretty goddess (or god-child, "godchen") of the wedding night and bedroom; "godkin" may echo Hamlet's "bare bodkin" (III. i. 76), but it more likely is a conflation of Hamlet's "God's bodkin, man!" (II. ii. 516—meaning "God's little body"), a term more appropriate in context: Issy-Ophelia's celestial little body. See entries for 403.14–15, 408.31–32, 443.14–15, and 449.30.

447.04 *till navel, spokes, and felloes hum like hymn:* Hodgart has mentioned (p. 742) that this line echoes the Player's description of violence and destruction, in *Hamlet:* "Break all the spokes and fellies from her wheel, / And bowl the round nave down the hill of heaven . . . " (II. ii. 483–84). Joyce seems to be using the line in quite an opposite sense, as Jaun calls for "Meliorism in mass quantities . . . till navel, spokes, and felloes hum like hymn"—that is, till the wheel (of Fortune perhaps—the line refers to "raffling" and "sweepstakes"), consisting of hub ("nave"), spokes, and "fellies" (rim segments), runs smoothly and hums like a hymn.

448.20 *'Tis an ill weed blows no poppy good:* the proverbial ill wind that blows no one good. In *Henry IV, Part 2* (V. iii. 85), Pistol refers to "the ill wind which blows no man to good." (See *Henry VI, Part 3*, II. v. 55: "Ill blows the wind that profits nobody.") Cf. entries for 20.35 and 28.09.

449.30 *hearing the wireless harps of sweet old Aerial:* the wireless and aerials through which Jaun's cables to Issy are to arrive with his "loveliest pansiful thoughts" (see entry for 446.03) and, perhaps, a wireless Ariel *(The Tempest).*

450.02–5 *What wouldn't I poach . . . flashing down the swansway:* recalls the legend of the Bard's (the Swan of Avon) deer-poaching incident, referred to in 209.14–15. "Swansway" may also refer to the "swan's road," a common

Anglo-Saxon kenning for the sky, and to Proust's *Swann's Way*. See entry for 465.28–35.

450.32–33 *But enough of greenwood's gossip:* As You Like It's "greenwood" world again. Cf. 30.14, 74.10, and 335.32.

Glasheen observes that "to tell a Greenwood" is to tell a lie—*AWN*, I, 5 (Oct. 1964): 10.

452.27 *nenni:* refers to Ophelia's "Hey non nony" (IV. v. 164); see entries for 307.F8 and 203.14.

455.11–13 *Postmartem is the goods. . . . Toborrow and toburrow and tobarrow! That's our crass, hairy and evergrim life:* here Jaun has an apocalyptic vision, and warns Issy that death is the only certainty—postmortem is the goods. Our life on earth is only a series of tomorrows, ending in burial under the sod ("tobarrow"). He echoes Macbeth's speech on the same theme: "Tomorrow, and tomorrow, and tomorrow, / Creeps at this petty pace . . ." (V. v. 19). See entry for 455.24–29.

455.24–29 *What a humpty daum earth looks our miseryme heretoday as compared beside the Hereweareagain Gaieties of the Afterpiece when the Royal Revolver of these real globoes lets regally fire of his mio colpo for the chrisman's pandemon to give over and the Harlequinade to begin properly SPQueaRking Mark Time's Finist Joke. Putting Allspace in a Notshall:* this passage concerns the Last Day as a Christmas pantomime; see chapter 3 of this study for a detailed explication. Shakespearean references are to the Gaiety Theatre and Globe Theatre, Michael Gunn, *Macbeth, Julius Caesar,* and *Hamlet.*

"SPQueaRking" cleverly describes the pandemonium of the Last Day, like the day Julius Caesar fell (on the Ides of March), when "The graves stood tenantless and the sheeted dead / Did *squeak* and gibber in the Roman streets" (*Ham.* I. i. 115–16); SPQR were the initials of Rome (*Senatus Populusque Romanus*, the Senate and People of Rome; cf. 454.35, "The seanad and pobbel queue's remainder"). Jaun summarizes the Judgment Day with an echo of *Hamlet:* "Putting Allspace in a Notshall." This could only happen on the Last Day, and doing so would please the spatialist Jaun-Shaun-Bottom, who might, like Hamlet or Brutus, say, "O God, I could be bounded in a nutshell and count myself a king of infinite space, were it not that I have bad dreams" (II. ii. 250). See Peery, p. 255 and Hodgart, p. 740; see also entry for 276.L2.

Glasheen suggests (p. 125) that "455.26–9 describes the burning of the Globe during a performance of Shakespeare's *Henry VIII*." In 1613 the Globe burned down because of a cannon fired in act IV.

See chapter 3 of this study to learn how the *Wake* is seen as a Christmas pantomime. The traditional English pantomime included performances by grotesque or buffoon-like characters, such as Harlequin or Scaramouch; Harlequin became a major character. The pantomimes evolved from elaborate fairy tale fantasies into a mixture of slapstick, vaudeville, and popular songs. They still preserve the tradition of having the "boy" (the hero of the fairy tale) played by a girl and his mother played by a male—a theme (i.e., sexual confusion and transvestitism) that repeatedly finds its way into the *Wake*. Even in this century, the pantomime has been the most popular form of Christmas entertainment in England ("Pantomime," *Encyclopaedia Britannica*). See also Adams, *Surface and Symbol*, pp. 76–82.

"Evergrim" is another theater reference—to W.W. Kelly's touring stage company, the Evergreen Touring Company. See Glasheen, p. 154.

456.10 *Oliviero:* this could be Laurence Olivier, famous for his interpretation of *Hamlet* (at the Old Vic in 1937; Joyce died in 1941) based on Ernest Jones's *Hamlet and Oedipus*.

456.20–24 *All the vitalmines is beginning to sozzle in chewn . . . kates and eaps . . . and xoxxoxo and xooxox xxoxoxxoxxx till I'm fustfed like fungstif:* Shaun is eating again; his eating habits are associated with Sir Toby Belch (see entries for page 423) and Falstaff (e.g., 7. 13, "fraudstuff"). Here again are Belch's "cakes and ale" (*TN* II. iii. 106) in "kates and eaps" (cf. 423.11) and Falstaff in "fungstif." After masticating his food down to the vitamins, all that is left of Shaun's victuals are little x's and o's; he's then fast-fed (or force-fed) like Falstaff—and "stuffed" ("fustfed" anagram).

457.03 *Ferdinand:* Miranda's match in *The Tempest*.

461.17,30 *my golden violents wetting. . . . Coach me how to tumble:* Issy's reply to her brother features key words of Ophelia's: violets ("I would give you some violets, but they withered all when my father died" in IV. v. 182–83; cf. entry for 143. 26) and "tumble" ("Before you tumbled me, / You promised me to wed" in IV. v. 62–63; Issy, too, is speaking of a "wetting"). See *Hamlet* section of Appendix 2, under IV. v. 174–83.

463.08 *Romeo: Romeo and Juliet*.

463.15–17 *Got by the one goat, suckled by the same nanna, one twitch, one nature makes us oldworld kin:* Jaun-Shaun describing his relationship with his twin, Dave-Shem, echoes Ulysses's lines from *Troilus and Cressida*: "One touch of nature makes the whole world kin" (III. iii. 174). See 139.01, "one touch of nature set a veiled world agrin"; see also Hodgart, p. 751.

463.19–20 *There's the nasturtium for ye that saved manny a poor sinker from water on the grave:* this seems to introduce Ophelia, who gave out flowers ("There's fennel for you, and columbines. There's rue for you . . ." in IV. v. 174–80) and who was a "poor sinker" and drowned in her watery grave. See 78.19.

463.36 *the prince of goodfilips:* after calling Dave-Shem a "demented brick," Jaun-Shaun names him the prince of goodfellows. Joyce also has Robin Goodfellow, *A Midsummer Night's Dream*'s Puck, in mind here, since this entry appears in the *Scribbledehobble* workbook: "prince of goodfellows: Robin" (*Scribbledehobble*, Thomas E. Connolly, ed., p. 97).

464.30 *costard:* Costard was the clown in *Love's Labor's Lost*, referred to, perhaps, also in 563.23, "costarred."

465.28–35 *As the curly bard said. . . . Be offalia. Be hamlet. Be the property plot. Be Yorick and Lankystare. Be cool. Be mackinamucks of yourselves. . . . Watch the swansway:* Jaun-Laertes is now urging Issy-Ophelia and Shem-Hamlet to go ahead and play around, reversing his earlier advice. In effect, Shaun says, "Go ahead—do anything and be anyone you want to. Be a flirt, an offal-ia (a trashy Ophelia). Be Hamlet. Be Yorick, even, or York and Lancaster, anything you want to. Be cool. Make a mess of yourselves." Jaun seems to be using Shakespeare's words as a guide: "the swansway" of "the curly bard" (see 450.05).

467.08 *A full octavium below me:* Octavius, Augustus Caesar. See entry for 468.03–4.

468.03–4 *How used you learn me, brather soboostius, in my augustan days? With cesarella looking on:* Jaun-Shaun speaks about his competition with Dave-Shem for the love of Issy. In the family triumvirate, Shaun is Augustus ("in my augustan days") Caesar, or Octavius, while Shem is "a full octavium below [him]" (467.08; perhaps Shem is Antony) and Issy is "cesarella," or Margareen-Cleopatra. "In my augustan days" echoes Cleopatra's "salad days" (*Ant.* I. v. 73) when Caesar (Julius) looked on; Shaun-Octavius, reversing the roles, now has Issy-Cleopatra looking on at his own salad days.

468.20–22 *But from the stress of their sunder enlivening, ay clasp, deciduously, a nikrokosmikon must come:* Jaun grasps ("ay clasp") that from the thunder and lightning ("sunder enlivening") of the sexual act (e.g., "They clasped and sundered, did the coupler's will" in *U*, 38) shall a child come, a microcosm of Nick and Mick. Or, as Stephen Dedalus argues about Shakespeare, the reconciliation comes only after a sundering: "Where there is a reconciliation . . . there must have been first a sundering. . . . There can be no reconciliation if there has not been a sundering. . . . What softens the heart of a man ? . . . A child, a girl placed in his arms, Marina" (*U*, 193, 195).

468.26 *mitching:* perhaps the *"miching mallecho"* of Hamlet (III. ii. 131; see "miching micher" in 291.22). See also Hodgart, p. 742. The context ("they put on my watchcraft . . . Mymiddle toe's mitching") seems to refer to witchcraft and recalls the Witch's "By the pricking of my thumbs, / Something wicked this way comes" in *Macbeth* IV. i. 44–45. Thomas Middleton ("middle toe") wrote *The Witch*, as well as, some believe, the witches' scene in *Macbeth*. See *RES*, p. 540.

468.34–35 *And, remember this, a chorines, there's the witch on the heath, sistra:* Jaun reminds sister Issy of the "weird sisters" of *Macbeth*, the witches on the blasted heath. See entries for 468.26 and 469.20–21.

469.20–21 *Lead on, Macadam, and danked be he who first sights Halt Linduff!:* Jaun bids his farewell with Macbeth's last words: "Lay on, Macduff, / And damned be him that first cries, 'Hold, enough!'" (V. vii. 33–34). Shaun, however, is, Macduff; the roles are reversed, and the line seems to be addressed by Macduff ("Linduff"; see entry for 438.31–36) to Macbeth ("Macadam," son of Adam). For both Jaun and Shakespeare's Macbeth, these words form their final farewell—"last fireless words of postludium" (469.29). See Peery, p. 253.

469.23 *Bennydick:* Much Ado's Benedick, possibly. Cf. 431.18.

471.30 *Sickerson, that borne of a bjoerne . . . hellyg Ursulinka:* Sickerson—the son of a holy Danish bear, or of a holy Ursuline nun—is also Sackerson, the famed Elizabethan bear mentioned in *The Merry Wives of Windsor* (I. i. 263–66) and in *Ulysses* on page 188. See entries for 429.18–19 and 530.22.

Bjorn is Danish for "bear"; *hellig* is Danish for "holy," and *Ursulinka* is, presumably, a diminutive *ursus*.

"Born" may refer to "man" (*beorn* in Anglo-Saxon).

Book III, Chapter 3

477.18–23 *in the back of their mind's ear. . . . And in their minds years:* another variant of Hamlet's "In my mind's eye, Horatio" (I. ii. 186). See 254.18 and 425.25.

478.16 *lead us to hopenhaven:* Copenhagen, a Danish haven, and a haven of hope in "the undiscovered country." See 143.10, 220.34, and 248.25.

481.07–8 *—Dream. Ona nonday I sleep. I dreamt of a somday. Of a wonday I shall wake. Ah!:* again Yawn has Bottom's dream-vision about non-days, somedays, one day, Monday, Sunday, etc. This is a direct echo of Shaun-Bottom's vision in 403.18–407.22: "Methought as I was dropping asleep somepart in nonland . . ." Bottom dreamed that he was an ass; the ass in *Finnegans Wake* is present in 475.30–35, 478.08, 479.09, 480.06–7, 482.14, 482.34–36, and 489.35. See entry for 482.34–36.

Glasheen suggests that "where no spider webbeth" (481.05) may be an echo of the song the Fairies sing Titania to sleep with in *A Midsummer Night's Dream:* "Weaving spiders, come not here: / Hence, you long-legged spinners, hence!" (II. ii. 18–19).

481.16 *old Romeo: Romeo and Juliet.*

482.34–36 *What can't be coded can be decorded if an ear aye sieze what no eye ere grieved for:* Boyle notes (in *James Joyce's Pauline Vision*, pp. vii–xii, 10) that this line echoes two lines from *A Midsummer Night's Dream:* Theseus's "How shall we find the concord of this discord?" (V. i. 60) and Bottom's "The eye of man hath not heard, the ear of man hath not seen" (IV. i. 209). The ass in *Finnegans Wake* laments that "Had I the concordant wiseheads of Messrs Gregory and Lyons alongside of Dr Tarpey's and I dorsay the reverend Mr McDougall's, but I, poor ass, am but as their fourpart tinckler's dunkey" (405.04–6). Man, however, is an ass if he goes about as a concordant wisehead, to expound or decode Bottom's dream. Boyle argues (p. x) that Joyce's point is "that the miraculous and inspired expression of [dreams and visions] may not be totally subject to the rational dissection of nonpoets."

483.16–18 *I'll see you moved farther, blarneying Marcantonio! What cans such wretch to say to I or how have My to doom with him?:* Yawn-Shaun regards with disdain his twin brother, whom he here calls Mark Antony. In asking "what can such a wretch say to me or what have I to do with him?" Yawn is echoing Hamlet's question about the Player: "What's Hecuba to him, or he to Hecuba?" (II. ii. 543). Yawn goes on to ask, "Been ike hins kindergardien?" (483.25; German for—"Am I my brother's keeper?"). Cf. 276.08–9.

485.17 *old fellow: Othello*, perhaps. See entry for 410.04 and *Ulysses*, p. 567 for the source of this pun.

486.09 *Mere man's mime:* another possible version of *Love's Labor's Lost.* See entry for 157.23.

488.18 *Ruemember, blither, thou must lie:* recalls Ophelia's "There's rosemary, that's for remembrance. Pray you, love, remember. . . . There's rue for you and here's some for me" (*Ham.* IV. v. 174–80). Remembering and rue are both used as motifs for Ophelia. See entry for 444.12.

488.19 *Oyessoyess!:* Yawn's vigorous affirmative is also King Hamlet's "List, list!" Cf. 85.31, "Oyeh! Oyeh!" The plural of "oyez" is "oyesses" *(Webster's).*

489.15–19 *I remember ham to me, when we were like bro and sis over our castor and porridge. . . . We were in one class of age like to two clots of egg:* Yawn-Shaun remembers his childhood days (of porridge and castor oil) with his twin (Castor and Pollux), Shem, who is referred to as ham and Hamlet. They were as alike as two clots in an egg. This is another indication of why ham, eggs, and other breakfast foods are used to indicate similarity, forgery, and plagiarism. See chapter 6 of this study.

The second sentence may echo Helena's lines in *A Midsummer Night's Dream:* "We, Hermia, like two artificial gods, / Have with our needles created both one flower. . . . So we grew together, / Like to a double cherry . . ." (III. ii. 203–9.)

489.33–35 *As you sing it it's a study. That letter selfpenned. . . . This nonday diary, this allnights newseryreel:* the letter and the *Wake* are Shakespearean—*As You Like It* and *Midsummer Night's Dream* (cf. Shaun-Bottom's dream-vision on "nonday" in "nonland" in 481.07–8 and 403.18–407.22), the all-night dream and the newsreel about HCE and his family.

491.07 *clapperclaws:* a reference to the curious epistle to the reader prefacing the first quarto edition of *Troilus and Cressida:* "Eternal reader, you have here a new play, never staled with the stage, never clapper-clawed with the palms of the vulgar, and yet passing full of the palm comical. . . ." See Hodgart, p. 751; cf. 614.30, "clappercoupling."

491.20 *the arkbashap of Yarak:* both the Archbishop of York and the skull ("boskop") of *Hamlet*'s Yorick; see entry for 190.19. Yorick is referred to several times in the *Wake.*

491.29 *My Mo Mum!:* "Fie, foh, and fum" again (*Lr.* III. iv. 174). See entries for 7.09, 133.17, and 367.23.

491.29 *He loves a drary lane:* Yawn says that HCE likes drama such as the fare presented at Drury Lane, the most famous of Shakespearean theaters. See 50.06 and 600.02.

492.34 *priesters crossing the singorgeous to aroint him . . . :* priests crossing one's sinful throat (*gorge* in French, and the Blessing of the Throats with the Sign of the Cross) to anoint one, the cross of Saint George, and *Macbeth*'s "Aroint thee, witch!" (I. iii. 6). Cf. 223.19 and 406.13.

493.18–19 *And there is nihil nuder under the clothing moon:* the Four Questioners express their doubts about ALP's story, echoing Cleopatra's lines at the death of Antony: "The odds is gone, / And there is nothing left remarkable / Beneath the visiting moon" (*Ant.* IV. xv. 66–67).

500.02 *They're playing thimbles and bodkins:* "bodkins" refers to Hamlet's "bare bodkin" (III. i. 76), with which one might his quietus make (or, per-

178   SHAKESPEAREAN ALLUSIONS

haps, his "God's bodkin, man!" in II. ii. 516). This line recalls 268.15, "And a bodikin a boss in the Thimble Theatre." Thus, what "they're playing" at the Thimble appears to be *Hamlet*. Cf. 79.20, "bare godkin." See entry for 268.15.

500.18 *Aure! Cloudy father!:* if, as the entry for 500.02 indicates, this page deals with *Hamlet*, then perhaps "Cloudy father" refers both to Hamlet's pseudofather, Claudius (cf. 121.01, "Claudian brother"), and to his real father, King Hamlet (see 18.23, where the King is "Head-in-Clouds"). "Aure!" may be a version of King Hamlet's "List!" (*aude* in Latin).

501.16 *Do you remember on a particular lukesummer night? . . . :* a reference to *Midsummer Night's Dream*, confirmed by the following three entries.

501.19 *the isles is Thymes:* recall "I know a bank where the wild thyme blows" (*MND* II. i. 249). See Boyle, p. 5.

502.29 *Miss Somer's nice dream: Midsummer Night's Dream.* The phrase is contrasted to "Mad Winthrop's [midwinter's] delugium stramens" (delirium tremens) in the same line—a nightmare of sorts.

503.21 *This stow on the wolds, is is Woful Dane Bottom?:* the woeful Dane may be Hamlet, but Bottom is the ass-man in "Miss Somer's nice dream" (502.29). This place (*stow* in Old English) in the woods (OE, *wold* and *weald*) may also be Hell, the woeful bottom of the universe. Wherever it is, it is mentioned three times elsewhere in *Finnegans Wake:* in 340.09, "warful doon's bothem"; in 369.12, "Woovil Doon Botham"; and in 594.12, "warful dune's battam" (see especially the entry for the latter).

Hodgart points out—in *AWN* No. 18 (Dec. 1963)—that Dean's Bottom is a locality in Kent. See also Louis Mink's note in *AWN*, XVII, 2 (Apr. 1980): 23; Boyle, (pp. 6–7) also sees both Hamlet and Bottom in this line.

504.16 *Your bard's highview, avis on valley:* maybe the Bard of Avon ("avis on"). *Avis* is Latin for "bird"; a bird's eye view (and a bard's high view) of the Avon valley. The "avis on" may be the Swan of Avon. Cf. 515.22.

507.35 *Shivering William:* Perhaps William Shakespeare. See Glasheen, p. 309. The phrase was in the *Scribbledehobble*, p. 96.

508.06 *twelfth day: Twelfth Night.*

508.23 *Clopatrick's:* Cleopatra and St. Patrick. Cf. 166.34 and 91.06.

509.27–28 *Lid efter lid. Reform in mine size his deformation:* eyelid after eyelid introduces another play on Hamlet's "In my mind's eye" (I. ii. 186). See 425.25 and 477.23. The presence of *Hamlet* in this passage lends some credence to the entry for 509.30–32.

509.30–32 *He could claud boose his eyes to the birth of his garce, he could lump all his lot through the half of her play, but he jest couldn't laugh through the whole of her farce . . . :* Hodgart (p. 751) reads this as a reference to the "play scene" in *Hamlet*, to, apparently, Claudius ("claud") and his inability to sit through the "Mousetrap" with equanimity.

510.16–17 *Awake! Come, a wake! Every old skin in the leather world, infect the whole stock company of the old house:* the apocalyptic message of the *Wake*, to awake and arise from the nether world. The world-as-theater metaphor is expressly stated here, where the world is peopled by members of a stock company. See chapter 3 of this study.

511.21 *Where letties hereditate a dark mien:* Letty Greene (see 161.30) and dark-faced ladies. The dark lady of the sonnets, perhaps.

512.26 *the sickly sigh from her gingering mouth:* Feste's addition to Sir Toby's query to Malvolio ("Dost thou think, because thou art virtuous, there shall be no more cakes and ale?") was, "Yes, by Saint Anne, and ginger shall be hot i'th'mouth too" (*TN* II. iii. 107). See 423.11.

513.09 *Delphin's Bourne:* perhaps, again, "the undiscovered country, from whose bourn . . ." (*Ham.* III. i. 80). Cf. entries for 190.21, 365.05, and 379.35.

515.07 —*A gael galled by scheme of scorn? Nock? / —Sangnifying nothing. Mock!:* a "tale told of Shaun and Shem" (215.35) and Macbeth's "A tale / Told by an idiot, full of sound and fury, / Signifying nothing" (V. v. 26–28). "A tale told . . ." of or by someone is a refrain in *Finnegans Wake*, as Hodgart has observed (p. 745). See lines 215.35, 275.24, 324,05, 396.23, 563.26, and 597.08.

515.23 *the same as a mind's eye view:* a bird's eye view (cf. 504.16, "a bard's highview") and Hamlet's "In my mind's eye" (I. ii. 186).

516.21 *Montague:* Romeo's family name in *Romeo and Juliet*.

516.24 *faketotem:* recalls Greene's *Groatsworth of Wit*, in which Robert Greene accuses Shakespeare of being a plagiarist (a "fake"), "an absolute *Iohannes factotum*, [who] is in his owne conceit the onely Shake-scene in a countrey."

521.13 *Jones's lame:* perhaps reference to Shakespearean critic and psychoanalyst Ernest Jones, who wrote *Hamlet and Oedipus*. Oedipus was "lame" with a swollen foot. See 434.19, "swell foot . . . to joy a Jonas."

Psychoanalysis does seem to be the theme to this and the next several pages. To the advice "Get yourself psychoanolised!" Yawn replies (as did Joyce to Jung) that "I can psoakoonaloose myself any time I want . . . without your interferences or any other pigeonstealer" (522.32–36).

523.02–4 —*Have you ever weflected, wepowtew, that the evil what though it was willed might newewtheless lead somehow on to good towawd the genewality?:* Sylvia Silence's analysis (given to a reporter—"wepowtew") of HCE may recall Brutus's reflections on the evil in Caesar's ambition: "If it be aught toward the general good" (I. ii. 85); "I know no personal cause to spurn at him, / But for the general" (II. i. 11–12). Silence's defence of HCE follows, here, the reverse logic, the logic of the *felix culpa*.

523.09 *as much sinned against as sinning:* like Lear, HCE (on trial here) is "a man / More sinned against than sinning" (*Lr.* III. ii. 59–60). In *Ulysses*, Gertie MacDowell thinks of Leopold Bloom as "more sinned against than sinning" (*U*, 358); Mulligan, in "Circe," says, "I believe him [Bloom] to be more sinned against than sinning" (*U*, 493).

530.22 *Sackerson:* Sackerson, the famed Elizabethan bear in the Bear Garden next to the Globe, is mentioned in *The Merry Wives of Windsor* (I. i. 306) and in *Ulysses*, page 188. See entries for 429.18 and 471.30.

531.18–21 *There's me shims and here's me hams and this is me jupettes. . . . He never cotched finer, balay me, at Romiolo Frullini's flea pantamine:* Shem, Ham, and Japhet; Romeo ("Romiolo") and Juliet ("jupette"); and a free Christmas pantomime are all here.

532.03 *Fa Fe Fi Fo Fum:* "Fie, foh, and fum" (*Lr.* III. iv. 174). See entry for 7.09.

532.04 *Arise, sir ghostus!:* see entry for 568.25.

535.11 *handshakey congrandyoulikethems, ecclesency:* once more Joyce ranks himself in the company of the world's greatest poets. Nathan Halper writes: "At several points in the *Wake*, Joyce gives us the triad Goethe, Shakespeare, and Dante. They are there as representatives of Western European culture. When he speaks of his peers, he omits the name of Goethe, e.g. 535.11—'handshakey congrandyoulikethems, ecclesency.' The one addressed—via Bloom of Eccles Street—is the Joyce of *Ulysses*. 'Congrandyoulikethems' is a reference to Can Grande to whom Dante reputedly addressed a letter dealing with the four levels of the Comedy. 'Shakey' alludes to Shakespeare. The three are gathered into a single family" (*AWN*, IV, 5 [Oct. 1967]: 96–97). They shake Joyce's hand in congratulations ("congrandyoulikethems") because he is "likethems." Cf. 28.04, 96.23, 344.05, and 539.05–9.

539.05–9 *I always think in a wordworth's of that primed favourite continental poet, Daunty, Gouty and Shopkeeper, A. G. . . . Like as my palmer's past policy I have had my best master's lessons:* HCE defends his virtue by citing his love for poetry; his masters are Wordsworth, Dante, Goethe, and Shakespeare. See entries for 47.19, 128.15–17, and 344.05–6. "Shopkeeper, A. G." is Sylvia Beach's Shakespeare & Company, which first printed *Ulysses*. Cf. 535.11.

539.32–33 *Hungry the Loaved and Hangry the Hathed:* two kings, one (Henry VIII) of which spawned a Shakespearean history play—Henry II (the Loved) and Henry the Eighth (and the Hated).

540.03–4 *This seat of our city it is of all sides pleasant, comfortable and wholesome . . . :* McHugh points out (p. 540) that HCE's praising depiction of Dublin in 540.03–8 is a direct quotation from the description of Dublin in Holinshed's *Chronicles*. The *Chronicles* was also Shakespeare's source for *Macbeth* (among other plays); this recalls Duncan's description of Inverness: "This castle hath a pleasant seat. The air / Nimbly and sweetly recommends itself / Unto our gentle senses" (*Mac.* I. vi. 1–3).

Shakespeare is much quoted in these pages (539–43), as if HCE wanted to prove his love for Dante, Goethe, and Shakespeare, expressed in 539.06.

540.15–16 *massed murmars march: where the bus stops there shop I:* another version of *Love's Labor's Lost*, and Ariel's song from *The Tempest*: "Where the bee sucks there suck I" (V. i. 88), amid a description of the modern metropolitan shopping malls of Dublin. See Hodgart, p. 749. A more oblique echo of Ariel's song occurs one line earlier: "Ubi pop jay piped, ibi pep goes the whistle." *Ubi* and *ibi* are Latin for "where" and "there"; "Pop goes the Weasel" is also heard. See entry for 541.06–7.

540.17–18 *From the hold of my capt in altitude till the mortification that's my fate:* another variant of King Hamlet's "cap-a-pe," head ("capt") to foot ("fate"). See entries for 234.11–12 and 583.29.

540.23 *fresk letties from the say:* fresh lettuce, fresh letters from the sea, and Letty Greene.

541.06-7 *by awful tors my wellworth building sprang sky spearing spires, cloud cupoled campaniles:* a reference to Prospero's "cloud-capped towers" in *The Tempest* (Ariel has been alluded to in the previous page). HCE, a creator like Prospero, is bragging about the buildings and the city he has built, as Prospero does. However, as will Prospero's creation, "The cloud-capped tow'rs ("tors" perhaps), the gorgeous palaces, / The solemn temples, the great globe itself . . . shall dissolve" (IV. i. 152–54). See entry for 607.32; see also Hodgart, p. 749.

542.29 *raped lutetias in the lock:* combination of Shakespeare's *Rape of Lucrece*, Pope's *Rape of the Lock*, a rape of Paris *(Lutetia)*, and "the Lock"—the popular name for Dublin's Westmoreland Lock Hospital for venereal disease, the "French" disease. See Louis O. Mink, *A Finnegans Wake Gazetteer*, p. 537.

543.01 *doubling megalopolitan poleetness:* within a description of the beauties of Dublin, this phrase stands for Dublin's metropolitan politeness and hospitality, and for the Dublin Metropolitan Police. Polonius also appears to be present (he is repeatedly connected with the metropolis; cf. 616.24, "metropolonians"). Here, HCE is also describing his "taughters" (543.15)—a daughter of Polonius, no doubt constantly being lectured to, would appropriately be a "taughter" *(Tochter* in German).

543.11 *Attent! Couch hear!:* List, list!

545.23 *Fee for farm:* "Fie, foh, and fum" *(Lr.* III. iv. 174).

546.05–7 *These be my genteelician arms. At the crest, two young frish, etoiled, flappant, devoiled of their habiliments, vested sable, withdrewers argent . . . :* HCE's coat-of-arms bears some verbal resemblance to John Shakespeare's: "This sheld or cote of Arms, viz. Gould, on a Bend Sables, a Speare of the first steeled argent. And for his creast or cogniζaunce . . ." (*RES*, 122). Joyce had already mentioned Shakespeare's coat of arms in *Ulysses*, p. 210: "Like John O'Gaunt his name is dear to him, as dear as the coat of arms he toadied for, on a bend sable a spear or steeled argent. . . ."

546.30–547.05 *faithful Fulvia . . . upon search of louvers, brunette men of Earalend . . . Fluvia . . . Fulvia Fluvia:* Fluvia is ALP, the flowing river and the wife of HCE; Fulvia was Mark Antony's faithful wife, whose death is announced to him in act I of *Antony and Cleopatra*. As ALP-Fulvia, Fluvia is in search of lovers in HCE and the "men of Ireland." Fulvia's man is "Earalend," since, in *Julius Caesar*, Mark Antony asked the Romans to "lend me your ears" (III. ii. 73) (Glasheen, p. 13). Cf. 278.L3.

549.31 *amiens:* in *As You Like It*, Amiens is a follower of the banished Duke in the Forest of Arden. He sings the song "Under the greenwood tree," referred to in 30.14, 74.10, 335.31–34, and 450.32–33. Three lines later there is a reference to "Adam," who was also referred to in 30.13 in union with Amiens's song; like Amiens, Adam was a character in *As You Like It*.

550.21 *a mopsa's broom to duist her sate:* Mopsa is a shepherdess in *The Winter's Tale*.

550.26 *to wring her withers limberly:* a reference to Hamlet's "Let the galled jade winch; our withers are unwrung" (III. ii. 234). See Hodgart, p. 742.

"Withers" are shoulders, parts of arms; thus "limberly" is a fitting adverb in context. See entry for 143.16.

551.35 *no porte sublimer benared my ghates:* porters at the gate, *portes* (French doors), and gates. See chapter 5.

553.05–6 *Cammomile Pass cuts Primrose Rise and Coney Bend bounds Mulbreys Island:* Coney Island and Mulberry Bend are locations in New York. Using the same sort of title-switching, we get Cammomile Rise and Primrose Pass. "Camomile Rinse" is an old-fashioned cosmetic trick: blondes rinse their hair with camomile tea to keep their hair from darkening. Primrose Pass may echo Ophelia's "primrose path of dalliance" (*Ham.* I. iii. 50). See *AWN*, IV, 4 (Aug. 1967): 104–5, on Coney Island and Mulberry Bend.

553.13 *Fra Teobaldo:* possibly Shakespearean scholar and forger Lewis Theobald. Cf. "theabild" in 159.32 and "theobalder" in 263.05.

553.16–17 *gregoromaios and gypsyjuliennes:* Greco-Roman Romeos and Gypsy Juliets.

Book III, Chapter 4

556.03–5 *when she took the veil, the beautiful presentation nun, so barely twenty, in her pure coif, sister Isobel:* as in 257.01, Issy appears to be *Measure for Measure*'s Isabella, sister to Claudio, and also a saintly novitiate.

558.29–30 *ru arue rue:* Ophelia's rue.

559.18 *Act: dumbshow:* as in *Hamlet*, perhaps. Cf. 88. 25 and 120.07–8.

561.20–21 *Here's newyearspray, the posquiflor, a windaborne and heliotrope; there miriamsweet and amaranth and marygold to crown:* in this description of Isobel (Issy, "dadad's lottiest daughterpearl" in 561.15), one of the "Porter babes," we have the now familiar identification of Issy with Ophelia, who also distributed flowers: "There's rosemary. . . . And there is pansies. . . . There's fennel for you, and columbines. There's rue for you . . ." (*Ham.* IV. v. 174–80).

563.26 *puck and prig:* Puck, possibly. In context, the reference seems to be to the two twins—one (Shem-Joyce) a Puck-like trickster, the other (Shaun-Stannie) a sanctimonious prig.

The word preceding, "costarred," may refer to *Love's Labor's Lost*'s Costard.

563.27–31 *How frilled one shall be as at taledold of Formio and Cigalette! What folly innocents! Theirs whet pep of puppyhood! Both barmhearts shall become yeastcake by their brackfest. I will to leave a my copperwise blessing between the pair of them, for rosengorge, for greenafang:* this is a description of the twin babes, Jerry and Kevin, in bed. Thus, it is again a "taletold" of Shem and Shaun, echoing Macbeth's famous last speech (see entry for 515.07), or it is a tale of the Ant ("Formio") and the Grasshopper ("Cigalette"). Formio and Cigalette echo *Romeo and Juliet*, another tale of the folly of innocents and of saccharine puppy love ("puppyhood" and "pep"-pepette). Twins, of course, are almost identical; so again we have breakfast ("brackfest") connected with similar identities and forgeries (see chapter 6 of this study). Finally, as twins, they are almost indistinguishable, like *Hamlet*'s Rosencrantz and Guildenstern—"rosengorge" and "greenafang."

The twins are also here as Jacob and Esau competing for their father's (Isaac) blessing: "I will to leave a my copperwise blessing between the pair of them."

564.21 *Listeneth!* List!

565.12 *Vortigern, ah Gortigern!:* another reference to Shakespearean forgeries. In 1796 William Henry Ireland claimed that he had discovered a lost play, *Vortigern and Rowena*, written by Shakespeare. Many believed that Ireland's earlier discoveries of lost Shakespearean papers and of this lost play were authentic, until the great Shakespeare scholar Edmond Malone exposed Ireland as a fraud. See chapter 6 of this study.

This allusion was noted earlier by Philip B. Sullivan in *AWN*, o.s. 9 (Jan. 1963), p. 5.

565.18–20 *You were dreamend, dear. The pawdrag? The fawthrig? Shoe! Hear are no phantares in the room at all, avikkeen. No bad bold faathern, dear one:* Shem-Jerry has been crying in his sleep and has had a nightmare; ALP tells him that he was only dreaming. Jerry's dream seems to involve his father (*padre* and "fawthrig") as a ghost ("phantares"); ALP assures him that there are no phantoms, no bad bold fathers, in the room. Given the constant identification of Shem with Hamlet and of HCE with the Ghost, it is possible that this vision of his father as a ghost is taken from the Ghost scenes in *Hamlet*. See chapter 4 of this study.

566.18–22 *The dame dowager to stay kneeled how she is, as first mutherer with cord in coil. The two princes of the tower royal, daulphin and deevlin, to lie how they are without to see. The dame dowager's duffgerent to present wappon, blade drawn to the full . . . :* Hodgart has determined (p. 744) that this passage (describing ALP and HCE) is a reference to *Macbeth;* this is questionable, though the passage may be based on Duncan's murder. Lady Macbeth-ALP-"dame dowager" is both the first mother and the "first murderer"—as accomplice in the murder of the King. "The two princes of the tower royal" seems to refer to the two princes (dramatized in *Richard III*) locked up in the Tower of London: in *Macbeth*, however, Duncan's two sons, Malcolm and Donalbain (or Kevin and Jerry), are also sleeping in the castle, oblivious to the murder: they "lie how they are without to see." Macbeth himself is the "dame dowager's duffgerent," who will "present the weapon" and slay Duncan ("Donkers," perhaps, in 566.31). However, the identifications are confused: "duffgerent" also seems to include Macduff and Duncan (the regent)—but, then, in *Finnegans Wake* everyone *is* everyone else.

Hodgart's identification of "How shagsome all and beastful!" (566.33) with Macduff's son's words to the Murderer ("Thou liest, thou shaghaired villain" in IV. ii. 81) is unconvincing.

566.23 *Isabella:* heroine of *Measure for Measure*. The identification of Issy with Isabella has occurred previously in 257.01, 279.F1, and 556.05.

567.17 *all the king's aussies and all their king's men:* Humpty Dumpty, king's horses, and king's men; also the King's Men, or the Chamberlain's Men. See other references to the King's Men in 47.26, 219.15, and 285.L2.

568.08–9 *Britus and Gothius shall no more joustle for that sonneplace but mark one autonement:* the atonement—or at-one-ment—of the warring opposites is Bruno's contribution to the *Wake*. Ernest Jones views Brutus and Cassius as filial figures, jostling for the place vacated by the Caesar-father ("joustle" for that son's place, and a place in the sun); the winner, however, is neither of them, but their at-oned union—"mark one autonement," or Marcus Antonius. See chapter 5 of this study.

See chapter 6 for further discussion of the importance of this passage.

568.25 *Arise, sir Pomkey Dompkey! Ear! Ear! Weakear!:* the ghost of King Hamlet identified with HCE (Humpty Dumpty). Cf. 532.04 "Arise, sir ghostus!" "Ear! Ear!" is Earwicker's ("Weakear") version of the Ghost's "List! List!" References to poison ("foison") and Denmark ("Caubeenhauben"—Copenhagen) are found in 568.28; Polonius is present in 568.36.

568.36 *will be poking out with his canule into the arras:* like Polonius. See Hodgart, p. 741.

569.28–35 *Mumm me moe mummers! What, no Ithalians? How, not one Moll Pamelas? Accordingly! Play actors by us ever have crash to their gate. Mr Messop and Mr Borry will produce of themselves, as they're two genitalmen of Veruno . . . all for love. . . . Such a boyplay! Their bouchicaulture! What tyronte power! Buy our fays!:* a joyous celebration is taking place, and there is a call for more dramatic entertainment: "Mumm me moe mummers!" We'll have plays at the celebration! Tindall notes (p. 298) that Richardson's *Sir Charles Grandison* ("Ithalians" and "Pamelas") and Synge's *Playboy* ("boyplay") are included among the plays. Messieurs "Messop" and "Borry" will produce Shakespeare's *Two Gentlemen of Verona* and Dryden's *All for Love*. Theatre is culture, and "bouchicaulture" (Dion Boucicault, author of *Arrah-na-Pogue*) is also here; by our faith ("Buy our fays!"), what a tyrant's power ("tyronte power") has the force of good drama—when acted by such as famed Irish actor William Grattan Tyrone Power and Willie and Frank Fay, actors at the Abbey Theatre. Senn writes (p. 8) that "Henry Mossop and Spranger Barry were rival actors in the Crow Street and Smock Alley theatres"; see entry for 184.21. Mossop and Barry's play about male friendships is appropriately "two genitalmen" and "such a boyplay!"

Irish actor Spranger Barry was not only the proprietor of Dublin's Crow Street Theatre, but was also "one of the greatest Shakespearean actors of his day, second only to David Garrick" (*RES*, 59). At the Drury Lane, he and Garrick became great rivals. The *RES* (pp. 558–59) reports that Henry Mossop played Shakespearean roles under the direction of both Garrick and Barry.

571.34 —*Wait! Hist! Let us list!:* List, list!

573.34–576.17: Hodgart writes (p. 748):

"The passage most closely touching The Man [Shakespeare] is the account of the law-suit in Book III, Chapter IV, pp. 573–6, where Ann Doyle the

plaintiff is not only Mrs. Earwicker (Anna Liffey) but Anne Hathaway, and the litigation concerns her pregnancy and the second-best bed, as well as contraception, the Church of England, forgery and Joyce's *Ulysses:*
    574/15 *Wieldhelm, Hurls* (William Hughes, Mr. W. H.)
    575/11 *Mr Brakeforth's* . . . /12 *nine months from date* . . . /15 *pinkwilliams* . . . /29 *Will Breakfast* (i.e. on the next morning Mr. Bloom will breakfast in bed)."

The allusions are a bit obscure and confusing, but in general Hodgart is correct. "Will Breakfast" is clearly Will Shakespeare, especially since breakfast and breakfast foods are often associated with Shakespeare and his forgers; see chapter 6 of this study. Leopold Bloom is repeatedly associated with Shakespeare in *Ulysses.* If Ann Doyle is Anne Hathaway in these pages, then HCE is Shakespeare—and, sure enough, on page 576 (see entry for 576.24) HCE is referred to as "mirrorminded."

Ulysses begins with Stephen, Mulligan, and Haines breakfasting; Joyce likes to end his books (i.e., Bloom's coming breakfast) where they begin.

574.15   *Wieldhelm, Hurls:* cf. entry for 573.34–576.17.

575.11   *Mr Brakeforth:* "Will Breakfast" (575.29) and Shakespeare. See entry for 573.34–576.17.

575.29   *Will Breakfast:* Will Shakespeare. See entry for 573.34–576.17 and chapter 6 of this study.

576.24   *mirrorminded:* HCE is being described as "Prospector, projector and boomooster giant builder of all causeways woesoever . . ." (576.16–18). He is thus a moving force of many facets and, appropriately, is "myriad-minded." This was Coleridge's adjective for Shakespeare, in chapter 15 of *Biographia Literaria*. HCE is later described as "synthetical" (596.32).

"Mirror"-minded is also an apt description. Joyce associated Shakespeare with mirrors. In "Circe," Stephen and Bloom look into a mirror together and see the face of Shakespeare, while Lynch comments, "the mirror up to nature" (*U*, 567); Hamlet had advised the Players that the purpose of drama was "to hold, as 'twere, the mirror up to nature" (III. ii. 20).

577.16   *Regies Producer with screendoll Vedette, peg of his claim and pride of her heart:* possibly another reference to Shakespearean actors Peg Woffington ("peg of his claim") and Thomas Sheridan; see entry for 413.02 "peg . . . and . . . tum." Again, the present context implies that Woffington and Sheridan were lovers: the line occurs within a bedtime prayer that HCE and ALP may have good sexual relations in bed—"that he may dishcover her, that she may uncouple him" (577.18). Thomas Sheridan was the manager of Dublin's Smock Alley Theatre and Peg Woffington was one of his stars; thus, "Regies Producer with screendoll Vedette," she was the "peg of his claim" and he, the "pride of her heart." Glasheen observes (p. 228) that *Peg O'My Heart* is also the title and the heroine of a play by J. H. Manner.

See entries for 210.25, 413.02, 436.09–11, 586.12, and 579.17.

577.30   *rue to lose:* rue and Ophelia.

578.16   *And who is the bodikin by him, sir?:* (The small body next to HCE is ALP.) Another of the references to "bodkin" in the *Wake;* this one, however, refers not to Hamlet's "bare bodkin" (or dagger), but to Hamlet's "God's bodkin, man, much better! Use every man after his desert, and who shall scape whipping?" (II. ii. 516–17). "Bodkin" here means "little body." See 79.20, 268.15, 446.05, and 500.02.

579.08–25 *. . . Goat to the Endth, thous slowguard! Mind the Monks and their Grasps . . . :* Hodgart writes (p. 741) that "The proverbs and advice on page 579 are like Polonius's"; so also, perhaps, are the ones on page 587, yet no direct echoes can be found in either.

579.17 *Peg the pound to tom the devil:* among a Polonius-like catalog of proverbs is this line—yet another reference to Peg Woffington and Thomas Sheridan. See entries for 413.02, 436.09–11, 577.16, and 586.12.

579.24 *Oil's wells in our lands: All's Well that Ends Well.*

581.23 *cloudious: Hamlet's* Claudius, possibly.

583.11 *And the twillingsons, ganymede, garrymore:* the twins (Danish, *tvilling*) have yet another set of identities. Ganymede is the name adopted by Rosalind in *As You Like It* when she goes into the Forest of Arden disguised as a boy; "Garrymore" may be the famous Shakespearean actor John Barrymore. Cf. 269.18.

583.29 *waxened capapee:* again, the ghost of King Hamlet, armed "cap-a-pe" (I. ii. 200). See entries for 58.25, 78.05, etc., for other references to this line.

Tindall (p. 294) implies that in context, however, "waxened capapee" may refer to the condom (the "ringasend as prevenient" in 585.09) HCE-Porter is using in bed with his wife. Rather, the reference is probably to "armor" and "armed cap-a-pe," since, as Margaret Solomon points out (in *Eternal Geomater*, p. 134), "'armor' is an eighteenth-century euphemism for condom and was so regarded by Stephen in the Circe episode of *Ulysses* when he misquoted Swift's epigram." *Ulysses*, p. 588; cf. Gifford and Seidman, p. 426.

585.26 *O yes! O yes! Withdraw your member! Closure. This chamber stands abjourned:* after HCE and ALP reach an ecstatic orgasm, the sexual act is over and HCE withdraws his member. The sexual act has been described in legal language; thus, when it is over, the Court stands adjourned (and ALP's sexual chamber is closed). Thus, "O yes! O yes!" is, once again, the "*Oyez! Oyez!*" (or "here-hear" in 584.36) used in chambers of law—in other words, "List! List!" Cf. entry for 85.31.

"O yes!" also represents Mrs. Bloom, and the joy of sexual affirmation.

586.12 *playing peg and pom:* another reference to illicit relationships, and to Shakespearean actors Peg Woffington and Thomas Sheridan. See entries for 210.25, 413.02, 436.09–11, 577.16, and 579.17. From these references, we can gather that "playing peg and pom" means not only playing roles in a Shakespeare play, but also having illicit sexual relations.

586.15 *Attention at all!:* List!

586.18 *Here is a homelet not a hothel:* the Porter's house and inn is a home, not a hotel or a brothel. "Homelet" is also Hamlet; cf. 59.30 and 230.07.

587.03 *Hiss!:* perhaps List!

587.08 *our Theoatre Regal's drolleries puntomine:* the Theatre Royal (or the King's House) was the original official designation of the Drury Lane ("drolleries") Theatre, the most famous theatre in English stage history, known for its Shakespearean productions, such as those of David Garrick. The *Wake* is repeatedly equated with a Christmas "puntomine" at an English or Irish (Gaiety) theatre. Schoenbaum (p. 256) notes that Christmas pantomimes were also a tradition at the Drury Lane, as at the Gaiety. See the numerous references to the Drury Lane as listed in Appendix 3; see also chapter 3 and entry for 455.24–29, regarding Christmas pantomimes.

590.02 *leareyed and letterish:* Lear, and Letty Greene.

Book IV

593.02 *Calling all downs. Calling all downs to dayne:* the call for the dawn and for the day of ricorso that opens book IV seems to be taken from the refrain of Ophelia's song: "You must sing 'A-down a-down, and you call him a-down-a'" (*Ham.* IV. v. 170–71). Hers is a "daynish" dawn. Cf. entry for 10.28.

593.05–6 *Here! Here!:* a spatialist version of "Hear!" and "List! List!"

593.11 *Calling all daynes to dawn:* calling all the days to dawn—and calling all Danes to rise. In this call for resurrection and ricorso, HCE-King Hamlet's reincarnation for the next Viconian cycle, his son, is going to rise like a phoenix (like the "Phoenican wakes" from the "Ashias" in 608.30–31) when the "cockcock crows for Danmark" (192.21), while his progenitor fades away with the end of the night of the dream, just as the ghost of Hamlet's father "faded on the crowing of the cock" (I. i. 157). Or, as Joyce writes in 598.09–10, "The has goning at gone, the is coming to come. Greets to ghastern, hie to morgning": this is the moment when the new greets the old, as the old is going and the new, coming.

Cf. entry for 593.02 and Ophelia's song.

594.12 *make sunlike sylp om this warful dune's battam:* echoes the "Woful Dane Bottom" of 503.21, with its references to *Hamlet* and *A Midsummer Night's Dream;* see entry for 503.21. Hart (in *Structure and Motif*, p. 104) notes that "OM is a symbol for the sun, which here shines out over the yawning gap of the Eddas as Earwicker uses Sunlight Soap to wash his craggy buttocks—the 'awful Dane's bottom.'" Once more, we find the Shakespearean pun of Bottom as the ass, arse, and bottom.

594.14–15 *Respassers should be pursaccoutred. Qui stabat Meins quantum qui stabat Peins:* trespassers should be prosecuted; the crime is theft, or equipping (accoutering) oneself with a purse. The Latin seems to echo Iago's lines: "Who steals my purse steals trash; tis something, nothing . . ." *(Oth.* III. iii. 157). See Hodgart, p. 751.

594.25–27 *Gaunt grey ghostly gossips growing grubber in the glow. Past now pulls. Cur one beast, even Dane the Great . . . .:* as the dawn ("glow") comes, the Ghost grows dimmer, pulled back by the past—until the old creator fades on the crowing of the cock ("Let shrill their duan Gallus" two lines later). Dane the Great is HCE as King Hamlet. Great Dane is, of course, a "cur," a beast, a dog—or, by Joycean equivalence, God. Thus, father-creators are again, ingeniously, equated with gods.

595.03 *Whake? Hill of Hafid, knock and knock:* it is time for ricorso and waking, and so, at the Hill of Howth, there is a new HCE (the son-Cad) knocking at the Gate—at Castle Knock Gate near Chapelizod (see Tindall, p. 308). See also chapter 5 for references to the porter at the gate.

595.32 *Fill stap:* Falstaff and full stop again; see entries for 366.25–30, 370.13, and 379.17–18. HCE-Falstaff's end is come, as he fades on the crowing of the cock. *Ricorso* brings a new HCE; thus, of the old Falstaff, Joyce writes: "So let him slap, the sap . . . He canease. Fill stap." (So let him sleep. *He* can rest *easy,* at a full stop.)

596.24 *freeflawforms:* "Fie, foh, and fum" *(Lr.* III. iv. 174).

596.36 *Will:* maybe Will Shakespeare. Cf. entry for 575.29.

597.16 *a story about brid and breakfedes:* the *Wake,* a story about bed and breakfast, about "Will Breakfast" (575.29), about sleep and ricorso, and a bird ("brid")—the phoenix.

597.20 *all-a-dreams:* like Hamlet's "John-a-dreams" (II. ii. 553).

598.02 *they just done been doing being in a dromo of todos:* the author tells us that it has been a long night, but the morrow is here. All the people that we've dreamed about have just been acting in a drama of "today" and of everything (a drama of *todos*)—just like the twins, the Dromios in *Comedy of Errors.* They've just been an "actaman housetruewith" (598.34)—an actormen's housetroupe (like the whole stock company of the house).

598.09–10 *Greets to ghastern, hie to morgning:* see entry for 593.11.

598.30 *Hear!:* List!

599.36–600.02 *the gist of the pantomime, from cannibal king to the property horse . . . in this drury world of ours:* many readers would like to know the gist of this pantomine, the *Wake,* from Hannibal (HCE), the cannibal king, down to the props of this dreary Drury Lane worldstage of ours.

600.36–601.01 *glaum is:* perhaps Macbeth, thane of Glamis and Cawdor. Cf. 250.14–18, "Glamours . . . Coldours. . . . Lack breath must leap no more."

603.01 *with that smeoil like a grace of backoning over his egglips of the sunsoonshine:* book IV is the Book of Ricorso, of morning—and of breakfast. The new day, the new ricorso, is a replica of the old; thus there is an association between breakfast and forgery in *Finnegans Wake.* The new HCE, Shaun-Francis Bacon, is thus described as having an oily smile and smell, with bacon grease all over his egg-smeared, breakfasting lips. The eclipse of the sun is odd in this passage, since the time is dawn. Surely the new "son" is shining.

Grace Abounding is also here.

603.15 *Dutiful wealker for his hydes of march:* since the ricorso signals the rise of the new HCE and the fall of the old, it brings beautiful weather for the Ides of March—for the fall of the old Caesar, dutifully walking in Hyde (or Phoenix) Park.

603.17 *The man was giddy on letties:* HCE was intoxicated with young women, like Letty Greene.

604.19 *Which aubrey our first shall show:* pages 604–6 give us a brief life of St. Kevin (Shaun), which is first announced in this line. John Aubrey (1626–97) was the author of *Aubrey's Brief Lives,* including the first biography of Shakespeare. Cf. 209.14–15.

Glasheen claims (p. 20) that 149.05–7 echoes Aubrey's "Beaumont and Fletcher."

604.22 *Oyes! Oyeses! Oyesesyeses!:* the brief life of Kevin begins with a call to "list!"—*oyez!*

606.04 *violet vesper vailed:* still another version, conceivably, of *Love's Labor's Lost.*

606.26 *What will not arky paper, anticidingly inked with penmark, push?. . .:* to what extent will ink and paper not go? Many readers have asked the same question of the *Wake,* with its many *Hamlet*-oriented Danish penmarks. See entry for 189.06.

607.09–10 *Messagepostumia . . . cymbaloosing:* Mesopotamia and Posthumus Leonatus ("postumia"), Imogen's husband in *Cymbeline* ("cymbaloosing").

607.32 *a clout capped sunbubble anaccanponied from his bequined torse:* compare with 541.06–7, "by awful tors . . . cloud cupoled campaniles"; both lines refer to Prospero's words, "The cloud-capped tow'rs, the gorgeous palaces . . ." (*Tmp.* IV. i. 152). See Hodgart, p. 749. "His bequined torse" is Copenhagen, Wellington's big white horse (with an equine torso), almost as ubiquitous in this book as the Four Old Men's Ass; but "torse" also refers to "awful tors" (541.06) and to Prospero's "tow'rs."

608.14 *This Mister Ireland? And a live?:* HCE and Anna Livia ("And a live"), both alive and well. Perhaps HCE is seen here as both an embodiment of Ireland and a fake—such as William Henry Ireland, Shakespearean forger, creator of *Vortigern and Rowena.* Cf. 565.12 "Vortigern." See *AWN,* o.s. 9 (Jan. 1963), p. 5.

608.18 *the voice of Alina:* ALP as, perhaps, *As You Like It*'s Aliena (Celia).

608.22 *I dhink I sawn to remumb or sumbsuch. A kind of thinglike . . .:* HCE wakes up and recalls having a dream: I think I seem to remember some such. . . . This scene recalls a parallel passage in *A Midsummer Night's Dream,* when Bottom wakens and says: "I have had a dream. . . . Methought I was—there is no man can tell what . . ." (IV. i. 203–7)—and the Ass's "mescemed somewhat came of the noised and somewho . . ." (404.09–10). See chapter 3 of this study.

608.31 *fierce force fuming:* "Fie, foh, and fum" (*Lr.* III. iv. 174).

609.19 *When the messanger of the risen sun (see other oriel):* maybe Ariel, Prospero's messenger in *The Tempest.* See other Ariels in 449.30 and 540.14–16. Oriel, of course, is also a projecting bay window—a transmitter of the rising sun.

611.33, 612.04 *Uberking Leary. . . . Ober King Leary:* HCE as both the Irish High King Leary and *King Lear.*

614.13, 30 *And the mannormillor clipperclappers. . . . with a clappercoupling:* the "clapper claws" mentioned in the Printer's Preface to *Troilus and Cressida.* See entries for 491.07 and 614.27–615.10.

614.27–615.10 *Our wholemole millwheeling vicociclometer . . . (. . . be he Matty, Marky, Lukey or John-a-Donk), autokinatonetically preprovided with a clappercoupling smeltingworks exprogressive process (. . . known as eggburst, eggblend, eggburial and hatch-as-hatch can) receives through a portal vein the dialytically separated elements . . . type by tope, letter from litter, word at ward . . . in fact, the sameold gamebold adomic structure of our Finnius the old One, as highly charged with electrons as hophazard can effective it. . . . Cockalooralooraloomenos, when cup, platter and pot come piping hot, as sure as herself pits hen to paper and there's scribings scrawled on eggs:* this passage is an important statement of Joyce's Viconian theory, especially in its application to literature, Shakespeare, and the scrambling of breakfast eggs. See chapter 6 of this study for a detailed discussion.

The Shakespearean allusions include *Hamlet*'s "John-a-Dreams," *Troilus and Cressida*'s "clapperclaws," and the breakfast of ricorso.

615.25 *backed in paladays last:* back in *Paradise Lost*, and in Cleopatra's "salad days," "when [she] was green in judgment, cold in blood" (*Ant.* I. v. 73–74). Cf. entry for 69.10.

615.31 *their bacon what harmed butter! It's margarseen oil:* Bacon (Francis), butter, margarine, and more breakfast.

616.24 *most eatenly appreciated by metropolonians:* the reference is to HCE (the "coerogenal *H*un") as a citydweller. Citydwellers seem to be connected with Polonius ("metropolonians"): cf. 543.01, "megalopolitan poleetness" (metropolitan politeness), etc. See Hodgart, p. 741. Having warned us to "Be sage about sausages" (616.22), Joyce now presents this Polonius as perhaps *bologna*—cf. 621.13, "roly polony."

619.20–22 *Lsp! . . . Lpf! . . . Lispn!:* Anna Livia begins her final, great monologue with a call to "List!" Her call is repeated four more times in the monologue: "Lst!" in 621.17, "Lss." in 624.06, "Lff!" in 628.07, and "Lps" in 628.15.

619.27 *Reclined from cape to pede:* ALP is addressing HCE, who is reclined from head to foot; she tells him to "Rise up, man of the hooths" (619.25—man of Howth Head), for it is time for ricorso. This is nearly the last of the many references to HCE as King Hamlet, armed "cap-a-pe" (I. ii. 200); the last occurs in 622.30. See entries for 58.25, 78.05, 191.14, 220.25–26, 221.29, 540.17, and 583.29.

ALP tells HCE to rise, for they are now to be displaced by the younger generation. She consoles him (619.31): "But there's a great poet in you too" (like in Hamlet-Joyce-Shakespeare). Leopold Bloom also had "a touch of the artist" about him (*U*, 235).

621.13 *With a taste of roly polony from Blugpuddels after:* with a taste of rolypoly bologna, after blood-pudding. Again, Polonius is a sausage. See entry for 616.24.

621.29–30 *I'll close my eyes. So not to see. Or see only a youth in his florizel, a boy in innocence:* as the book draws to a close, and the aged Anna Livia flows toward the sea, there is a very moving passage in Anna Livia's love song. She tells HCE that she still loves him, that she'll close her eyes so as not to see his old age—or pretend to only see what he once was, a flowering tree (the "flourishing . . . buaboabaybohm" of 29.02) in youthful innocence.

Florizel was, in *The Winter's Tale*, the young Prince of Bohemia, as young and innocent as his Perdita.

622.30 *capapole:* King Hamlet's "cap-a-pe" again, and for the last time. Here, ALP even addresses HCE ("evers the Carlton hart") as "capapole": "And you needn't host out with your duck and your duty, capapole. . . ."

623.16 *vim vam vom:* "Fie, foh, and fum" (*Lr.* III. iv. 174).

623.34 *hath an an:* Anne Hathaway, and Anna Livia.

627.28–30 *How she was handsome, the wild Amazia, when she would seize to my other breast! And what is she weird, haughty Niluna . . . :* Hodgart has suggested that, in the final pages of the *Wake*, in Anna Livia's tragic monologue as she flows into the sea and dies, we find, appropriately, allusions to the final words of Shakespeare's tragic heroines, as well as to tragic operatic heroines. A watery death, of course, recalls Ophelia. Perhaps Desdemona is pleading here, like Marlowe's Faustus, for time—"But half an hour! . . . But while I say one prayer" (*Oth* V. ii. 81–83): "That I prays for" (623.30), and "moananoaning" (628.03—Desde*mona*). [Faustus's own last speech may be here in "Sea, sea!" (626.07): "See, see, where Christ's blood streams in the firmament!" (V. ii. 143).] Dying, ALP cries out, Faustus-like: "I see them rising! Save me from those therrble prongs!" (628.04–5). Practically the last words of Lady Macbeth are "Out, damned spot! Out, I say! . . . All the perfumes of Arabia will not sweeten this little hand. Oh, oh, oh!" (V. i. 47–48); in 624.24, ALP refers to her "parafume . . . with a spot of marashy" (perfumes of Arabia; damned spot), and later says, "No! Nor for all our wild dances in all their wild din" (627.26–27).

The most apt analogy to HCE and ALP in these final pages, however, is to the aging lovers, Antony and Cleopatra. Dying and flowing out to sea, ALP addresses her husband as Cleopatra did in her final speech ("Husband, I come"—V. ii. 286). Cleopatra apotheosizes the dead Antony, describing him as a Colossus: "His legs bestrid the ocean: his reared arm / Crested the world" (V. ii. 82–83); so also Anna Livia addresses Humphrey: "Steadyon, Cooloosus! Mind your stride or you'll knock" (625.22). Earlier in the play, Cleopatra had called Antony "The demi-Atlas of this earth" (I. v. 23); ALP now refers to HCE as an "atlas" (626.13). Cleopatra's final words, as she applies a second asp to her breast, are, "Dost thou not see my baby at my breast / That sucks the nurse asleep? . . . As sweet as balm, as soft as air, as gentle— / O Antony! Nay, I will take thee [the asp], too" (V. ii. 309–11). In ALP's final monologue is found "Softly so" (624.21), "Gently" (627.12), "Bussoftlhee" (628.14—practically the last words of the *Wake*); "as soft as air" is echoed in 628.08, "So soft this morning, ours [air]." Lines 627.28–30 seem a clear reference to Cleopatra with the asp at her breast: "How she was handsome . . . when she would seize to my other breast! And what is she weird, haughty Niluna . . ." (Antony had called Cleopatra "my serpent of old Nile" in I. v. 25). Both women's deaths have a sad but noble grandeur.

See entry for 628.13–14.

Anna Livia, as the Liffey, is a river; the Nile (along with the moon, "luna") and the Amazon ("the wild Amazia") are mentioned here. Glasheen further suggests (p. 8) that in *Finnegans Wake*, the Nile and the Amazon are "Shakespeare's queens, Cleopatra and Hippolyta. 'Amazon' is usually derived from 'without breast' or from the Circassian word for 'moon.'"

628.13–14 *End here. . . . Bussoftlhee, mememormee!:* as Anna Livia flows out to the sea, more Shakespearean heroines surface (see entry for 627.28–30). Leo Knuth wrote in his "Last Leaf"—in *AWN*, XII, 6 (Dec. 1975): 103–5—that "Anna Livia's 'End here' echoes Marina's [Marina, the heroine of *Pericles*, "Called Marina / For I was born at sea"—V. i. 157] 'I will end here' (V. i. 154). Another Shakespearean heroine. . . . Juliet uses these words to express her despair: '. . . end motion here' (*Romeo and Juliet*, III. ii. 59). It is the sight of Juliet at the window that inspires Romeo's soliloquy, 'But soft! What light through yonder window breaks?' Compare 'Bussoftlhee'. . . . The last words of Isabella's [Isabella, heroine of *Measure for Measure*] instructions to Mariana, her stand-in, '. . . but, soft and low, / Remember now my brother' (IV. i. 68–69) are echoed in 'Bussoftlhee, mememormee!'" See entry for 628.14–15.

Knuth maintains that the Ghost's "But soft, methinks I scent the morning air" (*Ham*. I. v. 58) is also here in "Bussoftlhee" and "So soft this morning, ours" (628.08). "Lff!" and "mememormee!" on this last page refer to more of the Ghost's lines from the same scene in *Hamlet* (see entries for 619.20–22 and 628.14–15).

See also entry for 627.28–30.

628.14–15 *Take. Bussoftlhee. . . . Lps. The keys to. Given! A way . . .:* "Lps" is both "List!" and Lips. Knuth—in *AWN*, V, 2 (Apr. 1968): 28—has observed that "Lips" are Dutch keys (in a popular Dutch commercial advertisement)— "The keys to. Given." Taking and giving lips (and soft kisses—"bussoftlhee," perhaps) at the dawn of ricorso and rerising have led Werner Morlang—in *AWN*, VII, 6 (Dec. 1970): 95—to compare these final words with Mariana's song in *Measure for Measure:*

> *Take*, O take those *lips away*,
> That so sweetly were forsworn;
> And those eyes, the *break of day*,
> Lights that do mislead the morn;
> But my kisses bring again, bring again . . .
>
> (IV. i. 1–5; my italics)

Morlang further notes that in a letter to Giorgio and Helen (28 Dec. 1934), Joyce called this Shakespearean lyric his "own favourite" song.

628.14 *mememormee!:* Anna Livia Plurabelle's parting words to her husband, HCE, as she passes away into the ocean, are a poignant echo of the same words HCE himself, in a previous Viconian incarnation as King Hamlet, had uttered, fading at dawn, to his son: "Adieu, adieu, adieu. Remember me!" (I. v. 91).

PART III

Shakespearean Allusions: Appendixes

Appendix 1: The Shakespearean World

William Shakespeare
- 28.04   Shakeshands
- 47.19   Suffoclose! Shikespower! Seudodanto! Anonymoses!
- 76.26   old knoll
- 96.23   shakeahand
- 123.24   our plumsucked pattern shapekeeper
- 128.16   no notion of shopkeepers
- 141.21   bacon or stable hand
- 143.22   all the rivals to allsea, shakeagain, O disaster! Shakealose!
- 145.24   More poestries from Chickspeer
- 152.33–34   our once in only Bragspear, he clanked, to my clinking, from veetoes to threetop, every inch of an immortal
- 154.05   allsall allinall
- 159.07   myriads of drifting minds
- 161.31   shakespill and eggs
- 172.28   he was in his bardic memory low
- 174.09–10   clasp shakers (the handtouch which is speech without words)
- 174.28   slowspiers counter quicklimers
- 175.20   where theirs is Will there's his Wall
- 177.23–32   Shem always blaspheming, so holy writ, Billy . . . his Ballade Imaginaire . . . by Maistre Sheames de la Plume . . . that he was aware of no other shaggspick, other Shakhisbeard
- 183.26   shopkeepers' wives
- 191.02   for the laugh of Scheekspair
- 229.08–9   nation of sheepcopers
- 242.31   allinall
- 248.23   Shake hands through the thicketloch! Sweet swanwater!
- 257.19–20   the baker's booth . . . Missy Cheekspeer
- 274.L4   *As Shakefork might pitch it*
- 295.04   As Great Shapesphere puns it
- 331.22–23   will is the littleyest, the myrioheartzed
- 344.05–6   which goateye and sheepskeer they damnty well know

422.31–32   Old Knoll and his borrowing
441.33   the goattanned saxopeeler upshotdown chigs peel of him
465.28–35   As the curly bard said. . . . Watch the swansway.
504.16   Your bard's highview, avis on valley
507.35   Shivering William
535.11   handshakey congrandyoulikethems, ecclesency
539.05–9   always think in a wordworth's of that primed favourite continental poet, Daunty, Gouty and Shopkeeper, A. G.
575.11   Mr Brakeforth
575.29   Will Breakfast
576.24   mirrorminded
596.36   Will

His small Latin and less Greek
125.14–15   Not Hans the Curier though had he had have only had some little laughings and some less of cheeks

John Shakespeare
172.05   John's is a different butcher's

The Shakespeare coat of arms
546.05–7   These be my genteelician arms. At the crest, two young frish . . . vested sable, withdrewers argent

The will
121.32   a grand stylish gravedigging with secondbest buns
413.17–18   This, my tears, is my last will intesticle wrote off in the strutforit about their absent female assauciations

Stratford
340.32   strait a way . . . from Piping Pubwirth
413.17   strutforit

Legends
209.14–15   I aubette my bearb it's worth while poaching on! Shake it up, do, do!
229.14   From the Mermaids' Tavern
340.32–34   strait a way . . . from Piping Pubwirth to Haunted Hillborough
450.02–5   What wouldn't I poach . . . flashing down the swansway

Problem plays and purple patches
31.23   the purchypatch of hamlock
32.32   performance of the problem passion play
111.02   patchpurple of the massacre
200.04   Theirs porpor patches!
316.23   paupers patch

Manuscripts, folios, and quartos
122.36–123.01   the toomuchness, the fartoomanyness, of all those four-legged ems
197.18   Don Dom Dombdomb and his wee follyo!

300.30 thur him no quartos
326.07–8 intra trifum triforium trifoliorum
425.20 my trifolium librotto, the authordux Book of Lief
428.19 Georges Quartos

Anne Hathaway
58.29 the first woman, they said, souped him . . . Lili Coninghams, by suggesting him they go in a field
114.17 thithaways . . . hithaways
338.31 when the morn hath razed out limpalove
411.27–28 The gloom hath rays, her lump is love
623.34 hath an an

Elizabeth Hall
80.17–18 the first babe of reconcilement
338.31 when the morn hath razed out limpalove.
411.27–28 The gloom hath rays, her lump is love

Letty Greene (see Part II, entry for 161.30)
20.24 lettice leap
43.28–29 lattice . . . green
161.30 Lettucia in her greensleeves
184.25 Litty fun Letty fan Leven
184.35 Layteacher Baudwin
203.29 Letty Lerck's lafing light
229.21 Lettyshape
344.11–12 *lefting the gat out of the big: his face glows green*
415.03 Auld Letty Plussiboots
422.33 Folletta Lajambe
456.26 Letternoosh, Letterspeak, Lettermuck
511.22 letties
540.23 fresh letties from the say
590.02 letterish
603.17 giddy on letties
620.10 let us . . . Rathgreany

Greene's *A Groatsworth of Wit Bought with a Million of Repentance*
137.34 a laughsworth of his illformation over a larmsworth of salt
170.03 for four testers one groat
181.01 trying to copy the stage Englesemen he broughts their house down
232.27–28 old cocker, young crowy, sifadda, sosson
288.F1 An ounceworth of onions for a pennyawealth of sobs
360.36 our groatsupper
414.20–419.08 [The fable of the Ondt and the Gracehoper—see entry in Part II]
516.24 faketotem

Biographers—Aubrey, Brandes
80.14 brandihands

209.14–15 I aubette my bearb it's worth while poaching on! Shake it up, do, do!
604.19 Which aubrey our first shall show

Lamb's *Tales from Shakespeare*
440.18–19 Mary Liddlelambe's flitsy tales, espicially with the scentaminted sauce

Ernest Jones
127.31–32 plays gehamerat when he's ernst
128.36 has an eatupus complex and a drinkthedregs kink
149.10 we don't think, Jones, we'd care to this evening
160.18 if I weren't a jones in myself
160.35–168.12 [an Ernest Jones-based lecture on Brutus, Cassius, and Caesar]
233.19–21 letting punplays pass to ernest: / —Haps thee jaoneofergs?
434.19,27 Put your swell foot foremost . . . to joy a Jonas

Stephen Dedalus's theory of Shakespeare
53.32 poleaxe your sonson's grandson
80.17–18 the first babe of reconcilement is laid in its last cradle of hume sweet hume
338.31 limpalove
411.27–28 The gloom hath rays, her lump is love
468.20–22 But from the stress of their sunder enlivening, ay clasp, deciduously, a nikrokosmikon must come.

Appendix 2: The Plays

The plays most frequently alluded to in Finnegans Wake. *The entries for each play are divided into: 1) title, characters, and miscellaneous references, and 2) allusions to the text (arranged by act, scene, and line).*

Hamlet, Prince of Denmark

Title
143.07 camelot prince of dinmurk

Hamlet, and King Hamlet (referred to in act I as "Denmark")
31.23 the purchypatch of hamlock
37.04 a sensible ham
41.18 Ebblinn's chilled hamlet
59.31 *Mon foie*, you wish to ave some homelette . . .
76.05–6 Ham's cribcracking yeggs
79.35 good King Hamlaugh's gulden dayne
82.11 a different and younger him of the same ham
84.32 that thuddysickend Hamlaugh

APPENDIXES 199

114.19 from tham Let Rise till Hum Lit
127.31–32 plays gehamerat when he's ernst
143.07 hapless behind the dreams of accuracy as any camelot prince of dinmurk
143.23 the signs of Ham
177.21–22 this hambone dogpoet pseudoed himself under the hangname he gave himself of Bethgelert
181.35 the excommunicated Drumcondriac, nate Hamis
187.22 Tamstar Ham of Tenman
189.06 small peace in ppenmark
193.10 Do you hear what I'm seeing, hammet?
199.20 a shinkobread (hamjambo, bana?)
201.08 *my old Dane*
214.32 you hamble creature
230.05–7 eggspilled him out of his homety dometry . . . because all his creature comfort was an omulette
301.F5 Very glad you are going to Penmark. Write to the corner.
323.36 ghustorily spoeking, gen and gang, dane and dare, like the dud spuk of his first foetotype
330.06 Danno the Dane
385.16 the mad dane
418.18 Moyhammlet
421.18,29 words as the penmarks used out in sinscript . . . the views of Denmark
452.02 perish the Dane
465.32 Be offalia. Be hamlet.
503.21 Woful Dane Bottom
532.04 Arise, sir ghostus!
565.18–20 [see Part II entry]
568.25 Arise, sir Pomkey Dompkey! Ear! Ear! Weakear!
586.18 Here is a homelet
593.11 Calling all daynes to dawn
594.12 om this warful dune's battam
594.27 Dane the Great
606.26 what will not arky paper, anticidingly inked with penmark, push?

Ophelia
31.18 Offaly
72.04 O'Phelim's Cutprice
105.18 Ophelia's Culpreints
110.11 the drame of Drainophilias
225.35 The flossies all and mossies all they drooped upon her draped brimfall
226.04–5 Poor Isa sits a glooming . . . around her swan's
465.32 Be offalia. Be hamlet.

Claudius
121.01 his Claudian brother

126.14 claud
500.18 Cloudy father
509.30 claud
581.23 cloudious

Polonius
388.01 Exeunc throw a darras
543.01 doubling megalopolitan poleetness
568.36 will be poking out with his canule into the arras
579.08–25 [see Part II entry]
616.24 metropolonians
621.13 roly polony

Gertrude
254.31–32 And insodaintly she's a quine of selm ashaker while as a murder of corpse . . .
287.19 meager suckling of gert stoan

Horatio
329.04 hip, hip, horatia!

Rosencrantz and Guildenstern
563.31 the pair of them, for rosengorge, for greenafang

Reynaldo
192.14 Reynaldo

The Dumb Show
88.25 the dumb scene
120.07–8 dummpshow . . . mute commoner
442.22 we'll dumb well soon show him
509.30–32 [see Part II entry]
559.18 Act: dumbshow

Saxo Grammaticus (source of Hamlet tale)
16.07 You phonio saxo?
304.18 By Saxon Chromaticus
388.31 sexon grimmacticals

I. i. 63 *HORATIO: He smote the sledded Polacks on the ice.*
28.06 Pollockses
53.32 poleaxe your sonson's grandson

I. i. 68 *HORATIO: But, in the gross and scope of my opinion*
78.05 from grosskopp to megapod

I. i. 115–16 *HORATIO: The graves stood tenantless and the sheeted dead Did squeak and gibber in the Roman streets.*
455.28 to begin properly SPQueaRking

I. i. 157 *MARCELLUS: It faded on the crowing of the cock.*
192.21 the cockcock crows for Danmark

APPENDIXES 201

594.25–30 Gaunt grey ghostly gossips growing grubber in the glow . . . even Dane the Great. . . . Let shrill their duan Gallus
598.10 Greets to ghastern, hie to morgning

I. ii. 76 *HAMLET: Seems, madam? Nay, it is. I know not 'seems.'*
143.26–27 what would that fargazer seem to seemself to seem seeming of, dimm it all?

I. ii. 129 *HAMLET: O that this too too sullied flesh would melt*
367.29 the bounds whereinbourne our solied bodies all attomed attain arrest.

I. ii. 150–51 *HAMLET: O God, a beast that wants discourse of reason*
  Would have mourned longer.
420.15–16 an infant sailing eggshells on the floor of a wet day would have more sabby

I. ii. 180–81 *HAMLET: The funeral baked meats*
  Did coldly furnish forth the marriage tables.
121.32 The gypsy mating of a grand stylish gravedigging with secondbest buns

I. ii. 185 *HAMLET: In my mind's eye, Horatio.* (and I. i. 112, *HORATIO: the mind's eye*)
254.18 to the mind's ear
425.25 in my mine's I
477.18,23 in the back of their mind's ear . . . and in their minds years
509.27–28 in mine size
515.23 the same as a mind's eye view

I. ii. 187–88 *HAMLET: 'A was a man, take him for all in all,*
  I shall not look upon his like again.
154.05 allsall allinall
242.31 allinall
392.23–24 in her beaver bonnet, the King of the Caucuses, a family all to himself

I. ii. 200 *HORATIO: Armèd at point exactly, cap-a-pe.* (see also entries under I. ii. 228, *From top to toe*)
58.25 cappapee
78.05 from grosskopp to megapod
191.14 from head to foot
220.25–26 (in the programme about King Ericus of Schweden and the spirit's whispers in his magical helmet), cap-a-pipe with watch and topper, coat, crest
221.29 Kopay pibe by Kappa Pedersen
540.17–18 From the hold of my capt in altitude till the mortification that's my fate
583.29 waxened capapee
619.27 Reclined from cape to pede

            622.30   capapole
I. ii. 228 *HAMLET: [Armed] From top to toe?*
              ALL: My lord, from head to foot.
   152.33   Bragspear he clanked, to my clinking, from veetoes to threetop,
            every inch of an immortal
   191.14   Immaculatus, from head to foot, sir
   234.11   childfather from tonsor's tuft to almonder's toe
   342.31   From Topphole to Bottom

I. ii. 230 *HORATIO: He wore his beaver up.*
   52.24   The first Humphrey's latitudinous baver
   392.23–24   in her beaver bonnet, the king of the Caucuses

I. iii. 1–43   (Laertes's sermon to Ophelia)
   431.01–6, 431.21 ff.   Sister, dearest . . . [see Part II, entry for 431.21]

I. iii. 50 *OPHELIA: . . . the primrose path of dalliance*
   361.22   before the bridge of primrose
   553.05–6   Cammomile Pass cuts Primrose Rise

I. iv. 2 *HORATIO: It is a nipping and an eager air.*
   132.06–7   a hunnibal in exhaustive conflict, an otho to return; burning body
            to aiger air

I. iv. 14–16 *HAMLET: . . . though I am native here,*
                And to the manner born . . .
   365.05   in my baron gentilhomme to the manhor bourne

I. iv. 70–71 *HORATIO: . . . the cliff*
                That beetles o'er his base into the sea.
   248.18   when he beetles backwards

I. v. 9–11 *GHOST: I am thy father's spirit*
              Doomed for a certain term to walk the night,
              And for the day confined to fast in fires.
   18.24   when Head-in-Clouds walked the earth
   177.04   his pawdry's purgatory was more than a nigger bloke could bear
   565.18–20   [see Part II entry]

I. v. 15–16 *GHOST: I could a tale unfold whose lightest word*
                Would harrow up thy soul
   19.25   What a meanderthalltale to unfurl

I. v. 22 *GHOST: . . . List, list, O, list!* (quoted by Stephen Dedalus in *U*, 188
            as "List! List! O List!")
   5.27   Heed! Heed!
   13.16   List! Wheatstone's magic lyer.
   15.08   Year! Year!
   21.02   Lissom! Lissom!
   51.09   lust!
   55.31   craving their auriculars to recepticle particulars

APPENDIXES 203

58.06   Lou! Lou!
58.18   lo! lo!
65.04   Now listen, Mr Leer!
68.25   Hear, O hear
76.11   Now hear
85.31   Oyeh! Oyeh!
95.33   hist! . . . hast!
96.01   Harik! Harik! Harik!
103.10 and we list as she bibs us
117.02 Here, Ohere!
147.03 Hearhere!
148.26 Liss, liss!
152.15 Audi, Joe Peters! Exaudi facts!
175.27 *Hirp! Hirp! for their Missed Understandings!*
200.33 Odet! Odet!
201.03–4 Listen now. . . . Tarn your ore ouse! Essonne inne!
238.23 List!
278.L3 *land me arrears*
287.18 husk, hisk, a spirit spires
337.26 heahear!
364.14 Attonsure! Ears to hears!
398.29 Hear, O hear
409.03 Ear! Ear! Not ay! Eye! Eye!
488.19 Oyessoyess
500.18 Aure! Cloudy father!
543.11 Attent! Couch hear!
553.04 oyir, oyir, oyir
564.21 Listeneth!
568.25 Ear! Ear!
571.34 Wait! Hist! Let us list!
584.36–585.01 here-hear
586.15 Attention to all!
587.03 Hiss!
593.05–6 Here! Here!
598.30 Hear!
604.22 Oyes! Oyeses! Oyesesyeses!
619.20–22 Lsp! . . . Lpf! . . . Lispn!
621.17 Lst!
624.06 Lss.
628.15 Lps.

I. v. 58 *GHOST: But soft, methinks I scent the morning air*
   628.08, 14   So soft this morning, ours. . . . Bussoftlhee

I. v. 91 *GHOST: Adieu, adieu, adieu. Remember me.* (and I. v. 110, *HAMLET: It is 'Adieu, adieu, remember me.'*)
   13.27   Adear, adear!
   158.20 Ah dew! Ah dew!

224.10 A dire, O dire!
250.07 ajew ajew
563.35 Adieu, soft adieu
628.14 mememormee!

I. v. 95, 97 *HAMLET: Remember thee? . . . Remember thee?*
230.35 Remember thee, castle throwen?

I. v. 188–89 *HAMLET: The time is out of joint. O cursèd spite*
  That ever I was born to set it right.
104.05 disjointed times
181.29–30 His jymes is out of job, would sit and write.

II. ii. 174 *HAMLET* [to Polonius]: *You are a fishmonger.*
29.26 fishmummer
144.30 the rubberend Mr Polkingtone, the quoniam fleshmonger
408.25, 36 Fishhands Macsorley . . . Piscisvendolor!

II. ii. 181–82 *HAMLET: For if the sun breed maggots in a dead dog, being a good kissing carrion . . .*
131.17 god at the top of the staircase, carrion on the mat of straw

II. ii. 187 *POLONIUS: Still harping on my daughter*
374.06 Still pumping on Torkenwhite

II. ii. 202 *HAMLET: . . . if, like a crab, you could go backward*
249.02–3 But if this could see with its backsight he'd be the grand old greeneyed lobster

II. ii. 203 *POLONIUS: Though this be madness, yet there is method in't.*
32.05 if so be you have metheg in your midness
126.09 fine artful disorder
159.30–31 baileycliaver though he's a nawful curilass and I must slav to methodiousness
173.34 with a meticulosity bordering on the insane
182.07 by the beerlitz in his mathness

II. ii. 251–53 *HAMLET: O God, I could be bounded in a nutshell, and count myself a king of infinite space, were it not that I have bad dreams.*
276.L2 *Omnitudes in a knutshedell*
455.29 Putting Allspace in a Notshall

II. ii. 483–84 *PLAYER: Break all the spokes and fellies from her wheel,*
  And bowl the round nave down the hill of heaven.
447.04 till navel, spokes, and felloes hum like hymn

II. ii. 490–93 *PLAYER: 'But who (ah woe!) had seen the mobled queen'*
379.18 queens mobbing him

II. ii. 516 *HAMLET: God's bodkin, man!*
79.20 bare godkin
268.15 And a bodikin a boss in the Thimble Theatre

446.05 The so pretty arched godkin of beddingnights
500.02 They're playing thimbles and bodkins
578.16 And who is the bodikin by him, sir?

II. ii. 543 *HAMLET: What's Hecuba to him, or he to Hecuba?*
276.08–9 What's Hiccupper to hem or her to Hagaba?
483.18 What cans such wretch to say to I or how have My to doom with him?

II. ii. 553 *HAMLET: Like John-a-dreams, unpregnant of my cause . . .*
61.04 John a'Dream's mews
399.34 So, to john for a john, johnajeams, led it be!
597.20 all-a-dreams
614.29 John-a-Donk

III. i. 56 ff. [See pages 65–66 of this study for a comparison of 143.03–28 with Hamlet's famous fourth soliloquy.]

III. i. 56 *HAMLET: To be or not to be—that is the question*
70.08–9 wider he might the same . . . other he would, with tosend and obertosend
110.14 me ken or no me ken Zot is the Quiztune
123.31–32 Hanno O'Nonhanno
182.19–21 in the act of reciting old Nichiabelli's monolook interyerear *Hanno, o Nonanno, acce'l brubblemm'as*
269.19–20 To me or not to me. Satis thy quest on.
319.28 at weare or not at weare

III. i. 57–58 *HAMLET: Whether 'tis nobler in the mind to suffer*
The slings and arrows of outrageous fortune
434.04–05 Where it is nobler in the main to supper than the boys and errors of outrager's virtue.

III. i. 60–61 *HAMLET: . . . To die, to sleep*
No more . . .
347.04 Steep Nemorn

III. i. 63–64 *HAMLET: 'Tis a consummation*
Devoutly to be wished
319.35 a satuation, debauchly to be watched for
432.14, 32–33 a consommation . . . where's the fate to be wished for

III. i. 66–68 *HAMLET: For in that sleep of death what dreams may come*
When we have shuffled off this mortal coil,
Must give us pause.
256.14–15 For here the holy language. Soons to come. To pausse.

III. i. 75 *HAMLET: When he himself might his quietus make*
40.30–32 . . . where he could throw true and go and blow the sibicidal napper off himself for two bits to boldywell baltitude in the peace and quitybus

III. i. 76 *HAMLET: With a bare bodkin?*
 79.20   bare godkin
 268.15 And a bodikin a boss in the Thimble Theatre
 446.05 the so pretty arched godkin of beddingnights
 500.02 They're playing thimbles and bodkins
 578.16 And who is the bodikin by him, sir?

III. i. 79–80 *HAMLET: The undiscovered country, from whose bourn*
 No traveller returns.
 31.32   I've mies outs ide Bourn
 143.10 old hopeinhaven [see Part II, entry for 143.03–28]
 190.21 your bourne of travail
 220.34 Poopinheavin
 248.25 cope of heaven
 365.04–5 to the manhor bourne
 366.14 bourne up pridely out of medsdreams
 367.29 the bounds whereinbourne our solied bodies all attomed attain arrest
 379.35 Beyond bournes and bowers
 478.16 lead us to hopenhaven
 513.09 Delphin's Bourne

III. i. 83 *HAMLET: Thus conscience does make cowards of us all.*
 319.07 and thus plinary indulgence makes columellas of us all

III. ii. 13 *HAMLET: It out-herods Herod.*
 127.11 if he outharrods against barkers

III. ii. 131 *HAMLET: Marry, this is miching mallecho; it means mischief.*
 291.22 that miching micher
 468.26 mitching

III. ii. 234 *HAMLET: . . . our withers are unwrung*
 143.16 comeliewithhers
 550.26 to wring her withers limberly

III. ii. 367 *POLONIUS: Very like a whale.*
 120.11 very like a whale's egg
 307.F2 Wherry like the whaled prophet in a spookeerie

IV. iv. 52–53 *HAMLET: . . . all that fortune, death, and danger dare,*
 Even for an eggshell.
 183.11–12 doubtful eggshells
 420.15–16 An infant sailing eggshells on the floor of a wet day would have had more sabby

IV. v. 25 *OPHELIA: By his cockle hat and staff . . .*
 41.02 Sant Iago by his cocklehat
 81.10 you may scallop your hat

IV. v. 62–63   *OPHELIA:* '*Before you tumbled me,*
                              You promised me to wed'
    461.30   Coach me how to tumble

IV. v. 164   *OPHELIA: Hey non nony, nony, hey nony*
    203.14   Neya, narev, nen, nonni, nos!
    307.F8   Eu, Monsieur? Nenni No, Monsieur!
    452.27   nenni

IV. v. 170–71   *OPHELIA: You must sing 'A-down a-down, and you call*
                              him a-down-a.'
    10.28   Downadown, High Downadown.
    593.02   Calling all downs. Calling all downs to dayne.

IV. v. 174 ff.   *OPHELIA: There's rosemary, that's for remembrance. . . . And there is pansies. . . . There's fennel for you, and columbines. There's rue for you. . . . There's a daisy. I would give you some violets*
    203.28–30   Afrothdizzying galbs . . . vierge violetian . . . throw those laurels now on her daphdaph teasesong
    215.07–8   Forgivemequick, I'm going! Bubye! And you, pluck your watch, forgetmenot.
    226.10–12   Bring tansy, throw myrtle, strew rue, rue, rue. She is fading out like Journee's clothes so you can't see her now.
    226.32   W waters the fleurettes of novembrance
    227.15–16   for they are the florals, from foncey and pansey to papavere's blush, forsake-me-nought
    389.02   forgetmenots
    463.19–20   There's the nasturtium for ye now that saved manny a poor sinker from water on the grave
    561.20–21   Here's newyearspray, the posquiflor, a windaborne and heliotrope; there miriamsweet and amaranth and marygold

IV. v. 175–76   *OPHELIA: And there is pansies, that's for thoughts.*
    226.10   Bring tansy, throw myrtle . . .
    227.15–16   for they are the florals, from foncey and pansey
    271.20   brood our pansies
    278.05–6   With a pansy for the pussy in the corner
    403.14–15   Pensée! The most beautiful of woman of the veilch veilchen veilde.
    408.31–32   what the eldest daughter she was panseying
    426.21   the wieds of pansiful heathvens
    443.14–15   He'll have pansements then for his pensamientos
    446.03   loveliest pansiful thoughts

IV. v. 180   *OPHELIA: There's rue for you, and here's some for me.*
    226.10–12   Bring tansy, throw myrtle, strew rue, rue, rue.
    227.14   Beatrice . . . and Rue
    279.F1   Then rue. . . This isabella I'm on knows the ruelles of the rut

208   APPENDIXES

    433.35–36 Wet your thistle where a weed is and you'll rue it
    444.12 Rue the day!
    488.18 Ruemember, blither, thou must lie
    558.29–30 ru arue rue
    577.30 rue to lose

IV. v. 182–83 *OPHELIA: I would give you some violets, but they withered all when my father died.*
    143.26 Violet's dyed!
    461.17 my golden violents wetting

IV. vii. 30–32 *KING: You must not think . . . That we can let our beard be shook with danger*
    177.32 he was aware of no other shaggspick, other Shakhisbeard

IV. vii. 159 *KING: A chalice for the nonce*
    131.30–31 nods a nap for the nonce

V. i. (The gravediggers' scene)
    121.32 a grand stylish gravedigging with secondbest buns
    171.15 the tragic jester
    189.28 premature gravedigger
    190.19 boskop of Yorek
    229.36–230.01 the grusomehed's yoeureeke
    283.14–15 tods of Yorek
    338.11–12 mottledged youth . . . is supposing to motto the sorry dejester
    465.32 Be Yorick
    491.20 *the arkbashap of Yarak*

V. i. 31 *CLOWN: 'A was the first that ever bore arms.*
    5.05 Of the first was he to bare arms and a name

V. i. 132 *HAMLET: . . . he galls his kibe*
    321.11 a kiber galler

V. ii. 10 *HAMLET: There's a divinity that shapes our ends.*
    278.F2 he's have a culious impressiom on the diminitive that chafes our ends

Macbeth

Macbeth, thane of Glamis and Cawdor
    188.27 Cold caldor
    189.14 Chalwador
    250.16–18 Glamours . . . Coldours . . . Lack breath must leap no more.
    250.34–36 Led by Lignifer, in four hops of the happiest, ach beth cac duff, a marrer of the sward incoronate
    290.06 poor MacBeth
    302.F1 I loved to see the Macbeths Jerseys knacking spots of the Plumpduffs Pants.

412.21   quoth mecback
566.18–22   the dame dowager . . . as first mutherer. . . . The two princes of the tower royal . . . to lie how they are without to see. The dame dowager's duffgerent to present wappon, blade drawn to the full
600.36–601.01   glaum is

Macduff, the thane of Fife
77.14   Dane to pfife
250.35   ach beth cac duff
302.F1   I loved to see the Macbeths Jerseys knacking spots of the Plumpduffs Pants
438.36   lucky duffs and light lindsays
469.20–21   Lead on, Macadam, and danked be he who first sights Halt Linduff!
566.20   duffgerent

The Witches on the Heath
3.11–12   all's fair in vanessy, were sosie sesthers wroth
151.13–14   the watches cunldron apan the oven, though it is astensably a case of Ket's rebollions
175.14   Not yet Witchywitchy of Wench struck Fire of his Heath
246.10–12   Ansighosa pokes in her pot still to souse at the sop be sodden enow and to hear to all the bubbles besaying: the coming man, the future woman.
251.11   most anysing maybefallhim from a song of a witch
468.35   there's the witch on the heath

Inverness
3.11–12   all's fair in vanessy, were sosie sesthers wroth
35.10   inverness
289.28   at Idleness
332.28   at Inverleffy

Birnam Wood
248.22   Dunckle Dalton of matching wools
250.16   For a burning would is come to dance inane.

I. i. 10   *WITCHES: Fair is foul, and foul is fair.*
3.11–12   all's fair in vanessy, were sosie sesthers wroth

I. iii. 6   *WITCH: 'Aroint thee, witch!'*
223.19   Arrest thee, scaldbrother!
406.13   arount it
492.34   aroint him

I. iii. 77   *MACBETH: Upon this blasted heath . . .*
194.15   windblasted tree of the knowledge of beautiful andevil
340.07–8   The field of karhags and that bloasted tree. Forget not the felled.
468.35   there's the witch on the heath

I. vi. 1–3   *DUNCAN: This castle hath a pleasant seat. The air*

     Nimbly and sweetly recommends itself
     Unto our gentle senses.
 540.03–4 This seat of our city it is of all sides pleasant, comfortable and wholesome

I. vii. 1–2 MACBETH: *If it were done when 'tis done, then 'twere well*
     It were done quickly.
 307.27 If You Do It Do It Now

II. i. 46 MACBETH: *And on thy blade and dudgeon gouts of blood*
 143.05 his gouty hands

II. i. 54–56 MACBETH: *. . . thus with his stealthy pace,*
     With Tarquin's ravishing strides, towards his design
     Moves like a ghost.
 278.F7 Strutting as proud as a great turquin weggin that cuckhold

II. ii. 34–42 MACBETH: *Methought I heard a voice cry 'Sleep no more!*
     Macbeth does murder sleep' . . .
     Glamis hath murdered sleep, and therefore Cawdor
     Shall sleep no more. Macbeth shall sleep no more.
 250.16–18 Glamours hath moidered's lieb and herefore Coldours must leap no more. Lack breath must leap no more.
 347.04 Steep Nemorn

II. ii. 61 MACBETH: *The multitudinous seas incarnadine*
 79.03 even the first wugger of himself in the flesh, whiggissimus incarnadined.

II. iii. 1–20 (The Drunken Porter's scene, the Knocking at the Gate)

II. iii. 1 ff. PORTER: *Here's a knocking indeed. . . . Who's there, i'th'name of Belzebub? . . . I'll devil-porter it no further.*
 64.09–11 This battering babel allower the door and sideposts . . . was not in the very remotest like the belzey babble of a bottle of boose

II. iii. 12–13 PORTER: *Faith, here's an English tailor come hither for stealing out of a French hose. Come in, tailor.*
 70.13–32 Humphrey's unsolicited visitor . . . bleated through the gale outside which the tairor of his clothes was hogcallering . . . that he would break his bulshewigger's head for him . . . that he would break the gage over his lankyduckling head . . . and went on at a wicked rate.

II. iii. 1–20 (Miscellaneous references to the Drunken Porter and the Knocking at the Gate)
 50.05 outandin brown candlestock
 51.24 the porty
 63.17–19 a most decisive bottle of single in his possession, seized after dark . . . temperance gateway was there in a gate's way
 63.32–35 trying to open zozimus a bottlop stoub by mortially hammering his

APPENDIXES 211

        magnum bonum . . . against the bludgey gate for the boots about the swan
- 65.35   the bottle at the gate
- 69.15ff.   A stonehinged gate . . . applegate . . . the iron gape, by old custom left open to prevent the cats from getting at the gout, was triplepatlockt on him on purpose by his faithful poorters.
- 72.02–3   Sublime Porter
- 72.28   at the wicket in support of his words
- 91.15   come on to Porterfeud
- 262.05–6   Thus come to castle./Knock.
- 330.30–32   Knock knock. War's where! Which war? The Twwinns. Knock knock. Woos without! Without what? An apple. Knock knock.
- 379.01   Kick nuck, Knockcastle!
- 530.32   Tipknock Castle!
- 551.35   no porte sublimer benared my ghates
- 595.03   Whake? Hill of Hafid, knock and knock.

II. iii. 115   *MACDUFF: Look to the Lady (*also Banquo in line 121)
- 105.22   Look to the Lady

III. ii. 22–23   *MACBETH: . . . Duncan is in his grave.*
                      After life's fitful fever he sleeps well.
- 74.16–19   Humph is in his doge. . . . When we sleep

IV. i. 10   *WITCHES: Double, double, toil and trouble*
- 134.04   double trouble
- 138.02–3   his troubles may be over but his doubles have still to come
- 250.34–36   ach beth cac duff . . . Will any dubble dabble on the bay?

IV. i. 80   *2. APPARITION: . . . for none of woman born*
                Shall harm Macbeth.
- 55.10   manorwombanborn
- 79.08–9   no man of woman born
- 365.04–5   to the manhor bourne

IV. i. 117   *MACBETH: What, will the line stretch out to th' crack of doom?*
- 11.04–5   when Thom's blowing toomcracks

V. i. 32   *LADY MACBETH: Out, damned spot! Out, I say!*
- 251.16–17   The specks of his lapspan are his foul deed thoughts, wishmarks of mad imogenation. Take they off! Make the off!
- 624.24   a spot of marashy [see Part II, entry for 627.28–30]

V. i. 47–48   *LADY MACBETH: Here's the smell of blood still. All the perfumes of Arabia will not sweeten this little hand.*
- 52.05–6   but all the bottles in sodemd histry will not soften your bloodathirst
- 624.24   parafume [see Part II, entry for 627.28–30]
- 627.26–27   No! Nor for all our wild dances in all their wild din. [see Part II, entry for 627.28–30]

V. iii. 22–23 MACBETH: *I have lived long enough. My way of life*
Is fall'n into the sear, the yellow leaf
  336.15 his awebrume hour, her sere Sahara of sad oakleaves

V. v. 18–19 MACBETH: *There would have been a time for such a word.*
To-morrow, and to-morrow, and to-morrow . . .
  250.16 Yet's the time for being now, now, now. For a burning would is come to dance inane . . .

V. v. 19–23 MACBETH: *To-morrow, and to-morrow, and to-morrow*
Creeps in this petty pace from day to day
To the last syllable of recorded time,
And all our yesterdays have lighted fools
The way to dusty death.
  104.12 Which of your Hesterdays Mean Ye to Morra
  280.06–7 tomorrows gone and yesters outcome
  455.11–13 Postmartem is the goods. . . . Toborrow and toburrow and tobarrow!

V. v. 23 MACBETH: *. . . Out, out, brief candle!*
  50.05 outandin brown candlestock
  276.09–10 Ough, ough, brieve kindli!

V. v. 26–28 MACBETH: *. . . It is a tale*
Told by an idiot, full of sound and fury,
Signifying nothing.
  515.07–8 —A gael galled by sheme of scorn? Nock?
—Sangnifying nothing. Mock!
  (See also: 215.35, A tale told of Shaun and Shem; 275.24, They are talles all tolled; 324.05, tail toiled of spume and spawn; 396.23, stole stale mis betold; 563.27, as at taledold of Formio and Cigalette; 597.08, Totalled in toldteld and teldtold.)

V. viii. 12 MACBETH: *I bear a charmèd life.*
  382.02 his charmed life

V. viii. 30 MACBETH: *Though Birnam Wood be come to Dunsinane* (also in IV. i. 93, V. iii. 60, and V. v. 44–45)
  248.22 Dunckle Dalton of matching wools
  248.28–29 Underwoods spells bushment's business. So if you sprig poplar you're bound to twig this.
  250.16–18 For a burning would is come to dance inane. Glamours hath moidered's lieb and herefore Coldours must leap no more. Lack breath must leap no more.
  417.31 Never did Dorsan from Dunshanagan dance it more devilry

V. viii. 33–34 MACBETH: *. . . Lay on, Macduff,*
And damned be him that first cries, 'Hold, enough!'
  469.20–21 Lead on, Macadam, and danked be he who first sights Halt Linduff!

Julius Caesar

Julius Caesar
- 150.09 seesers
- 161.36 Caesar outnullused
- 162.01 The older sisars (Tyrants, regicide is too good for you!)
- 162.02–5 (the compositor of the farce of dustiny however makes a thunpledrum mistake by letting off this pienofarte effect as his furst act as that is where the juke comes in) having been sort-of-nineknived ...
- 162.08 who never quite got the sandhurst out of his eyes
- 167.23 Merus Genius to Careous Caseous! *Moriture, te salutat!*
- 207.24 Leste, before Julia sees her!
- 219.13 Caesar-in-Chief
- 237.12 we herehear, aboutobloss, O coelicola, thee salutamt.
- 271.03–6 Sire Jeallyous Seizer ... and the tryonforit of Oxthievious, Lapidous, and Malthouse Anthemy
- 306.L2 *Julius Caesar*

Brutus and Cassius
- 161.12 Burrus and Caseous
- 161.17 Burrus ... yet unbeaten as a risicide
- 163.06 *Butterbrot ... Schtinkenkot!*
- 166.34–167.01 A cleopatrician in her own right she at once complicates the position while Burrus and Caseous are contending for her misstery by implicating herself with an elusive Antonius, a wop
- 167.04 This Antonious-Burrus-Caseous grouptriad
- 281.15–16 Bruto and Cassio
- 366.25 ff. when booboob brutals and cautiouses ... blows the gaff off mombition and thit thides or marse
- 568.08–9 Britus and Gothius shall no more joustle for that sonneplace but mark one autonement

Mark Antony
- 152.22 My hood! cries Antony Romeo
- 167.01 an elusive Antonius, a wop
- 167.04 This Antonious-Burrus-Caseous grouptriad
- 271.03–6 ... the tryonforit of Oxthievious, Lapidous and Malthouse Anthemy
- 483.17 blarneying Marcantonio
- 568.08–9 Britus and Gothius ... but mark one autonement

I. i. 61 *FLAVIUS: See whe'r their basest mettle be not moved.*
- 359.04 Under the selfhide of his bessermettle

I. ii. 18–23 *SOOTHSAYER: Beware the ides of March.*
- 27.08 his olde by his ide
- 31.32 I've mies outs ide Bourn
- 35.03–4 one happygogusty Ides-of-April morning (the anniversary, as it fell out, of his first assumption of his mirthday suit ...)

214   APPENDIXES

    40.10   eyots of martas
    43.12   roman easter
    85.27   calends of mars
    97.03   Juletide
    128.32   three hundred sixty five idles
    274.L3   *till the calends of Mary*
    289.27–28   on the Ides of Valentino's, at Idleness
    354.24   their murdhering idies
    366.29–30   thit thides or marse makes a good dayle to be shattat
    455.28   to begin properly SPQueaRking [see Part II, entry for 455.24–29]
    603.15   hydes of march

I. ii. 85   *BRUTUS: If it be aught toward the general good*
    523.02–4   the evil . . . might nevewtheless lead somehow on to good towawd the genewality

I. ii. 140   *CASSIUS: The fault, dear Brutus, is not in our stars*
    278.L3   *Dear Brotus, land me arrears.*

III. ii. 21–22   *BRUTUS: Not that I loved Caesar less, but that I loved Rome more.*
    281.22–23   What if she love Sieger less though she leave Ruhm moan?

III. ii. 26–28   *BRUTUS: There is tears for his love; joy for his fortune; honor for his valor; and death for his ambition.*
    282.01–3   With sobs for his job, with tears for his toil, with horror for his squalor but with pep for his perdition.

III. ii. 73   *ANTONY: Friends, Romans, countrymen, lend me your ears.*
    55.31   craving their auriculars to recepticle particulars
    278.L3   *Dear Brotus, land me arrears.*
    546.30–33   Fulvia. . . . Earalend

III. ii. 92   *ANTONY: Ambition should be made of sterner stuff.*
    366.29–30   mombition . . . thit thides or marse. . . . Fall stuff.

V. v. 68   *ANTONY: This was the noblest Roman of them all.*
    84.15   nobiloroman
    419.21–22   nobly Roman as pope

A Midsummer Night's Dream

Title
    501.16   lukesummer night
    502.29   Miss Somer's nice dream

Bottom
    93.18   he was dovetimid as the dears at Bottome
    319.06   bully bluedomer
    340.09   warful doon's bothem

APPENDIXES 215

    342.31   *eeridreme*. . . . From Topphole to Bottom
    369.12   Woovil Doon Botham
    503.21   Woful Dane Bottom
    594.12   om this warful dune's battam

Puck
    210.34–35   a putty shovel for Terry the Puckaun
    227.29   a puck on the plexus
    278.13   pack, puck
    326.03   As puck as that Paddeus
    369.29   her chilikin puck
    425.30   pucktricker's
    463.36   the prince of goodfilips
    563.26   puck and prig

Lantern and Wall
    69.05–7   the whole of the wall . . . wallhole
    321.04   lampthorne . . . wand

Demetrius
    319.05–6   ringing rinbus round Demetrius for . . . bully bluedomer

Helena
    71.29   *Hellena*

Flute
    343.36   Flute!

Oberon and Titania
    339.14   Obriania's beromst!

I. ii (The scene in which Peter Quince's "rude mechanicals" prepare their play)
    359.31–360.16   [See Part II entry.]

I. ii. 75   *BOTTOM: I will roar you as gently as any sucking dove.*
    93.17–18   he was dovetimid as the dears at Bottome
    245.18   sucking loves
    403.16   dhove's suckling

II. i. 164   *OBERON: In maiden meditation, fancy free*
    208.16   fancyfastened, free

II. i. 249   *OBERON: I know a bank where the wild thyme blows*
    430.29   wild thyme
    501.16–21   lukesummer night. . . . The isles is Thymes.

II. ii. 18   *1. FAIRY: Weaving spiders, come not here*
    481.05   where no spider webbeth [see Part II, entry for 481.07–08]

III. i. 7   *QUINCE:* . . . *bully Bottom* (also Flute, in IV. ii. 18)
    319.06   bully bluedomer

III. i. 64–65   *QUINCE: Come sit down, every mother's son* . . .
    212.15   ilcka madre's daughter

216 APPENDIXES

  360.03 Let everie sound of a pitch keep still [see Part II entry]

III. ii. 203–9 *HELENA: We, Hermia, like two artificial gods*
      Have with our needles created both one flower . . .
      . . . So we grew together,
      Like to a double cherry . . .
  489.19 We were in one class of age like to two clots of egg.

III. ii. 338 *DEMETRIUS: Follow? Nay, I'll go with thee, cheek by jowl.*
  168.11 jack by churl
  215.19 He married his markets, cheap by foul.

IV. i. 203 ff. *BOTTOM: I have had a most rare vision. . . . Man is but an ass if he go about to expound this dream. Methought I was. . . . Methought I was, and methought I had . . .*
  403.18–405.07 Methought as I was dropping asleep somepart in nonland . . . arrah, methought. . . . And lo, mescemed. . . . Yet methought . . . but I, poor ass, am but as their fourpart tinckler's dunkey
  481.07–08 —Dream. Ona nonday I sleep. I dreamt of a somday. Of a wonday I shall wake. Ah!
  489.35 This nonday diary, this allnights newseryreel
  608.22 ff. I dhink I sawn to remumb or sumbsuch. A kind of thinglike . . .

IV. i. 209 *BOTTOM: The eye of man hath not heard, the ear of man hath not seen . . .*
  482.34–36 What can't be coded can be decorded if an ear aye sieze what no eye ere grieved for

V. i. 16–17 *THESEUS: Turns them to shapes, and gives to airy nothing*
      A local habitation and a name.
  52.50 Mary Nothing

V. i. 60 *THESEUS: How shall we find the concord of this discord?*
  405.04–6 Had I the concordant wiseheads . . . but I, poor ass . . .
  482.34–36 What can't be coded can be decorded if an ear aye sieze what no eye ere grieved for

V. i. 412 *PUCK: If we shadows have offended . . .*
  319.03–6 [see Part II entry]
  404.13 Whom we dreamt was a shaddo

Other plays alluded to in Finnegans Wake. These plays are arranged alphabetically by title.

All's Well that Ends Well

Title
  40.01 All Swell that Aimswell

150.30   by Allswill
279.05   alls war that end war
295.21   All's fair on all fours
418.35   ail's weal
579.24   Oil's wells in our lands

Antony and Cleopatra

Cleopatra
91.06   Cliopatrick (the sow) princess of parked porkers
104.20–22   Cleopater's Needlework . . . on the Sahara . . . and the Parlourmaids of Aegypt
164.07–8   on this stage there pleasantly appears the cowrymaid M.
166.34 ff.   A cleopatrician in her own right . . . implicating herself with an elusive Antonius, a wop
254.07   Clio's
271.L2   *Cliopatria, thy hosies history*
508.23   Clopatrick's
627.30   haughty Niluna

Antony
152.22   My hood! cries Antony Romeo
167.01   an elusive Antonius, a wop
167.04   This Antonius-Burrus-Caseous grouptriad
271.03–6   Sire Jeallyous Seizer . . . and the tryonforit of Oxthievious, Lapidous and Malthouse Anthemy
483.17   blarneying Marcantonio
568.08–9   Britus and Gothius . . . but mark one autonement

Octavius and Lepidus
271.03–6   the tryonforit of Oxthievious, Lapidous and Malthouse Anthemy
467.08   A full octavium below me
468.03–4   in my augustan days? With cesarella looking on.

Enobarbus
157.27   Enobarbarus

Charmian
20.03   has still to moor before the tomb of his cousin charmian

Fulvia
546.30–547.05   faithful Fulvia . . . Earalend . . . Fluvia . . . Fulvia Fluvia

Miscellaneous
328.22   from Coxenhagen till the brottels on the Nile

I. v. 73   CLEOPATRA: *My salad days* . . .
69.10   lost paladays
468.03–4   in my augustan days? With cesarella looking on.
615.25   paladays last.

218   APPENDIXES

IV. xv. 66–67   CLEOPATRA: *The odds is gone,*
And there is nothing left remarkable
Beneath the visiting moon.
    493.18–19   And there is nihil nuder under the clothing moon.

V. ii. 308–10   CLEOPATRA: *Dost thou not see my baby at my breast*
That sucks the nurse asleep? . . .
As sweet as balm, as soft as air, as gentle . . .
    624.21   Softly so
    627.12   Gently
    628.08   So soft this morning, ours [see Part II, entry for 627.28–30 on these three references]

As You Like It

Title
    489.33   As you sing it

Jaques
    245.18–24   Darkpark's acoo with sucking loves. Rosimund's by her wishing well. . . . Jacqueson's Island.
    422.33   the jaquejack

Rosalind (Ganymede)
    245.18   Rosimund's by her wishing well . . . Jacqueson's Island
    269.18   glib Ganymede
    583.11   And the twillingsons, ganymede, garrymore

Celia (Aliena)
    147.11   Celia
    608.18   the voice of Alina

Amiens
    549.31   amiens

Orlando
    74.05   orland

II. v. 1   AMIENS: *Under the greenwood tree . . .*
    30.13–14   the grand old gardener was saving daylight under his redwood tree
    74.10   green woods
    335.32–34   And it was . . . in the green of the wood . . . and jollyjacques spindthrift on the merry
    450.32–33   But enough of greenwood's gossip

II. v. 48 ff.   AMIENS: *Ducdame, ducdame, ducdame.*
    15.17   duncledames

II. vii. 28   JAQUES: *And thereby hangs a tale.*
    143.15   and the thereby hang of the Hoel of it
    224.08   Towhere byhangs our tales

II. vii. 139   *JAQUES: All the world's a stage . . .*
   33.03   our worldstage's practical jokepiece
   278.13   All the world's in want

II. vii. 142–43   *JAQUES: And one man in his time plays many parts,*
                                His acts being seven ages . . .
   316.16   seven oak ages

III. ii. 98   *TOUCHSTONE: If the cat will after kind . . .*
   394.28   katte efter kinne

The Comedy of Errors

Title
   425.24   Outragedy of poetscalds! Acomedy of letters!

Dromio(s)
   89.03   Two dreamyums in one dromium? Yes and no error.
   211.08   Dromilla
   598.02   they just done been doing being in a dromo of todos

Aemelia
   410.23   Speak to us of Emailia.

Coriolanus

Title
   118.13   Coccolanius
   228.11   the coriolano
   354.33   corollanes'

Cymbeline

Cymbeline
   292.25   hark back to lark to you symibellically
   607.09–10   Messagepostumia . . . cymbaloosing

Imogen (Fidele)
   6.25   dusty fidelios
   251.17   mad imogenation
   300.L1   *Ultimogeniture*

Posthumus Leonatus
   316.34   a warry posthumour's expletion
   377.09   Postumus
   422.14   Obnoximost posthumust!
   563.04   Here are posthumious tears
   607.09–10   Messagepostumia . . . cymbaloosing

II. iii. 19   *CLOTEN: Hark, hark, the lark at heaven's gate sings . . .*
   292.25   hark back to lark to you symibellically

IV. ii. 258–63 *GUIDERIUS: Fear no more the heat o' th' sun,*
Nor the furious winter's rages;
Thou thy worldly task hast done,
Home art gone and ta'en thy wages.
Golden lads and girls all must,
As chimney-sweepers . . .

    256.11–12 Home all go. Halome. Blare no more ramsblares. . . . And cease your fumings.

IV. ii. 262–63 *GUIDERIUS: Golden lads and girls all must,*
As chimney-sweepers, come to dust.
    6.25 dusty fidelios
    20.30 golden youths

The First Part of King Henry the Fourth

Falstaff
    7.13 fraudstuff
    50.02–5 [see Part II entry]
    366.30 Fall stuff.
    370.13 Fool step!
    379.18 Fell stiff.
    456.24 I'm fustfed like fungstif
    595.32 Fill stap.

Hotspur (Harry Percy)
    50.02–5 cockspurt [see Part II entry]
    352.10 the enemay the Percy rally got me

Miscellaneous
    347.12 freshprosts of Eastchept

II. iv. 514–15 *PRINCE: O monstrous! but one halfpennyworth of bread to this intolerable deal of sack!*
    137.34 a laughsworth of his illformation over a larmsworth of salt
    288.F1 An ounceworth of onions for a pennyawealth of sobs

The Second Part of King Henry the Fourth

III. ii. 203 *FALSTAFF: We have heard the chimes at midnight, Master Shallow.*
    403.19–21 I heard . . . midnight's chimes

IV. v. 92 *KING: Thy wish was father, Harry, to thy thought.*
    147.19–20 Whoses wishes is the farther to my thoughts

V. iii. 85 *PISTOL: . . . the ill wind which blows no man to good.*
    448.20 'Tis an ill weed blows no poppy good

Henry the Fifth

II. iii. 16   HOSTESS: . . .*and 'a babbled of green fields* (Folio version: *and a table of green fields*)
    10.34   A verytableland of bleakbardfields!

Henry the Eighth

Title
    138.32   hahnreich the althe
    307.14   Henry Tudor
    539.32–33   Hungry the Loaved and Hangry the Hathed

King John

IV. ii. 11–12   SALISBURY: . . . *to paint the lily,*
                        To throw a perfume on the violet . . .
    434.18   if you can't point a lily get to henna out of here

King Lear

Title and King Lear
    13.17   Wheatstone's magic lyer.
    65.04   Now listen, Mr Leer!
    398.23   kingly leer
    590.02   leareyed and letterish
    611.33   Uberking Leary
    612.04   Ober King Leary

Fool (Whetstone)
    13.17   Wheatstone's magic lyer

Cordelia
    289.29   Liv's lonely daughter

Goneril
    349.02   gonorrhal stab

I. ii. 15   EDMUND: *Got 'tween asleep and wake.*
    192.20   fame would come to you twixt a sleep and a wake

III. ii. 59–60   LEAR: *I am a man*
                       More sinned against than sinning.
    523.09   as much sinned against as sinning

III. iv. 174–75   EDGAR: *His word was still, 'Fie, foh, and fum,*
                         I smell the blood of a British man'
    7.09   Finfoefom the Fush
    133.17   fiefeofhome
    367.23   fare fore forn

    370.28   the feof of the foef of forfummed
    491.29   My Mo Mum
    532.03   Fa Fe Fi Fo Fum
    545.23   Fee for farm
    596.24   freeflawforms
    608.31   fierce force fuming
    623.16   vim vam vom

IV. vi. 104   *LEAR: I am not ague-proof.*
    112.20   Ague will be rejuvenated.

IV. vi. 106   *LEAR: Ay, every inch a king.*
    152.34   every inch of an immortal
    268.04–5   All every inch of it

Love's Labor's Lost

Title
    74.03   lost leaders live!
    99.06   Morse nuisance noised
    157.23   but it was all mild's vapour moist
    435.16   All blah! Viper's vapid vilest
    486.09   Mere man's mime
    540.15   massed murmars march
    606.04   violet vesper vailed

Costard
    464.30   costard
    563.25   costarred

Longaville
    347.26   all feller come longa villa finish

III. i. 169   *BEROWNE: This signor-junior, giant-dwarf, Dan Cupid*
    445.22   if you think I'm so tan cupid

V. ii. 909   *WINTER: While greasy Joan doth keel the pot*
    138.03   the lobster pot that crabbed our keel

Measure for Measure

Title
    336.05   measures for messieurs

Duke Vincentio
    38.26   Mr Browne, disguised as a vincentian

Isabella
    257.01   So angelland all weeping bin that Izzy most unhappy is.
    279.F1   isabella
    556.03–5   when she took the veil, the beautiful presentation nun, so barely twenty, in her pure coif, sister Isobel.

566.23   Isabella

Angelo
257.01   angelland

Claudio
121.01   his claudian brother

IV. i. 1–6   *MARIANA and BOY: Take, O take those lips away,*
That so sweetly were forsworn;
And those eyes, the break of day,
Lights that do mislead the morn;
But my kisses bring again, bring again . . .
628.14–15   Take. Bussoftlhee. . . . Lps. The keys to [see Part II, entry for 628.14–15]

IV. i. 68–69   *ISABELLA: . . . but, soft and low,*
'Remember now my brother.'
628.14   Bussoftlhee, mememormee!

The Merchant of Venice

Title
105.01   *When the Myrtles of Venice Played to Bloccus's line*
435.03   the Smirching of Venus

Launcelot Gobbo
319.20   And be the coop of his gobbos

Pound of flesh
192.17   to give you your pound of platinum and a thousand thongs a year

IV. i   (The Quality of Mercy versus Shylock's Justice scene)
187.21 ff.   in mercy or justice . . .

V. i. 83–84   *LORENZO: The man that hath no music in himself*
Nor is not moved with concord of sweet sounds . . .
167.35–36   That mon that hoth no moses in his sole nor is not awed by conquists of word's law . . .

The Merry Wives of Windsor

Title
227.01–2   The many wiles of Winsure

Falstaff
(see listings under *1H4*)

I. i. 263–66   *SLENDER: You are afraid if you see the bear loose, are you not? . . . I have seen Sackerson loose twenty times.*
429.18–19, 430.06–7   restant, against a butterblond warden of the peace, one comestabulish Sigurdsen . . . the first human yellowstone landmark (the bear, the boer, the king of all boors)

224   APPENDIXES

    471.30   Sickerson, that borne of a bjoerne . . . hellyg Ursulinka
    530.22   Sackerson

II. iii. 20   *CAIUS: Vat be all you, one, two, tree, four, come for?* (also III. iii. 208, *CAIUS: If dere be one, or two, I shall make-a de turd.*)
    282.29   caiuscounting

Much Ado About Nothing

Title
    227.33   McAdoo about nothing
    290.09   MacAdoo

Beatrice
    227.14   Beatrice

Benedick
    469.23   Bennydick

III. v. 15   *DOGBERRY: Comparisons are odorous.*
    59.10   while it is odrous comparisoning to the sprangflowers
    163.26   odiose by comparison

Othello

Othello the Moor
    20.03   has still to moor before the tomb of his cousin charmian
    281.17–21   ('tis demonal!) . . . Sickamoor's so woful sally.
    343.22–23   in the tragedoes of those antiants their grandoper
    390.04   his old fellow
    390.27   That old fellow
    410.04   my oldfellow's
    485.17   old fellow

Iago
    41.02   Sant Iago
    281.21   Ancient's aerger

Cassio
    281.16   Cassio

Desdemona
    281.17–21   ('tis demonal!) . . . Sickamoor's so woful sally.
    281.18   il folsoletto nel falzoletto col fazolotto dal fuzzolezzo [the handkerchief; see Part II entry]

Emilia
    410.23   Speak to us of Emailia

I. i. 88–89   *IAGO: . . . an old black ram*
                         Is tupping your white ewe.
    396.14–15   What would Ewe do? With that so tiresome old milkless a ram.

I. iii. 338 ff. *IAGO: Put money in thy purse.*
    422.18–19 May we petition you, Shaun illustrious, then, to put his prentis' pride in your aproper's purse

II. iii. 64–65 *IAGO: And let me the canakin clink, clink;*
    And let me the canakin clink.
    118.04–5 And let us bringtheecease to beakerings on that clink

III. i. 8–9 *CLOWN: O, thereby hangs a tail.*
    MUSICIAN: Whereby hangs a tale, sir?
    143.15 and the thereby hang of the Hoel of it
    224.08 Towhere byhangs ourtales

III. iii. 157 *IAGO: Who steals my purse steals trash . . .*
    594.14–15 Respassers should be pursaccoutred. Qui stabat Meins quantum qui stabat Peins.

III. iii. 165–66 *IAGO: O, beware, my lord, of jealousy!*
    It is the green-eyed monster . . .
    88.15 And how did the greeneyed mister arrive at the B.A.?
    94.17 one old obster
    193.10 to make you go green in the gazer
    249.02–3 But if this could see with its backsight he'd be the grand old greeneyed lobster

IV. iii. 40–41 *DESDEMONA: 'The poor soul sat sighing by a sycamore tree,*
    Sing all a green willow . . .'
    281.17–21 ('tis demonal!) . . . Sickamoor's so woful sally

V. ii. 81–83 *DESDEMONA: But half an hour! . . . But while I say*
    one prayer!
    623.30 That I prays for [see Part II, entry for 627.28–30]

Pericles

Title
    306.L2 *Pericles.*
    327.13 periglus

V. i. 154 *MARINA: I will end here.*
    628.13 End here.

Richard the Second

Miscellaneous
    345.15 bagot
    352.10 the enemay the Percy rally got me

IV. i. 201 *RICHARD: Ay, no; no, ay; for I must nothing be . . .*
    409.03 Ear! Ear! Not ay! Eye! Eye!

Richard the Third

Richard III (Crookback)
    127.17–19 Dook Hookbackcrook upsits his ass booseworthies jeer and junket but they boos him oos and baas his aas when he lukes like Hunkett Plunkett
    134.10–11 in Silver on the Screen but was sequenced from the set as Crookback by the even more titulars, Rick, Dave and Barry
    138.33 writchad the thord
    319.20 Reacher the Thaurd
    373.14 the magreedy prince of Roger. Thuthud.

Buckingham
    318.21 backonham

The Two Princes (Edward and Richard)
    566.19–20 The two princes of the tower royal

I. i. 1–2 *RICHARD: Now is the winter of our discontent*
                      Made glorious summer by this son of York
    318.20–21 Now eats the vintner over these contents oft with his sad slow munch for backonham

V. v. 7, 13 *RICHARD: A horse! a horse! my kingdom for a horse!*
    104.11 *Buy Birthplate for a Bite*
    134.08 twiceynurseys fore a drum
    152.22 My hood! cries Antony Romeo
    193.31 My fault, his fault, a kingship through a fault
    352.09 my oreland for a rolvever
    373.15 Heigh hohse, heigh hohse, our kingdom from an orse!

Romeo and Juliet

Romeo and Juliet
    81.10 And if he's not a Romeo you may scallop your hat
    144.14 Like Jolio and Romeune
    148.13 not for all the juliettes in the twinkly way
    152.22 My hood! cries Antony Romeo
    157.08–9 Nuvoletta in her lightdress . . . leaning over the bannistars
    200.09 Madame Delba to Romeoreszk
    291.12 juwelietry
    303.02 Romeopullupalleaps
    350.23 rawmeots and juliannes
    391.21 from Roneo to Giliette
    441.11 what stuck to the Comtesse Cantilene [see Part II entry]
    463.08 Romeo
    481.16 old Romeo
    516.21 Montague

531.18–21 this is me jupettes . . . at Romiolo Frullini's flea pantamime
553.16–17 gregoromaios and gypsyjuliennes
563.27–29 How frilled one shall be as at taledold of Formio and Cigalette! What folly innocents! Theirs whet pep of puppyhood!

I. i. 12–15 GREGORY: . . . *for the weakest goes to the wall.*
 SAMPSON: *'Tis true; and therefore women, being the weaker vessels, are ever thrust to the wall.*
 79.33–34 as her weaker had turned him to the wall

I. iv. 53 ff. (Mercutio's Queen Mab speech)
 379.17–18 One bed night he had the delysiums that they were all queens mobbing him.

II. ii. 33 JULIET: *O Romeo, Romeo! wherefore art thou Romeo?*
 416.18 Iomio! Iomio!

III. ii. 59 JULIET: *. . . end motion here.*
 628.13 End here.

The Tempest

Ariel
 449.30 hearing the wireless harps of sweet old Aerial
 609.19–20 When the messanger of the risen sun (see other oriel)

Ferdinand
 457.03 Ferdinand

I. ii. 378–79 ARIEL: *The wild waves whist,*
 Foot it featly here and there
 292.21 what stale words whilom were woven with and fitted fairly featly for

IV. i. 152–53 PROSPERO: *The cloud-capped tow'rs, the gorgeous palaces,*
 The solemn temples, the great globe itself . . .
 541.06–7 by awful tors my wellworth building sprang sky spearing spires, cloud cupoled campaniles
 607.32 a clout capped sunbubble anaccanponied from his bequined torse.

V. i. 88 ARIEL: *Where the bee sucks, there suck I . . .*
 540.14–16 Ubi pop jay piped, ibi pep goes the whistle. . . . Where the bus stops there shop I

Timon of Athens

Characters
 306.L4 *Alcibiades*

III. iii. 6 SERVANT: *They have all been touched and found base metal.*
 359.04 under the selfhide of his bessermettle

Titus Andronicus

Titus, Caius, Sempronius
    128.15   Titius, Caius and Sempronius

Lavinia
    40.11   lavinias
    327.12   and all the Lavinias of ester yours

Troilus and Cressida

Characters
    154.18   achilles
    306.L2   *Ajax.*

Epistle to the Reader ('A never writer, to an ever reader. News'): *Eternal reader, you have here a new play, never staled with the stage, never clapper-clawed with the palms of the vulgar, and yet passing full of the palm comical* . . .
    491.07   clapperclaws
    614.13, 30   And the mannormillor clipperclappers. . . . with a clappercoupling

III. iii. 174   *ULYSSES: One touch of nature makes the whole world kin.*
    138.36–139.01   with one touch of nature set a veiled world agrin
    463.16–17   one twitch, one nature makes us oldworld kin

Twelfth Night

Title
    508.06   twelfth day

Illyria
    281.06   *la pervenche en Illyrie*

Viola
    223.07   Viola

Sir Toby Belch
    406.25   hurrah there for tobies
    423.13   thank the Bench
    423.33   negertoby

I. iii. 103   *BELCH: Art thou good at these kickshawses, knight?*
    291.12   kickychoses

II. iii. 106   *BELCH: Dost thou think, because thou art virtuous, there shall be no more cakes and ale?*
    423.11   Does he drink because I am sorely there shall be no more Kates and Nells.
    456.22   kates and eaps

II. iii. 107 *FESTE: Yes, by Saint Anne, and ginger shall be hot i'th'mouth, too.*
  512.26   the sickly sigh from her gingering mouth

The Two Gentlemen of Verona

Title
  569.31   two genitalmen of Veruno

Valentine
  20.34   volantine, valentine eyes.
  249.04   Valentine

IV. ii. 39 *HOST: Who is Silvia? What is she . . .*
  211.35–36   for Who-is-silvier—Where-is-he?
  256.23   and why is limbo where is he

The Winter's Tale

Title
  201.11   winter's doze

Camillo, Mamillius
  211.08   Camilla, Dromilla, Ludmilla, Mamilla
  492.13   Capilla, Rubrilla, and Melcamomilla

Mopsa
  550.21   a mopsa's broom to duist her sate

Florizel
  621.30   a youth in his florizel, a boy in innocence

III. iii. 57 (STAGE DIRECTION): *Exit* [Antigonus], *pursued by a bear.*
  55.25   pursue the bare

The Poems

The Sonnets

Mr. W. H. (William Hughes?)
  257.34–35   When the h, who the hu, how the hue, where the huer?
  574.15   Wieldhelm, Hurls

Dark Lady
  15.17   duncledames
  511.21   Where letties hereditate a dark mien

Sonnet 111: *And almost thence my nature is subdued*
  To what it works in, like the dyer's hand

230   APPENDIXES

    226.12   Still we know how Day the Dyer works

Sonnet 129: *Had, having, and in quest to have . . .*
    143.12   the course of his tory will had been having recourses

Sonnets 134, 135, 136 (for example)
    175.20   where theirs is Will there's his Wall

Venus and Adonis

Line 158:   **Can thy right hand seize love upon thy left?**
    27.04   when the ritehand seizes what the lovearm knows.

The Rape of Lucrece

Miscellaneous
    278.F7   Strutting as proud as a great turquin weggin that cuckhold
    542.29   raped lutetias in the lock

Appendix 3: The Shakespearean Theatre World

Shakespearean Theatres

Blackfriars
    48.03   The Blackfriars

The Globe
    455.26   the Royal Revolver of these real globoes

Bankside Theatre District
    201.05–6   By earth and the cloudy but I badly want a brandnew bankside, bedamp and I do, and a plumper at that!

The Old Vic
    62.06   the old vic
    330.13   Old Vickers sate down on their airs

The Phoenix (Cockpit Theatre)
    205.25   Phoenix Tavern
    219.02   Feenichts Playhouse
    321.18   by night in the Phoenix! Music.
    427.34   out there in Cockpit

Drury Lane (Theatre Royal, King's House)
    50.06   druriodrama
    79.27–28   she pulls a lane picture for us, in a dreariodreama setting
    491.29–30   He loves a drary lane
    587.08   our Theoatre Regal's drolleries puntomine
    600.02   in this drury world of ours

Dublin Theatres

The Gaiety (King Street Theatre, managed by Michael Gunn and his wife, Bessy Sudlow; Royce and Vousden acted there)

- 32.10–26 Madame Sudlow . . . king's treat house
- 50.15 volunteer Vousden
- 72.25 Gonn
- 98.11 Turk of the theatre (first house all flatty: the king, eleven sharps)
- 130.26 long gunn but not for cotton
- 132.18 Thorker the Tourable
- 179.35–180.04 an entire operahouse (there was to be stamping room only in the prompter's box and everthemore his queue kept swelling) . . . in their gaiety pantheomime
- 205.29 royss in his turgos the terrible
- 220.24 HUMP (Mr Makeall Gone)
- 242.10 gunnfodder
- 257.34 Gonn the gawds, Gunnar's gustspells
- 434.08–10 playing breeches parts for Bessy Sudlow in flesh-coloured pantos instead of earthing down in the coalhole trying to boil the big gun's dinner
- 439.17 Venerable Val Vousdem
- 455.25–27 the Hereweareagain Gaieties of the Afterpiece when the Royal Revolver of these real globoes lets regally fire of his *mio colpo* for the chrisman's pandemon
- 481.19 We speak of Gun, the farther
- 513.21–22 Edwin Hamilton's Christmas pantaloonade, *Oropos Roxy and Pantharhea* at the Gaiety
- 520.02 a tarrable Turk
- 531.05 Master's gunne he warrs the bedst
- 590.24 begum by gunne!
- 596.15 Gunnar, of The Gunnings, Gund
- [Note: Joyce was a friend of Gunn's and Bessy Sudlow's son, Selskar Gunn, who is also referred to a number of times in the *Wake;* see Glasheen, p. 113.]

The Smock Alley Theatre (managed by Thomas Sheridan; see also references to Mossop and Barry, to Woffington and Sheridan, and to Othello's "green-eyed monster")

- 60.32 S.S. Smack and Olley's
- 105.25–26 *From Abbeygate to Crowalley Through a Lift in the Lude, Smocks for their Graces*
- 147.32 Smock Alley the first night
- 184.24 Sharadan's *Art of Panning*
- 249.03 the grand old greeneyed lobster

The Crow Street Theatre

- 105.26–27 *From Abbeygate to Crowalley . . . Smocks*
- 184.21 Currageen moss and blaster of Barry's

210.17   Buck Jones, the pride of Clonliffe [see Glasheen, p. 147]
323.28–324.16   [refers to a particular performance of *Hamlet* at the Crow—see Part II entry]
569.30   Mr Messop and Mr Borry

Theatre Royal (of Dublin)
127.17–19   [on a performance there of *Richard III*:] Dook Hookbackcrook upsits his ass booseworthies jeer and junket but they boos him oos and baas his aas when he lukes like Hunkett Plunkett
587.08   our Theoatre Regal's drolleries puntomine

The Adelphi Theatre
219.14   As played to the Adelphi

The Thimble Theatre
268.15   And a bodikin a boss in the Thimble Theatre
500.02   They're playing thimbles and bodkins

Shakespearean Actors and Actresses

King's Men (Chamberlain's Men) and Queen's Men (Queen Elizabeth's Men)
47.26   And not all the king's men nor his horses . . .
219.15–16   Before all the King's Hoarsers with all the Queen's Mum
285.L2   *Arthurgink's hussies and Everguin's men*
567.17   all the king's aussies and all their king's men

Richard Burbage, David Garrick, Barry Sullivan (as Richard III)
134.11   Crookback by the even more titulars, Rick, Dave and Barry

David Garrick, Thomas Elrington (and F. Elrington Ball)
55.33–36   hearing in this new reading of the part . . . the new garrickson's grimacing . . . of that once grand old elrington bawl
121.02–8   [see Part II entry on this passage about Garrick acting Hamlet]

Edmund Kean and James Quin
305.18–20   Old Keane . . . Where is that Quin

Henry Mossop and Spranger Barry
184.21   Currageen moss and blaster of Barry's
569.28 ff.   Mumm me moe mummers. . . . Mr Messop and Mr Borry will produce of themselves, as they're two genitalmen of Veruno

Peg Woffington and Thomas Sheridan
184.24   Sharadan's *Art of Panning*
210.25   Magpeg Woppington
413.02   there is a peg under me and there is a tum till me
436.10–11   like Population Peg on a hint or twim clandestinely does be doing to Temptation Tom
577.16   Regies Producer with screendoll Vedette, peg of his claim and pride of her heart

579.17 Peg the pound to tom the devil
586.12 playing peg and pom

Marie Ney (as Ophelia)
203.14 Neya, narev, nen, nonni, nos!

Ellen Terry (as Puck)
210.34–35 a putty shovel for Terry the Puckaun

John Barrymore
583.11 garrymore

Laurence Olivier
456.10 Oliviero

Note: See Senn, pp. 7–8, for a listing of other Irish actors possibly referred to in the *Wake*.

Appendix 4: Shakespearean "Forgery"

Forgers

Lewis Theobald (Pope's "Tibbald"; see also Atherton, pp. 69–70)
28.05 Boald Tib
117.19 tell Tibbs has eve
159.32 theabild
236.08 Saint Tibble's Day
263.05 theobalder
424.29 till tibbes grey eves
553.13 Fra Teobaldo

William Henry Ireland
565.12 Vortigern, ah Gortigern!
608.14 This Mister Ireland?

John Payne Collier
343.02 And you collier carsst on him

Claimants

Francis Bacon
(see "Bacon and Francis Bacon" section)

Delia Bacon
111.05 Belinda of the Dorans
208.29 the dowce little delia
423.25 till that hag of the coombe rapes the pad off his lock
(See also "Bacon and Francis Bacon" section)

Earl of Rutland
    42.36   Rutland heath
    148.08   For Rutland blue's
    437.05   Rutland Rise

Ignatius Donnelly
    261.27   cryptogam
    281.F3   You daredevil donnelly [see Part II entry]

Elizabeth I
    145.30   the Lady who Pays the Rates [see Part II entry]

John Sheffield, Duke of Buckingham
    318.21   backonham

Nicholas Breakspear and the Jesuits
    152.33–34   Bragspear, he clanked . . . every inch of an immortal [see Part II entry]

Collaborators

William Rowley
    330.14   Red Rowleys
    376.31   Rowley

Thomas Middleton
    468.26   Mymiddle toe's mitching [see Part II entry]

Bacon and Francis Bacon

    7.10   Whase be his baken head?
    41.13–15   make bakenbeggfuss . . . and a shinkhams topmorning with his coexes
    71.12   *York's Porker* [see Part II entry]
    141.21   bacon or stable hand
    199.16–20   her meddery eygs, yayis, and staynish beacons on toasc . . . and a shinkobread (hamjambo, bana?) for to plaise that man hog
    205.18   their dinners of cheeckin and beggin
    257.15,22   his place of beacon. . . . the prize of a pease of bakin
    267.12   Belisha beacon
    318.21   backonham
    339.03–4   Like old Dolldy Icon when he cooked up his iggs in bicon
    345.30   *salt bacon*
    363.17   baccon!
    382.11   her beaconegg
    405.33   the half of a pint of becon with newled googs
    406.03–4   and bacon with . . . a pair of chops
    603.01   with that smeoil like a grace of backoning
    615.31   their bacon what harmed butter! It's margarseen oil

Breakfasts: Hamlet and Bacon, Shakespill and Eggs, Will Breakfast

12.14–15 there'll be iggs for the brekkers come to mournhim, sunny side up with care
16.36 He was poached on in that eggtentical spot
19.09 Owlets' eegs
26.03 eggynaggy
41.13–15 make bakenbeggfuss . . . and a shinkhams topmorning with his coexes
54.24 moyliffey eggs
59.30–32 *Mon foie*, you wish to ave some homelette, yes, lady! Good, mein leber! Your hegg he must break himself.
71.12 *York's Porker*
76.05–6 Ham's cribcracking yeggs
79.01 ham
124.09–15 à grave Brofèsor; àth é's Brèak—fast—table . . . and smearbread and better and Him and newlaid ills . . . by him Brotfressor Prenderguest
161.31 shakespill and eggs
163.06 *Butterbrot. . . . Schtinkenkot!*
177.20–22 one Davy Browne-Nolan his heavenlaid twin (this hambone dog-poet pseudoed himself under the hangname he gave himself of Bethgelert)
183.11–12 doubtful eggshells
184.18–32 whites and yolks and yilks . . . his oewfs . . . his avgs . . . his uoves, oves, and uves . . . his ochiuri . . . his Frideggs à la Tricarême
199.06 eygs
199.16–20 her meddery eygs, yayis, and staynish beacons on toasc and a cupenhave so weeshywashy of Greenland's tay or a dzoupgan of Kaffue mokau . . . and a shinkobread (hamjambo, bana?) for to plaise that man hog
220.29 due to egg everlasting
229.01 With harm and aches till farther alters!
230.05–7 eggspilled him out of his homety dometry . . . because all his creature comfort was an omulette
253.24 yam ham
267.19–20 Yggely ogs Weib
285.04 yeggs
288.05 eggways
296.21 Eggsmather
318.20–21 Now eats the vintner over these contents oft with his sad slow munch for backonham
320.09 hamd till hem . . . with his pudny bun brokfost
339.03–4 Like Old Dolldy Icon when he cooked up his iggs in bicon
351.03 meggs and teggs
359.22 a ham . . . a ham pig

366.25–26   when booboob brutals and cautiouses only aims at the oggog hogs in the humand
394.27   saga abooth a gooth a gev a gotheny egg
406.32   ham and jaffas
407.17   rawsucked frish uov
423.19   eggschicker
437.21   Stamp out bad eggs
453.11–12   turning breakfarts into lost soupirs
457.16   refond of eggsized
458.23   the Homesworth breakfast tablotts
473.23   lightbreakfastbringer
483.23–25   healtheous as is eggs . . . braod . . . buttyr . . . hogsfat
484.36   *Eggs squawfish*
489.15–19   I remember ham to me, when we were like bro and sis over our castor and porridge. . . . We were in one class of age like to two clots of egg
497.33–34   the two salaames and the Halfa Ham
528.06   diamants blickfeast
541.25   fastbroke down in Needer thorpe
563.29–30   Both barmhearts shall become yeastcake by their brackfest
575.11   Mr Brakeforth's
575.29   Will Breakfast
586.18   Here is a homelet
597.16   a story about brid and breakfedes
603.01   with that smeoil like a grace of backoning over his egglips of the sunsoonshine
613.11–12   little eggons, youlk and meelk, in a farbiger pancosmos. With a hottyhammyum all round
613.23   breakfarsts
614.32   eggburst, eggblend, eggburial, and hatch-as-hatch can
615.09–10   cup, platter and pot . . . eggs
615.31   their bacon what harmed butter! It's margarseen oil.
616.20,22   knowing the size of an eggcup. . . . Be sage about sausages!

Appendix 5: *Wake* Chapter Summaries of Shakespearean Themes

Note: See the plot synopses provided by Glasheen (pp. xxiii–lxxi) and Campbell and Robinson (pp. 15–23) for an overview of the *Wake*. The present summaries provide only a rough and brief index to the usage and frequency of Shakespearean allusions and motifs in each chapter of *Finnegans Wake*.

Book I, Chapter 1: Pages 3–29

This chapter introduces the common elements of the *Wake*, and recapitulates the story of the fall several times. The Shakespearean allusions here are relatively infrequent, and no major clusters or patterns emerge. Page 11 includes the first description of the Hen's letter from Boston, which comes to symbolize all literature and history. The Hen's act of digging is symbolic of scholarship, as argued in chapter 2 of this study; there will be new Shakespeares and new scholars, for there are always ricorsos and breakfasts: "there'll be iggs for the brekkers come to mournhim" (12.14)—mourning brings morning, and a "wake" leads to awake. The motif of breakfast becomes associated with Shakespeare (symbolic of literature) and ricorso. The players and elements of our eternal family drama are cast on page 13, to be sung forever by an Irish bard ("ollaves" in 13.19)—an old man, his wife, their maiden daughter, and twin boys (pen and post)—in this play by the "worldwright from the excelsissimost empyrean" (14.19). On pages 18–19, at the end of the Mutt and Jute episode, we have the first description of the middenheap and burial mound, symbol of past "litterature," scholarship, and history: thousands of life stories have fallen here, thick as snowflakes, litters and letters from aloft, all the letters swallowed by the same ancestral mound, an "allforabit" (19.02). The earth is but dust, and the same returns; he who can read the signs will understand history. The past is our world, and the world is the WORD: the source of alphabet, letters, and literature. Page 20 is about the origin of paper and books. Joyce comments on the interminable fecundity of literature and of literary interpretations, using the *Wake* (book of Dublin's giant and double-ends joined) as the symbol of all literature: "So you need hardly spell me how every word will be bound over to carry three score and ten toptypsical readings throughout the book of Doublends Jined" (20.13–16).

Book I, Chapter 2: Pages 30–47

This chapter is largely about the overthrow of a father figure (HCE) by a son (Cad, Hosty, etc.); this is a very Shakespearean theme and, consequently, Shakespearean references are more frequent here. On page 31 we find the first connection between Father and Son (in the Holy Trinity) with the father-and-son problem in Hamlet ("the purchypatch of hamlock" in 31.24). Pages 32–33 contain the first important statement of the *Wake*'s theatre metaphor: that all the world's a stage ("worldstage" in 33.03), symbolized by a Shakespearean performance at Michael Gunn and Bessy Sudlow's Gaiety Theatre on King Street, Dublin. The rebellious encounter of the Cad with HCE, and the subsequent overthrow of old by young, is accompanied by a number of references to the Ides of March and to *Julius Caesar*, a day and a play of rebellions, of filial figures overthrowing father figures. Hosty's rann, "The Ballad of Persse O'Reilly," is symbolic of the new bard and book (like Joyce and the *Wake*) toppling and replacing the old "Shikespower" (47.19).

Book I, Chapter 3: Pages 48–74.

This chapter is about gossip and uncertainty, about incommunicability and the impossibility of learning the truth, and about the attempts of literature and scholarship to do so by fabricating sundry accounts and interpretations of every incident. Again, life is assumed to be a Shakespearean play—a "druriodrama" (50.06) at Drury Lane, "Blackfriars" (48.03), or the "old vic" (62.06). The chapter contains various tellings of the story of HCE's encounter with the Cad and of HCE's fall; this "play" is constantly subject to new interpretations, such as those by David Garrick ("this new reading of the part . . . the new garrickson" in 55.34), for "the unfacts, did we possess them, are too imprecisely few to warrant our certitude" (57.16–17). All is slander and gossip, poison poured in the porches of one's ears. The differing opinions of men on the street ("evidencegivers by legpoll" in 57.17) are like the various interpretations of literary critics—mostly lies, for nothing can be proved. On page 58 one of the three soldiers even suggests that HCE-King Hamlet ("cappapee") was done in, like Stephen Dedalus's Shakespeare, because a woman seduced him in a field (see 58.29). The rest of the chapter recounts a number of versions of the encounter between HCE, whose name is Porter (see pp. 560 ff.), and the Cad at Castle Knock Gate near HCE's pub in Chapelizod. The versions of this encounter are thus accompanied by numerous references to *Macbeth*'s Porter and to the "Knocking at the Gate." Page 66 includes a short digression about the letter.

Book I, Chapter 4: Pages 75–103

The fourth chapter continues the investigation into different versions of HCE's fall, and includes a trial in which HCE is judged "Nolans Brumans" (93.01). HCE's history is compared to that of Shakespeare and Anne Hathaway in 80.17–18. "Dreariodreama" (79.28) reminds us that we're still at Drury Lane, or at the Gaiety (98.11). More versions of the encounter with the Cad and HCE's fall follow, with appropriate allusions to *Macbeth* (also a play about falls, about sons overthrowing fathers), *Hamlet*, and *Julius Caesar*. I have found no particularly dominant pattern of Shakespearean allusion in this chapter.

Book I, Chapter 5: Pages 104–125

This is a chapter about the letter, about scholarship and textual studies; in it Joyce tries to equate his works (the letter is the *Wake* as well as all literature) with Shakespeare's. Shaun begins his lecture on scholarship here. As with Shakespearean scholarship and controversy, the question is asked: "who in hallhagal wrote the durn thing anyhow?" (107.36). The chapter contains a number of references to forgers and Shakespearean imitators (such as Lewis Theobald), and to Shakespearean manuscripts (e.g., the "fourlegged ems" in 123.01). Shaun discusses the manuscript and the interpretations of the letter. There are a number of references to *Hamlet* here; 114.19 is a prediction that the *Wake* will eventually enjoy a literary pre-eminence similar to that of *Hamlet* (see the final pages of Part I of this study). Joyce includes in this chapter parodies of various schools of literary criticism. As with the Book of Kells and the Shakespearean folios, the letter (the *Wake*) raises questions of authorship and interpretation; a study of specific letters is like Shakespearean scholarship, "a grand stylish gravedigging with secondbest buns" (121.32). Shaun's views hover close to those of psychoanalyst Ernest Jones, who seems to be partaking of a literary breakfast (page 124). But who was the scribe who penned the letter? It was not Shaun the Post, a forger playing at being Shakespeare ("Hans the Curier" with "some little laughings and some less of cheeks" in 125.14–15), but the odious Shem the Penman.

Book I, Chapter 6: Pages 126–168

This chapter contains many Shakespearean references; *Hamlet, Julius Caesar,* and *The Merchant of Venice* are particularly important. Professor Shaun-(Ernest) Jones answers twelve questions at length. Question nine (on page 143) is full of *Hamlet* references, and concerns the plight of the artist (Shem-Joyce-Hamlet); this important passage may be, at least in part, a reconstruction of Hamlet's "To be or not to be" speech (see chapter 4 of this study). Passage 145.24–34 contains a reference to questions of the authorship of Shakespeare's plays; several other references to Shakespearean authorship (e.g., 161.31 "shakespill and eggs") follow in this chapter. Question eleven contains several long digressions: in the Mookse and Gripes episode, Nuvoletta's drowning (pp. 157–59) recalls Ophelia's; following is Shaun-Jones's lecture (161–67) on the "Antonius-Burrus-Caseous grouptriad," based on Ernest Jones's psychoanalytic reading of Shakespeare's *Julius Caesar* (see chapter 5 of this study). Finally, Shaun turns down his brother's plea for a loan, appealing to Shylock's philosophy in *The Merchant of Venice* for his defense (see 167.35–168.01), setting up the Justius-Mercius (and the quality of mercy) contrast in book I, chapter 7.

Book I, Chapter 7: Pages 169–195

This is the "Shem" chapter; as we might expect in a chapter about the "artist," there are many references to Shakespeare. Three main charges, all Shakespearean in nature, are brought against Shem: madness, plagiarism (or forgery), and artistic conceitedness. First, Shem's "meticulosity bordering on the insane" (173.34) is like Hamlet's method-in-madness, and in this chapter Shaun repeatedly accuses Shem of being mad; this charge may be the main reason for the many *Hamlet* references here. Second, as a "semidemented zany" (179.25), Shem is accused of fantasizing about success as a playwright in the "gaiety pantheomime" (180.04), but of being, in fact, a forger, who is "trying to copy the stage Englesemen" (181.01; as in Greene's accusation of Shakespeare), and a "pelagiarist" (182.03). Furthermore, like Greene's "only Shake-scene in a countrie," Shem is said to think of himself as the greatest penman, "aware of no other shaggspick, other Shakhisbeard" (177.32). Shaun accuses Shem of being obsessed with himself and of writing only about himself. In exile, Shem cooks and defecates (creative acts). Shaun's accusations about Shem are a searing examination-of-conscience of Joyce by Joyce, culminating in the charge: "Sh! You are mad!" (193.28). However, in an important passage (192.20), Joyce compares his fame to that of Christ and *Hamlet*, and predicts that his artistic reputation will see a resurrection. The chapter ends with the confrontation between Shaun-Justius-Shylock, the prosecutor and spokesman of Justice, and Shem-Mercius-Portia, the spokesman of Mercy and art, whose pen and lifewand can make the dumb speak.

Book I, Chapter 8: Pages 196–216.

This chapter, like chapter 3, is about gossip and the "gossipaceous" Anna Livia. There are a number of Shakespearean references, but no single dominant pattern or cluster. The gossip is, again, about HCE's crime and fall in the park; ALP, as the Hen with her nabsack, tries to vindicate her husband's reputation. What exactly happened in Phoenix Park? ALP tries to serve HCE a Shakespearean breakfast (on page 199) to cheer him up about his "wee follyo"—his folly and his folio. The rhyme ALP composes on page 201—a version of the letter—is a Joycean plea for understanding, for a proper audience (a "brandnew bankside," like Shakespeare's, in 201.05), so that the *Wake* may receive its deserved recognition. As the River Liffey, ALP's voyage to the ocean contains a number of references to Ophelia, another drowned river woman.

Book II, Chapter 1: Pages 219–259

This chapter, *The Mime of Mick, Nick and the Maggies*, is a play; as a play, the chapter is a microcosm of the *Wake* and of all history. This very important (and difficult) chapter is the one in which the dramatic metaphor is the most insistent; the entire section is a play. As would be expected in a chapter about drama, there are many Shakespearean allusions here. *The Mime* is a family drama, a play given by the children before their parents, a pantomime of temptation and frustration. Like the *Wake* and like a Viconian cycle, it has four acts. This chapter, particularly the theatre-metaphor of pages 219 to 221, is explicated in chapter 3 of this study.

The playbill opens with an announcement for the production at the Elizabethan Phoenix Playhouse, acted by a stock company ("with nightly redistribution of parts") while the stage manager (and father) looks on. The family cast includes Glugg (Shem), Izod (Issy), Chuff (Shaun), Ann (ALP), and "HUMP (Mr Makeall Gone)," or HCE, as Michael Gunn, manager of the Gaiety (220.24). Numerous *Hamlet* references indicate that this play, "adopted from the Ballymooney Bloodriddon Murther" (219.19), may be Senecan or *Hamlet*-like. Following a list of the stage props is the argument of the play.

The Mime is about the competition between Mick-Chuff and Nick-Glugg for the love of the Maggies (the Floras, or flower girls), led by Issy-Izod, who repeatedly appears amid references to Ophelia and to Ophelia's flowers. Glugg-Shem's plights and problems seem to be those of Joyce himself. Toward the end of the mime, Chuff returns to battle Glugg for rights to Izod. These pages (248–52) contain a dense cluster of allusions to *Macbeth;* Chuff is seen as Macduff, come to wreak vengeance on Glugg-Macbeth: "For a burning would is come to dance inane. . . . Lack breath must leap no more." Glugg is defeated. At this point in the play, the fourth act (ricorso) of the mime begins: the "hour of closing" (255.06) is at hand—for pub and play—and "the producer (Mr John Baptister Vickar)", producer of history (Vico), arrives to close the play. The parents have come back, and the kids are sent upstairs to bed, as Chuff and Glugg are still competing, this time for a piece of bacon (or Shakespeare, perhaps). The curtain falls, on page 257, to loud applause: "Byfall. / Upploud! / The play thou schouwburgst, Game, here endeth. The curtain drops by deep request."

Book II, Chapter 2: Pages 260–308

This dense and difficult, albeit hilarious (especially the marginal notes and footnotes), chapter is about the children's study period, and contains some fine parodies of scholarship. However, Shakespearean allusions are fairly infrequent, and don't exhibit any major pattern. There are a number of allusions to Shakespeare (such as 295.04 "Great Shapesphere" and 274.L4 "*Shakefork*"), to forgery (for example, 263.05 "theobalder" and 281.F3; see Part II entries), to *Hamlet*, and to *Julius Caesar*, a good play for schoolboys. When Issy is struck with melancholy and contemplates suicide, she is compared (in 279.F1) with Ophelia, a depressed suicide. As Margareen-Cleopatra, she bemoans the fact that Burrus and Caseous (Shaun and Shem) are studying rather than attempting romance—thus the references to *Julius Caesar* and *Antony and Cleopatra* in this chapter. Kevin and Dolph (Shaun and Shem) study geometry; when Dolph reveals the vaginal triangle to a marveling Kev, the latter accuses him of being a fake and a forger (300.03). Dolph-Mercius shows Kev how to write and compose "All the charictures in the drame" (302.31)—for which favor Kev-Justius decks Dolph.

Book II, Chapter 3: Pages 309–382

This long and immensely difficult chapter contains a series of phantasmagorical occurrences at HCE's tavern. For such a long section, there are relatively few Shakespearean allusions; those present are largely to *Hamlet, Macbeth, Richard III*, and *Henry IV*. HCE is compared a number of times to Richard III; and the Russian General, at his demise, is alluded to a few times (in 370–79) as Falstaff. Beyond the contextual explanations I have provided in Part II for this chapter's Shakespearean allusions, however, I have not discovered any significant pattern.

Book II, Chapter 4: Pages 383–399

This short chapter (on the four old men watching Tristan and Isolde make love), following the long and difficult previous chapter, is relatively simple. It, too, however, has rather few Shakespearean allusions (which are explained in Part II), and those present occur in no discernible clusters or patterns.

Book III, Chapter 1: Pages 403–428

This chapter contains a fairly dense cluster of Shakespearean allusions for a number of reasons. Here HCE dreams about Shaun; the Shakespearean parallel is Bottom's dream in *A Midsummer Night's Dream*. There are in fact a number of allusions to Bottom's dream, to *A Midsummer Night's Dream*, and to midnight here. Furthermore, the dream seems to be dreamt by the "ass" of the *Wake*—thus another tie to Bottom. In the dream, Shaun has the drinking and gourmandizing habits of Falstaff or Sir Toby Belch, and these are described with a number of allusions to both Falstaff (e.g., 403.21, "midnight's chimes") and Belch (e.g., 423.11, "Does he drink because I am sorely there shall be no more Kates and Nells"). In the dream, Shaun speaks of his love for Issy-Ophelia (who is repeatedly characterized by allusions to Ophelia's "there is pansies, that's for thoughts") and his scorn for Shem. Shaun plans to compose a letter or a play, which turns out to be a will for his beloved, with references to Shakespeare's will (413). He then launches into the fable of the Ondt and the Gracehoper (414.20 ff.), which Joyce may have patterned on Robert Greene's *A Groatsworth of Wit*. Shaun accuses Shem-Joyce's letter (the *Wake*) of being trash. Then, illogically, he claims the letter for his own; and, on pages 422–25, he launches into another great accusation against Shem of plagiarism and forgery, with references to Shakespearean "forgers" Theobald, Bacon, Delia Bacon, as well as to other forgers like James Macpherson. Shaun claims that Shem (clearly identified here with Joyce) stole the works from Shaun himself; the accusations are reminiscent of similar ones in book I, chapter 7: "Every dimmed letter in it is a copy. . . . The lowquacity of him! . . ." (424.32 ff.) Shaun claims to be as talented as his brother, and boasts that his own "trifolium librotto" (425.20) will be much better than Shem's "Acomedy of letters" (425.24).

Book III, Chapter 2: Pages 429–473

This chapter contains Jaun-Shaun's lecture to Issy and to the leap year girls. The lecture is based on Laertes's parting sermon to Ophelia (see chapter 4 of this study); Jaun-Laertes gives advice to Issy-Ophelia about maintaining her virtue and warns her about Dave-Shem-Hamlet. Consequently, there are many echoes from *Hamlet* (e.g., 447.04 "till navel, spokes, and felloes hum like hymn") in this chapter, as well as one to Ernest Jones's *Hamlet and Oedipus* in 434.19,27. Thoughts about Ophelia again contain allusions to "pansies." Jaun continues to give advice about many things, and he declares his own love for Issy along the way. On page 455 he warns her about death and the afterlife, and creates a vision of the apocalyptic worldstage, the Last Day as the Globe Theatre (see Part II, entry for 455.24 ff.). On page 456 Jaun's eating is again accompanied by references to Belch and Falstaff. Toward the end of his lecture, Jaun-Laertes abruptly reverses his earlier advice, introduces Dave-Hamlet to Issy-Ophelia, and urges them to make love: "Be offalia. Be hamlet. . . . Shuck her!" (465.32 ff.). Shaun then bids farewell and disappears in a burst of glory, quoting *Macbeth* (469.20–21).

Book III, Chapter 3: Pages 474–554

Although there are numerous Shakespearean allusions in this chapter, they are relatively infrequent, considering the chapter's great length; nor do there appear to be any major clusters or patterns. Much happens in this chapter, and all originates with Yawn-Shaun, whose vision (beginning in 481.07; see Part II entry) is still part of Bottom's dream; thus, there are recurrent references in this chapter to Bottom, to asses and donkeys, and to "Miss Somer's nice dream" (502.29). References to the "whole stock company of the old house" (510.17) and to the "Christmas pantaloonade . . . at the Gaiety" (513.21) remind us of the dramatic metaphor. This section includes a trial during which HCE defends his virtue by referring to his love for poetry and for Shakespeare (539.06–9) and by proclaiming his achievements as a builder of cities, quoting Shakespeare in his speech.

Few patterns of Shakespearean allusion emerge; contextual explanations of individual allusions are provided in Part II.

Book III, Chapter 4: Pages 555–590

This entertaining passage takes place in HCE and ALP's bedroom, with the four old men as bedposts. There are a fair number of Shakespearean allusions, but they form no pronounced patterns. Pages 560 ff. reveal that our archetypal family is called "The Porters." Page 569 contains a joyous call for more theatre, with a number of dramatic and Shakespearean references (e.g., "two genitalmen of Veruno"). The account of the lawsuit (in pages 573–76; see Part II, entry for this passage) between Anna Livia and HCE contains allusions to Shakespeare ("Will Breakfast" in 575.29), Anne Hathaway, and Shakespeare's will. However, at the end of the chapter, HCE and ALP make love in bed as the four men watch.

Book IV: Pages 593–628

The fourth and last book of *Finnegans Wake*, the Book of Ricorso, of renewal, is Joyce's call for the rising sun and for a new dawn; it is also a call to breakfast, a symbol of morning. References to Shakespearean "brarkfarsts" (613.23) abound in this final section. The eggs of breakfast provide an important explanation of the message of the *Wake*, in 614.27–615.10 (see chapter 6 of this study). All literature and history are Viconian cycles; a new dawn brings a new HCE, a new lifetree, a new Shakespeare-father-creator, receiving the new elements. As with the letter from the litterheap, however, the new cycle is really the same as the old: the old HCE is reincarnated as the new HCE, and all new works of scholarship and literature are only retellings, recombinations, and reworkings of the same forged letter; the morning comes to serve up new breakfasts and new Shakespeares. Pages 615–19 contain the last and fullest version of ALP's letter (symbolic of the *Wake*) to HCE. ALP's lovely final monologue, as she fades out to sea, contains numerous references to Shakespeare's tragic heroines, and ends with a call to her husband to remember her, echoing HCE-King Hamlet's own words: "mememormee!" (628.14).

Notes

Chapter 1

1. As recalled by Frank Budgen, according to Clive Hart in *Structure and Motif in Finnegans Wake* (Evanston, Ill.: Northwestern Univ. Press, 1962), p. 163. Hart does not supply a date for this putative statement, but implies that it occurred during the years Joyce spent writing the *Wake*.

2. According to Herbert Gorman, *James Joyce: A Definitive Biography* (New York: Farrar and Rinehart, 1939), p. 112. Such comparisons remained in Joyce's consciousness. For example, while later working on *Ulysses*, Joyce wrote that *"J'ai 35 ans. C'est l'âge que Shakespeare a eu quand il a conçu sa douleureuse passion pour 'la dame noire'"* (*Letters*, II, p. 432; also discussed in Bernard Benstock, *James Joyce: The Undiscovered Country* [New York: Barnes and Noble, 1977], p. 99). Inevitably, critics, too, have gotten into the habit of comparing; one recent commentator asserts that Joyce is "the major writer in English since Shakespeare." See Colin MacCabe, *James Joyce and the Revolution of the Word* (New York: Barnes and Noble, 1979), p. 3.

Joyce's admiration of Shakespeare was lifelong. As early as 1900, the young Joyce, although praising Ibsen and attacking *Macbeth*, wrote (in "Drama and Life"): "Shakespeare was before all else a literary artist; humour, elegance, a gift of seraphic music, theatrical instincts—he had a rich dower of these. . . . It was far from mere drama, it was literature in dialogue." See *The Critical Writings of James Joyce*, ed. Ellsworth Mason and Richard Ellmann (New York: Viking Press, 1964), p. 39. In 1905 Joyce wrote Stannie that "In my history of literature I have given the highest palms to Shakespeare, Wordsworth and Shelley" (*Letters*, II, p. 90).

3. An absurd possibility suggested by Sir Dunbar Plunket Barton in *Links Between Ireland and Shakespeare* (1919), and fueled by, among other things, the fact that in *Hamlet* I. v. 137, the protagonist swears by St. Patrick. In *Ulysses*, John Eglinton refers to this fact in the "Scylla and Charybdis" chapter: "Has no-one made [Hamlet] out to be an Irishman? Judge Barton, I believe, is searching for clues. He swears (His Highness not His Lordship) by Saint Patrick" (*U*, 198). See Gifford and Seidman, pp. 182, 266.

4. Patrick W(eston) Joyce's books include *Ancient Irish Music* (1972), *Old Irish Folk Music and Songs* (1909), *As We Speak It in Ireland* (1910), and *Social History of Ancient Ireland* (1903). Among the books in Joyce's personal library were two books by Patrick W. Joyce: *An Illustrated History of Ireland*, and *The Origin and History of Irish Names of Places*. These two volumes proved invaluable in writing the *Wake*. See Thomas E. Connolly, *The Personal Library of James Joyce: A Descriptive Bibliography*, University of Buffalo Studies, vol. 22, no. 1 (Buffalo: Univ. of Buffalo Press, 1955).

5. James S. Atherton, *The Books at the Wake: A Study of Literary Allusions in James Joyce's* Finnegans Wake (Carbondale, Ill.: Southern Illinois Univ. Press, 1959), p. 162.

6. William M. Schutte, *Joyce and Shakespeare: A Study in the Meaning of* Ulysses (New Haven: Yale University Press, 1957). Among early critics, perhaps the best material on Shakespeare in *Ulysses* is that in S.L. Goldberg's *The Classical Temper: A Study of James Joyce's*

Ulysses (New York: Barnes & Noble, 1961), and Harry Levin's *James Joyce: A Critical Introduction* (New York: New Directions, 1941).

7. Levin, p. 133.

8. Goldberg, pp. 219–20. Levin's, Schutte's, and Goldberg's early contentions about the importance of Shakespeare in the Joyce canon have become accepted givens in Joyce scholarship. One recent study, for example, begins with the assumption that Shakespeare and Homer were the two greatest influences on Joyce. See Mary T. Reynolds, *Joyce and Dante: The Shaping Imagination* (Princeton: Princeton Univ. Press, 1981), p. 3.

9. Adaline Glasheen, *Third Census of* Finnegans Wake (Berkeley: Univ. of California Press, 1977), pp. xxii, 260. Glasheen's contributions to *Wake* studies are immense, and her books *(A Census, A Second Census,* and *Third Census)* have been most valuable in the research for this study.

10. Atherton, p. 45. A quick glance through Parts II and III of this study will attest that Atherton's comment is in fact a vast understatement.

11. Atherton (p. 164) similarly noted (in 1974) that "this article [Hodgart's] is the fullest treatment of the theme yet published." Both Hodgart's and Peery's works, however, were very creditable early lists of Shakespearean allusions; I wish to acknowledge my debt to both for providing me with some initial clues in my research. L.A.G. Strong, in his book *The Sacred River,* also listed a few Shakespearean allusions. Hodgart, "Shakespeare and *Finnegans Wake,*" *The Cambridge Journal* 6 (1953): 735–52; Peery, "Shakhisbeard at *Finnegans Wake,*" *University of Texas Studies in English* 30 (1951): 243–57; Strong, *The Sacred River: An Approach to James Joyce* (New York: Pellegrini & Cudahy, 1951), pp. 68–75.

12. Hodgart, p. 735.

13. Atherton, pp. 45, 151.

14. Ibid., p. 164.

15. —"that ideal reader suffering from an ideal insomnia" (120.13–14).

16. Compare Hamlet's ". . . he galls his kibe" (V. i. 132) and the Player's "Break all the spikes and fellies from her wheel, / And bowl the round nave down the hill of heaven" (II. ii. 483–84).

17. These other sources could include the *Skeleton Key,* the *Reader's Guide,* and the "Synopsis" in the *Third Census.* Joseph Campbell and Henry Morton Robinson, *A Skeleton Key to Finnegans Wake* (New York: Viking Press, 1944); William York Tindall, *A Reader's Guide to Finnegans Wake* (New York: Farrar, Straus & Giroux, 1969); Glasheen, *A Third Census,* pp. xxiii–lxxi.

18. "James Joyce," *Encyclopaedia Britannica* (1970), Vol. 13 (Chicago: William Benton). The entry was contributed by James Atherton.

19. Goldberg, *The Classical Temper,* p. 67.

20. Glasheen, p. 260.

21. I have provided a chapter-by-chapter summary of usage and frequency of Shakespearean allusions in appendix 5, in Part III of this study.

22. Hodgart, p. 735.

23. Peery, p. 243. Peery follows with two straightforward examples; the second is a well-known allusion from the first page of the *Wake:* "Sometimes Joyce is fairly obvious, as when he writes 'odiose by comparison' (163) for Dogberry's 'Comparisons are odorous' (*Mac.* 3. 5. 18). But of another sort altogether are the allusions in a passage like the following: 'not yet, though all's fair in vanessy, were sosie sesthers wroth with twone nathandjoe' (3). Readers familiar with the Bible may hear in 'sosie sesthers wroth' the names of Susanna, Esther and Ruth; and in this context 'in vanessy' may evoke 'in the vain game of love,' with overtones of Swift and Vanessa. But to comparatively few readers would 'in vanessy' suggest Inverness, the castle of Macbeth, who was undone by three sisters."

24. Ibid., p. 244.

25. The first example echoes "what dreams may come . . . must give us pause" (*Ham.* III. i. 66–68); the second echoes "Can thy right hand seize love upon thy left?" (*Ven.* 158) See Hodgart, "Work in Progress," *The Cambridge Journal* 6 (1953): 23–29, on the first example, and Glasheen, *AWN*, I, 4 (Aug. 1964): 5, on the second.

26. This line is explicated in greater detail in Part II of this study.

27. The passage on page 455 is explicated at length in Part II. This pun, as well as that on "pansies," was pointed out by Hodgart, pp. 740–41.

28. Frank Budgen, *James Joyce and the Making of* Ulysses (Bloomington: Indiana Univ. Press, 1960), p. 284.

29. *Letters*, III, pp. 401–2.

30. Levin, p. 106.

31. In a sense, however, that is what the *Wake* is really all about. Glasheen is one who at times gets sucked into the *Wake*'s Charybdis, seeing Shakespeare in everything. Still, her contributions to *Wake* studies have been so immense that they easily overshadow any excess in zeal.

32. Thanks are extended especially to Atherton, Begnal, Benstock, Glasheen, Hart, Hayman, Hodgart, McHugh, O Hehir, Rose, and Senn—among others—for their central and continuing contributions to *Wake* studies.

Chapter 2

1. Willard Farnham, "Introduction" to *Hamlet*, in *William Shakespeare: The Complete Works*, ed. Harbage *et al.* (Baltimore: Penguin Books, 1969), pp. 931–32.

2. Stephen's words here, of course, do quote the traditional Catholic liturgy: *Sicut erat in principio, et nunc, et semper: et in saecula saeculorum.* ("As it was in the beginning, is now, and ever shall be: world without end.")

The movement of history towards "the manifestation of God" was a popular idea among Victorian historians; see, for example, J.P. Kenyon's review of J.W. Burrow's *A Liberal Descent: Victorian Historians and the English Past*, in *TLS*, 4 December 1981, p. 1408.

3. T.S. Eliot, *"Ulysses,* Order, and Myth," *The Dial* 75 (Nov. 1923): 480–83.

4. "Arise and fly / The reeling Faun, the sensual feast; / Move upward, working out the beast, / And let the ape and tiger die." From *In Memoriam A.H.H.*, section 118.

5. Eliot, *"Ulysses,* Order, and Myth," p. 483.

6. Quoted in *Literary History of the United States*, 3rd ed., Spiller et al., eds., (New York: Macmillan, 1963), p. 1342. I have been unable to locate the original source.

7. Stephen is quoting ("the livid final flame" in *The Marriage of Heaven and Hell*) and paraphrasing Blake.

8. Sonnet 19.

9. *Nec iam pater* (VIII. 231); see page 73 in chapter 5 of this study, on how Stephen reaches this conclusion by using Shakespeare as an example.

10. "—Art, said Stephen, is the human disposition of sensible or intelligent matter for an esthetic end" (*P*, 207).

11. In his *Shakespeare's Lives* Samuel Schoenbaum has described the countless attempts that have been made at a Shakespearean biography, and has proven that Shakespearean biography is a mirror that reflects the biographer more than the subject; in the process, Shakespeare *is*, to paraphrase Haines, the happy hunting ground of many minds who have lost their balance (Oxford: Clarendon Press, 1970).

12. Goldberg, p. 67.

13. In the classic Japanese film (and novel) *Rashomon*, a sequence of events centered around a rape is reenacted four different times in four significantly different versions—as recollected

by the raped woman, then by the rapist, by the woman's husband (tied to a tree and forced to witness the rape), and, finally, by an unsuspected fourth witness to the crime. Such literary relativity in shifting points of view is masterfully explored by modern writers such as Ford, Faulkner, and Durrell. Joyce would have been familiar with similar effects in Browning's *The Ring and the Book*.

14. Similarly, Hart notes in *Structure and Motif* (pp. 65–66) that "In *Finnegans Wake* [Joyce] was particularly concerned to reproduce relativity and the uncertainty principle. The latter functions in the book exactly as it does in the physical world. The large cyclic books of the constituent material are both clearly defined and predictable, but the smaller the structural units we consider, the more difficult it is to know how they will function.... There is in fact no absolute position whatever in *Finnegans Wake*.... From whichever standpoint we may examine the Joycean phenomena, all other possible frames of reference, no matter how irreconcilable or unpalatable, must be taken into account as valid alternatives."

15. It is fun, though, to speculate. See page 78 of chapter 5 for a discussion of the date of HCE's fall, as suggested by the Shakespearean allusions.

16. The Ghost's actual words, in his speech of I. v. 9–23, include: "I am thy father's spirit, / Doomed for a certain term to walk the night.... List, list, O list! / If thou didst ever thy dear father love—."

Leopold Bloom also has these lines on his mind during the day, but, typically, he gets the quotation wrong; in "Lestrygonians" he thinks: "That is how poets write, the similar sounds. But then Shakespeare has no rhymes: blank verse. The flow of the language it is. The thoughts. Solemn. *Hamlet, I am thy father's spirit / Doomed for a certain time to walk the earth*" (*U*, 152). And in "Circe," he hears the voice of Paddy Dignam: "Bloom, I am Paddy Dignam's spirit. List, list, O list!" (*U*, 473).

17. In the *Hamlet* section of Appendix 2 are listed the fifty or so of these variations. Here are a few examples: "Heed! Heed!" (5.26); "List!"(13.16); "Year! Year!" (15.08–9); "Lissom! Lissom!" (21.02); "lust!" (51.09); "Lou! Lou!" (58.06); "lo! lo!" (58.18); "Hear, O hear" (68.25); "Oyeh! Oyeh!" (85.31—'Oyez, oyez!'); "Liss, liss!" (148.26); "List!" (238.23); "land me arrears" (278.L3, or Mark Antony's famous line in *Julius Caesar);* "Ear! Ear! ... Eye! Eye!" (409.03); and "Oyes! Oyeses! Oyesesyeses!" (604.22).

18. These will be discussed in chapter 5 of this study.

19. See Part II, entry for 134.10–11, for another reference to famed Shakespearean actor David Garrick.

20. The "problem plays" is a term first used by F.S. Boas to describe four Shakespearean plays containing great problems of interpretation; these include *Hamlet* ("the purchypatch of hamlock"), a play full of purple passages (also commonly known as purple patches).

21. However, as Oscar Wilde's Algernon Moncrieff (in *The Importance of Being Earnest*) said, "The truth is rarely pure and never simple. Modern life would be very tedious if it were either, and modern literature a complete impossibility." The same is true of the seeming jumble of words that is the *Wake*.

22. Tindall, p. 98.

23. See Jackson I. Cope's revealing account of the Egyptological source of the *Wake*'s middendump in *Joyce's Cities* (Baltimore: Johns Hopkins Univ. Press, 1981), pp. 114–16.

24. The important connection made in the *Wake* between Shakespeare and breakfasts shall be discussed in chapter 6 of this study.

25. "O'c'stle" is also perhaps a reference to Shakespeare's Falstaff, via Sir John Oldcastle. See Part II, entry for 18.06.

26. Joyce's notion of scavenging and feeding on the past is a central theme of *Finnegans Wake* (as it is in *Ulysses*). In book I, chapter 7, Shem-Joyce conducts some probing self-questioning (via Shaun), an examination of conscience about his own self-cannibalism: "Sniffer of carrion, premature gravedigger ... blind poring upon your many scalds and burns and blisters ..." (189.28–32).

27. The *Hamlet* references in the chapter include the following: "disjointed times" (104.05), "Ophelia's Culpreints" (105.18), "the drame of Drainophilias" (110.11), "me ken or no me ken Zot is the Quiztune" (110.14), "from tham Let Rise till Hum Lit" (114.19), "dummpshow" (120.07–8), "very like a whale's egg" (120.11), "his Claudian brother" (121.01), "a grand stylish gravedigging" (121.32), and "Essex" (125.17).

28. Glasheen argues (p. 21) that Biddy Doran, the hen who tries to resurrect the memory of HCE, is linked (through Delia-Artemis the goddess) to Delia Bacon (1811–59), the first Baconian and American authoress of *The Philosophy of Shakespeare's Plays Unfolded*. Delia Bacon believed that by breaking into Shakespeare's tomb, she could prove that Francis Bacon was the playwright Shakespeare; she never did rape the lock of Shakespeare's tomb, but went mad instead. See entries for 208.29 and 423.25 in Part II.

29. The hen, too, is a capable literary scholar, for she is a "Misthress of Arths" (112.29). Though she has an M.A. degree, she still "is not out to dizzledazzle with a graith uncouthrement of postmantuam glasseries [a great accoutrement of postman's and post-Mantuan (postpastoral) glossaries] from the lapins and the grigs [from the Latins and the Greeks]" (113.01–2).

30. In these pages, the letter is equated not only with *Hamlet*, but also with Joyce's works: "The teatimestained terminal . . . is a cosy little brown study all to oneself [like *Dubliners* or *Chamber Music*, perhaps] . . . or just a poor trait of the artless *[A Portrait of the Artist]*" (114.29–32).

31. Atherton, (pp. 67–70) has pointed out some other references to Shakespearean manuscripts and forgers in this chapter, including "those fourlegged ems" (122.36–123.01): "This must refer to the suggestion made first by the MS. of the *Play of Sir Thomas More* that putting four legs to occasional m's was Shakespeare's besetting sin as a writer." Joyce refers to "this kind of paddygoeasy partnership" as "the ulykkhean" (123.16), since he used it in *Ulysses*, where he fed off the *Odyssey* of Homer's "wretched mariner" (123.23–24) and patterned the shape of his own tale on Shakespeare ("our plumsucked pattern shapekeeper" in 123.24). See also chapter 6 of this study, where forgers in the *Wake* are discussed at greater length.

Chapter 3

1. His one extant attempt at being a dramatist—*Exiles*, in 1918—was a failure.

2. Early critics made a similar comparison between Joyce's artistic progression and Stephen's aesthetics in *Portrait*, pp. 214–15. See, for example, Levin, pp. 44–45, and Hugh Kenner, in *James Joyce: Two Decades of Criticism*, ed. Seon Givens (New York: Vanguard, 1948), p. 149. I say that Joyce followed this progression only in "a vague sense" because this popular notion is somewhat facile: in another sense, all of Joyce's novels were essentially dramatic.

3. Goldberg, p. 32. Furthermore, Goldberg shows that the "themes [are] realized dramatically" (p. 39), that Stephen's argument about Shakespeare (in *Ulysses*) "is dramatically presented" (p. 69), and that the dramatic "allows Joyce his coveted artistic objectivity" (p. 77).

4. Hamlet on his father: "'A was a man, take him for all in all, / I shall not look upon his like again" (I. ii. 187–88). Stephen, referring to God as "the playwright who wrote the folio of the world and wrote it badly," continues: "the lord of things as they are . . . is doubtless all in all in all of us" (*U*, 213).

5. Operas are one of the forms of drama in the *Wake*. A recurrent theme in this drama of Viconian history is the force of destiny, or Verdi's *La Forza Del Destino*.

6. I owe my awareness of some Michael Gunn references to Glasheen's three *Censuses*.

7. As the shaper of puns and the wielder of a sharpened pencil, Joyce-Shem-Stephen

("Kinch, the knife-blade" in *U*, 4) is a "punsil shapner" (98.30). As Shaun might say, "Shun the Punman!" (93.13). Like Dr. Johnson's Shakespeare, a quibble was also to Joyce the fatal Cleopatra for which he lost the world and was content to lose it.

Hart has clearly stated the relation between "pen" and "gun" in *Finnegans Wake*, referring to Michael Davitt's celebrated "pen letter": "The document came to be known as the 'pen letter' because in it Davitt referred to the murder-weapon (a revolver) by the usual Fenian cant term, 'pen.' Throughout *Finnegans Wake* 'pen' and 'Letter' go together, of course; it is Shem the Penman, modelled partly on Davitt himself, who writes the Letter, and it is he who brandishes a revolver under Earwicker's nose in I.2. The word 'pen' is often used in contexts of fighting and bloodshed, which suggests that Joyce is using it in the Fenian sense" (*Structure and Motif*, p. 201).

8. The identity of the Ass—whether he is Christ, Shaun, Johnny MacDougal, or whoever—has become an enigma comparable to that of the Man in the Macintosh in *Ulysses*.

Joyce, who was obsessed with female bottoms, no doubt found the pun (by Shakespeare in *MND*) of ass-"arse"-Bottom very appealing—and, as usual, appropriated it. See, for example, Part II, entry for 594.12.

9. A reference, in addition, to Falstaff's line: "We have heard the chimes at midnight, Master Shallow" (*2H4* III. ii. 203). Since we are amid *A Midsummer Night's Dream*, "vixen" may recall Hermia, who "was a vixen when she went to school" (III. ii. 324). "Shaddo" may echo Puck's epilogue: "If we shadows have offended . . ." (*MND* V. i. 412).

Michael H. Begnal writes about the quoted lines from page 403: "It is quite possible that the Ass who narrates the first three chapters of Book III, as the beast of burden of the Four Old Men and as Bottom of 'A Midsummer Night's Dream,' is actually Shem who takes this opportunity to make light of his more serious brother. His opening: 'Methought as I was dropping asleep somepart in nonland of where's please' (403.18) is a good deal reminiscent of Shem's Shakespearean imitations . . ." (*Narrator and Character in* Finnegans Wake [Lewisburg: Bucknell Univ. Press, 1975], p. 58).

10. Boyle, *James Joyce's Pauline Vision: A Catholic Exposition* (Carbondale, Ill.: Southern Illinois Univ. Press, 1978), p. x.

11. Boyle, *James Joyce's Pauline Vision*, p. 102.

12. Boyle, *James Joyce's Pauline Vision*, p. 5.

13. However, as Father Boyle felicitously notes, "In terms of the wilder aspects of Shem-Bottom's own vision, on *FW* 502, we find the dream turned into a nightmare of delirium tremens. But not that either, since it really is 'delugium stramens,' a deluge of straw, a most happy situation for an ass!" (*James Joyce's Pauline Vision*, p. 6).

14. Atherton, p. 149.

15. "Under the greenwood tree" and the Green World are alluded to elsewhere in the *Wake:* in 74.09, "green woods"; in 335.32–34, "And it was . . . in the green of the wood . . . and jollyjacques [Jaques?] spindthrift on the merry"; and in 450.33 "greenwood's gossip." Jaques's "worldstage" metaphor is perhaps echoed again in 278.13: "All the world's in want."

16. The sennet of invitation has perhaps been sounded (though softly) in 15.17, "duncledames." Jaques's "Ducdame," according to the *Pelican Shakespeare*, has been "variously explained as deriving from gypsy 'dukra me,' a fortune-teller's cry to the gullible, from Welsh 'dewch'da mi,' meaning 'come with me,' etc."—all are "come hither"' s. See Part II, entry to 15.17.

17. See the discussion of Christmas pantomimes at the Gaiety in Robert M. Adams's *Surface and Symbol: The Consistency of James Joyce's* Ulysses (New York: Oxford Univ. Press, 1962), pp. 76–82.

18. Polonius: "Though this be madness, yet there's method in't" (II. ii. 203).

Joyce said that Book III is a Way of the Cross, being traveled by a carrier of the Word

(Shaun the Post): "... Shawn ... is a description of a postman travelling backwards in the night through the events already narrated. It is written in the form of a *via crucis* of 14 stations but in reality is only a barrel rolling down the river Liffey" (*Letters*, I, p. 214).

19. Since "business per usuals" refers to sons (see 37.09-10, in which the Cad "went about his business ... as a metter of corse," and elsewhere), such as Prince Hamlet, then "puritas of doctrina" may be God the Father, and the purchypatch may be the Holy Ghost— or, as we shall later see, it may be the ghost of "hamlock"'s father, HCE himself.

20. Senn, "Notes" on Dublin theaters, in *AWN*, Old Series 2, p. 6.

21. Recall T.S. Eliot's line about Joyce: "One has the sense of everything happening at once."

22. Atherton, p. 163. On Bankside (from *RES*, 56): "... a district within the borough of Southwark on the South Bank of the Thames, and the site of most of the Elizabethan public theatres, including the Hope, the Rose, the Globe, and the Swan. ... In 1596 Shakespeare was living in or near the Bankside."

23. The Phoenix Playhouse was originally designed as an amphitheatre for cockfighting. "And old lotts have fun at Flammagen's ball": "lots of fun at Finnegan's Wake" is the chorus from "The Ballad of Tim Finnegan."

24. The Old Vic is also referred to, in "the old vic" (62.06) and "Old Vickers sate down on their airs" (330.13).

25. Perhaps one of these "sons" of Garrick is another famous Shakespearean actor, Thomas Elrington.

26. See, for example, *RES*, pp. 700, 833. Glasheen (p. 24) believes that the references are to Burbage, Garrick, and Spranger Barry. The use of first names (Rick, Dave, Barry), however, would argue a reference to Barry Sullivan, famed for his portrayal of Richard III.

27. The King's Men (Chamberlain's Men) and the Queen's Men (Queen Elizabeth's Men) are mentioned several times in the *Wake*, in conjunction (naturally) with the line about "all the King's horses and all the King's men" in the "Humpty Dumpty" nursery rhyme; "Hump" (or Crookback) or "Humpty" is another role of HCE and Michael Gunn; see "HUMP (Mr Makeall Gone)" in 220.24. These references are listed under the "Actors and Actresses" section of Appendix 3.

28. In addition to all examples previously quoted, see also "Gonn" (72.25); "the theater (first house all flatty: the king, eleven sharps)" in 98.11; "long gunn but not for cotton" (130.26); "playing breeches parts for Bessy Sudlow in flesh-coloured pantos instead of earthing down in the coalhole trying to boil the big gun's dinner" (434.08-10); "Master's gunne he warrs the bedst" (531.05); "begum by gunne!" (590.24); and "Gunnar, of The Gunnings, Gund" (596.15).

29. See Part II, entry for 127.17, and Senn's "Notes" on Dublin theaters, p. 7, for the details of this amusing incident.

30. Senn (p. 8) writes: "The rivalry between the threatres was so keen as to be mutually injurious, and was fanned by their respective patrons. For instance, Lord Mornington (266.11), father of the Duke of Wellington, induced Kane O'Hara to write *Midas*, made up of Dublin jokes and by-sayings, in opposition to the Italian burletta at Smock Alley. O'Hara may appear at 580.32 and 610.03. *Midas* is named several times: 158.07, 481.33, 482.04." O'Hara (O'Mara, etc.) is one of the characters who, in book I, chapter 2, composes and spreads the "Ballad of Persse O'Reilly," symbolic of the *Wake* itself; *Midas* (and the golden ass's ears) may, thus, be Bottom's dream, or the *Wake* itself.

The *RES*, p. 386, reports: "During the 18th Century the Smock Alley was the center of Irish theatrical life.... Members of this company who were later to win fame in London as Shakespeareans were James Quin, Peg Woffington, and Thomas Sheridan, who was also manager of the theatre for ten years. In 1758 two other distinguished Irish actors, Spranger Barry and Charles Macklin, opened up a second theatre in Dublin, known as the Crow St.

Theatre. Unfortunately, the resultant competition proved unprofitable for both theatres, and they were eventually combined under the leadership of another Shakespearean actor, Henry Mossop."

31. Barry is even better-known for his rivalry at the Covent Garden in London with Garrick at Drury Lane; his Romeo provoked the "Romeo and Juliet War" (*RES*, 59).

32. From Fitzpatrick's *Dublin*, p. 249, as quoted by Senn on page 5. Nat Lee (1653?–1692) was a dramatist who went insane. Released from Bedlam, he died thus: "According to Oldys, when returning one night, overladen with wine, from the Bear and Harrow in Butcher Row, through Clare St. to his lodgings on Duke St., Lee 'fell down on the ground as some say, according to others on a bulk, and was killed or stifled in the snow' [sic]." See *The Dictionary of National Biography*, ed. Sir Leslie Stephen and Sir Sidney Lee (London: Oxford Univ. Press, 1921–22), vol. 11, p. 808.

33. Glasheen, p. 228.

34. *RES*, p. 957. The possibility that Woffington and Sheridan were lovers did cause a minor scandal in Dublin. For three years Woffington was Sheridan's leading lady at the Smock Alley (1751–53); the acting duo of Peg and Tom were the darlings of the Dublin theater public. I cite Esther K. Sheldon's biography of Sheridan: "Indeed, Dublin gossips suspected the worst when, during Christmas week of 1752, Sheridan and Woffington took off together . . . [to] the Sheridan country home, leaving Mrs. Sheridan behind, possessed—again according to Dublin gossip—by 'raging Fits of Jealousy.'" In truth, according to Sheldon, Sheridan—a model of respectability—was taking Woffington to talk to a clergyman he knew, in an attempt to convert the scandalous actress. See *Thomas Sheridan of Smock-Alley* (Princeton: Princeton Univ. Press, 1967), pp. 187–88. The biography contains much detailed information on the Dublin theaters and on Sheridan, Woffington, Mossop, Barry, Digges, Garrick, and others.

Obviously Joyce was steeped in Shakespearean stage history, both British and Irish. I have noted some major references in Irish Shakespearean stage history; for guidance on general Irish stage history in the *Wake*, readers should see Senn, Fitzpatrick, McHugh (in *AWN* XVI, 5 [Oct. 1979]: 72), and Sheldon's biography of Sheridan.

35. Schoenbaum (p. 256) assures us that Christmas pantomimes were also a tradition at the Drury Lane. See Part II, entry for 455.24–29, on the English tradition of Christmas pantomimes.

36. Glasheen, p. 116. "Turko the Terrible" is mentioned in both *Ulysses* and *Finnegans Wake*: *U*, 10, 57; *FW*, 98.10, 132.18, 205.29, 520.02.

37. In the opening pages of the book, *Finnegans Wake* is already compared to a Christmas pantomime. A wake, of course, carries connotations at once of death, birth (a-wake), and *ricorso*—and is thus appropriately associated with Christmas and its similar connotations: "Fillagain's chrissormiss wake" (6.14–15), *Finnegans Wake* as a Christmas pantomime.

38. *SPQR* was the motto of Rome (*Senatus Populusque Romanus*—the Senate and People of Rome; see "The seanad and pobbel queue's remainder" in 454.35), and so combines with "squeak and gibber in the Roman streets" to form "SPQueaRking."

39. Glasheen suggests (p. 125) also that "455.26–9 describes the burning of the Globe during a performance of Shakespeare's *Henry VIII*." On June 29, 1613, the debut date of *Henry VIII*, the Globe "burned to the ground, set afire by a cannon fired in the royal salute at the entrance of the King in the fourth scene of Act I" (*RES*, 350). The passage includes the line: ". . . when the Royal Revolver of these real globoes lets regally fire of his *mio colpo*. . . ."

In 569.28–35, Joyce writes another passage about stage history; it is a call for more theatre: "Mumm me moe mummers! What, no Ithalians? How, not one Moll Pamelas? Accordingly! Play actors by us ever have crash to their gate. Mr Messop and Mr Borry will produce of themselves, as they're two genitalmen of Veruno . . . all for love. . . . Such a boyplay! Their bouchicaulture! What tyronte power! Buy our fays!" Here are references to Mossop and Barry, among other actors, and to *Two Gentlemen of Verona*, among other plays. See Part II, entry for 569.28–35 for an explication of the allusions.

40. *Letters*, I, p. 295.

41. See *Letters*, I, p. 406; Tindall, p. 153; and Roland McHugh's *The Sigla of* Finnegans Wake (Austin: Univ. of Texas Press, 1976), pp. 55–61.

42. McHugh calls these pages "programme notes." He also notes the play's similarities to Christmas pantomimes at the Gaiety. See *The Sigla of* Finnegans Wake, pp. 57–58.

43. This "Bloodriddon Murther," played by the "Brothers Bratislavoff," may be *Der Bestrafte Bruder-Mord* (Fratricide Punished), an early 18th-century German version of *Hamlet*. The Ballyhooley Blueribbon Army was an Irish temperance organization. "Bluechin Blackdillain" includes Bluebeard, famed wife-killer in another bloody murder story (and a popular English pantomime), and "black villain"; Glasheen believes (p. 32) that the "Black Man" in *Finnegans Wake* is Hamlet (in *Ulysses*, p. 208, Stephen Dedalus refers to "Hamlet, the black prince"). Blue Chin and Black Dillon, as McHugh notes (p. 219), are characters in Le Fanu's *The House By The Churchyard*.

44. The *Freeman's Journal* of December 24 and 26, 1892, carried an ad for a Christmas pantomime at the Gaiety, including the climactic "THE GRAND TRANSFORMATION/ Entitled/WINTER AND SUMMER." Adams shows that page 678 of *Ulysses* is based on this ad; it describes a show "commissioned by Michael Gunn, lessee of the Gaiety Theatre, 46, 47, 48, 49 South King Street . . . the grand annual Christmas pantomime . . . [(]under the supervision of Mrs Michael Gunn, ballets by Jessie Noir, harlequinade by Thomas Otto) and sung by Nelly Bouverist principal girl." See Adams, *Surface and Symbol*, pp. 76–82; and McHugh, *The Sigla of* Finnegans Wake, p. 58.

45. *Cap-a-pe* is a leitmotif for King Hamlet. If HCE = King Hamlet, then Cad-Shem = Prince Hamlet; or, as we shall see, the ghost is Shakespeare and the son is Joyce. See chapter 4 of this study for an extended discussion of this leitmotif.

46. See Part II, entry for 256.11–15. "Halome" may also contain *Salome*, another play, by Oscar Wilde.

Chapter 4

1. Cf. Dounia Christiani's *Scandinavian Elements of* Finnegans Wake (Evanston, Ill.: Northwestern Univ. Press, 1965).

2. This theory is parodied in the *Wake* in "poleaxe your sonson's grandson" (53.32). "Poleaxe" refers to Hamlet's father, who "smote the sledded Polacks on the ice" (I. i. 63); Stephen says that "Not for nothing was he [Shakespeare] a butcher's son wielding the sledded poleaxe and spitting in his palm" (*U*, 187). Bloom, having thought earlier about butchers, reflected on those "Wretched brutes there at the cattlemarket waiting for the poleaxe to split their skulls open" (*U*, 171).

3. Hodgart suggests that "Joyce . . . sees Dublin as a primarily Danish and secondarily English city" ("Work in Progress," *The Cambridge Journal*, 6 [Oct. 1952–Sept. 1953], p. 35).

4. Echoes of this line from *Hamlet* also occur in *Ulysses* on pages 18 and 37.

"Penmark": Glasheen notes (p. 229) that "Penmarch" is the French "village . . . where, some say, Tristan died. . . . thus uniting Tristan and Hamlet, which are important roles of Shem the Penman."

5. References to Danish Copenhagen (which is also the name of Duke Wellington's "big wide harse"—8.21), abound in the *Wake;* see "Poopinheavin" (220.34), "kokkenhovens"

(324.29), "Cominghome" (388.13), "cupandnaggin" (548.32), "Caubeenhauben" (568.28), and more.

6. Tindall (p. 102) claims that "*Ulysses* [is] Joyce's purple-patched 'massacre' (110.22–111.02)." However, John Bishop has convincingly shown that "the patchpurple of the massacre" refers to, among other things, the Battle of the Boyne and the mouth of the Boyne River, precious artifacts buried by the Vikings at that site, and the Danish "invaders"; once again we have our connections with Denmark. Bishop, in *The End: An Introductory Study of* Finnegans Wake, dissertation at Stanford University (1981), pages 21–25, 708.

7. Hodgart (p. 751) reads lines 590.30–33 as a reference to the "play scene" in *Hamlet*, in which the conscience of the king is caught: "He could claud boose his eyes to the birth of his garce, he could lump all his lot through the half of her play, but he jest couldn't laugh through the whole of her farce. . . ." Hodgart recognizes in these lines Claudius's ("claud") inability to sit through the "Mousetrap" with equanimity; I'm not fully convinced.

8. Ernest Jones, "The Problem of *Hamlet* and the Oedipus-Complex," Introduction to *Hamlet* (London: Vision Press, 1947), p. 9; also in *Hamlet and Oedipus* (New York: Doubleday, 1949), pp. 25–26.

9. Farnham, Introduction to *Hamlet*, in *William Shakespeare: The Complete Works*, ed. Harbage *et al*. (Baltimore: Penguin Books, 1969), p. 932.

10. As much as Joyce made fun of Ernest Jones in *Finnegans Wake*, his story of a father-son relationship in the *Wake* parallels Jones's and Freud's Oedipal interpretations of *Hamlet*. This topic is treated at greater length in chapter 5. Hodgart comments (pp. 738–39): "Shem, who is the mother's boy of the twins, represents the workings of the Oedipus-complex: in fantasy he kills his father Earwicker. . . . This is elaborated in the story of how Buckley shot the Russian General, told most fully in Book II, chapter iii, which is paralleled by Hamlet's working himself up to kill Claudius. Whenever this theme is found, the quotations from *Hamlet* thicken."

11. "God" and "dog" is a frequent pun in *Ulysses* and the *Wake;* see, for example, 482.01: "Dodgfather, Dodgson and Coo" as the Trinity of God the Father, God the Son, and the Holy Ghost (or dove), *à la* Lewis (Dodgson) Carroll; or, for example, see in *Ulysses:* "Dog of my enemy" (*U*, 45).

12. It is noteworthy that the cast of characters in this mock play of Mulligan's corresponds exactly to the cast of characters of *Finnegans Wake*, to the seven members of HCE's "howthold of nummer seven" (242.05). Even in "Scylla and Charybdis," Joyce is already using Shakespeare as a model for the archetypal family drama.

13. Campbell and Robinson, in *Skeleton Key* (p. 81), call this chapter: "HCE—His Demise and Resurrection."

14. Perhaps also a reference here to "for the weakest goes to the wall. . . . therefore women, being the weaker vessels, are ever thrust to the wall" (*Rom*. I. i. 12–15). See Peery, p. 243.

15. The number 32 in Joyce's works always has the gravity of a fall or demise. See *Ulysses*, p. 72, for example, where Bloom thinks "Thirty-two feet per second, per second. Law of falling bodies." (Cf. *U*, 550). Coincidentally, "that thuddysickend Hamlaugh" is printed on the thirty-second line of the page; Joyce would have expected no less!

16. "Grosskopp" also echoes Horatio's "The gross and scope of my opinion" (I. i. 68), spoken after seeing the Ghost, armed "cap-a-pe." Horatio's gross and scope, or general view, was that "This bodes some strange eruption to our state" (I. i. 69).

17. "Cap-a-pipe" may also refer to the Cad with his pipe; the Cad's pipe (Hosty's pen, Buckley's revolver) seems instrumental in causing HCE-King Hamlet-Russian General's downfall—thus the reference in 221.28 to "Kopay pibe by Kappa Pedersen," another echo of "cap-a-pe" and "cap-a-pipe." Glasheen (p. 152) observes that "Kapp and Peterson" was a firm of Dublin pipe and tobacco makers. Only one other time does "cap-a-pe" appear to refer

to filial figures and not to HCE: in 58.25, the three soldiers are described as "cockaleak and cappapee"—presumably that means they were heavily armed, from head to foot. A motif similar to "cap-a-pe," however, seems to refer to Shaun; this is not surprising because Shaun, resembling HCE, is his father's boy and the next HCE. Hamlet, incredulous, asks again in act I, scene ii about the Ghost: "HAMLET: [Armed] From top to toe? / ALL: My lord, from head to foot" (I. ii. 228). "Top to toe" and "head to foot" seem to refer to Shaun. On page 152 the Mookse (Shaun) is described as armed, carrying his father's sword: "our once in only Bragspear, he clanked, to my clinking, from veetoes to threetop, every inch of an immortal" (152.33–34, with references to Nicholas Breakspear, Shakespeare, and King Lear; see Part II, entry for 152.33). Later, Shaun-Stanislaus, as the pure one of the twins, is referred to as "that other, Immaculatus, from head to foot, sir, that pure one" (191.14). Finally, in *The Mime* chapter, Chuff-Kevin-Mookse is described thus: "How he stud theirs with himself mookst kevinly . . . the churchman childfather from tonsor's tuft to almonder's toes" (234.10–11).

18. As Tindall has suggested in *A Reader's Guide*, p. 294.

19. "Remember me!" is also heard, as Hart has noted (*Structure and Motif*, p. 231), in the final aria from Purcell's *Dido and Aeneas*.

20. Compare with the Ghost's own words: "Fare thee well at once. / The glowworm shows the matin to be near / And gins to pale his uneffectual fire. / Adieu, adieu, adieu. Remember me" (*Ham.* I. v. 89–91).

21. Goldberg, p. 78–79. Cyril Connolly, in a 1929 essay called "The Position of Joyce" (the information of which Connolly claims to have gotten from Joyce himself), calls Stephen Dedalus "the Hamlet young man" with "his minor poet melancholy." See *The Condemned Playground* (London: Routledge, 1945), pp. vii, 2.

22. Hodgart, pp. 738–39.

23. Ibid., p. 740. Hayman's *A First-Draft Version* reads "quietness," and describes Hosty as "feeling suicidal" (*A First-Draft Version of* Finnegans Wake, ed. David Hayman [Austin: Univ. of Texas Press, 1963], p. 65).

24. Hamlet, ham, eggs, bacon, Francis Bacon, pork, and breakfasts are associated in the *Wake* with Shakespeare; see chapter 6 of this study. "Hambone"-*jambon* appears again in 199.18–21, with bacon, as "beacons and hamjambo."

25. Glasheen, pp. 28, 93. Many of us have become familiar with this traditional Welsh story through William Robert Spencer's popular ballad. The *Encyclopaedia Britannica* (1970) tells the tale thus: "*Gellert*, in Welsh tradition, was the trusted hound given by King John to his son-in-law, Prince Llewellyn the Great of Wales. Being left one day in 1205 to guard his master's infant son, he killed a huge wolf which tried to attack the child. Llewellyn, returning to find the baby missing and Gellert's muzzle stained with blood, assumed that the dog had destroyed his son and stabbed him. He later found the child lying unharmed beneath the overturned cradle, with the wolf's corpse beside him. The remorseful prince caused Gellert to be honourably buried on Mt. Snowdon and named the place Beddgelert; i.e., grave of Gelert [sic]" (p. 55).

There are at least two references in the *Wake* to Saxo Grammaticus, whose *Historiae Danicae* was the source of the Hamlet tale: "By Saxon Chromaticus" (304.18), and "Sexon grimmacticals" (388.31—along with Anglo-Saxon grammar books). Perhaps "You phonio saxo?" (16.07) also refers to Grammaticus.

26. See also "Putting Allspace in a Notshall" (455.28). Shem-Jerry's "bad dreams," as was seen earlier, have to do with Hamlet-like visions of his father's ghost.

27. Polonius's line was, of course, "Though this be madness, yet there is method in't" (II. ii. 203). The charge of madness is repeatedly made against Shem and against Joyce, and "madness and method" form a major theme in the *Wake*.

28. Joyce's first draft of *Finnegans Wake* (edited by Hayman) shows that many of the

Shakespearean echoes of this passage—"gouty," "sleepish," "hapless beyond the dreams of accuracy as any camelot, prince of dinmurk," "hopeinhaven"—were first-level additions. There seemingly was a conscious effort to give this passage Shakespearean resonances.

29. McCarthy remarks: "This question demonstrates the many levels of appearance through which reality is filtered in the 'dimm' dream: while Hamlet knew not 'seems,' Joyce's dreamer knows little else" (*The Riddles of* Finnegans Wake [Cranbury, N.J.: Associated Univ. Presses, 1980], p. 76).

30. Variations of *O felix culpa!* compose a ubiquitous motif for HCE's crime. Hart lists twenty-four such puns in *Structure and Motif*, p. 236.

31. "Tumble" is also used in this sense in *Ulysses*. Stephen, lecturing on Shakespeare, says, "[Ann Hathaway] is a boldfaced Stratford wench who tumbles in a cornfield a lover younger than herself" (*U*, 191). Bloom thinks, "Tumble her. Columble her" (*U*, 512), and "sixteen years ago I twenty-two tumbled . . ." (*U*, 563).

Other lines from Ophelia's song occur in Joyce's works. "By his cockle hat and staff" (IV. v. 25) is echoed in the *Wake* by "Sant Iago by his cocklehat" (41.02); in *Ulysses* Stephen mentally calls for "My cockle hat and staff" (*U*, 50). "By Cock, they are to blame" is changed by Stephen into "By cock, she was to blame" (*U*, 191) in the same passage about Anne Hathaway as above.

32. "You must sing 'A-down a-down, and you call him a-down-a'" (IV. v. 170), another line from this song, is echoed twice in the *Wake:* "Downadown, High Downadown" (10.28) and "Calling all downs. Calling all downs to dayne" (593.02).

33. This is discussed by Begnal in "Shaunspeare in *Finnegans Wake*," AWN, II, 4 (Aug. 1965): 4.

34. It is possibly a coincidence, or just another case of Joycean serendipity, but in 1925 famed Shakespearean actress Marie Ney played Ophelia at the Old Vic, with Ernest Milton as Hamlet. See *RES*, p. 291.

35. In a footnote, Issy-Ophelia replies with a quote from *Hamlet:* "he'd have a culious impressiom on the diminitive that chafes our ends" (278.F2; Hamlet said, "There is a divinity that shapes our ends" in V. ii. 10). Issy is saying that if the twins were sitting on a stool as hard as her own, she would bet her bottom dollar they'd also have a curious impression and a pain on their diminutive bottoms, chafing their derrières.

The French word *pensée* is the actual root word of the English "pansy." "Pansy" can also mean an effeminate or a homosexual male.

36. This possibility was first suggested by Hodgart, p. 741.

37. In reference to these lines (434.04–5), to "Put your swell foot foremost" (434.19), and to "joy a Jonas" (434.27), Tindall (pp. 240, 249) has pointed out that "Ernest Jones' *Hamlet and Oedipus* is brought to mind by 'errors of outrager's virtue' from *Hamlet* (434.4–5), 'swell foot' or Oedipus (434.19), and 'Jonas' (434.27)." Jones, a psychoanalyst and a Shakespearean critic, was somewhat of an authority on incest—which is what Jaun-Laertes is proposing to Issy-Ophelia. As will be found in the "Burrus and Caseous" history, "Professor Jones" is a surrogate for Shaun-Jaun. See chapter 5 of this study.

38. These are not the only correspondences. A glance at the *Hamlet* section of Appendix 2 shows references to, or quotes by, Claudius, Polonius, Horatio, Rosencrantz and Guildenstern, etc.—even to Reynaldo!

Chapter 5

1. See Ovid's *Metamorphoses*, VIII, 231. Joyce may have had this passage about Stephen's namesake in mind while writing both the *Portrait* and "Scylla and Charybdis."

2. The issue is basically the same as that between "History and Possibility," discussed in

chapter 2 of this study: does the father create the son or the son the father? do we make history, or does history make us? do we create the past, or are we created by the past?

3. Goldberg, pp. 80–81.

4. Margot Norris writes: "As the Daedalus myth governs *Portrait*, and the Odyssey *Ulysses*, so *Finnegans Wake* is founded on the involuted patterns of the Oedipus myth" (*The Decentered Universe of* Finnegans Wake [Baltimore: Johns Hopkins Univ. Press, 1974], p. 28).

5. *Letters*, I, p. 396.

6. Glasheen, p. 47.

7. Sheldon Brivic notes in his psychoanalytic study of the *Wake:* "The defeat of the father is not merely a singular event, but an archetypal pattern. The shooting of the General by Buckley corresponds to all the scenes in which the soldiers see the crime of H.C.E., and to all occurrences of the everyday situation of a follower recognizing a weakness in his leader" (*Joyce Between Freud and Jung* [Pt. Washington, N.Y.: Kennikat Press, 1980], p. 214). Before Brivic, Tindall wrote (p. 198) about the encounter between Buckley and the Russian General in book II, chapter 3: "The Cad's interview with Earwicker provides precedent and parallel. *Cadet* and *bouchal* are plainly the same young man. Each kills father, the first by asking the time, the second by pulling a trigger. Echoes of Chapter II abound. Hosty's wren reappears...."

8. Levin, pp. 170–173, 133.

9. Goldberg, pp. 219–20.

10. Quoted in Gorman's *James Joyce*, p. 112.

11. Again, as Atherton remarked, "Joyce saw himself as Shakespeare's rival—possibly his greatest rival."

12. As father to be overthrown, HCE is frequently equated with Shakespeare in the *Wake*. See, for example, 58.29—"the first woman, they said, souped him . . . Lili Coninghams, by suggesting they go in a field"—in which HCE and Anna Livia are placed parallel to Shakespeare and Anne Hathaway (the latter of whom, according to Stephen Dedalus, seduced the young William in a cornfield, which Best amends to "ryefield"—*U*, 191) and to Bloom and Molly (the latter of whom tumbled Leopold in a ryefield); the same comparisons occur in "the fields of heat and yields of wheat where corngold Ysit? shamed and shone" (75.10). The comparison between HCE and Stephen's Shakespeare is alluded to also in "the first babe of reconcilement is laid in its last cradle of hume sweet hume" (80.17–18) and "when ginabawdy meadabawdy" (95.06–7). In pages 573–76, the details of the litigation between Ann Doyle (ALP) and Honuphrius (HCE) connect them to Shakespeare and Anne Hathaway. For more detailed explications, see the corresponding entries in Part II for 58.29, 80.17–18, and 573.34–576.17.

13. Joyce himself did not deny the validity of Freud's theories, but remarked "that Freud had been anticipated by Vico." See Richard Ellmann, *James Joyce*, p. 351.

14. For example, the professor in book I, chapter 5 is called Jones (149.10); at one point he attempts psychoanalytic literary criticism as one of those "old Sykos who have done our unsmiling bit on 'alices, when they were yung [Jung] and easily freudened" (115.21–23). "Errors of outrager's virtue" (434.04) is a quote from *Hamlet* ("arrows of outrageous Fortune"), "swell foot" (434.19) refers to Oedipus, and "Jonas" (434.27) refers to Ernest Jones. Professor Shaun-Jones's account of Burrus and Caseous (161–62) is based on a discussion of *Julius Caesar* in *Hamlet and Oedipus*. Tindall writes (p. 249), "Not only one of Shaun's authorities, Ernest Jones seems one of his surrogates."

15. *Hamlet and Oedipus* is the final version of Jones's work-in-progress, which went through several rewritings and expansions, and took on several new titles in a span of forty years. The essay was first written in 1909, as an exposition of a footnote in Freud's *Interpretation of Dreams;* the essay was published in January of 1910, in *The American Journal of*

Psychology, under the title, "The Oedipus Complex as an Explanation of Hamlet's Mystery." In 1911 a German translation appeared as a brochure in the series *Schriften zur angewandten Seelenkunde*, under the title of "Das Problem des Hamlet und der Oedipus-Komplex." In 1923 the essay, titled "A Psycho-Analytic Study of Hamlet," was the first chapter of Jones's *Essays in Applied Psycho-Analysis* (long out of print). The original version was reintroduced (with the adoption of the German title, though translated back into English) as the introduction to an edition of *Hamlet* (London: Vision Press, 1947); it was called "The Problem of Hamlet and the Oedipus-Complex." Finally, revised and expanded into book form, the material appeared as *Hamlet and Oedipus* in 1949; this is the only easily accessible edition of the work nowadays (Jones's ideas, however, do not differ between earlier and later versions). Both "The Problem of Hamlet and the Oedipus-Complex" and *Hamlet and Oedipus* (Garden City: Doubleday, 1949) have been used in this study.

16. Jones, "The Problem of Hamlet and the Oedipus-Complex," in *Hamlet* (London: Vision Press, 1947), p. 9.
17. Ibid., p. 15.
18. Ibid., p. 15.
19. Ibid., p. 22. Notice the applications to Joyce: HCE in the *Wake*, a father figure, dreams of incest with Issy (as in, for example, 75.05–11), and is thus brought into competition with the twins, who also desire Issy; in the *Portrait*, Stephen as a boy is greatly attached to his mother and wishes for his father's death (the importance of John Joyce in his son's life and works has been often noted); and, in book I, chapter 2, the Cad, having confronted and replaced HCE, acts out the Oedipal wish and marries HCE's wife (*FW*, 37–38; see also Tindall, p. 60).

We learn from "the bynames . . . put under him" that "our old offender [HCE in the park] was humile, commune and ensectuous" (29.30). For an analysis of the insect-incest tie, see Fritz Senn's "Insects Appalling," in *Twelve and a Tilly*, Jack P. Dalton and Clive Hart eds. (Evanston: Northwestern Univ. Press, 1965), pp. 36–39.

20. Jones, "The Problem of Hamlet and the Oedipus-Complex," p. 22.
21. Ibid., p. 29.
22. Jones, *Hamlet and Oedipus*, p. 124.
23. As Stephen Dedalus points out in the library, "He [Shakespeare] wrote the play in the months that followed his father's death" (*U*, 207).
24. Jones, "The Problem of Hamlet and the Oedipus-Complex," pp. 21, 30. The quotation also applies admirably to the family drama of the *Wake*, as do a few other comments by Jones on *Hamlet:* "Spying and overhearing play . . . a central theme of the story" (Jones, p. 35); this is also true of the "gossipaceous" (195.04) *Wake*, with its many calls to "List!" to the various versions of Hosty's overheard "Ballad of Persse O'Reilly." Jones writes that the "revolt of youth" is "the deepest problem . . . since the beginning of time" (p. 42); Joyce makes the encounter in the park between HCE and the Cad the "basis" of his book about universal history.
25. Jones, *Hamlet and Oedipus*, p. 137.
26. Ibid., p. 138.
27. Ibid., p. 139.
28. Ibid., pp. 140–41. Jones points out, however, that Shakespeare's suppressed knowledge "seems to leak through in Brutus' apology to Antony for the murder of Caesar (Act III, Sc. 1): 'Our reasons are so full of good regard that were you, Antony, the son of Caesar [i.e. as I am], you should be satisfied.' "
29. This line from *Julius Caesar* (III. ii. 21–22) also finds its way into the *Wake:* "What if she love Sieger less though she leave Ruhm moan?" (281.22–23).
30. HCE, in an inverness raincoat, meets his fate at the hands of a revolutionary (Cad)

who is about to displace and replace him; another "father figure," Duncan, proceeded to Macbeth's castle, Inverness, for a similar assignation.

31. Other references to the Ides of March are listed in the *Julius Caesar* section of appendix 2 and annotated in Part II.

32. Like Hosty in his ballad, Joyce in the *Wake* "overthrows" the father (Shakespeare) by rendering the father's works in the form of a cosmic farce.

33. Levin, p. 170.

34. The world of the "worldwright" is reaffirmed in these opening pages of chapter 3 of *Finnegans Wake* with a cluster of references to the dramatic metaphor: "The Blackfriars" (48.03, famous Elizabethan theatre); "the mime mumming the mick and his nick miming their maggies" (48.10–11; the family drama—*The Mime of Mick, Nick and the Maggies*—at the Gaiety); "utility man of the troupe capable of sustaining long parts at short notice . . . baring this stage" (49.20, 29—the players of a stock company); "Me drames" (49.32: the dream-vision as drama); "druriodrama" (50.06: a Drury Lane drama, or a play about fairies—druries—like *MND*, with its "airy nothings"; cf. "Mary Nothing" in 52.20).

35. Tindall writes (p. 76): "Either by falling against the gate or by trying to open a bottle of stout against it he may have caused a disturbance."

36. Hodgart, p. 736.

37. This is how Campbell and Robinson, in their *Skeleton Key* (p. 76), interpret it. McHugh notes (p. 67), however, that *dún an doras* is Irish for "shut the door."

38. The coincidental parallel between the Porter's comments about the English tailor and John Joyce's story of the Dublin Tailor (Kersse) and the Norwegian sea captain must have pleased Joyce.

39. Though pages 63 to 72 contain the major cluster, there are a number of other references to gates, knocking, and porters, "as the gates may be" (149.33), in the rest of the *Wake*. Some are listed in the *Macbeth* section of Appendix 2.

The same Shakespearean connection has been mentioned by Margot Norris in *The Decentered Universe* (p. 38): "The precedent for a porter who is drunk is, of course, the famous gatekeeper in *Macbeth*. The porter in *Finnegans Wake* is also wakened by the knocking at the gate (64.2, 67.19)."

40. In an investigation of 3.15–24 (the second paragraph of *FW*), John Bishop shows how the dreaming HCE imagines his own inert body to be defined by Dublin's easternmost extremity of Howth Head ("the humptyhillhead of humself" in 3.20) and "to the west his tumptytumtoes . . . at the knock out in the park" (3.21–22—Castle Knock, a hill at the western end of Phoenix Park). Bishop has observed and others before him have pointed out that "Dubliners have handed down over the years a piece of folklore according to which one can see in the contours of the hills extending between Howth and Castle Knock the prone form of the slain Celtic demi-god and giant, Finn MacCool, his head buried under the Hill of Howth and his toes sticking up under the soil at Castle Knock." From Bishop, *The End: An Introductory Study of* Finnegans Wake, p. 144.

41. Tindall notes (p. 249) that "Professor Jones's history of Burrus and Caseous seems to owe something to Ernest Jones's account of Brutus and Cassius in *Hamlet and Oedipus*."

42. "Caesar outnullused" is also the Machiavellian Caesar Borgia's motto, *Aut Caesar aut nihil*—"Either Caesar or nothing." This is adapted from Suetonius, *Caligula* 37: *Aut Caesar aut nullus*. See Tindall, p. 122, and McHugh, p. 161.

43. Leigh Hunt wrote in 1812: "*Brutus*, however, is clearly the hero of the story, and . . . should have given his name to the piece; for *Caesar* appears but in two short scenes and is dispatched at the beginning of the third act, whereas Brutus . . . is the arbiter of all that succeeds." Bernhard Ten Brink made similar criticisms in 1895. See *RES*, pp. 415–16. In like manner, the lines simultaneously allude to Verdi's "kettledrum mistake" in his prelude (to *La Forza del Destino*), letting so much depend on that powerful opening triple crash;

latecoming royalty ("the juke") would thus miss the most powerful effect of that "furst act."

44. A perversion of the martial salute of the gladiators and Caesar's armies: *Ave Caesar, morituri te salutant!*—"Hail, Caesar, they who are about to die salute you!" Cf. 237.12: "we herehear, aboutobloss, O coelicola, thee salutamt."

Glasheen suggests (p. 41) that Brutus and Cassius appear as chewable foods because in Dante's *Inferno* they are chewed in Satan's own mouth.

45. See, for example, *Macbeth* I. iv. 49 and I. vii. 27 for the usage of "o'erleap" in the sense of usurpation through "vaulting ambition."

46. Macbeth might have been prophesying the arrival of Shaun, Shem, and the washerwomen when he said: "Stones have been known to move and trees to speak" (*Mac.* III. iv. 123).

47. See 469.20–21 for a direct echo of this line, and 624.24 for another echo of Lady Macbeth's words.

48. One of these guises is, like that of the Mookse and the Gripes, that of the Ondt and the Gracehoper in 414.20–419.08. Joyce apparently modeled this version less on La Fontaine's fable of the Ant and the Grasshopper than on Greene's *Groatsworth of Wit*, which was mentioned by Joyce in *Ulysses* on pages 187, 204, and 210. While the *Groatsworth* is famous for Robert Greene's alleged verbal attack on Shakespeare, Greene also retells in it the fable of the Ant and the Grasshopper to illustrate his earlier story of the two brothers, Lucanio and Roberto; both stories tell the tale of Greene's own dissipated life (Greene, of course, is Roberto the Grasshopper). Joyce's treatment is similar: Joyce-Shem is the Gracehoper, whose Greene-like libidinous living is decried by the miserly Ondt (Shaun) and who finally, like Greene and Roberto, comes to naught. The descriptions of the Gracehoper's excesses (e.g., "Now whim the sillybilly of a Gracehoper had jingled through a jungle of love and debts . . . and horing after ladybirdies . . . he fell joust as sieck as a sexton and tantoo pooveroo quant à churchprince [*tant pauvre qu'un* churchmouse], and wheer . . . to find a hospes, alick, he wist gnit" in 416.08 ff.) are similar to those in Roberto's tale. In his debased and poverty-stricken final state, the Gracehoper summarizes his dissipated life (pages 418–19) in rhymed verse, just as the fable in Greene's *Groatsworth* ends with the Grasshopper's self-composed epitaph written in rhymed verse. In "our groatsupper" (360.36) Joyce hints at the tie between *Groatsworth* and grasshopper; I believe that Joyce's fable and the *Groatsworth* bear a close resemblance.

In his own "Notes on the English Drama," Joyce made the following entry, misremembering Greene's controversial lines about Shakespeare: "Robt Greene: deserted his wife, having debts and no money / to buy Clothes went to bed, owing money / to his landlord, drank Rhenish wine and / ate pickled herring with Nash: death   *Dying Exhortation* / (Shakes) 'an upstart crow beautiful with our feathers that with a tiger's head wrapt in a player's hide supposes he is able to bombast out a blank verse as the best of you and being an absolute Johannes Factotum is in his own conceit the only Shakescene in the country' / [Flodden Field] (Shake) 'feeding on crumbs that fall from the translator's trencher.'" See William H. Quillan, "Composition of Place: Joyce's Notes on the English Drama," *James Joyce Quarterly* 13, no. 1 (Fall 1975): 4–26.

In *Ulysses*, Stephen Dedalus refers to Greene and his *Groatsworth* four times: "A deathsman of the soul Robert Greene called him" (*U*, 187); "He had a good groatsworth of wit" (*U*, 190); "Chettle Falstaff who reported his uprightness of dealing" *(U*, 204—Chettle wrote an apology for the *Groatsworth)*; and "dearer than his glory of greatest shakescene in the country" (*U*, 210). See chapter 6 of this study for other echoes of Robert Greene in the *Wake*.

49. The motif of "A tale told of Shaun and Shem" is another link between *Macbeth* and the struggle of "brothers," a link made clear in 515.07-8: "—A gael galled by scheme of scorn? Nock? / —Sangnifying nothing. Mock!" Here we have Mick and Nick, and *Macbeth's* "a tale /

Told by an idiot, full of sound and fury, / Signifying nothing" (V. v. 26–28). "A tale told . . ." of or by someone is a refrain and leitmotif in the *Wake*, as Hodgart (p. 745) and others have pointed out—for example: "A tale told of Shaun or Shem" (215.35); "They are talles all tolled" (275.24); "tail toiled of spume and spawn" (324.05); "stole stale mis betold" (396.23); "as at taledold of Formio and Cigalette" (563.26); "Totalled in toldteld and teldtold" (597.08); and so on.

50. Begnal has noticed that "In actuality . . . Antonius is not a new character at all; he is the entity formed by the fusion of Burrus and Caseous as Bruno's philosophy again comes into play" (*Narrator and Character in* Finnegans Wake, p. 94).

51. One statement of Shakespeare as master appears in Hosty's rann: "Suffoclose! Shikespower! Seudodanto! Anonymoses!" (47.19). The same acknowledgment of Dante and Shakespeare—and also Goethe—as his literary masters is made in "Which goatheye and sheepskeer they damnty well know" (344.05–7), in "the goattanned saxopeeler upshotdown chigs peel" (441.33), and in "always think in a wordworth's of that primed favourite continental poet, Daunty, Gouty and Shopkeeper, A.G." (539.05–06).

Chapter 6

1. Glasheen notes (p. 257) that "according to Mr. Ellmann, [Schott was] Joyce's 'no. 1 pupil' in Trieste. 'What's he like?' 'A horseface,' Joyce said. In *FW*, Schott becomes Joyce, lectured to by Professor Jones."

2. See chapter 4 of this study. The purgatory of Shem-Joyce's "Our Father" is linked with that of the ghost of Hamlet's own *padre*, "doomed for a certain term to walk the night" (I. v. 10) in purgatory. For Hamlet, also, this revelation was more than he could bear. Cf. Stephen Dedalus's "Our Father who art in purgatory. Khaki Hamlets don't hesitate to shoot" (*U*, 187).

3. See page 63 and endnote 25 for chapter 4 of this study to discover how "hambone dogpoet" and "Bethgelert" refer to Hamlet (see also 199.17–20 "beacons" and "hamjambo"). Ham and Bacon, or Shakespeare/Hamlet and Francis Bacon, are the same (or, so the Baconians claimed), disguised here under a pseudonym-agnomen.

4. Possibly "faketotem" in 516.24 is derived from this charge of a Jack-of-all-trades as a fake. See also endnote 48 for chapter 5 about Greene's *Groatsworth* and Joyce's fable of the Ondt and the Gracehoper.

5. "Boskop of Yorek" is an appropriate description of Shem as both the "tragic jester" and the "premature gravedigger." In context, Shaun-Stanislaus is accusing Shem-Joyce of not taking a steady job (at the Guinness Brewery or as a priest) "like any boskop of Yorek"—like any old skull of yore, like any man in the past, like any Bishop of York.

6. Shaun echoes critical objections to Joyce's work as self-obsessed feeding on his own sensations and emotions, as solipsistic feeding on his own closed world. D.H. Lawrence, for example, said that Joyce's novels were "childishly interested in the phenomenon. 'Did I feel a twinge in my little toe, or didn't I?' asks every character of Mr. Joyce. . . . The people in the serious novels [like *Ulysses*] are so absorbedly concerned with themselves and what they feel or don't feel, and how they react to every mortal button. . . ." From "Surgery for the Novel—Or a Bomb," *International Book Review*, April 1923; reprinted in Lawrence's *Selected Criticism*, ed. Anthony Beal (New York: Viking, 1971), pp. 114–15. The lines quoted above from the *Wake* (189.31–190.08), along with "quashed quotatoes" and "messes of mottage," may refer directly to (or else may echo uncannily) the words of Lawrence himself, speaking about the *Wake*: "I had a copy of *Transition*. . . . My God, what a clumsy *olla putrida* James Joyce is! Nothing but old fags and cabbage-stumps of quotations from the Bible and the rest, stewed in the juice of deliberate, journalistic dirty-mindedness— what old and hard-worked staleness, masquerading as the all-new!" Joyce must have found

in Lawrence and in that author's views about Joyce the ideal model for Shaun. See the letter to Aldous Huxley, 15 August 1928; reprinted in Lawrence's *Selected Literary Criticism*, p. 148.

7. The liturgical *Dominus Vobiscum* means "May the Lord be with you." The *mea culpa* usually translates as "through my fault, through my fault, through my most grievous fault." Shem's version, of course, echoes "Reacher the Thaurd" (319.20): "A horse! a horse! My kingdom for a horse!" (*R3* V. v. 7, 13).

8. Polonius commented thus on Hamlet's words and behavior: "Though this be madness, yet there is method in't" (*Ham*. II. ii. 203). Despite Peery's disaffirmation (p. 256)—"I find in the *Wake* no echo of Polonius' 'Though this be madness, yet there is method in't' "—I note several echoes in the text above.

"Metheg in your midness" refers both to Polonius's method-in-madness and to mead (metheglin = mead, beer) in your belly or midsection. Shem-Joyce's mad method is attributed by Shaun, typically, to his brother's drunkenness, for "under the mollification of methaglin" (92.04—under the influence), when one is "soaked in methylated" (85.31), metheg becomes method—and beer-soaked madness: "the beerlitz in his mathness" (182.07). The author of the *Wake*, Shem-Joyce, taking a swig of metheglin, is in these references taking a swipe at his own mad method and matter: "he took a svig at his own methyr" (132.24).

9. Shaun is being pretty clever himself, making a hidden accusation of forgery; we have Lewis Theobald here, a very clever forger hidden amid the Charge of the Light Brigade at Balaclava. In 1728 Theobald printed a play entitled *Double Falsehood*, which he claimed to be a modernized version of a lost Shakespearean play, *Cardenio*. Nothing has ever turned up to substantiate his claim. Theobald is alluded to several times in the *Wake*.

10. Joyce had been a teacher at the Berlitz schools in Italy.

11. See the last chapter of Robert Polhemus's *Comic Faith* (Univ. of Chicago Press, 1980) for an illuminating discussion on the meaning of this passage in particular, and of "Shem" in general.

12. Shaun, on the other hand, "only had some little laughings and some less of cheeks" (125.15). See "Chickspeer's" (145.24), "Missy Cheekspeer" (257.20), and "first on the cheekside . . . and over on the owld jowly side" (230.02–4).

13. Such is the case, for example, with the italicized paragraph on page 281, which is lifted verbatim from the historian Edgar Quinet's *Introduction à la Philosophie de l'Histoire de l'Humanité*. See Atherton, p. 34.

14. Joyce himself admitted to an inability to invent stories. Tindall has observed (pp. 132–33) that "All art, according to Joyce . . . is forgery or fake. Stephen Dedalus at the end of *A Portrait* is about to 'forge' something in the 'smithy' of his soul, after the fashion of Daedalus, that 'fabulous artificer' or smith. . . . And Earwicker's sacramental body, hammered out by Joyce, is 'fraudstuff' (7.13). Naturally Shem-Joyce agrees that he is a fraud and a sham." However, "forging" to Joyce was a creative talent, not merely one with purely negative associations.

In her article entitled "Originality and Repetition in *Finnegans Wake* and *Ulysses*," Jennifer Schiffer Levine shows how, in the *Wake*, "we may see writing as pious transcription or as deception and theft: total originality, given the shared nature of language, is impossible. . . . What looks like change is only, perhaps, recycling, and we are bound to a wheel of repetition. . . . Total newness, total originality, is impossible, and so the writer's guilt becomes that of the thief and the conman. No wonder then that the letter smells like dung: it is recycled language . . ." (*PMLA* 94, no. 1 [Jan. 1979]: 106–20).

15. These are listed in appendix 4. Tindall provided an early list of references to fraud, forgery, and fakes in his *Reader's Guide*, p. 138.

16. Atherton, p. 165.

17. *Letters*, III, p. 157. Glasheen writes (p. 145) that *"Jim* the Penman—James Townshend Saward (fl. 1831–56) was so known. This respectable English barrister forged £100,000 worth of checks." *Jim the Penman* was also a play by Sir Charles Young.

18. *The Index Manuscript* lists numerous entries in the Ossian index, derived from Macpherson's *The Poems of Ossian.* See Rose's *James Joyce's The Index Manuscript: Finnegans Wake Holograph Workbook VI. B.46* (Colchester: A Wake Newslitter Press, 1978), pp. 34–44.

19. Ham (Hamlet), bacon (Francis), omelette (Hamlet), Shakespeare, eggs, and other breakfast foods seem to refer to this problem of identity and authorship.

20. Both of these passages deserve some elucidation:
Passage 145.24–34 reads: "More poestries from Chickspeer's. . . . O, you mean the strangle for love and the sowiveall of the prettiest? Yep, we open hap coseries in the home. And once upon a week I improve on myself I'm so keen on that New Free Woman with novel inside. I'm always as tickled as can be over Man in a Surplus by the Lady who Pays the Rates. But I'm as pie as is possible. Let's root out Brimstoker and give him the thrall of our lives. It's Dracula's nightout. For creepsake don't make a flush! Draw the shades, curfe you . . ." Poetry from Shakespeare, struggle for love and life, Darwinian survival of the fittest, feminism, female novels, a Man (or a Priest—in a surplice) who is dressed as a Lady (or vice versa) and is "as easy as pie," "curfews," and Bram Stoker, Irish author of *Dracula.* Glasheen asserts (p. 272) that this passage "becomes more comprehensible if you know that Stoker wrote a jesting piece, claiming Elizabeth I was really a man. The piece was taken seriously by a Mr. Titterton, who claimed in *New Witness,* 1913, that Elizabeth-the-man wrote Shakespeare's plays."

Lines 152.33–34 read: "our once in only Bragspear, he clanked, to my clinking, from veetoes to threetop, every inch of an immortal." "Bragspear" is both English Pope Nicholas Breakspear (Adrian IV) and Shakespeare (as well as Arthur, our once and future king). That Shakespeare is being alluded to is revealed in the description of a king in clanking armor: both King Hamlet (who was "Armed . . . from top to toe" in *Ham.* I. ii. 228—or *cap-a-pe,* "from veetoes to threetop") and King Lear, "every inch a king" (*Lr.* IV. vi. 106). John Garvin asserts in *James Joyce's Disunited Kingdom,* p. 170, that "our once in only Bragspear" is reminiscent of Robert Greene calling Shakespeare "the only Shakescene." The verbal pun between Shakespeare and Breakspear has led enthusiasts to another connection, of which Joyce (who was well-versed in Shakespearean matters, as "Scylla and Charybdis" and Schutte's book have shown), as a Jesuit product, was probably aware; Schoenbaum writes (p. 595): "An equally beguiling suggestion was made by Harold Johnson in *Did the Jesuits write Shakespeare?* (1910). Noting that the only English Pope, Adrian IV (1154–59), bore the name of Nicholas Breakspear, Johnson proposes that the pontiff inspired the pseudonym [i.e., "Shakespeare"] adopted by members of the Society of Jesus as they varied their devotions by busying themselves with *Romeo and Juliet* and *Antony and Cleopatra.*"

21. Joyce was aware that the forgery accusation would be made about *Finnegans Wake,* too (an accusation Joyce wouldn't deny, having based all his work on the middenheap of the past); he also knew what the *Wake* would do to his literary reputation: "You'll have loss of fame from Wimmegame's fake" (375.16–17).

22. See entries for 111.05 and 281.F3 in Part II.

23. The line reads: "Beerman's bluff was what begun it, Old Knoll and his borrowing" (422.31–32). "Beerman" and "Old Knoll" are HCE as the publican and as Howth Head; but, as Glasheen reminds (p. 157), Old Knowell (cf. "old knoll" in 76.26) was the role Shakespeare was believed to have played in Ben Jonson's *Everyman in His Humour.* If so, then Joyce is saying that the letter, symbol for the *Wake* and for all literature, was originally written (or begun) by Shakespeare, who was himself accused of "borrowing" from others.

24. The line obviously refers to Pope's "The Rape of the Lock." The context, however, is

about plagiarism and forgery; and, because Shakespeare-Shem was accused of plagiarizing Bacon-Shaun, the "hag" may be Delia Bacon, the first real Baconian, who tried to prove that Bacon was Shakespeare by attempting to rape the lock of Shakespeare's tomb. See Part II, entry for 423.25. Perhaps "sygnus the swan" (423.21) is the Swan of Avon.

25. The Duke of Buckingham was Richard's henchman in *Richard III*. Because ham and bacon are rivals, however, the reference to "backonham" may be to two "rivals" to Shakespeare's authorship: Francis Bacon, and John Sheffield, Duke of Buckingham, an "adapter" and rewriter of Shakespeare's plays.

26. Hodgart has maintained (p. 748) that "the passage most closely touching the Man [Shakespeare] is the account of the law-suit in Book III, Ch. IV, pp. 573–6, where Ann Doyle the plaintiff is not only Mrs. Earwicker (Anna Liffey) but Anne Hathaway, and the litigation concerns her pregnancy and the second-best bed, as well as contraception, the Church of England, forgery and Joyce's *Ulysses:* 574/15 *Wieldhelm, Hurls* (William Hughes, Mr. W.H.) 575/11 *Mr Brakeforth's* . . . /12 *nine months from date* . . . /15 *pinkwilliams* . . . /29 *Will Breakfast* . . . (i.e., on the next morning Mr. Bloom will breakfast in bed)." See also Part II, entry for 573.34 ff.

27. From the "Preface" to *Troilus and Cressida*. See also "clipperclappers" (614.13) and "clapperclaws" (491.07).

28. Hart notes: "At least one version of the Letter is written on the shells of these eggs—'there's scribings scrawled on eggs'" (*Structure and Motif*, p. 199).

29. "Very like a whale's egg" describes the Protean qualities of the *Wake*, which, like the cloud observed by Hamlet and Polonius, takes on many shapes—even that of a whale: "Very like a whale" (III. ii. 367).

30. Having complained about his lack of an appreciative Bankside (like Shakespeare's), Joyce goes on to say on page 201 that he is "waiting for my old Dane . . . to wake himself out of his winter's doze" (201.08–11)—waiting for the hibernating *Wake* and his literary reputation to wake and rise from the ashes.

31. Tindall, p. 247; see Tindall, pages 247–48, for other insights into this passage.

32. This line is a direct echo of Edmund's words about his brother Edgar in *King Lear:* "Got 'tween asleep and wake" (I. ii. 15).

33. "Thithaways" and "hithaways" may refer, here, to Shakespeare via Anne Hathaway.

Bibliography

Primary Works

Joyce, James. *The Critical Writings of James Joyce.* Edited by Ellsworth Mason and Richard Ellmann. New York: Viking, 1959.
———. *Dubliners.* New York: Viking, 1961.
———. *Finnegans Wake.* New York: Viking, 1959.
———. *The Letters of James Joyce.* Vols. 1–3. Edited by Stuart Gilbert (1) and Richard Ellmann (2, 3). New York: Viking, 1957, 1966, 1966.
———. *A Portrait of the Artist as a Young Man.* New York: Viking, 1964.
———. *Ulysses.* New York: Random House, 1961.
Shakespeare, William. *The Complete Works.* Edited by Alfred Harbage, et al. Baltimore: Penguin Books (Pelican), 1969.

Works Related to Shakespeare

Brandes, Georg Morris Cohen. *William Shakespeare, A Critical Study.* 1893. New York: Macmillan, 1911.
Greene, Robert. *Greene's Groats-worth of Wit.* In *Shakspere Allusion-Book, Part I*, edited by C.M. Ingleby. London: New Shakspere Society, 1874.
Harris, Frank. *The Man Shakespeare and His Tragic Life-story.* New York: M. Kennerly, 1909.
Jones, Ernest. *Hamlet and Oedipus.* Garden City: Doubleday, 1949.
———. "The Problem of Hamlet and the Oedipus-Complex." In *Hamlet.* London: Vision Press, 1947.
Lee, Sir Sidney Lazarus. *A Life of William Shakespeare.* New York: Macmillan, 1916.
The Reader's Encyclopedia of Shakespeare. Edited by Oscar J. Campbell and Edward G. Quinn. New York: Thomas Y. Crowell, 1966.
Schoenbaum, Samuel. *Shakespeare's Lives.* Oxford: Clarendon Press, 1970.
Spevack, Marvin. *The Harvard Concordance to Shakespeare.* Cambridge, Mass.: Belknap Press, 1973.

Selected Works Related to Joyce

A full bibliography for Joyce studies (up to 1977) can be found in Robert H. Deming, *A Bibliography of James Joyce Studies.* The selection below includes works cited in the text and other works that were helpful in the conception or composition of this study.

Adams, Robert M. *Surface and Symbol: The Consistency of James Joyce's* Ulysses. New York: Oxford Univ. Press, 1962.

Atherton, James S. *The Books at the Wake.* Carbondale: Southern Illinois Univ. Press, 1959.

Beckett, Samuel, et al. *Our Exagmination Round His Factification for Incamination of Work in Progress.* Paris: Shakespeare and Company, 1929.

Begnal, Michael H. "Shaunspeare in *Finnegans Wake.*" *A Wake Newslitter,* II, 4 (Aug. 1965): 3–6.

———, and Eckley, Grace. *Narrator and Character in* Finnegans Wake. Cranbury, N.J.: Associated Univ. Presses, 1975.

Begnal, Michael H., and Senn, Fritz, eds. *A Conceptual Guide to* Finnegans Wake. University Park: Pennsylvania State Univ. Press, 1974.

Benstock, Bernard. *James Joyce: The Undiscover'd Country.* New York: Barnes and Noble, 1977.

———. *Joyce-Again's Wake.* Seattle: Univ. of Washington Press, 1965.

Bishop, John. "The End: An Introductory Study of *Finnegans Wake.*" Ph.D. dissertation, Stanford Univ. 2 vols. 1981.

Boldereff, Frances M. *Reading* Finnegans Wake. Woodward, Pa.: Classic Nonfiction Library, 1959.

Bonheim, Helmut. *Joyce's Benefictions.* Berkeley: Univ. of California Press, 1964.

———. *A Lexicon of the German in* Finnegans Wake. Berkeley: Univ. of California Press, 1967.

Boyle, Robert, S. J. *James Joyce's Pauline Vision: A Catholic Exposition.* Carbondale: Southern Illinois Univ. Press, 1978.

Brivic, Sheldon. *Joyce Between Freud and Jung.* Pt. Washington, N.Y.: Kennikat Press, 1980.

Budgen, Frank. *James Joyce and the Making of* Ulysses. Bloomington: Indiana Univ. Press, 1960.

Campbell, Joseph, and Robinson, Henry Morton. *A Skeleton Key to* Finnegans Wake. New York: Viking, 1944.

Christiani, Dounia. *Scandinavian Elements of* Finnegans Wake. Evanston, Ill.: Northwestern Univ. Press, 1965.

Connolly, Thomas E., ed. *James Joyce's Scribbledehobble: The Ur-Workbook for* Finnegans Wake. Evanston: Northwestern Univ. Press, 1961.

———. *The Personal Library of James Joyce: A Descriptive Bibliography.* University of Buffalo Studies 22, no. 1. Buffalo: Univ. of Buffalo Press, 1955.

Cope, Jackson I. *Joyce's Cities: Archaeologies of the Soul.* Baltimore: Johns Hopkins Univ. Press, 1981.

Dalton, Jack P., and Hart, Clive, eds. *Twelve and a Tilly.* Evanston: Northwestern Univ. Press, 1965.

Deming, Robert H. *A Bibliography of James Joyce Studies.* Boston: G.K. Hall, 1977.

Eliot, T.S. "*Ulysses*, Order, and Myth." *The Dial* 75 (Nov. 1923): 480–83.

Ellmann, Richard. *James Joyce*. London: Oxford Univ. Press, 1959.
Garvin, John. *James Joyce's Disunited Kingdom*. New York: Barnes and Noble, 1977.
Gifford, Don, and Seidman, Robert J. *Notes for Joyce*. New York: E.P. Dutton, 1974.
Gilbert, Stuart. *James Joyce's* Ulysses. New York: Random House (Vintage), 1955.
Glasheen, Adaline. *Third Census of* Finnegans Wake. Berkeley: Univ. of California Press, 1977.
Goldberg, S.L. *The Classical Temper: A Study of James Joyce's* Ulysses. New York: Barnes and Noble, 1961.
Gorman, Herbert. *James Joyce, A Definitive Biography*. New York: Farrar and Rinehart, 1939.
Hart, Clive. *A Concordance to* Finnegans Wake. Minneapolis: Univ. of Minnesota Press, 1963.
——. *Structure and Motif in* Finnegans Wake. Evanston: Northwestern Univ. Press, 1962.
——, and Senn, Fritz, eds. *A Wake Digest*. Sydney: Sydney Univ. Press, 1968.
Hayman, David. *A First-Draft Version of* Finnegans Wake. Austin: Univ. of Texas Press, 1963.
Hodgart, Matthew J.C. *James Joyce: A Student's Guide*. London: Routledge and Kegan Paul, 1978.
——. "Shakespeare and *Finnegans Wake*." *The Cambridge Journal* 6, no. 12 (Sept. 1953): 735–52.
——. "Work in Progress." *The Cambridge Journal* 6, no. 1 (Oct. 1952): 23–29.
——, and Worthington, Mabel P. *Song in the Works of James Joyce*. New York: Columbia Univ. Press, 1959.
James Joyce Quarterly. Edited by Thomas F. Staley. 1963–1982.
Kenner, Hugh. *Dublin's Joyce*. Boston: Beacon Press, 1956.
Levin, Harry. *James Joyce: A Critical Introduction*. New York: New Directions, 1941.
Levine, Jennifer Schiffer. "Originality and Repetition in *Finnegans Wake* and *Ulysses*." *PMLA* 94, no. 1 (Jan. 1979): 106–20.
Litz, A. Walton. *The Art of James Joyce*. London: Oxford Univ. Press, 1964.
MacCabe, Colin. *James Joyce and the Revolution of the Word*. New York: Barnes and Noble, 1979.
McCarthy, Patrick A. *The Riddles of* Finnegans Wake. Cranbury, N.J.: Associated Univ. Presses, 1980.
McHugh, Roland. *Annotations to* Finnegans Wake. Baltimore: Johns Hopkins Univ. Press, 1980.
——. *The Sigla of* Finnegans Wake. Austin: Univ. of Texas Press, 1976.
Mink, Louis O. *A* Finnegans Wake *Gazetteer*. Bloomington: Indiana Univ. Press, 1978.
Norris, Margot. *The Decentered Universe of* Finnegans Wake. Baltimore: Johns Hopkins Univ. Press, 1974.
O Hehir, Brendan. *A Gaelic Lexicon for* Finnegans Wake. Berkeley: Univ. of California Press, 1967.

———, and Dillon, John M. *A Classical Lexicon for* Finnegans Wake. Berkeley: Univ. of California Press, 1977.

Peery, William. "Shakhisbeard at *Finnegans Wake*." *University of Texas Studies in English* 30 (1951): 243–57.

Polhemus, Robert M. *Comic Faith: The Great Tradition From Austen to Joyce.* Chicago: Univ. of Chicago Press, 1980.

Quillan, William H. "Composition of Place: Joyce's Notes on the English Drama." *James Joyce Quarterly* 13, no. 1 (Fall 1975): 4–26.

Reynolds, Mary T. *Joyce and Dante: The Shaping Imagination.* Princeton: Princeton Univ. Press, 1981.

Rose, Danis. *James Joyce's The Index Manuscript:* Finnegans Wake *Holograph Workbook VI. B. 46.* Colchester, England: A Wake Newslitter Press, 1978.

Schutte, William. *Joyce and Shakespeare: A Study in the Meaning of* Ulysses. New Haven: Yale Univ. Press, 1957.

Senn, Fritz. "'Notes' on Dublin Theatres." *A Wake Newslitter*, Old Series 2 (Apr. 1962), pp. 5–8.

Solomon, Margaret. *Eternal Geomater.* Carbondale: Southern Illinois Univ. Press, 1969.

Strong, L.A.G. *The Sacred River: An Approach to James Joyce.* New York: Pellegrini and Cudahy, 1951.

Thornton, Weldon. *Allusions in* Ulysses: *An Annotated List.* Chapel Hill: Univ. of North Carolina Press, 1968.

Tindall, William York. *A Reader's Guide to* Finnegans Wake. New York: Farrar, Straus, and Giroux, 1969.

A Wake Newslitter. Edited by Clive Hart and Fritz Senn. 1962–1982.

Index of Authors Cited

Matters pertaining directly to Joyce and Shakespeare are listed and classified in the appendixes that constitute Part III of this study. This index lists other authors cited or referred to in the pages of this book.

Adams, Robert M., 174, 250, 253
Aristotle, 20–23, 30, 125
Atherton, James S., 1, 2, 3, 33, 38, 43, 97, 98, 113, 115, 125, 126, 133, 140, 146, 150, 152–53, 163, 168, 233, 245, 246, 247, 249, 250, 251, 257, 262
Aubrey, John, 134, 141, 189, 197–98

Bacon, Delia, 97, 99, 100, 125, 141, 168, 233, 242, 249, 264
Bacon, Francis, 8, 96–106, 121, 125, 129, 132, 135, 140, 141, 146, 150, 152–53, 155, 162, 168, 188, 190, 233, 234–36, 242, 249, 255, 261, 263, 264
Ball, F. Elrington, 119
Barton, Sir Dunbar Plunket, 245
Beal, Anthony, 261
Beaumont, Francis, 145, 189
Beckett, Samuel, 149
Beerbohm, Max, 12
Begnal, Michael H., 131, 164, 247, 250, 256, 261
Belleforest, François de, 142
Benstock, Bernard, 245, 247
Bishop, John, 254, 259
Blake, William, 2, 247
Boas, F.S., 56, 116, 248
Boucicault, Dion, 33, 184
Boyle, Robert, S.J., 37, 165, 169, 176, 178, 250
Brandes, Georg Morris Cohen, 123, 169, 197

Brecht, Bertolt, 34, 143
Brink, Bernhard Ten, 259
Brivic, Sheldon, 257
Browning, Robert, 121, 248
Bruno, Giordano, 5, 9, 74, 88, 103–5, 117, 135, 184
Budgen, Frank, 11, 245, 247
Bunyan, John, 164
Burrow, J.W., 247

Campbell, Joseph, 156, 236, 246, 254, 259
Carew, Thomas, 145
Carroll, Lewis. *See* Dodgson, Charles Lutwidge
Chambers, E.K., 159
Chesterton, G.K., 117
Christiani, Dounia, 253
Clemens, Samuel Langhorne [pseud. Mark Twain], 49
Coleridge, Samuel Taylor, 132, 158
Collier, John Payne, 233
Congreve, William, 51
Connolly, Cyril, 255
Connolly, Thomas E., 174, 245
Cope, Jackson I., 248
Coryate, Thomas, 145–46

Dalton, Jack P., 258
Dante, 117, 127, 137, 159, 171, 180, 246, 260, 261
Dickinson, Emily, 144

Digges, Leonard, 155
Dodgson, Charles Lutwidge [pseud. Lewis Carroll], 2, 254
Donne, John, 145
Donnelly, Ignatius, 97, 99, 150, 152–53, 234
Dryden, John, 184
Dumas, Alexandre *(père)*, 1
Durrell, Lawrence, 248

Eliot, T.S., 18–19, 247, 251
Ellmann, Richard, 245, 257, 261

Farnham, Willard, 17, 57, 247, 254
Faulkner, William, 24, 248
Fitzpatrick, Samuel, 42, 127, 252
Flaubert, Gustave, 2
Fletcher, John, 145, 189
Ford, Ford Madox, 24, 248
Freud, Sigmund, 7, 31, 35, 75–78, 90, 146, 254, 257

Garvin, John, 131, 263
Gifford, Don, 169, 186, 245
Gilbert, W.S., 32
Givens, Seon, 249
Glasheen, Adaline, 2, 6, 46, 47, 63, 75, 113, 114, 115, 116, 121, 123, 125, 126, 128, 130, 132, 135, 137, 139, 140, 141, 142, 144, 150, 151, 155, 156, 158, 159, 164, 168, 171, 173, 174, 176, 178, 181, 185, 189, 192, 231, 232, 236, 246, 247, 249, 251, 252, 253, 254, 255, 257, 260, 261, 263
Goethe, Johann Wolfgang von, 127, 137, 159, 171, 180, 261
Goldberg, S.L., 2, 22, 33, 62, 74, 75, 245–46, 247, 249, 255, 257
Goldsmith, Oliver, 42, 45, 60
Gorman, Herbert, 245, 257
Greene, Robert, 8, 89, 92–93, 96, 98, 101, 128, 131, 134, 136, 146, 153, 160, 167, 179, 197, 239, 242, 260, 261, 263

Halper, Nathan, 154, 180
Hamilton, Edwin, 47
Hart, Clive, 125, 130, 187, 245, 247, 248, 250, 255, 256, 258, 264
Hayman, David, 117, 247, 255
Hodgart, Matthew J.C., 2, 3, 5, 7, 62, 80, 113, 117, 118, 119, 120, 121, 122, 123, 126, 127, 128, 139, 140, 142, 146, 147, 149, 150, 151, 152, 153, 154, 155, 156, 158, 160–61, 162, 163, 165, 170, 172, 173, 174, 175, 177, 178, 179, 180, 181, 183, 184–85, 186, 187, 189, 190, 246, 247, 253, 254, 255, 256, 259, 261, 264
Homer, 6, 18, 93, 98, 100, 126, 136, 246, 249
Horace, 162
Hughes, Rev. S., 119
Hunt, Leigh, 259
Huxley, Aldous, 262

Ibsen, Henrik, 2, 32–33, 52, 54–55, 245
Ireland, William Henry, 93, 97, 136, 183, 189, 233

Johnson, Harold, 131, 263
Johnson, Samuel, 250
Jones, Ernest, 7, 9, 31, 35, 57, 62, 70, 75–78, 83–85, 88, 90, 92, 98, 101, 102, 127, 130, 132, 133, 146, 170, 174, 179, 184, 198, 239, 242, 254, 256, 257, 258, 259
Jonson, Ben, 145, 168
Joyce, Patrick W., 1, 245
Jung, Carl G., 179, 257

Kenner, Hugh, 249
Kenyon, J.P., 247
Knuth, Leo, 192
Kyd, Thomas, 56–57

La Fontaine, Jean de, 260
Lamb, Charles, 171, 198
Lamb, Mary, 171, 198
Lang, Andrew, 158
Lawrence, D.H., 261
Lee, Nat, 46, 252
Lee, Sir Sidney Lazarus, 158, 252
Le Fanu, Joseph Sheridan, 253
Levin, Harry, 1, 12, 75, 246, 247, 249, 257, 259
Levine, Jennifer Schiffer, 262
Lewis, Wyndham, 151

MacCabe, Colin, 245
McCarthy, Patrick A., 129, 256
McHugh, Roland, 113, 118, 119, 121, 127, 128, 131, 133, 139, 141, 145, 148, 153, 160, 162, 169, 170, 171, 172, 180, 247, 252, 253, 259
Macpherson, James, 97, 100, 126, 168, 242, 263
Mallarmé, Stéphane, 2, 62

Malone, Edmond, 183
Manner, J.H., 185
Marlowe, Christopher, 191
Mason, Ellsworth, 245
Middleton, Thomas, 158, 175, 234
Milton, John, 20
Mink, Louis O., 178, 181
Morlang, Werner, 192

Norris, Margot, 257, 259

O Hehir, Brendan, 247
Ossian. *See* Macpherson, James
Ovid, 21, 73, 256

Pascal, Blaise, 151, 164
Pater, Walter, 124
Paul, Saint, 37
Peery, William, 2, 3, 7–8, 122, 133, 134, 151, 168, 173, 175, 246, 254, 262
Plutarch, 77
Polhemus, Robert M., 262
Pope, Alexander, 97, 115, 125, 150, 168, 181, 233, 263
Proust, Marcel, 173

Quillan, William H., 146, 260
Quinet, Edgar, 152, 156, 262

Reynolds, Mary T., 246
Richardson, Samuel, 24, 184
Robinson, Henry Morton, 156, 236, 246, 254, 259
Rose, Danis, 124, 135, 140, 143, 152, 157, 171, 247, 263
Rowley, William, 157–58, 234

Saxo Grammaticus, 63, 103, 115, 135, 154, 163, 200, 255
Schoenbaum, Samuel, 131, 132, 137, 146, 187, 247, 252, 263
Schopenhauer, Arthur, 11
Schutte, William, 2, 245, 246, 263
Seidman, Robert J., 169, 186, 245
Senn, Fritz, 42, 45, 127, 143, 148, 155, 184, 233, 247, 251, 252, 258

Sheldon, Esther K., 252
Shelley, Percy Bysshe, 245
Sheridan, Richard Brinsley, 46
Sheridan, Thomas, 46, 71, 137, 148, 166, 171, 185, 186, 231, 232, 251, 252
Socrates, 11
Solomon, Margaret, 186
Sophocles, 117
Spencer, William Robert, 135, 255
Spiller, Robert Ernest, 247
Spinoza, Baruch, 11
Stein, Gertrude, 153
Stephen, Sir Leslie, 252
Sterne, Laurence, 24, 93, 138
Stoker, Bram, 130, 263
Strong, L.A.G., 3, 115, 151, 162, 246
Suetonius, 133, 259
Sullivan, Arthur, 32
Sullivan, Philip B., 183
Swift, Jonathan, 2, 9, 99, 113, 119, 186
Swinburne, Algernon, 56, 71, 171
Synge, John Millington, 32, 184

Tennyson, Alfred, Lord, 18, 132, 247
Theobald, Lewis, 80, 97–101, 114, 115, 125, 132, 146, 150, 168, 182, 233, 242, 262
Thomas Aquinas, Saint, 21–22, 30
Tindall, William York, 27, 107, 126, 133, 140, 162, 170, 171, 184, 186, 188, 246, 248, 253, 254, 255, 256, 257, 258, 259, 262, 264
Toye, Peter, 153
Twain, Mark. *See* Clemens, Samuel Langhorne

Vico, Giambattista, 5, 9, 18–19, 28, 31, 32, 34, 41, 43, 48, 61, 76, 88, 104–5, 109, 190, 192, 240, 241, 243, 249, 257

Wilde, Oscar, 71, 149, 248, 253
Wills, W. G., 32–33
Wilson, J. Dover, 142
Wordsworth, William, 180, 245
Worthington, Mabel P., 131

Yeats, William Butler, 62, 169
Young, Sir Charles, 263